The Art of Ana Clavel
Ghosts, Urinals, Dolls, Shadows and Outlaw Desires

LEGENDA

LEGENDA, founded in 1995 by the European Humanities Research Centre of the University of Oxford, is now a joint imprint of the Modern Humanities Research Association and Routledge. Titles range from medieval texts to contemporary cinema and form a widely comparative view of the modern humanities, including works on Arabic, Catalan, English, French, German, Greek, Italian, Portuguese, Russian, Spanish, and Yiddish literature. An Editorial Board of distinguished academic specialists works in collaboration with leading scholarly bodies such as the Society for French Studies, the British Comparative Literature Association and the Association of Hispanists of Great Britain & Ireland.

MHRA

The Modern Humanities Research Association (MHRA) encourages and promotes advanced study and research in the field of the modern humanities, especially modern European languages and literature, including English, and also cinema. It also aims to break down the barriers between scholars working in different disciplines and to maintain the unity of humanistic scholarship in the face of increasing specialization. The Association fulfils this purpose primarily through the publication of journals, bibliographies, monographs and other aids to research.

Routledge
Taylor & Francis Group
LONDON AND NEW YORK

Routledge is a global publisher of academic books, journals and online resources in the humanities and social sciences. Founded in 1836, it has published many of the greatest thinkers and scholars of the last hundred years, including Adorno, Einstein, Russell, Popper, Wittgenstein, Jung, Bohm, Hayek, McLuhan, Marcuse and Sartre. Today Routledge is one of the world's leading academic publishers in the Humanities and Social Sciences. It publishes thousands of books and journals each year, serving scholars, instructors, and professional communities worldwide.

www.routledge.com

STUDIES IN HISPANIC AND LUSOPHONE CULTURES

Studies in Hispanic and Lusophone Cultures are selected and edited by the Association of Hispanists of Great Britain & Ireland. The series seeks to publish the best new research in all areas of the literature, thought, history, culture, film, and languages of Spain, Spanish America, and the Portuguese-speaking world.

The Association of Hispanists of Great Britain & Ireland is a professional association which represents a very diverse discipline, in terms of both geographical coverage and objects of study. Its website showcases new work by members, and publicises jobs, conferences and grants in the field.

www.legendabooks.com/series/shlc

STUDIES IN HISPANIC AND LUSOPHONE CULTURES

1. *Unamuno's Theory of the Novel*, by C. A. Longhurst
2. *Pessoa's Geometry of the Abyss: Modernity and the* Book of Disquiet, by Paulo de Medeiros
3. *Artifice and Invention in the Spanish Golden Age*, edited by Stephen Boyd and Terence O'Reilly
4. *The Latin American Short Story at its Limits: Fragmentation, Hybridity and Intermediality*, by Lucy Bell
5. *Spanish New York Narratives 1898–1936: Modernisation, Otherness and Nation*, by David Miranda-Barreiro
6. *The Art of Ana Clavel: Ghosts, Urinals, Dolls, Shadows and Outlaw Desires*, by Jane Elizabeth Lavery
7. *Alejo Carpentier and the Musical Text*, by Katia Chornik
8. *Britain, Spain and the Treaty of Utrecht 1713-2013*, edited by Trevor J. Dadson and J. H. Elliott
9. *Books and Periodicals in Brazil 1768-1930: A Transatlantic Perspective*, edited by Ana Cláudia Suriani da Silva and Sandra Guardini Vasconcelos
10. *Lisbon Revisited: Urban Masculinities in Twentieth-Century Portuguese Fiction*, by Rhian Atkin
11. *Urban Space, Identity and Postmodernity in 1980s Spain: Rethinking the Movida*, by Maite Usoz de la Fuente
12. *Santería, Vodou and Resistance in Caribbean Literature: Daughters of the Spirits*, by Paul Humphrey
13. *Reprojecting the City: Urban Space and Dissident Sexualities in Recent Latin American Cinema*, by Benedict Hoff

The Art of Ana Clavel

Ghosts, Urinals, Dolls, Shadows and Outlaw Desires

❖

Jane Elizabeth Lavery

Routledge
Taylor & Francis Group
LONDON AND NEW YORK
2015

First published 2015 by Modern Humanities Research Association and Routledge

2 Park Square, Milton Park, Abingdon, Oxfordshire OX14 4RN
52 Vanderbilt Avenue, New York, NY 10017

Routledge is an imprint of the Taylor & Francis Group, an informa business

First issued in paperback 2020

ISBN 978-1-907975-65-3 (hbk)
ISBN 978-0-367-60170-6 (pbk)

CONTENTS

❖

I dedicate this book to Ana Clavel, to my husband Simon, and to my daughters, Sienna Catherine and Lucia Jessica, both of whom were born during the writing process

ACKNOWLEDGEMENTS

This book is a true mosaic of voices and therefore I would like to express my deepest gratitude to those who have contributed to this study. A heartfelt thanks to Ana Clavel for enabling this project by providing me with invaluable insights into her work and material on her literary and multimedia work, as well as by offering very useful comments on the manuscript. Thanks to an amicable professional relationship with Clavel, I have had privileged access to unpublished material which the author has supplied to me and which is invaluable data that has contributed to the ground-breaking dimension of this monograph. I am also grateful for her kindness in welcoming me into her home during my research trip to Mexico in 2008 which fostered a wonderful friendship. During this time, I was directly involved in helping Clavel to set up the exhibition for *Las Violetas son flores del deseo* which gave me an important insight into how the author worked across a number of disciplines (art, performance, music, photography) as well as giving me access to the different people involved in this and Clavel's other multimedia endeavours, including web designers, performers, artists, and photographers. The original data I obtained during my stay has allowed me to address in my monograph existing *lacunae* in our understanding of Clavel's work with an approach that is thematically and analytically innovative.

I gratefully acknowledge the contributions, insights, and careful readings of a number of scholars. I am thus deeply indebted to Nuala Finnegan, Claire Taylor, Sarah Bowskill, Niamh Thornton, Irma López, Loraine Day, Claire Firth, Lorraine Kelly, Anna Kemp, Mark Dinneen, Philip Swanson, Trevor Dadson, Ros Mitchell, and Mike Kelly. I am grateful to the various IT experts and artists whom I interviewed and who have collaborated in Clavel's multimedia projects. They are: Lourdes Fernández, Gabriel Macotela, Mauricio Baeza, Arturo Rivera, Rocío Caballero, Saúl Kaminer, Alejandro Escalante, Maribel Portela, Rubén Maya Moreno, Gustavo Monroy, Jocelyne Marmottan, Luis Manuel Serrano, Rogelio Cuéllar, and Arturo Buitrón.

I am also very thankful to the British Academy for providing me with a small grant award which allowed me to go to Mexico City to attend the multimedia exhibition of Clavel's *Las Violetas son flores del deseo*. I am indebted to Southampton University's Modern Languages Section for their financial support to cover production costs. I am also very grateful for the financial support to cover production costs provided by Southampton University's MEXSU (Centre For Mexico-Southampton Collaboration) and the Institute for Language and Culture with its Impacts and Outputs Support Fund. I am similarly thankful to the University of Southampton for supporting my project by granting me a full year's sabbatical to dedicate this time to write the book. Finally, I would also like to thank my editor at Legenda, Graham Nelson, and

Trevor Dadson, general editor of Legenda's *Studies in Hispanic and Lusophone Cultures* series, for believing in my work as well as for their expertise, patience, and support.

A.C., Southampton University, December 2014

INTRODUCTION

❖

Ana Clavel and the *Boom Femenino*: Continuities and Queer Disruptions

Contexts

Ana Clavel, born in Mexico City in 1961, is an extraordinary writer of fiction, yet her works have received scant critical attention.[1] The aim of this monograph is thus to attest to Clavel's particular contribution to Hispanic letters, which arguably is as significant as that of more established Spanish American women writers. The study also demonstrates how Clavel continues the tradition of both her predecessors and contemporaries by focusing on questions of gender, but also how she queers the more conventional narrative themes and genres associated with some of the more 'canonical' writers of the *boom femenino* and actively resists the commodification of literature endorsed by market forces in Mexico today. There is a growing interest in Clavel in the form of a few articles, PhD theses and conference papers, but there are currently no major publications in monograph form on this author or studies which examine specifically the interrelationship between Clavel's different internet, artistic, and literary outputs.[2] Despite a general growing interest in art and literature using multimedia and digital technologies in Latin America, very few serious studies in the area have been produced to date.[3] There is thus a clear need for this study, as the analysis of Clavel's literary, multimedia, and cyber interventions will constitute an important contribution to the growing scholarly interest in the emerging 'canon' of Latin American artists and writers in these areas.

In order to situate Clavel's work within a broader Mexican cultural context, this introduction furnishes readers with a brief overview of Spanish American and specifically Mexican women's writing of the *boom femenino* produced from the 1970s onwards.[4] Clavel is a relatively unknown author who belongs to this wave which is characterized by the dramatic emergence of women's voices in the cultural sphere in Mexico and is due, in part, to a globalized cultural environment that has seen rapid change in all areas of women's lives.[5] It must be noted that the literary *boom femenino* is not a uniquely Mexican phenomenon as it is used to refer to the broader explosion in publishing by women writers throughout Spanish America. Furthermore, the term cannot be understood without, albeit brief, reference to the *boom* and *post-boom*.

The *boom* is a widely-known term used to refer to Spanish American literature and the explosion of literary activity after the 1960s, much of which was translated and found an international public. Whilst some *boom* narratives have come to be associated with complex and inaccessible forms of writing, *post-boom* writing, which refers to Spanish American literary production after the 1970s, is described as a counter-project to the *boom* in its accessibility, less flamboyant experimentation, and focus on the quotidian rather than complex philosophizing.[6] The *boom* is invariably associated with male writers, especially with the so-called 'big four' — Gabriel García Márquez, Julio Cortázar, Mario Vargas Llosa, and Carlos Fuentes — , whilst women writers rarely feature as part of this elite group. However, as Irma López points out,[7] from the 1970s onwards, new spaces opened up for other writers, in particular women writers who came to be associated with the *boom femenino*.[8] According to Dawn Slack, while the *boom* is studied by international literary and cultural critics and even recognized, to an extent, by non-academics, the myriad of Mexican (and Spanish American) women writers publishing since the 1980s have received comparatively little critical acclaim, in spite of (or perhaps because of) their productivity and popularity.[9] The intention of this monograph is therefore, in part, to redress this imbalance and to give the urgent critical attention which Ana Clavel and more broadly the *boom femenino* authors deserve.

At the heart of the work by these contemporary women writers, there lies similar preoccupations with issues, for instance, of gender inequality, the socio-historical marginalization of women or other perceived minority groups such as gays or Jews, the (female) body, and sexuality. Many of the *boom femenino* texts are centred on the experiences of women and their identities (López, 'The Will to Be', pp. 32–33). Lorraine Kelly highlights shared concerns of the writers pertaining to the *boom femenino*, such as the fight for equity and equality, and their desire to draw our attention to women's daily struggles to overcome the social, moral, and sexual constraints imposed by society.[10] In this way, she argues, this fiction becomes part of a theoretical meditation on the place of women in contemporary society. However, despite certain aesthetic and thematic commonalities, the *boom femenino* cannot be appraised as a unified literary 'movement'. Indeed, it is characterized by diverse thematic concerns as well as a diversity of generic form generally. The principal literary genres associated with the *boom femenino* are the novel (Cristina Rivera-Garza, Ana García Bergua, Ana Clavel), and, to a lesser extent, poetry (María Baranda, Pura López Colomé), but the chronicle (*crónica*) (Elena Poniatowska, Guadalupe Loaeza, Cristina Pacheco), and theatrical productions (Sabina Berman, Carmen Boullosa) have also contributed significantly to the increased visibility of women writers. Alongside this has been a willingness to embrace new multi-media forms that incorporate new technologies of communication such as the work of Eve Gil and Ana Clavel.

Despite the rich cultural output of this literary 'movement', the *boom femenino* frequently carries derogatory connotations as it is invariably linked to 'commercialism,' the concept of the 'best-seller' and by inference, 'light writing'. It is popularly associated with Mexicans Ángeles Mastretta, *Arráncame la vida* (1985) and *Mal de amores* (1996), and Laura Esquivel, *Como agua para chocolate* (1989); and Chilean Isabel Allende, *La casa de los espíritus* (1982). Notwithstanding the commercial success of their work, it is perhaps because of the Mastretta, Allende, and Esquivel best-seller 'phenomenon' that until recently the Mexican and more generally Spanish American literary establishments have rejected much of the writing of the *boom femenino*, considered as unworthy of critical attention.[11] The negative connotations associated with the *boom femenino* can be understood in the context of wider changes within the publishing industry in Mexico and globally in the past three decades. In the 1980s the economic crisis afflicting the country led to the drastic reconfiguration of the Mexican publishing industry, most notably in the merging of local presses with large multinational publishing corporations, such as the case of Grijalbo, which was bought by the Italian publishing house Mondadori (now part of the Random House/Mondadori group).[12] Finnegan also notes that the trend towards the globalization of the publishing industry has had a deep impact 'in the way texts are selected for publication' and how 'target markets for various authors and texts are constructed' (p. 157). Mexican publishing houses like Grijalbo and Joaquín Mortiz had historically been associated with left-wing agendas and the promotion of so-called *literatura difícil* written by young, experimental writers, but following their merging with global publishing giants the original visions of these companies have virtually disappeared due to a need for profit via increased sales of books (*Ambivalence, Modernity, Power*, p. 165). Now the strategy of globalized presses is the creation of specialized publication lines in the form of best-selling series represented in the main by female writers and directed at female readers. Thus the 'globalisation of publishing and the marketability of certain kinds of stories written by certain kinds of women seems to explain the dramatic rise in the "readable novel"' (*Ambivalence, Modernity, Power*, p. 176). This point also helps us to understand the increased backlash against women-authored, women-centred literature at the heart of the *literatura difícil* versus *literatura light* debate.

Until the 1980s the methods of production, publishing, and distribution in Mexico had been controlled in the main by a literary elite represented by national presses such as Grijalbo, as well as critics and writers including amongst others, Fernando Benítez, Carlos Fuentes, and Elena Poniatowska, who championed 'quality' literature as epitomized in the Mexican literary output of the 1960s (*Ambivalence, Modernity, Power*, p. 168). The rise of the 'readable' novel was seen as an affront to those belonging to this closed literary circle, and Mastretta's works, considered the epitome of *ligereza*, bore the brunt of their verbal wrath. Ironically perhaps, Elena Poniatowska — the figurehead of Mexico's literary elite — is a staunch defender of women's rights in her own novels and is also representative of the *boom femenino* wave,[13] but rather than praising the best-selling works of Mastretta, Allende, and Esquivel for giving voice to women's experiences in a *machista* conservative society, as they clearly do, she dismisses them outright as examples of trashy 'women's literature' serving as entertainment only: 'entran en la literatura como fenómenos comerciales y hacen "literatura femenina"' [in literature they are commercial phenomena and they write 'female literature'].[14] Mastretta and Esquivel are reviled by the Mexican literary establishment for seeking to conform to the exigencies of the marketplace and for bowing to publishers' pressures to produce 'light' entertainment that achieves high sales. Their best-selling novels are certainly attractive to a female readership for their portrayal of rebellion by strong female characters who resist patriarchal oppression and traditional gender roles. But Mastretta and Esquivel have been critiqued for entertaining readers with romantic love formulas such as forbidden love, without challenging the bases of heterosexual gender relations or upsetting the status quo.[15] It is undeniable that Mastretta, Esquivel, and Allende are rather conservative in terms of their engagement with exclusively heterosexual gender relations, provide attractive images of women, and write in a way that is characterized by its accessibility. Other Mexican *boom femenino* writers who are perceived as transmitting conservative messages include Boullosa, Nissán, Loaeza, and Sefchovich.[16]

But these in themselves are not necessarily examples of 'bad' writing. It must be stressed that some of the limited evaluations of specifically Mastretta's and Esquivel's best-sellers as merely *literatura light* contrast sharply with the more nuanced standpoint in which some critics have examined the multifaceted and often ambivalent features of their narratives, frequently framed within postmodern play.[17] These more sophisticated critiques highlight the value of these writer's novels, which lies in their ability to combine 'writerly' features in the form of narrative experimentation with other elements, including the enjoyment these works offer the reader, the use of the popular such as romance, and the ethical element in the form of consciousness-raising about the oppression of women.

With the publication of their best-sellers, Allende, Mastretta, and Esquivel were propelled into the literary limelight. Their best-seller status and their wider media popularity as literary celebrities have not only won them millions of fans across the globe but brought awareness to national and international markets of later *boom femenino* writers, including Clavel. The continued long-seller status and popularity of the best-sellers of Allende, Mastretta, and Esquivel have conceivably been fomented by their film adaptations, namely, *Como agua para chocolate* (1992, dir. Alfonso Arau), *The House of the Spirits* (1993, dir. Billie August), and *Arráncame la vida: el corazón no se gobierna* (2008, dir. Roberto Sneider). However, it could be argued that current global perceptions amongst the general public and certain members of the Spanish American literati of women's writing of this region as 'light', marketable literature have been fomented in great part by the adaptation of these *boom femenino* best-seller novels for the big screen, as well as by the *superescritora* status of Allende, Mastretta, and Esquivel.

The term *literatura light* in reference to the work by some women writers in Spanish America has triggered heated discussions around concepts such as 'women's writing' and the nature of literature and its place in a global world. In Mexico, there is wide dissension amongst scholars of women's writing concerning the location of women writers within the Mexican literary tradition. There is also strong evidence of a questioning of traditional feminist classifications and renewed focus on the usefulness (and indeed theoretical difficulty) of the use of the category of the 'woman writer' or, even more problematically, 'women's writing'. The reliance on these two distinct categories is further complicated in the Mexican context by a paradoxical situation in which such labelling is actively embraced by some, whilst a widely articulated hostility towards such classification and labelling is similarly evinced. Though there is ample evidence to support the continued existence of resentment towards women writers and often unchallenged assumptions about the content of their writing, it is also the case that many women writers actively seek recognition on the basis of their prose being written about and for women, and that their success as women writers frequently rests entirely on their gendered positioning within the Mexican literary sphere. Examples of this include work by Mastretta, Esquivel, Nissán, and Loaeza, who address an almost exclusively female readership. Yet quite a number of Mexican female writers are also reluctant to acknowledge that they are female writers or belong to the *boom femenino* for fear of derogatory pigeonholing. It could be argued that the defensive position adopted by many writers in Mexico is symptomatic of a continuing chauvinism, the legendary Mexican *machismo* that continues to relegate women writers to a kind of sub-category. María Luisa Puga has admitted, for example, to a dislike of labels and even to a fear of distinctions.[18] Ana Clavel is quite candid about her aversion to labels, because of the particularly negative effect that it has had on women's writing, and its reception, in Mexico.[19]

It must also be noted however that many writers, including Clavel, welcome the increasing scholarly attention paid to their work. At the same time, just as many contemporary writers are now repudiating the Mexican *boom femenino* altogether because of its association with the idea that women writers exclusively write *literatura light*, so too are many critics calling for fellow academics to start to look for alternative ways of discussing and writing about this group of writers and their works which move beyond labelling based on notions of agency and gender categorizations. There appears to be a division between some scholars (hostile in the same way as the writers they study) to the classification of women writers as a separate sub-category and others who insist on the political importance of the category of 'woman writer' and the feminist necessity to continue to study it as separate.[20] The divergent, even contradictory, positions and remarks on these issues reveal the complex web of meanings and attitudes that surround the terms 'feminine' or 'women's' literature, and the dilemmas women authors face regarding this classification. Yet, as Irma López points out, many:

> agree that as changes in culture and mentality continue to take place in Mexican society there will be less of a need for such distinctions, they will eventually disappear, and the literary skill of a genderless 'writer' will be discussed instead. ('The Will to Be', p. 32)

It is in the context of such debates and the generalized perception of the *boom femenino* as the primer of light writing, or as conveying heterosexual conservatism in the works of especially the first generation of female writers such as Mastretta, Esquivel, Loaeza, or Nissán, that a second generation of writers associated with this wave are consciously writing fiction which seeks to set itself apart from their predecessors. Whilst second generation writers such as Clavel, Cristina Rivera-Garza, or Ana García Bergua, for instance, see their work as broadly convergent with certain strands of the Mexican *boom femenino*, for example their feminist principles which include notions of gender inequality, as well as their focus on sexuality, the body, and the voices of marginalized sectors of society, they consciously write works of fiction which are not of the best-seller type associated with certain Mexican women's writing of the *boom femenino*. Clavel was particularly adamant on this point in our 2008 interview (unpublished), and such views are equally powerfully captured in the title of an article entitled 'Ana Clavel asegura que está al margen del "best seller"' [Ana Clavel affirms that she is on the margins of the 'best seller'].[21] Here Clavel tells us that she does not divert her attention away from writing literature in order to 'tomar el atajo y la ruta del "best seller"' [to take a shortcut down the 'best seller' path]. Clavel's desire to break away from formulaic forms of writing and her need to challenge certain stereotypical assumptions about the content of *boom femenino* writing is reflected in her queer aesthetics, as we shall discuss next.

The Queer

In order to understand Clavel's queer aesthetics, as well as the development of her literary and multimedia output, a chronological approach will be taken to her work, beginning with an examination of her collections of short stories, *Fuera de escena* (1984) [Behind the Scenes], *Amorosos de atar* (1992) [Stark Mad Lovers], *Paraísos trémulos* (2002) [Quivering Paradises], and *Amor y otros suicidios* (2012) [Love and Other Suicides]; her short stories published in (online) literary magazines, and others which are unpublished.[22] Then will follow an exploration of her novels *Los deseos y su sombra* (2000) [Desire and its Shadow] and *Cuerpo náufrago* (2005) [Shipwrecked Body], followed by her novella *Las Violetas son flores del deseo* (2007) [Violets are Flowers of Desire] and novel *El dibujante de sombras* (2009) [The Shadow Artist].[23] All of Clavel's works are united by the themes of queer sexuality and desire which recur throughout these texts. By engaging with Clavel's particular exploration of variegated desire from her early work to her more recent output, this will provide the reader with an understanding of how her conception of desire permeates her literary trajectory. Thus, it will be discussed how whilst *Cuerpo náufrago* and *Las Violetas* deal almost exclusively with erotic desire, her other works, that is some of her short fiction as well as *Los deseos* and *El dibujante*, deal not uniquely with sexual desire, but also with other types of (non-) desire including, for instance, a desire for (self-) recognition or a desire for creative and ideological freedom. As will be demonstrated, Clavel can be seen to be driven by the need to highlight the way in which human sexual instinct, even as symbolic forces seek to control it, is irrepressible. Specifically, this study seeks to unravel how notions of 'compulsory heterosexuality' are both reinforced and simultaneously challenged through the texts' diverse forms of sexual desire. Clavel's interest in incest, paedophilia, homosexuality, lesbianism, transgender, transvestism, doll or urinal fetish, and other 'non-mainstream' themes which pepper her works, offers a decidedly fresh perspective than the more dour approach — some critics would argue — of various mainstream *boom femenino* writers such as Esquivel and Mastretta, who focus on heteronormative (sexual) relations. Clavel's exploration of non-heterosexuality is in line with other second generation *boom femenino* writers such as García Bergua or Susana Pagano.

Clavel's works are thus notable for their queerness and transgressive thrust. In my study, the queer is used in relation to the author's work firstly as an example of 'outer-circle' sexualities.[24] Secondly, the queer refers to Kaminsky's understanding of the term, which according to the critic, not only 'serves to destabilize and denaturalize notions of sex and gender but also to unsettle notions of the normal'.[25] This particular reading of queer is also supported by David Halperin who remarks that 'queer' need not necessarily refer to sexuality, but also to anything which defies normalcy.[26] Thus as I hope to demonstrate, Clavel's queering stands, as Kaminsky notes, 'for that unbalancing act, the disturbance of the status quo that requires a re-visioning, in Adrienne Rich's words, of all our categories' (p. 210). Clavel disturbs conceptions of the normal not only by representing 'outlaw' sexualities and 'dark' desires but also by incorporating into her fictive world that which is at odds with normalcy as illustrated in the presence of carnivalesque viscerality, the fantastical, the shadow, ghosts, cyborgs, dolls, golems, and even urinals, all of which serve to question notions of the proper by verbalizing the 'unsaid' of rationalism. Clavel's works are linked by their need to queer certain 'givens', whether these be religious, moral, sexual, cultural, or historical, and by repeatedly seeking to transgress various 'taboos du jour'. It will be shown how Clavel's works as a whole create an illuminating portrait of (Mexican) society's particular fears, anxieties, and disavowed desires. In true postmodern spirit, Clavel can be seen as seeking to destabilize monological meaning, and general concepts such as 'essence', 'origins', 'authenticity', 'truth', and 'aura'[27] are queered via intertextuality and multimediality, or the exploration of notions, for instance, of replica, simulacra, and the 'liquidation of referentials'.[28] One feature which strongly emerges in all of her works in the context of the queer is the notion that texts, in all their variegated forms, resist the notion of singular authorship. At the same time Clavel's multimedia works in particular evince a tension in the sense that whilst they suggest the idea of art as collaboration, they also assert Clavel's authority as choreographer of the overall multimedia exhibits and in particular the creator of her literary works. Even though Clavel is influenced by the feminist thrust of Spanish American *boom femenino* writing, her adoption in some of her fiction of the male narrative voice represents an intentional queering of some of the early *boom femenino* writing where female writers often felt obliged to write about women and their experiences because of the prevailing second-wave feminist thinking, but in particular because of the pressures of the book publishing industry for women writers to produce marketable 'women's writing'. This move can be understood as a wider concern expressed by many contemporary Mexican female writers about the gendering of literature, and their particular hostility towards any form of classification or labelling.[29]

The queer also serves to highlight the various interlocking disruptions which are apparent in the author's works at the level of genre and the way in which she destabilizes disciplinary and discursive boundaries. Genre trouble in her *oeuvre* is predominantly suggested in the manner in which Clavel incorporates and plays with non-literary genres including (digital) photography, art in the form of sketches, and illustrations. What is particularly queer about Clavel's work is that, unlike many *boom femenino* writers who work exclusively with the literary written form, the author endorses both the literary form and multimedia. Clavel's works embrace an array of hybrid forms including the audiovisual, internet-enabled technology such as YouTube or web pages, as well as other media such as art installation, (video) performance, and photographic exhibition which have been displayed in various public spaces and cultural centres in Mexico. Therefore the concept of multimedia is central to my analysis of her work. I use this term in both senses of the word provided by the *OED* to refer to Clavel's 'use of more than one medium of communication and artistic expression', as well as to the way in which she incorporates 'a number of media, such as text, audio, video, and animation' within individual outputs.[30] I also use multimedia in the way that the different media — text, sound, image, and video — are 'presented together synchronously yet remain distinct'.[31] Finally, intermediality, an extension of multimedia, will also be used to explore the manner in which Clavel draws on different media such as painting and photography, and contemporary media such as computer technology, and how it is through their interaction that a new artistic mediation emerges.[32] In terms of Clavel's trajectory, it will be shown how her interest in non-literary forms can be traced back to her early fiction, and how since then she has increasingly embraced other media such as cyber technology or installation art which extend beyond the textual form. Her literary trajectory thus follows a queer path in the sense that she has moved from singular modes of creative expression in the form of literary writing, a traditional print medium, towards other non-literary forms, which has the effect of queering but similarly enriching each distinct medium she draws from.

Clavel is part of a bigger wave of other Spanish American writers who have also used multimedia, such as Doménico Chiappe, Verónica Gerber, or Mario Bellatin. Like Clavel, writers often use different media beyond the printed medium, particularly cyber technology, to promote their works and media personalities and to broaden their reading public. Blogsites, for instance, are a particular popular medium for this. Mexican female and male writers such as Cristina Rivera Garza, Eve Gil, Dolores Dorantes, Ángeles Mastretta, Amaranta Caballero, and Jorge Volpi, are a few of the many existing Mexican authors who have been writing blogs for several years. These accessible online blogs range from merely text-based blogs to audiovisual formats combined with text. Clavel also has her own website (<http://www.anaclavel.com/>) which she uses to publicize her works and to assert her status as multimedia writer in the form of a blog. Clavel also uses Facebook and Twitter for this same purpose.[33] What makes Clavel's particular mode of multimedia innovative is its range and its interconnectedness, with its involvement of relatively large-scale exhibitions and the participation of artists, performers, or 'back-stage' helpers such as IT experts. *Los deseos*, *Cuerpo náufrago*, *Las Violetas*, and *Las ninfas a veces sonríen* have formed the basis of such wider multimedia projects. Three of Clavel's works (*El dibujante*, *Amor y otros suicidios*, and *Las ninfas*) have also been publicized in book trailer format on YouTube (to be explored in Chapter 10) and similarly assert the sheer range of multimedia mediums with which the author engages. An author who compares broadly with Clavel's multimedia endeavours is the Chilean Diamela Eltit (b. 1949) who exemplifies the writer who has straddled diverse fields, as we see in relation to her novel *Lumpérica* (1983), for instance. Many have described this piece as more of a multimedia performance than a novel because of its appropriation of other non-literary techniques in the form of theatre, performance, video installation, and photography.[34] In an interview given in 1985, the author mentions that she does not seek to compartmentalize her visual and literary practices (Green, p. 25), which of course resonates deeply with Clavel's own aesthetics. Another Chilean writer and visual artist whose work has synergies with that of Clavel is Eugenia Prado who has written a number of multimedia works including *Hembros: novela instalación* which is underscored by its gender and genre bending thrust. The Guatemalan Regina José Galindo (b. 1974), though primarily known for her performance art, also moves in and out of various mediums including poetry, (video) performance, and cyber technologies in the form of blog writing which comprises essays, photographs, poems, and short stories. By examining Clavel's overall multimedia interventions, I will argue that Clavel is not merely a writer but a multimedia writer and, by extension, multimedia artist, whose engagement with the non-literary evinces a strong artistic sensibility and prowess. In exploring Clavel's multimedia endeavours, this study also seeks to establish whether, in an age when the transformation of culture in the twenty-first century is being fuelled with new technologies and different media, so-called traditional written cultures are being threatened or enhanced by such innovations. It will similarly be argued here that whilst Clavel is principally driven by a preoccupation with the conceptual intention behind her *oeuvre*, her overall multimedia efforts as well as her extensive media exposure also show a sharp sense for business and self-promotion of her public persona as (multimedia) writer. In this study I will discuss the relationship between queerness, multimedia interventions, and literature in Clavel's works and her multimedia public persona. In doing so, this study may be seen to contribute towards a possible theoretical framework within which to conceptualize the emerging 'canon' of (Latin American) writers and artists and their personas working with literature, cyberspace, and multimedia.

Having provided readers with an overview of Clavel's queer art, a brief chapter-by-chapter explanation of the study's contents and structure is needed. This monograph takes a chronological approach to Clavel's literary and multimedia output, from her earliest to more recent cultural production. It comprises ten chapters, each focusing on one or more texts or multimedia intervention by the author, and a conclusion. Thus, in Chapter 1 it will be argued how outlaw sexualities and (sexual) desire are a key motif in Ana Clavel's hitherto practically unexplored collections of short stories *Fuera de escena*, *Amorosos de atar*, *Paraísos trémulos*, *Amor y otros suicidios*, and other stories, either published or unpublished. In this respect, the short stories to be examined here encapsulate some of the concerns that come fully to the fore in the later works of Ana Clavel, as we shall see. Particular areas that will be explored in this chapter include Clavel's interest in 'no-deseos'. This term is one which Clavel often uses to refer to outlaw and forbidden sexual desires both in, and in relation to, her entire *oeuvre*. Non-desires also relate to repressed or unfulfilled desires, in the context of popular culture for instance, or to desires which are linked to, for example, feminism, motherhood, and writing and their particular relationship to life and death. Whilst Clavel's short stories do not engage extensively with non-literary disciplines such as photography or art, a number of them do nevertheless incorporate images and evince an interest in cinema, thus signalling the early stirrings of Clavel's nascent interest in multimedia.[35] Here the links between the literary and the non-literary will be examined in order to expand upon the diverse themes of (non-) desire.

This study then centres on the novels *Los deseos* (Chapter 2) and *Cuerpo náufrago* (Chapters 3, 4, and 5), both in terms of their literary and multimedia dimensions. In *Los deseos* the defiance of notions of historical 'truth' and the reconstruction of alternative conceptions of national identity are inexorably interwoven with the creation of a non-patriarchal conception of female subjectivity. Here Clavel's exploration of the female subject is analyzed in the context of Kristeva's theories of subjectivity in relation to the *sujet en procès* (1977) and the abject (1982).[36] Central to Clavel's work are the tropes of (dis)embodiment, invisibility, and the magical, which are linked to the concept of non-conformism. Finally, this chapter will explore briefly Clavel's notion of 'poética de sombras' [shadow poetics] in the context of her book as well as the relatively small-scale multimedia intervention for the promotion of *Los deseos*.

Cuerpo náufrago (Chapter 3) explores questions of the self, the corporeal, and desire in the context of wider issues which are connected to (trans)gender construction and sexual politics in Mexico. What marks out *Cuerpo náufrago* as a queer text is seen in its fantastical dimension as well as in its scope of 'outer-circle' sexualities (Rubin, 'Thinking Sex') which serve Clavel as a vehicle to examine Judith Butler's discussions on the subject of 'doing gender' and performativity (1990) and the postmodern perception of the (sexual) self as inchoate.[37] The multimedia dimension of *Cuerpo náufrago* is then examined in Chapter 4. This chapter focuses on the notion of discursive and genre trouble by exploring the connections between text and image in the context of the Barthesian notions of 'plaisir' ('pleasurable reading') and 'jouissance' ('erotics of reading'), and Kristeva's abjection (*Powers of Horror*).[38] Image and text also work together as a means of sustaining and challenging conventional discourses of bodily control and cleanliness which are inherent in the 'civilizing process' in Western and non-Western cultures, as well as gender and sexual categories. Questions relating to the clean, civilized body, the role of sanitation, toilets, and gender, are explored in relation to a number of works such as those of Laporte on the role of 'shit', Kristeva on the abject (in *Powers of Horror*), Douglas on 'matter out of place', Bakhtin on the grotesque, Tenorio-Trillo on Mexico's civilizing project, and Gershenson and Penner on the manner in which toilets are shaped by concepts of hygiene, propriety, and the binary gender division.[39] Chapter 5 offers an exploration of the interrelationship between the literary and multimedia by looking at notions of intertextuality, intermediality, and hypertextuality and how they serve to challenge the category of the originary itself and concepts of 'authority', 'authenticity', and 'uniqueness' which traditional conceptions of art and literature sustain. Intermediality will be examined so as to highlight the manner in which Clavel fuses a number of historically incongruous media such as the traditional (painting, the sculptural, and photography) with the new (cyber digital technology) in order to create a fresh type of mediation which involves a self-reflective process. Given the close synergies between *Cuerpo náufrago* and *Las*

Violetas in terms of their hypertextual dimension, I will examine hypertextuality in this chapter in relation to both works of fiction. Finally, *Cuerpo náufrago*'s broader *proyecto multimedia*, which consisted of a mural and urban space intervention, an art installation, a web page, performance, and photographic exhibition, suggests troubling of various kinds.

I then provide an analysis of Clavel's *Las Violetas flores del deseo* (Chapters 6, 7, and 8). Chapter 6 will discuss how Clavel explodes sexual taboos in the form of incest, rape, or paedophilia in *Las Violetas*. By comparing the novella to Vladimir Nabokov's *Lolita* (1955), it will be argued that the reason why *Las Violetas* so intensely perturbs resides in the manner in which the narrative obliges the reader to become an accomplice and partner in crime. Julián's doll fetish, a prime example of the queer, and the central theme of substitution underpins the key notions relating to the real and the simulacra. It is in this context that I will explore the manner in which Clavel's Violetas are avatars of the Golem figure in Jewish Kabbalistic tradition and *Las Hortensias* (1949) by Felisberto Hernández. Clavel deconstructs the female Golem myth given that the (unruly and monstrous abject) maternal/female presence in the process of (pro)creation cannot be eradicated. Drawing from the cyborg and cyber theories of Donna Haraway and Rosi Braidotti, the fusion of the real and unreal Violetas and notions of disembodiment provides feminist renewal as it highlights possibilities latent in the posthuman which disrupt traditional patriarchal understandings of reality, identity, and the body.[40] The real/hyperreal, original/replica opposition gains relevance in relation to notions of 'aura' (Benjamin, 'The Work of Art'), uniqueness, mimesis, intertextuality, authenticity, and authority.

My examination of the multimedia dimension of *Cuerpo náufrago* as an example of the queer is continued in the context of *Las Violetas* and its cover (Chapter 7), as well as its multimedia project (Chapter 8), which consisted of four distinct, but interrelated, areas: an exhibition of fourteen papier-mâché dolls, a performance, an installation, and a website. I examine the dust jacket image of *Las Violetas* which also formed part of the exhibition. The negative reception of the cover's explicit image may be understood because of the way in which the image plays upon a visible incongruity between innocent childhood and sexualized child-teenager, and consequently resists offering a safe interpretation. I take my cue from Gérard Genette's notion of paratextuality,[41] and specifically peritextuality as well as from Pauline Harris's and Barbara McKenzie's own ideas on these concepts.[42] I will analyse the text's peritextual elements in order to suggest that peritextuality both serves to anchor the viewer-reader's understanding and to disrupt interpretations. In Chapter 8 I move onto an examination of the photographic art installation of the multimedia exhibition, the cyber representation of this installation, as well as the doll exhibition. Drawing from the works of Mulvey, Halberstam, McGrath, and Suleiman, it will be argued that the installation and various paratextual elements draw the spectator's attention to the manner in which the signifier does not educe one meaning but multiple interpretations.[43] I examine the dolls which draw their inspiration from those of Bellmer and Hernández, the Mexican Lupita, and compare them to the 'real' sex dolls manufactured by Abyss Creations and Orient

Industry. The dolls represent an ambiguous oscillation between both the human and non-human as well as epitomizing Creed's notion of the monstrous-feminine and the Kristevan abject.[44] The dolls are a fusion of creative sources: they embody an interpretation(s) of Clavel's text as well as drawing directly from the personal creative styles of the artists who intervened on them. Finally, the performance and its various multimedia dimensions serve as vehicles to explore (non-) textual constructedness as well as prompting the spectator to engage critically with questions of child sexualization, (paedophilic) sexual violence, reader-spectator complicity, and female objectification.

Before detailing the content of the chapter on *El dibujante* (Chapter 9), it is important to provide a brief explanation to the reader as to why I have chosen to dedicate more extensive readings to *Cuerpo náufrago* and *Las Violetas* over a number of other texts examined in this study. Whilst *Los deseos* and *El dibujante* engage with multimedia forms, Clavel's use of the non-literary component is much more comprehensive and extensive in *Cuerpo náufrago* and *Las Violetas* and therefore one chapter is deemed insufficient to furnish readers with an in-depth understanding of these two 'texts'. Given that Clavel perceives herself foremost as a writer, it is important to provide a literary analysis of *Cuerpo náufrago* and *Las Violetas*. At the same time, a 'non-literary' approach is also warranted given the sheer variety of multimedia forms Clavel engages with in, and in relation to, these 'texts', firstly by using the visual in the actual work of fiction in the form of photographs, sketches, or illustrations, and secondly by exploiting in the context of art exhibitions a number of mediums comprising performance, mural and urban space interventions, internet, art installation, or photographic display. The argument in each subsequent chapter about *Cuerpo náufrago* and *Las Violetas* will thus deal with different dimensions of the texts and will also shift emphasis in theoretical and conceptual terms in each case. At the same time, it will become apparent that the central themes of these works of fiction are ones which reappear in their multimedia dimension, and therefore the theoretical approaches used and overall focus in each chapter will frequently dovetail and complement one another.

Chapter 9 will provide an analysis of *El dibujante de sombras*. This novel has inexorable connections to Clavel's previous works in its exploration of notions of the split subjectivity, replica, origins, intertextuality, (non-) conformity, (erotic) desire, and in particular its need to question religious, moral, sexual, cultural, or historical assumptions. Clavel's obsession with the 'poética de las sombras', which pervades *Los desesos*, and to an extent her other works, is central to our appreciation of *El dibujante,* and is intimately linked to the opposition between shadow and light and a myriad of other binary contrasts. Set in the Enlightenment, *El dibujante* requires a new historical and postmodern treatment given that it centres on real past events and persons which are simultaneously fictionalized, and focuses on the underbelly of history, and on those aspects of 'truth' which some of the official biographies of Johann Kaspar Lavater appear to have omitted. The ambiguities surrounding this character's life and relationship with his assistant Giotto are explored in particular in the context of Lavater's theological thinking and his 'science' of physiognomy. The proliferating references to shadow art and the camera obscura, as well as

Clavel's use of illustrations throughout the text, address interesting questions in the context of notions such as 'essence', 'aura' (Benjamin, 'The Work of Art'), 'authenticity', authority, mechanical reproduction, digital (replication) imitation, and intertextuality. Similarly, Clavel unqueers the negative otherness typically attached to the shadow in the history of art by exploring the myths of origins in relation to the birth of art, knowledge, representation, and projection. The shadow is a typically neglected area of interest in art history criticism perhaps because of its archetypal connotation of death, nothingness, and disembodiment.

The multimedia project in the form of a book trailer which ensued from *El dibujante* will be discussed in Chapter 10. Here I will also provide some remarks about Clavel's overall works of fiction, a brief analysis of her latest novella, *Las ninfas* and its multimedia dimension, as well as discussing Clavel's further wider multimedia involvement, including her YouTube, Facebook, and blog interventions, which have helped to promote her public persona and her status as multimedia writer. It will be discussed here how her literary multimedia ventures raise interesting questions relating to reader/user participation, consumer persuasion, and questions of multi-authorship. The conclusion will provide some final thoughts on Clavel's queer status as multimedia artist-writer, and literature's overall 'representational privilege'.[45]

In keeping with Clavel's queer fiction, my own theoretical approach in examining her literary and multimedia works is 'queered' in the sense that my book seeks to dislodge familiar disciplinary divides as well as the theoretical and methodological categories attending them. My approach to the question of sexuality, gender, and desire will be informed by theoretical work which stems predominantly from (Latin American) gender, queer, feminist and literary studies (Butler, Domenella, Finnegan, Norriega, Prieto, Prieur). Various visual art, music, intermedial, cyborg and cyberspace theories and works on these areas (Chiappe, Castillo, Haraway, Mahon, Landow, Rajewsky Rycenga, Rubin Suleiman, Taylor, Will) will also serve as important sources to enhance our understanding of Clavel's literary and multimedia interventions. This book involves a continual self-interrogating practice which draws attention to both the strengths and weaknesses of some of the theoretical paradigms applied to the texts.

This book will also draw from extensive unpublished interviews I conducted with Ana Clavel between 2008 and 2011, as well as ongoing email and telephone exchanges. They will be an important contribution to the overall study given that they shed new light on our understanding of her literary and multimedia works. Here I discuss with the author topics which are relevant to the monograph's overall thematics, such as her position within the Mexican *boom femenino*, the function of sex and desire in her work, and the role of non-literary genres such as photography and multimedia. It is often argued that the view of the author is of little or no relevance in relation to the content of their works. By drawing from excerpts from the interviews my intention is not to concede 'authority' to Clavel's views, but rather to show how the author's opinions on her own creation add to the richness which the multiple interpretations her literary and multimedia texts elicit in readers, participants, critics, and author alike.

Notes to the Introduction

1. Clavel also writes non-fiction with contributions to *El Universal*, for instance, and has written a book of essays entitled *A la sombra de los deseos en flor: ensayos sobre la fuerza metafórica del deseo* (Mexico: Universidad Autónoma de la Ciudad de México, 2008) [In the Shadow of the Apogee of Desires. Essays on the Metaphorical Power of Desire].
2. Existing criticism on Clavel will be used throughout this study. Significant contributions to our understanding on Clavel's work include, for example, Irma López's work on the author in *Confluencias y demarcaciones: Generaciones literarias y expresiones estéticas en la novela mexicana, 1998–2008*, 18, Ensayo (Mexico: Ediciones y Gráficos Eón, 2011), pp. 143–75; and Luzma Becerra's 'Otra forma de estar en el mundo, o la ciudad subterránea en *Los deseos y su sombra*, de Ana Clavel', Instituto Tecnológico y de Estudios Superiores de Monterrey, *Revista Iztapalapa*, 52 (2002), 245–59.
3. Edmundo Paz-Soldán and Debra A. Castillo (eds.), *Latin American Literature and Mass Media*, Hispanic Issues, 22 (New York: Garland, 2001); Claire Taylor and Thea Pitman (eds.), *Latin American Cyberculture and Cyberliterature* (Liverpool: Liverpool University Press, 2007).
4. For works on the Mexican *boom femenino* see the bibliography. Nuala Finnegan, and Jane E. Lavery (eds.), *The Boom Femenino in Mexico: Reading Contemporary Women's Writing* (Newcastle Upon Tyne: Cambridge Scholars Publishing, 2010) is a collection of essays that focuses on literary production by women in Mexico over the last three decades. The book is the first of its kind to engage critically with the notion of *boom femenino*.
5. Clavel's fiction is nevertheless becoming increasingly well known, particularly as a number of her works have been translated into English and other languages and has received numerous literary prizes including, amongst others, the Société académique's 'Arts-Sciences-Lettres' silver medal in 2004.
6. Donald L. Shaw, *The Post-Boom in Spanish American Fiction*, Suny Series in Latin American and Iberian Thought and Culture (Albany: State University of New York Press, 1998). Shaw's definition of the *post-boom* is rather narrow since *boom femenino* writers associated with the *post-boom* also demonstrate a keen interest in complex issues such as literary theory, philosophy, or technical creativity, as does Clavel. Any form of categorization is fraught with risk and indeed many critics have debated where the origins of the *boom* lie as well as questioning both its usefulness and appropriateness. For further detail on these debates, see Finnegan and Lavery.
7. Irma López, '"The Will to Be": Mexican Women Novelists from the late 1960s to the 1990s', in Finnegan and Lavery (eds.), *The Boom Femenino in Mexico*, pp. 26–47 (p. 27).
8. Whilst *post-boom* refers to the writing of both male and female writers, the *boom femenino* is a term specifically used to refer to Spanish American (Mexican) women's writing and its association, as we shall see, with the (Mexican) global publishing industry and with debates relating to, for instance, 'light literature' and to notions of 'women's writing'. Various sections in both this introduction and throughout this study appear in Jane Lavery, 'The *Superescritora* Ángeles Mastretta: The Strategies of a Best-Seller Writer in Projecting and Maintaining (Literary) Superstardom', *Journal of Iberian and Latin American Research*, 16:2 (2010), 117–31, <www.tandfonline.com> [accessed July 2014]. Various sections in this chapter also appear in Finnegan and Lavery (eds.), *The Boom Femenino in Mexico* (published with permission of Cambridge Scholars Press).
9. Dawn Slack, 'If a Mexican Woman Wrote, and No One Read Her, Did She Really Write? An Examination of Cristina Pacheco's Contributions to the *B(l)oom Femenino* in Mexico', in Finnegan and Lavery (eds.), *The Boom Femenino in Mexico*, pp. 92–107 (p. 104).
10. Lorraine Kelly, '"La Pieza desquiciante de la jerarquía": Reading the Work of Brianda Domecq as a Philosophy of Feminism', in Finnegan and Lavery (eds.), *The Boom Femenino in Mexico*, pp. 149–65 (p. 150).
11. As discussed by Nuala Finnegan '"Light" Women/"Light" Literature: Women and Popular Fiction in Mexico Since 1980', *Donaire*, 15 (2000 a), 18–22. It is not only the likes of Esquivel and Mastretta who are dismissed because they produce 'light' commercial literature: the same criticism is directed at male authors, such as Mexican novelist Elmer Mendoza, who in the past

ten years have jumped onto the bandwagon of popularity of the so-called *narco literatura* and *literatura de violencia*.

12. Nuala Finnegan, *Ambivalence, Modernity, Power: Women and Writing in Mexico since 1980* (Oxford: Peter Lang, 2007), p. 160.
13. Poniatowska represents a dual position in the sense that she was writing fiction during the *boom* and was one the few female writers who came to form part of, and was widely respected in, the elite circle of mainly male writers of the *boom*. But this author also continued to write during the *boom femenino* and her writing is widely perceived as reflecting the concerns of this wave, as discussed earlier.
14. Elena Poniatowska, 'Los éxitos y las críticas', *Clarín*, 2 September 2003, <http://edant.clarin.com/diario/2003/02/09/ s04003.htm> [accessed 10 May 2014]. Here, and unless stated otherwise elsewhere, the English translation is mine.
15. Debra A. Shaw, 'Bestsellers', in Verity Smith (ed.), *Encyclopedia of Latin American Literature* (London: Fitzroy Dearbourn, 1997), pp. 115–18; Lavery, 'The *Superescritora*', p. 210.
16. For an analysis on the conservatism of these writers see Emily Hind, 'Six Authors on the Conservative Side of the Boom Femenino, 1985–2003: Boullosa, Esquivel, Loaeza, Mastretta, Nissán and Sefchovich', in Finnegan and Lavery (eds.), *The Boom Femenino in Mexico*, pp. 48–72.
17. Jane Lavery, *Ángeles Mastretta: Textual Multiplicity* (Woodbridge: Tamesis, 2005); Claire Taylor, *Bodies and Texts: Configurations of Identity in the Works of Griselda Gambaro, Albalucía Ángel and Laura Esquivel*, MHRA (Leeds: Maney, 2003).
18. Beth K. Miller, *A la sombra del volcán: conversaciones sobre la narrativa mexicana actual* (Guadalajara: Universidad de Guadalajara/Xalli, 1990), p. 249.
19. Jane Lavery, unpublished interview with Ana Clavel, 2008. In her acceptance speech for the Premio Iberoamericano de Novela Elena Poniatowska 2013, for *Las ninfas a veces sonríen*, Clavel states her position very clearly vis-à-vis classificatory terms used for female writers by stating that 'I am not a woman ... I am a writer'. Ana Clavel, <http://anaclavel.com/blog/2013/10/18/palabras-al-recibir-el-premio-iberoamericano-de-novela-elena-poniatowska-2013/> [accessed 10 June 2014].
20. Nuala Finnegan and Jane E. Lavery, 'Introduction', in Finnegan and Lavery (eds.), *The Boom Femenino in Mexico*, pp. 1–25 (p. 9). This disparity is reflective, perhaps, of a wide debate in feminist scholarship which, in rudimentary terms, is divided between a feminism 'of equality' and a feminism 'of difference'.
21. 'Ana Clavel asegura que está al margen del "best seller"', no author, *Informador*, Thursday 8 March (2009), <http://www.informador.com.mx/cultura/2009/161631/6/ana-clavel-asegura-que-esta-al-margen-del-best-seller.htm> [accessed 8 June 2014].
22. Ana Clavel, *Fuera de escena* (Mexico City: Letras Nuevas, 1984), *Amorosos de atar* ([Culiacán]: Dirección de Investigación y Fomento de Cultura Regional del Estado de Sinaloa, 1992), *Paraísos trémulos* (Mexico City: Alfaguara, 2002), *Amor y otros suicidios* (Mexico City: B de Bolsillo, 2012); 'La Imagen del espejo' [The Image of the Mirror], in *Antología*, ed. by Yolanda Medina Haro, (Mexico City: taller de creación Colegio de Bachilleres # 1, plantel El Rosario, 1979) pp. 11–15; 'Un deseo realizado' [A Desire Fulfilled], *Revista de la Universidad de México*, 65 (2009), 68–69, <http://www.revistadelauniversidad.unam.mx/6509/conten.html> [accessed 8 June 2014].
23. Ana Clavel, *Los deseos y su sombra* (Mexico City: Alfaguara, 2000), English translation: *Desire and its Shadow*, trans. by Jay Miskowiec (Minneapolis: Aliform, 2006); *Cuerpo náufrago* (Mexico City: Alfaguara, 2005), English translation: *Shipwrecked Body*, trans. by Jay Miskowiec (Minneapolis: Aliform Publishing, 2008); *Las Violetas son flores del deseo* (Mexico City: Alfaguara, 2007), French translation: *Les Violettes sont les fleurs du désir,* trans. by François Gaudry (Paris: Métailié, 2009), and Arabic translation (Lebanon: Dar-Al-Farabi, 2011); *El dibujante de sombras* (Mexico City: Alfaguara, 2009), French translation: *Le Dessinateur d'ombres*, trans. by Brigitte Jensen (Paris: Éditions Anne Carrière, 2013). For reasons of space I will not examine in depth Clavel's latest novella, *Las ninfas a veces sonríen* (Mexico City: Alfaguara, 2012) [When Nymphs Smile], nor the multimedia dimension, although I will briefly allude to their significance in the context of her wider works in Chapter 10. Clavel has kindly given me permission to reproduce various images throughout the monograph which I will use for my analysis of her overall literary and multimedia works.

24. Gayle Rubin, 'Thinking Sex: Notes for a Radical Theory of the Politics of Sexuality', in Carole S. Vance (ed.), *Pleasure and Danger: Exploring Female Sexuality* (Boston: Routledge, 1984), pp. 267–319.
25. Amy Kaminsky, 'The Queering of Latin American Literary Studies', *Latin American Research Review*, 36:2 (2001), 209–19 (p. 210).
26. David M. Halperin, *Saint Foucault: Towards a Gay Hagiography* (Oxford: Oxford University Press, 1995), p. xxiii.
27. Walter Benjamin, 'The Work of Art in the Age of Mechanical Reproduction', in *Illuminations* (London: Pimlico, 1999), pp. 211–44.
28. Jean Baudrillard, *Simulations* (New York: Semiotext(e), 1983).
29. The exploration of 'no-deseos' [non-desires] from the perspective of a male narrator or character preponderates not only in Clavel's short stories but also in a number of her subsequent works. The predominance of the male narrative voice is linked to her desire to 'tomar distancia de todas las escritoras que hablaban de sus pequeños mundos de cocina y de costura' [distance myself from those female writers who talk about an inward-looking world of cooking and sewing]. Jorge Luis Herrera, 'Escritora de deseos y sombras: entrevista con Ana Clavel', [n.d.], <http://www.uaemex.mx/plin/colmena/Colmena%2051/Conversaciones/Ana.html> [accessed 3 June 2014]. Here Clavel notes that 'good' literature is not necessarily about speaking about one's own 'true' experiences which are linked to one's 'authentic' gender, but rather about offering readers a singular literary vision. Clavel's desire to speak about diverse (sexual) identities, whether male, female, or (non-) heterosexual could also be seen as a strategy to queer the perception that all *boom femenino* writers address an almost exclusively female readership.
30. *Oxford English Dictionary*, 'Multimedia', (2011), <http://www.oed.com/viewdictionaryentry/Entry/123564> [accessed 10 June 2014].
31. Yvonne Spielmann, 'Synesthesia and Intersenses: Intermedia in Electronic Images', *Leonardo*, 34:1 (2001), 55–61 (p. 57).
32. Ibid., p. 55; Ginette Verstraete, 'Intermedialities: A Brief Survey of Conceptual Key Issues', Acta Univ. Sapientiae, *Film and Media Studies*, 2 (2010), 7–14 (p. 10).
33. In Chapter 10 there will be further comments on Clavel's blog, Twitter, and Facebook interventions.
34. Mary Green, *Diamela Eltit: Reading the Mother* (Woodbridge: Tamesis, 2007), p. 25.
35. As will be discussed in Chapter 10, Clavel's *Amor y otros suicidios* does engage nevertheless with multimedia as it was promoted via two book trailers on YouTube.
36. Julia Kristeva, 'Le Sujet en procès', in *Polylogue* (Paris: Seuil, 1977), pp. 55–106, and *Powers of Horror: An Essay on Abjection*, trans. by Leon S. Roudiez (New York: Columbia University Press, 1982).
37. Judith Butler, *Gender Trouble: Feminism and the Subversion of Identity* (New York: Routledge, 1990).
38. Roland Barthes, *The Pleasure of the Text*, trans. by Richard Miller, note by Richard Howard (New York: Hill and Wang, 1975).
39. Dominique Laporte, *History of Shit*, trans. by Nadia Benabid and Rodolphe El-Khoury, intro. by Rodolphe El-Khoury (Cambridge, MA: MIT Press, 2000); Mary Douglas, *Purity and Danger: An Analysis of Concepts of Pollution and Taboo*, in *Collected Works*, 2 vols (London: Routledge, 2003), II; Mikhail M. Bakhtin, *Rabelais and his World*, trans. by Hélène Iswolsky (Bloomington: Indiana University Press, 1984); Mauricio Tenorio-Trillo, *Mexico at the World's Fairs: Crafting a Modern Nation*, The New Historicism: Studies in Cultural Poetics (Berkeley: University of California Press, 1996); Olga Gershenson, and Barbara Penner (eds.), *Ladies and Gents: Public Toilets and Gender* (Philadelphia: Temple University Press, 2009).
40. Donna Haraway, 'A Cyborg Manifesto: Science, Technology, and Socialist-Feminism in the Late Twentieth Century', in *Simians, Cyborgs and Women: The Reinvention of Nature* (New York: Routledge, 1991), pp. 149–81; Rosi Braidotti, *Nomadic Subjects: Embodiment and Sexual Difference in Contemporary Feminist Theory* (New York: Columbia University Press, 1994).
41. Gérard Genette, *Paratexts: The Thresholds of Textuality*, trans. by Jane E. Lewin, Literature, Culture, Theory, 20 (New York: Cambridge University Press, 1997).
42. Pauline Harris, 'At the Interface Between Reader and Text: Devices in Children's Picture Books that Mediate Reader Expectations and Interpretations', AARE Conference Paper,

Parramatta (2005), 1–17, <http://www.aare.edu.au/05pap/har05606.pdf> [accessed 22 June 2014]. Pauline Harris and Barbara McKenzie, 'Inviting Dissent: Classroom Practices for Nurturing Communities of Readers in the Early School Years', AARE Conference Paper, Parramatta, (2005), <http://www.aare.edu.au/05pap/har05289.pdf> [accessed 22 June 2014].

43. Laura Mulvey, 'Visual Pleasure and Narrative Cinema', *Screen* 16:3 (1975), 6–18; Judith Halberstam, *Female Masculinity* (Durham, NC: Duke University Press, 1998); Roberta McGrath, 'Re-reading Edward Weston: Feminism, Photography and Psychoanalysis', in Liz Wells (ed.), *The Photography Reader* (New York: Routledge, 2003), pp. 325–37; Susan Rubin Suleiman, 'Dialogue and Double Allegiance: Some Contemporary Women Artists and the Historical Avant-Garde', in Whitney Chadwick (ed.), *Mirror Images: Women, Surrealism, and Self Representation* (Cambridge, MA: MIT Press, 1998), pp. 128–55.

44. Creed, Barbara, *Monstrous-feminine: Film, Feminism, Psychoanalysis* (New York: Routledge, 1993).

45. Paz-Soldán and Castillo (eds.), *Latin American Literature and Mass Media*, p. 13.

CHAPTER 1

'Outlaw' Sexualities and Desires in Ana Clavel's Short Fiction

Desire is a key motif in Ana Clavel's hitherto academically virtually unexplored collection of short stories *Fuera de escena* (1984), *Amorosos de atar* (1992), *Paraísos trémulos* (2002) and *Amor y otros suicidios* (2012), as well as a number of short stories either published in online journals or unpublished ones which were personally provided to me by the author. It is vital to give attention to this particular thematic area of interest given that desire, in all its multifarious guises, remains a constant throughout Clavel's literary and multimedia work, as will become apparent in subsequent chapters. In this respect, the short stories form an early basis on which the later works by Clavel are built, in the sense that the issues raised by these short stories in relation to desire and in particular 'outlaw' sexualities are, in a way, embryonic in that they provide the seeds for Clavel's concerns in later writing. In the short stories, as we also see very clearly in Clavel's *Los deseos y su sombra*, *Cuerpo náufrago*, *Las Violetas son flores del deseo*, or *El dibujante de sombras*, Clavel's exploration of specifically sexual desire in its various configurations — heterosexual, lesbian, homosexual, transgender —, has a celebratory function aimed at mocking taboo and prohibition. By examining 'no-deseos' [non-desires], that is repressed or unfulfilled desires and specifically 'outlaw' sexuality such as transgender desire, lesbianism, extramarital affairs, orgiastic sex, and even sexual relations between cousins, Clavel can be seen as disturbing the reader's comfort zone in order to make him or her reflect upon notions of 'proper' or 'improper' relations. In particular, sexual multiplicity paradoxically serves both to bolster, and yet to challenge, the idea of desire as uniquely heterosexual, which is ultimately a product of (Mexican) culture's symbolic order and its organizing practices. Shaped by their sociocultural environment and by the narratives in circulation, it will be shown how some of the characters in the short stories are stifled by the prevailing heteronormative discourses of gender and sexuality. As many of the characters thus alternately struggle with and give in to their desires, these desires are occasionally disproportionally intensified, at times leading to lack and frustration. However, Clavel appears to demonstrate how other characters are also able to represent themselves, and thus negotiate a position that defies repressive ideologies. Sexual multiplicity also reinforces but similarly queers traditional heteronormative romance as encapsulated in various popular cultural forms such as the *novela rosa*, fairy tales, and cinema. The popular plays a particularly important role in the lives of a number of the characters in Clavel's short fiction as it functions to express their fantasies of ideal love, as well as of unfulfilled desire. Whilst fantasy offers sentimental and emotional escapism for the characters, so too do their fairy-tale notions of love and existence contrast dramatically with the dowdy monotony of life, a disparity which Clavel portrays through the use of humour and irony. Even though the stories expose the ways in which mass culture can perpetuate sexual and gender stereotypes, they similarly show the ability of a number of her characters to be not passive, but rather dynamic, consumers of mass culture, who can actively interpret it and use it to (sexually) creative ends, thus bestowing upon them a sense of freedom from restrictive lifestyles. Finally, 'no-deseos' also become intertwined with questions of feminism, (non-) motherhood, the role of creativity, life, and death, concerns which also crop up in Clavel's later fiction, as we shall see.

Sexualities in their various configurations, and specifically the connections and disconnections between the sexual desires between men and women in Clavel's short fiction (and indeed her subsequent writing), can be briefly contextualized in the broader cultural inscription of changing patterns of sexuality in the closing decades of the twentieth century and into the twenty-first century in Mexico. Even though Mexico is still defined by its time-honoured *machismo*, since approximately the 1960s second-wave feminism and the LGBT movement have served in particular to bring to light the significance of sexuality, gender, and desire in the construction of identity in a specifically Mexican context. The modernization of Mexican society and its increasingly globalized environment since this period have led to significant changes in the lives of women and so-called sexual minorities. These sweeping changes have been widely documented and have had social, cultural, and political ramifications throughout Mexican society.[1] These transformations have had a number of positive effects on these sectors including the widening access of women to education and professional labour markets and the decriminalization of consensual intimacy between same-sex couples (1998) thanks to the feminist and sexual rights movements. Yet in a society which is characterized in the main by a keen interest in restricting sexuality to chaste behaviour and monogamous heterosexual marriage, changing gender roles and the increased visibility of diverse sexual orientations and behaviours have led to a repressive backlash.[2] The increased breakdown of the traditional patriarchal family unit, growing divorce rates and single-parent families, and the liberation of sexual mores or identities have often been seen as an assault on traditional notions of masculinity. This perceived 'crisis of masculinity', that is the anxieties Mexican men have had to confront when faced with the family crisis, has been blamed, for example, for domestic violence against women or particularly savage outbursts of discriminatory reactions against homosexual men or other sexual minorities. At the same time, whilst conventional gender categories have not been completely shattered, Mexico's modernization process has meant that men's traditional roles and their attitudes towards traditional forms of sexuality and desire have had to change and accommodate women's new roles. Ultimately, by engaging with a range of 'outlaw' sexual desires, it may be suggested that it is thus Clavel's intention, both in her short stories as well as her subsequent works of fiction, not only to bring to light Mexican society's repressive heteronormativity and its particular fears, anxieties, and disavowed desires, but equally to celebrate those prohibited zones of pleasure, albeit in an often ambiguous, and not always positive, way.

Heterosexuality

Heterosexual and non-heterosexual desire is linked to Clavel's particular interest in her, notwithstanding ambivalent, representation of popular culture. References to popular culture abound in the author's short stories. Popular culture links the various characters emotionally or physically, as well as serving to express their fantasies of ideal love or sense of lack. For example, in the story 'En un vagón de metro Utopía' (*Amor*, pp. 15–28). [In the Carriage of the Utopia Metro], the male narrator and his partner Leonora draw from popular cultural forms to spice up their sexual lives. The childhood innocence typically attached to the fairy tale of 'Little Red Riding Hood' and the myth of Father Christmas are perverted as they become imbued with eroticism. Leonora enjoys sexual role-playing by enacting 'Little Red Riding Hood'; and encouraging the male narrator to assume the role of the ferocious wolf. Whilst the narrator has clearly enjoyed a fulfilled sexual life with Leonora which results in the birth of various children, he grows bored of his monogamous 'conventional paradise' (book blurb) and the drudgery of everyday life. He comes to perceive Leonora's penchant for sexual role-playing as repetitive: 'últimamente ha comenzado a repetirse, como si solo supiera jugar a la Caperucita, o cuando más, a la Bella Durmiente — si bien debo reconocer que aunque todavía bella cada vez más durmiente' [Lately she has started to be boring, as if she only knew how to pretend to be Little Red Riding Hood, or at most, Sleeping Beauty — although I must admit that whilst she is still beautiful she is ever more sleepy] (p. 20). An avid fantasist who creates his own 'pequeño teatro erótico personal' [personal miniature erotic theatre] (p. 20), the narrator seeks fulfilment by fantasizing of extramarital sexual affairs with unknown women, such as a waitress, and orgiastic sex with the 'Chicas Santa Clos del metro' [Santa Claus girls of the Underground] (p. 20), whom he starts stalking in the underground in the hope that he will be the object of their sexual attention (p. 20). For the narrator, the underground becomes a 'sistema arterial de leyendas, deseos y temores' [an arterial system of legends, desires and fears] (p. 21), and in many ways the female Santa Clauses represent those innate fears and desires. As the narrator seeks out these women in the underground, he compares his childhood excitement at the magic of Christmas with his sexual anticipation of coming across the women and engaging in sexual intercourse (p. 21). Once on the train, he conjures up in his mind an explicitly described scene in which he engages in orgiastic sex with three Santa Clauses of various striking or exotic appearances. But the narrator does not actually consummate the sexual act which ultimately remains in the realms of fantasy. Indeed, he is brutally shaken out of his fantasy dream as the ethereal beauties turn into threatening women who are there not to offer sexual services to the male passengers but rather, as one of the female Santa Clauses, gun in hand, crassly informs the narrator, 'órale, cabrón, o ¿necesito decirte que esto es un asalto navideño?' [come on, hurry up you bastard, or do I need to spell it out that this is a Christmas robbery] (p. 27). Even though Clavel can be seen to be challenging the borders of acceptability by exploring what some may perceive as morally challenging forms of sexuality in the way of extramarital and orgiastic sex, the clichéd view that dreams do not always live up to one's expectations is brashly reinforced here with humorous irony. The final comical twist embodies perhaps the narrator's fear of having to be confronted with the realization that sexual otherness enacted via fantasy does not necessarily lead to a form of bliss which, in his mind at least, can only be found beyond the 'conventional paradise' of monogamy.

The liberating yet equally entrapping effect of popular culture on the individual is no where better explored than in Clavel's short story 'Turbias lágrimas de una simple durmiente' (*Amorosos*, pp. 69–76) [The Cloudy Tears of a Sleeping Simpleton]. Here the critique of (Mexican) heteronormativity is evinced via the prism of traditional heteronormative romance as encapsulated in certain popular cultural forms, including the *novela rosa*, fairy tales, and cinema. 'Turbias lágrimas' gives us a glimpse into the dreary marriage of a Mexican couple, Jorge and Marga, both of whom are representative of Mexico's ideal social model of heteronormativity. Although fantasy provides sentimental escapism for the characters, their fairy-tale idea of love contrasts sharply with the drab mundaneness of their married life, a discrepancy which is captured through the author's use of acerbic irony. The title of this story immediately alerts us to the ambiguous role of fantasy: 'turbias lágrimas' [cloudy tears], suggesting the lacrimose sentimentality of the *novela rosa*, the *folletín*, or Hollywood soap, and 'durmiente' [sleeping], a clear allusion to the fairy tale of *Sleeping Beauty* indirectly mentioned in the short story (p. 70), clash with the word 'simple' which translates not only as 'simple' in the sense of uncomplicated, but also as 'dim-witted'.

Reference is made to the final romantic scene of the Hollywood cult movie *Blade Runner* (1982, dir. Ridley Scott) in which the main characters played by actors Sean Young and Harrison Ford are seen driving off in their car into the sun-drenched mountains. In Clavel's story, the Hollywood movie has a specifically *mise-en-abyme* function. Indeed, Jorge's loose reconstruction of the sexually and emotionally intense relationship between the two characters Rachel and Rick in *Blade Runner* has a special resonance given that it serves as an ironic counterpoint to Jorge's own lacklustre relationship with Marga. Jorge renames Harrison Ford's character from Rick to George as a way of impersonating the character in order to get closer to his female heroine Sean Young/Rachel, who represents the ideals of romance, beauty, and luxury. Jorge's conception of ideal romantic love is based on a fantasy which must be maintained via an impeccably choreographed performance. Performativity becomes particularly apparent via the references to the filming process, in which the film director intervenes, thus foregrounding, for instance, the illusion of romance (p. 69) or physical perfection as encapsulated in Sean Young/Rachel:

> Limitada por las líneas que algún guionista dibujó en torno a ella, Sean sólo pudo mostrar su lado de mujer perfecta, perfeccionada aún más por la meticulosidad de Pitt que detenía las escenas sólo para que la maquillista le polveara el rostro. (*Amorosos*, p. 70)

> [Restricted by the lines which were written specifically for her character by some scriptwriter, Sean was only able to project an image of a perfect woman, perfected even more so by the meticulousness of Pitt who would constantly stop the scenes in order to allow the makeup artist to retouch her face]

Ironically, Jorge — who has a 'predisposición casi innata para la infelicidad, ese sentimiento de que la vida tiene que ser una película y, además, trágica' [an almost innate predisposition to unhappiness and that sense that life has to be lived like a film and, what's more, a tragic one] (p. 72) — lives his own life as a performance, enacting the role of a tragic victim of a melodramatic *folletín*. Yet even as the popular entraps Jorge, so too does it liberate him. Following Clavel's view that 'lo que te define es el no ser' [what defines you being what you are not],[3] Jorge seeks to overcome his tragic sense of self by becoming other by vicariously living through the fictive artifice of Hollywood film.[4] The creative reconstruction of the movie permits Jorge to express his darkest inner self, thus liberating him from falling into the trappings of an emotionally repressed existence. However the emotional and sexual freedom that the popular offers is only transitory as the reader is poignantly reminded about the illusory nature of fantasy. George becomes engaged in a sexually steamy exchange with Sean/Rachel and, in contravention of the script, the male actor starts performing oral sex on the female actress. The film director is appalled by the idea of the characters having full-blown sex because 'entonces cómo imaginar la segunda parte' [how can one possibly imagine the second part] (p. 73). Jorge is similarly horrified at such a prospect given that to consummate the sexual act would be to kill the fantasy of the ideal. Intercourse threatens Jorge as it becomes a reminder of Sean/Rachel's visceral physicality and imperfection, like that of Marga: 'sumida en la ordinariez de la carne y el hueso' [immersed in flesh and blood ordinariness] (p. 73). Such recognition is linked to Jorge's horrified realization that he depends on the flesh-and-blood Marga to be able to recreate and sustain his fantasy of the unreal: 'reprime la arcada al pensar de qué manera esta imperfecta mujer de carne y hueso le es tan necesaria para configurar el deseo por las otras que busca en la pantalla' [stops himself from retching as he thinks how this imperfect flesh-and-blood woman is so utterly important for him in recreating those other women whom he seeks out on the screen] (p. 74). For Jorge, Marga must become one of his co-actors in his filmic recreation(s) to prolong the illusion:

> Por primera vez, Jorge se da cuenta de que también por Marga la escena ha de volverse Sísifo a repetirse. Pitt diría: un poco más de rímel para enturbiar esas lágrimas de víctima que, al fin cómplice, Marga acepta derramar. (*Amorosos*, p. 74)
>
> [For the first time, Jorge realizes that for Marga too the scene must constantly repeat itself in Sisyphean manner. Pitt would say: apply a little bit more makeup to the eyes in order to produce an effect of mascara-filled victim tears, which Marga, accomplice at last, willingly sheds]

Marga, much like her husband, perceives herself as a tragic victim of melodrama and in order to escape the harsh realities of a marriage comprised of unrequited love, she too draws from popular sources, this time in the form of fairy tales. Influenced by *Sleeping Beauty*, Marga has had the princess fantasy of finding her 'príncipe azul' [Prince Charming], whom Jorge comes to embody, since childhood. Despite his rejection of her, the only time when Marga feels a fleeting physical and emotional connection with him is when they make love (p. 74). It is thus why Marga agrees to participate in Jorge's play-acting fantasies since this will allow both of them to express a reciprocal desire for the unattainable, permitting, in the case of Marga, the feeling of being loved by her husband by enacting her role as passive 'chingada' [fucked one] and, in the case of Jorge in his role as 'chingón' [fucker], the illusion of embarking upon an idyllic romance with or making love to 'perfect' cinema icons. Whilst their particular reworking of popular genres and gender role-playing may save their marriage from disintegration, Clavel's short story is an indictment of the manner in which fantasy functions to maintain the illusion of the 'perfect' Mexican marriage, as well as the Sisyphean heteronormativity which popular forms promote. The male to female relationships which the story explores via the popular serve to critique the staunch gender stereotypes ingrained in Mexican and North American patriarchy which posit men such as Jorge/George as the prototypical sexually active 'chingón' against the passive female 'chingada', as embodied in the figure of Marga/Sean/ Rachel. Even though Marga (like Sean/ Rachel) colludes with this arrangement, it is through it that Clavel can be seen to be attacking the manner in which heteronormativity is strongly informed by relations of unavailing domination and subordination, reinforcing the heterosexual pact whereby the social and sexual power of men over women is emphasized.

Homosexuality

The emotional and physical (dis)connection between characters which popular culture foments is also seen in 'Una advertencia y tres cartas en el mismo sobre' (*Paraísos*, pp. 65–70) [A Warning and Three Letters in a Single Envelope], where the popular has a specifically healing, even if fleeting, function. Here Luis is staying in the flat of his lover Samuel and both these men are closet homosexuals. Whilst Samuel is studying abroad in Liverpool, Luis wallows in his frustrated love and writes letters to Samuel which will never be sent. In one of his letters to Samuel, Luis mentions Samuel's passion for Hendrix's music and how he gave Samuel Hendrix's *Electric Ladyland* (1968). Though Hendrix's album partially represents an ode to the singer's female fans and lovers, thus underlining a distinct heterosexual thrust, in Clavel's story the music becomes a medium to express homosexual desires. Though the Hendrix tunes remind Luis of his lover's physical absence, paradoxically, listening to them reminds him of Samuel listening to the melodies, which in turn helps Luis to bridge, emotionally at least, the gap which exists between himself and his absent lover (p. 66). But for all the energizing features of such popular cultural forms, the stigma of homosexuality nevertheless prevails. One senses a deep resentment in the letters which underscore Luis's umbrage at Samuel's decision to abandon him in order to pursue his studies in Liverpool. But more so than this, it is Samuel's decision to return to Mexico in order to resume his heterosexual relationship with Lorena which riles Luis. Samuel's choice leads Luis to reflect upon his own sense of being and the idea of the homosexual-heterosexual double self. Whilst we get only a relatively brief glimpse into the relationship between Luis and Samuel, it becomes evident that it has been built on the basis of an uneven relationship marked by the unequal roles of the 'active' male and the 'passive' male, a notion which is discussed in greater detail in Chapter 3. Whereas Samuel possesses prototypical virile traits such as athleticism and good looks with his body described as having a 'bronceado envidiable' [enviable tan] (p. 68), Luis is endowed with 'feminine' traits as epitomized in his 'enclenque' [skinny] and 'debilucho' [weakling] body (p. 68). Luis increasingly resents his role as (effeminate) appendage to Samuel (p. 68). Whilst at Samuel's apartment, Luis decides to emulate his lover's life by acquiring a bronzed colour of a '*Latin Lover*' (p. 67), becoming muscular by going to Samuel's gym and by frequenting the company of Samuel's female friends from the club (p. 67). His decision to usurp Samuel's identity is ambiguous: it appears that he assumes the role of his lover's fake double as a way of feeling closer to him but the last letter he writes to Samuel reveals a much more sinister intention:

> Eres un maldito mentiroso [...] Bueno, comprendo que quisieras salvar el orgullo [...] No quiero llegar tarde a mi boda. Hazme caso y no vengas, no tanto por las propiedades de que me he adueñado sino porque conoces a Lorena y dices amarla. Le causaría una grave crisis enterarse de la existencia de dos Samueles. (*Paraísos*, p. 70)

> [You're a bloody liar [...] Ok, I get why you wanted to save your pride [...] Must rush, don't want to be late for my wedding. Just listen to me and don't come. I am asking you not to come not so much because of the whole business of the properties of which I have taken ownership, but more so because you know Lorena and you say you love her. It would tip her over the edge if she found out about the existence of two Samuels]

Throughout the story the reader has felt an element of empathy for Luis because of Samuel's betrayal, but such feelings soon wane as the final twist reveals a deeply calculating character. Luis's decision to emulate Samuel's life, and in particular take possession of his flat and marry Lorena, make it clear that such actions have been made out of spite for his homosexual lover's snub. It is deeply ironic that Luis heavily criticizes Samuel for his 'double standards' given that Luis's self also comprises 'dos Luises', the private homosexual versus the public heterosexual. Like Samuel, Luis decides to reject his 'other', 'improper' gay self in favour of the straight, 'proper' self. Such rejection becomes particularly evident in the manner in which Luis refuses to look at his image reflected in the mirror (p. 68). If one's reflection in the mirror is the embodiment of the psychological otherness of self, then Luis's denial suggests his fear of his (true) other self, a fear which Samuel also clearly shares. Luis's empathetic 'comprendo que quisieras salvar el orgullo', which mirrors his own desire to save face, can be understood in the wider context of a deeply ingrained anxiety in Mexico about homosexuality. Homophobia is so rife in public life in Mexico that gays have been forced to hide their sexuality out of fear of reprisal, an apprehension which Samuel and Luis indirectly may share. As discussed in further detail in Chapter 3 which examines *Cuerpo náufrago*, homosexuality is often seen as the epitome of effeminacy, and so Samuel's and Luis's desire to salvage their pride and avoid being associated with socially disapproved behaviours leads them to conceal their true identities.[5] Despite their homosexual desires, it is their choice to be part of the heteronormative pact by assuming 'proper' roles which posit each as the heterosexual macho 'who makes it both with men and women without ever yielding an iota of his masculine persona'.[6] Regardless of the fact that Luis has behaved as he has towards his friend and the fact that both he and Samuel choose to desert their true desires in favour of social acceptability, the reader cannot perhaps but feel some empathy for both men who are ultimately victims of repressive patriarchal standards.

Transgender

Queer self-denial and the critique of heteronormativity also become apparent in Clavel's 'Tu bella boca Rojo Carmesí' (*Fuera de escena*, pp. 5–9) [Your Beautiful Bright Red Lips] in which the closet transgender Carlos can only give vent to 'his' 'no-deseos' in the absence of the prying eyes of his family. This is a cleverly written text given that Clavel tricks her reader into believing that the character being described here is female. This is achieved in a number of ways since the character's name is not mentioned until the very end and Clavel avoids using declined nouns to express the female or male subject being described, or gender-specific pronouns to accompany the verbs. The context of the story also leads to stereotypical assumptions about the gender of the character. Once, when the character is left alone at home whilst 'her' mother and sisters go out for a stroll, 'she' comes across a magazine snippet in which a model is donning a glamorous outfit by which 'she' is particularly taken. Recalling a similar dress which 'her' mother owns, 'she' goes to 'her' mother's bedroom to retrieve the robe from the cupboard. The character puts it on as well as various accessories and meticulously applies 'her' mother's makeup. Having dressed 'herself' in the provocative outfit, 'she' ventures out into the street where 'she' becomes the object of the lascivious attention of a milkman and a married man whose wife strikes him out of jealousy. The assumption that the character of the story is female is based upon the direct or indirect popular cultural references to fashion (pp. 5–9), princess fairy tales (p. 7), and *folletín*-esque romance (as suggested in the title of the short story, p. 5), all of which are stereotypically associated with women's fantasies and interests. 'Her' gender is bolstered by the stereotyped perception that all women have an obsessive fascination with clothes and preening rituals such as applying make-up or body lotions (p. 8). When we are told that 'she' has a penchant for John Field's nocturnes, this only serves to reinforce further our perception of the gender of the character as female. Field's nocturnes have historically been pigeonholed as a 'feminine' musical genre with their ornate melodies and excessive sentimentality, and therefore are perceived as predominantly appealing to the female listener because of women's own (similarly typecast) proneness to over-romanticization.[7] The feminine also becomes apparent in the story as we are told that the character occasionally wears 'her' mother's wedding dress, a gesture which signals women's princess fantasy yearning for the happily-ever-after life with her Prince Charming. In particular, 'her' fantasy of embodying a mythical nymph as encapsulated in the art of Jean Auguste Ingres and Pygmalion ('la illusión de ser ninfa de una fuente; o tal vez la escultura de un Pigmalión en espera del beso' [the illusion of being a fountain nymph; or perhaps the sculpture of some Pygmalion awaiting to be kissed], p. 8) encapsulates a woman's desire to possess the beauty and grace of these highly idealized figures, traits which are far beyond the reach of ordinary women. But our suppositions surrounding the sex of the character are powerfully queered at the end of the story. Indeed, shortly upon returning from 'her' escape, the character hears her/his family entering and frantically removes 'her' mother's dress as the mother calls out:

> ¡Carlos, Carlos ya estamos aquí! — escuchó que gritaba su madre al tiempo que, nervioso y con la sensación de las paredes transformadas en rejas, sólo atinaba a untarse crema en los labios para desvanecer la huella del carmesí del bilé. (*Fuera de escena*, p. 9)
>
> [Carlos, Carlos, we're back! — he heard his mother shouting, at the same time as he, feeling nervous and sensing that the walls had suddenly transformed into prison bars, only managed to dab some cream onto his lips to get rid of any traces of the crimson lipstick]

This quotation underpins the paradoxical role of the private realm in the context of Carlos's 'outlaw' and straight identities. Whilst the private allows Carlos to momentarily express her queer self as transgender, the private space also becomes imbued with repressive meaning and lack of self-acceptance, thus disallowing her to 'come out' publicly. In her brief analysis of this story, Velasco notes that the private represents a paradoxical locus:

> Prisión que también incrementa el deseo por despertar a ese otro Carlos que lucha por sustituir a aquel que conoce su familia: ese otro que infringirá las reglas si se prende el fuego que niega al varón. Carlos intuye que es diferente y lo disfruta, pero todavía no puede aceptar públicamente, el placer que le provoca experimentar el sueño de ser mujer. No obstante, tiene fe.[8]
>
> [A prison which enhances the desire to awaken that other Carlos who struggles to substitute that other person whom his family know: that other who will break the rules if the fire of desire is lit which denies the male. Carlos senses that he is different and enjoys this, but he still cannot accept publicly the pleasure he gains when he experiences the dream of being a woman. He does, however, have faith]

It is ironic perhaps that even as Carlos's self-repression is owed to oppressive heteronormative discourses which disavow sexual diversity and advocate strict gender binaries, she colludes with that same rhetoric. Her fantasy is to become part of a heterosexual relation in which she embodies the ideal woman like the Ingresian or Pygmalion nymphs, the passive recipient of the active male lover whose 'manos amantes que al desnudar acarician' [the caressing hands of the lover as he undresses her] (p. 7). This collusion is further bolstered by the delight Carlos takes ('disimulando la satisfacción de su éxito' [hiding the satisfaction of her success], p. 9) at being leered at by the milkman and the husband, suggesting that she is happy to partake in the dynamics of heterosexual relations which posit women in an inferior and objectified position relative to the dominant 'macho'. Carlos's joy is significant nevertheless since the (mis)recognition by others of her as a female signals perhaps that her desire to become a real woman is not confined to the realm of fantasy in the form of cross-dressing, but is a genuine possibility thanks to, for instance, body modification techniques which, whilst drastic, are nevertheless liberating for transgender people. This sense of satisfaction also highlights the view that even as Carlos's transgender person has as yet not realized its full potential due to familial repression, her ability to move between the male and female selves and to perform freely either genders, ultimately raises awareness in Carlos of the latent possibilities which lie beyond strict gender conventions. This particular point underpins the importance of Judith Butler's gender performativity, a notion which links 'Tu bella boca Rojo Carmesí' to 'Una advertencia' and 'Turbias lágrimas'. Whether Margo's and Jorge's appropriation of Hollywood movie gender stereotypes involving the passive 'Seans' and the active 'Georges', Luis's appropriation of Samuel's straight fake double or Carlos's interchangeable female and male selves, it is their performance of gender, that is their 'stylized repetition of acts' that shapes the presentation of the 'abiding gendered self', which ultimately signals the view that gender and sexuality are not innate but rather socially constructed.[9] *Cuerpo náufrago* has many synergies with these stories given that, as will be extensively discussed in Chapter 3, gender performativity is powerfully embodied in the transgender Antón/ia as a means of both reinforcing but equally refuting the time-honoured perception that gender and sexual categories are immutable. As will be argued, Butler's thesis regarding the traditional performances of either the masculine or the feminine also points to the idea that subjects can liberate themselves from the constraints linked to their sex and take on multiple gender (sexual) identities, which is demonstrated in the text's celebration of Antón/ia's myriad sexual identities as woman, man, bisexual, homosexual, and transgender. Whereas Luis is entrapped by his performance of the 'macho' straight self which denies his other gay half, Margo, Jorge, and Carlos all ultimately find a sense of freedom in their performances of gender.

Interfamilial Relationships

Queer sexual 'non-desires' continue to find their expression in other stories such as 'Un Deseo realizado' (2009) [A Desire Fulfilled] — renamed 'Después del paraíso' [After Paradise] in its republished version in *Amor y otros suicidios* — in which Clavel explores the taboo subject of interfamilial relationships between cousins.[10] Here the young cousins Felisa and Miguel begin an incestuous sexual and amorous relationship which they conduct under Felisa's bed, but are caught out by her family and subsequently subjected to accusations of immoral, illicit conduct. Deeply ashamed by their behaviour, Felisa and Miguel are 'expulsados de ese paraíso [...] para ya no reencontrarnos jamás' [expelled from that paradise [...] only to never meet again] (p. 69). Even though relations and marriage between cousins are legally sanctioned in Mexico, Felisa's and Miguel's sense of shame and the family's wrath at the couple's misdemeanour are rooted in questions of social respectability, moral objections incited by religious dogma, and, indirectly perhaps, the prevailing, and unmerited, myth that sexual relations between cousins invariably leads to the production of children born with congenital disorders. Clavel can be seen as attacking Mexico's public renunciation of cousin relations by provocatively suggesting that even whilst such relationships are not openly endorsed, these are common amidst the private lives of many families (p. 69). The author thus underpins the idea that the definitions of normalcy and deviance which form the basis of moral standards of society are merely artificial social constructs which are constantly flouted. In doing so, Clavel can be seen as unqueering the characters' 'bizarre' relationship by transforming it at the end of the story from a perceived 'crime' into a celebratory sexual and emotional reencounter between two persons whose unadulterated desire for one another embodies a universal experience which will resonate with most, if not all, readers.

Accompanying Clavel's 'Un deseo realizado' is an image of French Surrealist René Magritte's oil painting *Les Amants* (1928) depicting, to draw from art critic Alyce Mahon, 'an apparently respectable bourgeois couple' whose faces are concealed beneath a white cloth.[11] Magritte subsequently painted *Les Amants II* (1928) in which we see the same couple whose faces are still shrouded behind the white cloth but who are kissing one another on the mouth. Both these images resist singular definition. In the context of Clavel's short story, the juxtaposition of text and the first of Magritte's paintings incites the reader to reflect upon notions of sexual taboo. The first image suggests perhaps a loveless heterosexual relationship between the man and the woman because of their veiled faces, but the proximity of their heads belies such an interpretation and instead hints at intimacy rather than emotional and physical distance. The cloth, whilst not affording one particular meaning, powerfully conjures up associations with that which is concealed or prohibited. The nature of the prohibition suggested in the painting proves difficult to ascertain and so the reader looks for textual clues which might yield signification. As we read the text it becomes apparent that the taboo subject of the interfamilial relationship between Felisa and Miguel is metonymically embodied in Magritte's couple and their veiled heads. The exploration of the taboo of incest or sexual prohibition is perhaps more explicit in Magritte's *Les Amants II* (1928). Mahon notes that the sheet on this second canvas may symbolize the violence of desire, orgasmic pleasure, or 'perhaps secrecy and the taboo of illicit or incestuous desire' (p. 127). This particular image, in conjunction with the first and Clavel's text, reinforces the thrust of much of Surrealist art which reveals not only the creator's fears as well as those of the spectator-readers, but equally seeks to expose repressed desires which are revealed through sexual symbolism (Mahon, pp. 127–28). Both text and image(s) also serve as a reminder that, despite religious or social discourses which serve to curtail outlaw desires, human instinct is ultimately irrepressible, as vigorously illustrated by Felisa's and Miguel's love-making in the final lines of the story.

Lesbianism

Lesbian desire is the subject of three of Clavel's short stories, namely, 'La Imagen del espejo' (*Antología*, pp. 11–15) [The Image of the Mirror], 'Cuando María mire el mar' (*Amorosos*, pp. 77–92) [When María Sees the Sea], and 'Un Hombre tiene la edad de la mujer que ama' (*Amor*, pp. 41–54) [A Man is as Old as the Woman he Loves]. 'La Imagen del espejo', unpublished, was written by Ana Clavel in 1978.

She contributed the story, along with another entitled 'Inmortalidad' (*Antología*, pp. 9–10) [Immortality], to an anthology of short stories and poems written by fellow students at her school Colegio de Bachilleres, plantel 1 El Rosario, in Mexico City which was compiled by their Spanish literature teacher, Yolanda Medina Haro.[12] Even before Clavel became an established writer, it is clear from 'La Imagen del espejo' that she revelled in exploring questions of erotic 'no-deseos', or forbidden love. Here creative expression, same-sex desire, and death become inexorably interwoven. The unnamed narrator discusses the demise of her friend Fernanda whose cause of death is being investigated by the police. The narrator explains that Fernanda had certain peculiar characteristics such as her apparent hatred of men or talking to herself in front of the mirror. Upon questioning Fernanda about the latter, the narrator's friend explained that it was a habit which allowed her to escape reality (p. 12). Also she explained to her that when she started to become delirious, she would record these ramblings on her tape recorder (p. 12), thus allowing her to give vent to creative expression and repressed desires. Shortly before her death, Fernanda asks the narrator to listen to a set of tapes she has recorded and it is upon hearing the confessions which 'descubrían sus tendencias e identidad' [revealed her tendencies and identity] (p. 11), that the narrator painfully comes to understand Fernanda's 'bizarre' attitude and behaviour in life, the cause of her death, and, crucially, that both loved each other (p. 11). The recordings bring to the narrator's attention how Fernanda would often speak to her mirror image as a way of engaging in dialogue with her lesbian uncanny other.[13] Unlike Luis from 'Una advertencia', who rejects outright his 'gay' other, as suggested in his inability to look at his reflection in the mirror, Fernanda appears, initially at least, to recognize and accept her 'uncanny strangeness' (Kristeva, p. 192). However, upon reading a book entitled *Lesbianismo*, written by an unnamed male author, Fernanda represses her gay self and decides to take her own life. The narrator thus comes to realize that the audio recordings are a kind of suicide note. In one such recording Fernanda notes that there is one sentence in the book she read on lesbianism which became etched on her brain and which ultimately propelled her towards her death: 'cuando se descubren a sí mismas, se suicidan, pues sienten pero no quieren hacerlo' [when they discover who they really are, they commit suicide, for they do not want to admit their true homosexual feelings] (p. 15). The narrator also comes to understand at this point the seemingly irrational hatred Fernanda has for men. Indeed, in the recordings Fernanda blames her decision to commit suicide on the author of the text whom she compares to a puppeteer, whilst she views herself as the marionette on the strings being pulled around by him: 'el hombre que me manejaba jalando delgados hilos' [the man that controlled me by pulling from threadbare strings] (p.14). Even as this text appears to serve positively to confirm Fernanda's identity as a lesbian, it has been written by a man who effectively condemns lesbianism. Unable to overcome the ingrained homophobia which represses lesbian desire encompassed in the fateful predicament of same-sex women as envisaged by the male author, Fernanda takes her own life. Once again, as with a number of the other stories thus examined, Clavel appears to be condemning the manner in which oppressive heteronormative discourses which disavow sexual diversity can lead to extreme forms of self-repression.

The downbeat tone of the above story contrasts sharply with the more optimistic exploration of lesbian desire in 'Cuando María mire el mar'. In this story, which was awarded the Premio Nacional de Literatura Gilberto Owen in 1991, Clavel's interest in sapphic 'no-deseos' becomes intertwined with feminism, (non-) motherhood, the role of creativity and writing, and their particular relationship to life and death. Before embarking upon an analysis of the story, it is worth noting briefly that the image adorning the book cover of *Amorosos de atar* is a celebration of lesbianism. The illustration is that of Auguste Rodin's pencil and watercolour *Deux femmes enlacées* (1911) which portrays two nude women embracing passionately, one seated on the thighs of the other. Given Clavel's penchant for exploring non-mainstream forms of sexual desire and her enjoyment in contravening boundaries of acceptability, it is not surprising that Rodin's work features on the cover of her collection of short stories. Whilst widely appraised in international art circles, Rodin's works caused controversy because of his recurring treatment of Sapphic eroticism.[14] In many ways the choice of Rodin's artwork projects forward to the edgy subject matter of the book cover of Clavel's *Las Violetas son flores del deseo* (2007) and because of which, as will be discussed in Chapter 7, the Mexican giant retail chain Grupo Sanborns refused to sell the novella on the grounds of the cover's explicit content.

In 'Cuando María mire al mar' the eponymous protagonist has fallen pregnant with her first child, the product of an apparently happy relationship between María and Javier. María however is undecided about whether she wants to have the child or not and takes a trip to the coast without Javier, in the company of her cousin and various others to determine whether she wants to proceed with a termination. The reasons to abort the child appear to be rather selfish: like a number of the characters described in Clavel's other short stories, María is influenced by the (heterosexual) princess fairy-tale fantasy of love (*Amorosos*, p. 87). María has a dream of the 'hombre de su vida' [man of her dreams] with whom she has passionate sex and he offers her 'un platillo colmado de cerezas' [a dish full of cherries] (p. 75), a stereotypical image suggesting perhaps ideal love and adulation of the male for the female, both sexually and emotionally. Javier appears to embody this prototype for María and her decision to possibly have an abortion appears to be fuelled by her terror that 'the happy ever after' fantasy and her sexual appeal might be destroyed with the birth of a child (p. 91). At the same time, she is also fearful that such a decision could lead Javier to stop loving her and to the subsequent failure of their relationship (p. 76). María's anxieties are also metonymically represented in the metaphor of the sea. On the one hand, the sea, emblematic of the unconscious, irrational fears, and sexual (repressed) desires, comes to be associated with María's sexual lust for Javier (p. 77). On the other hand, the sea, a symbol of masculinity for María (p. 78), also embodies a source of terror as the protagonist is overcome by the fear that the fish inhabiting the big blue will devour her (p. 102). The image of a school of fish which swims up towards her womb connotes male sperm impregnating the female body, signalling the protagonist's fear of pregnancy. Horrified by the viscerality of her pregnant body, pregnancy becomes inexorably imbued with a Kristevan sense of abjection:

> Me veo con los intestinos desparramados, con un hoyo en la panza mientras mi salamandra aletea agónica como un pez en la playa [...] la picantez en los senos,

> la pesantez del vientre, esta saliva que no es la mía sino la de otro [...] ¿Y cómo no sentir asco ante estos efluvios? ¿Y si me invade toda y crece y me llena de su sangre y me come toda? No, qué horror. (*Amorosos*, p. 80)
>
> [I see myself with my intestines spilling out, with a hole in my stomach whilst my salamander flaps around dying like a fish washed up on a beach [...] the itchiness of my breasts, the heaviness of the belly, this saliva which is not mine but someone else's [...] How can I not feel disgust about these excretions? And what if it invades my whole body, fills me up with its blood and eats me all up? What a horrid thought]

The negative portrayal of motherhood, which focuses on the grotesque physicality of childbirth, is found in several other Mexican female writers of the *boom femenino*, including Brianda Domecq and Ángeles Mastretta. The refusal to romanticize motherhood could be understood as the influence on these writers of discourses prevalent in second wave feminism which often questioned the essentialist view that women's prerogative is solely to breed offspring, and promoted the idea that women have choices, such as participating in public life beyond the family. In a Mexican context, Clavel, like many other *boom femenino* writers, thus challenges the Malinche/Virgen de la Guadalupe dichotomy which is central to the construction of Mexican (non-) motherhood. The negative treatment of motherhood can be seen as an attack on the patriarchal myth which perpetuates the notion that childbirth is beautiful. The sense that pregnancy is an uncanny experience and is something which has been imposed on the female body comes across powerfully in Clavel's story. The representation of pregnancy as something vile, whereby María's body and identity are invaded by the monster foetus, becomes an indictment of Mexican patriarchal structures that restrict women's lives and their ability to choose possibilities which lie beyond motherhood. The denunciation of motherhood is also interrelated to creative freedom. There is a brief instance in the story in which we hear the narrator's voice in which s/he has the desire to intervene in the unfolding plot ('salirse del papel de narrador o testigo' [to step out of my role as narrator or witness], p. 79) in order to confront María with the aim of encouraging the protagonist finally to make a decision about what she wants to do with the child she is carrying in her womb. Such intervention draws the reader's attention to artistic self-consciousness and serves to foreground the role of the author in the creative process. In an interview Clavel explained to me that the story had a highly personal dimension as she had written the story of María as a reflection on her own experiences of pregnancy with her son.[15] Whilst Clavel was elated at the prospect of being a mother, at the same time she felt a deep sense of terror that motherhood would curtail her creative freedom. But Clavel also hastened to add that these were irrational fears for motherhood only served to nurture and enrich her writing and her personal life in ways that she had not imagined possible. It is perhaps this realization which serves to explain the positive ending of 'Cuando María mire el mar' since María decides to not proceed with the termination. Thus, the birth of a child as affirmation of life offers rejuvenating possibilities and becomes a metonym of the writing process which leads to the materialization of that endeavour in the form of a skilfully architected narrative and ultimately to the assertion of Clavel's creative voice.

It is interesting to note here that the protagonist's decision to have the baby is not propelled by her love for Javier but rather as a result of a lesbian encounter. Even though María claims to love Javier, one senses that she does not love a flesh and blood person, but rather a virtual, idealized Adonis that she has recreated in her sexual fantasies. Javier is also physically and emotionally absent: he does not accompany her to the coast and therefore is excluded from the important decision-making process in relation to their baby's future. María does not appear in any way disturbed by his absence and is happy to be able to take ownership of her situation and resolve it on her own, thus suggesting that their relationship is not a tightly woven unit. This point is reinforced by the fact that she welcomes and corroborates the desiring gaze of another man (p. 85), and in particular because she engages in a sexual relation with another woman, namely Claudia, one of the people accompanying María on her trip to the coast. Whereas sexual intercourse with the 'unreal' Javier is described in violent terms ('la embiste', [rams up her], p. 75), Claudia's and María's erotic encounter is imbued with gentle sensuousness and a sense of immediacy (pp. 89–90). Importantly, whereas during the sexual relations between Javier and María the foetus is referred to in monstrous terms, the erotic moment between María and Claudia does not exclude the foetus. Whilst Claudia's caresses are evidently sexual, so too do they evince a motherly tenderness for as she touches María she is careful not to hurt mother or her unborn child (p. 90). It is Claudia's protective gestures which seem to bring out María's own maternal instinct: 'la cercanía de ese cuerpo inofensivo la sedaba, como si alguien por fin, hubiera atendido el llanto de esa niña que llevaba dentro' [the proximity of that harmless body calmed her, as if someone, at long last, had heard the cries of that baby girl whom she carried in her womb] (p. 90). The Sapphic moment brings a sense of lucidity to María. She comes to the realization that a woman, rather than a man, is able to satisfy her both emotionally and physically. Indeed, unlike with Javier, with whom true communication appears to be almost entirely lacking, she is able to talk freely with Claudia. Furthermore, 'las manos [...] de Claudia conociéndola como ningún hombre — ni siquiera Javier — la ha conocido' [Claudia's hands discovering her like no other man, not even Javier, had done so] (p. 92). More pertinently, it is María's liaison with Claudia which has a positive effect on her as she seeks forgiveness from her unborn child for her initial selfishness, and ultimately helps her to embrace her pregnancy wholeheartedly: 'María ya no pudo pensar: "Lo que veo, mi salamandra puede verlo. También a ella — o a él — puede llegarle el perdón"' [María could no longer think: 'What I see, my salamader also sees. She or he too is capable of forgiveness'] (p. 92).

To conclude, it is clear that a key overarching element in the short fiction of Ana Clavel is that of desire in its variegated forms ranging from the sexual, creative self expression to maternal instinct. As will become apparent to the reader, these areas similarly represent the concerns that come fully to the fore in Clavel's later works of fiction.

Notes to Chapter 1

1. Tessa Cubitt, *Latin American Society* (London: Longman, 1995); Christa Wichterich, *The Globalized Woman: Reports from a Future of Inequality* (London: Zed, 2000); Sylvia Chant, 'Single-Parent Families: Choice or Constraint? The Formation of Female-Headed Households in Mexican Shanty Towns', in Denise A. Segura and Patricia Zavella (eds.), *Women and Migration in the U.S.-Mexico Borderlands: A Reader*, Latin America Otherwise (Durham, NC: Duke University Press, 2007), pp. 360–68.
2. Edgar González Ruiz notes that 'una larga tradición de intolerancia religiosa y cultural, ejercida en el México colonial por el Santo Oficio y que hoy pervive bajo diversas formas, es el caldo de cultivo del activismo de ciertos grupos que pretenden imponer a toda la sociedad una ética basada en la idealización de la abstinencia e influida por viejos prejuicios sexistas. En nombre de "la moral y las buenas costumbres" se oponen a la conquista de espacios de libertad y tolerancia para las minorías sexuales' [a long tradition of religious and cultural intolerance, exerted by the Holy Office in colonial Mexico and prevails today under various guises, is the breeding ground for the activism of certain groups who seek to impose on all of society an ethic which is based on the idealization of abstinence and antiquated sexist prejudices. In the name of 'morality and good behaviour' they are opposed to the triumph of those spaces of liberty and tolerance reserved for sexual minorities], *La Sexualidad prohibida: intolerancia, sexismo y represión* (Mexico City: Plaza y Janés, 2002). p. 105.
3. Lavery, unpublished interview with Clavel, 2011.
4. In this respect, Jorge bares certain comparison with Julián Mercader and his Violeta replicas in *Las Violetas son flores del deseo*, in the sense that both find emotional and sexual reprieve in the hyperreal.
5. Robert McKee Irwin, 'The Famous 41: The Scandalous Birth of Modern Mexican Homosexuality', *GLQ: A Journal of Lesbian and Gay Studies*, 6:3 (2000), 353–76 (p. 355).
6. David William Foster, *Sexual Textualities: Essays on Queer/ing Latin American Writing* (Austin: University of Texas Press, 1997), p. 3.
7. Jeffrey Kallberg, 'The Harmony of the Tea Table: Gender and Ideology in the Piano Nocturne', *Representations*, 39 (1992), 102–33 (p. 105).
8. Raquel Velasco, 'De amores marginales: el juego de la diferencia', *La Palabra y el Hombre*, Universidad Veracruzana, 135 (2005), 7–19 (p. 9), <http://cdigital.uv.mx/handle/123456789/451> [accessed 9 June 2014].
9. Butler, *Gender Trouble*, p. 140.
10. The analysis of the story in this chapter will be in relation to 'Un deseo realizado'.
11. Alyce Mahon, *Eroticism and Art* (Oxford: Oxford University Press, 2005), p. 127.
12. Yolanda Medina Haro (ed.), *Antología* (Mexico City: taller de creación Colegio de Bachilleres # 1, plantel El Rosario, 1979), printed in a limited edition of 500 copies.
13. The uncanny is used here in the Kristevan sense of the word which encompasses the idea of the 'other-in-the-self' and the recognition of one's 'uncanny strangeness'. Julia Kristeva, *Strangers to Ourselves*, trans. by Leon S. Roudiez (Hemel Hempstead: Harvester Wheatsheaf, 1991), p. 192.
14. Upon her reading of this chapter, Ana Clavel explained that 'cuando escogí la imagen de Rodin sólo me fascinó la fuerza del trazo que reflejaba la pasión de los amantes. No me di cuenta sino mucho después que eran dos mujeres' [when I chose the image by Rodin I was fascinated by the power of the strokes which reflected the passion of the lovers. It is only much later that I realized that they were two women].
15. Lavery, unpublished interview with Clavel, 2008.

CHAPTER 2

Los deseos y su sombra
Truth, (Ghostly) Selves, and (Multimedia) Luminous Shadows

Los deseos y su sombra (2000), which was the runner-up for the Premio Internacional Alfaguara de Novela 1999, is an outstanding novel in which the author skilfully interweaves the historical, the fictional, and the fantastic to create an original story of sexuality, desire, and the phantasmagoric.[1] It is a socially engaged novel, which explores questions of gender and sexuality within a broad Mexican socio-political context. Clavel's interest in contemporary socio-historical gender roles and relations reflects the concerns of a number of contemporary *boom femenino* Mexican writers such as Susana Pagano, Rosa Beltrán, and Sara Sefchovich. Unlike most of her other fiction which centres almost entirely on the private lives of individuals, *Los deseos* focuses both on the private and on national political realities. The correlation between the individual and the national is a focus which also strongly aligns Clavel's *Los deseos* with many *boom femenino* writers. In the vein of various *boom femenino* writers, Clavel's endeavour to challenge monological versions of historical 'truth' and to reconstruct alternative conceptions of national identity is intimately linked to the creation of a non-patriarchal conception of female subjectivity. In establishing Soledad's identity as a complex Kristevan 'sujet en procès' [subject in process], I propose an allegorical connection with the text's reconstruction of an alternative conceptualization of national identity. This chapter will focus primarily on Clavel's treatment of her female character within a psychoanalytical framework, although brief treatment of the socio-historical and political perspective is deemed necessary as it is intertwined with the development of the character as a subject in the process of becoming. It seems appropriate to provide a psychoanalytical reading of *Los deseos* given Clavel's own interest in psychoanalysis in her overall literary work. I will thus examine Clavel's exploration of the female subject in *Los deseos* in the context of Kristeva's theories of subjectivity in relation to the 'sujet en procès' and the abject applied specifically to the mother-daughter relationship, (sexual) desire and (dis) embodiment, the role of the mirror in the construction of subjectivity, and the idea of the alter ego or double.[2] As will be seen, central to Clavel's work are the tropes of (dis)embodiment, invisibility, and the supernatural which are inexorably linked to the concept of the queer. These motifs are also linked to 'no-deseos', as well as to the desire for (self-) recognition and for creative freedom. Invisibility is linked to the play of shadow and light, a central theme of the novel which is also connected to Clavel's notion of 'poética de las sombras' [shadow poetics] and her fascination with photography, which foregrounds the author's own intense interest in this area in much of her later literary and multimedia *oeuvre*. Finally, this chapter will explore briefly Clavel's relatively small-scale multimedia intervention for the promotion of *Los deseos*, demonstrating her nascent interest in this area.

(Exploding) Conceptions of Truth and Nation

Set between the 1960s and mid-1980s, *Los deseos* traces the life of Soledad García, an introverted young woman struggling to define her own sense of identity in a socially repressive society. She embarks upon a journey of self-discovery, exploring the unchartered territory of the dark side of desire and a magical Mexico City where she encounters historical and fictional characters. Clavel focuses on those radical elements which the hegemonic power chooses to silence but which threaten to upset the status quo. The city's liminal voices form part of what Edward Said terms 'the ignored group', encompassing 'the hidden or suppressed accounts of numerous groups — women, minorities, disadvantaged or dispossessed groups, refugees, exiles, etc'.[3] According to Dawn Slack the term 'etcetera' points to the plight of the subaltern; it refers to the 'gaps, absences, lapses, ellipses' (Said, p. vii, quoted by Slack, p. 223). Michel de Certeau depicts these sectors as 'unassigned, unreadable, and unsymbolized [...] a silent majority'.[4] This is portrayed through the female protagonist Soledad, who becomes both literally and metaphorically disembodied, a ghost who meanders through the labyrinthine streets of Mexico City.

Clavel's account of the city's underworld and its inhabitants is linked to socio-historical and political criticism. Although there are various references to the historical realities of Mexico, the text focuses almost entirely on the invented world of the imaginary character Soledad and on the impossibility of unravelling the 'truth' about this character, whose life is shrouded in mystery. The unknowability of her truth becomes interconnected with the text's comments on historic reality, symbolically illustrating that what we might perceive as reality or 'truth' is ultimately an imaginative construct. Even though historical realities are subordinated to social and psychological issues, the physical violence suffered by Soledad and various other characters reflects the experiences of silenced Mexicans under the PRI (Partido Revolucionario Institucional) between the 1950s and 1980s. Mexico City after the 1960s was far from a homogenous space, where the 'coherence' of the alleged miracle of *desarrollismo* (Mexico's process of modernization between 1940 and 1968) became increasingly questioned by the silenced sectors of society.[5] Mexico's empty discourse of modernization, social justice, national unity, and economic plenty, was undermined by destructive socio-political realities and an authoritarian rule which monopolized political power. Mexicans' questioning of *desarrollismo* and the state's undemocratic system came to a head during the 1968 Tlatelolco riots, an event to which Clavel makes reference in her text (*Los deseos,* p. 60). The insurgence resulted in the massacre of many innocent civilians by the army under orders from the ruthless PRI government. Their 'disappearance' is metaphorically signalled by Soledad's own invisibility. Soledad documents the event, but her friend Rosa belies the whole incident by claiming that it never actually took place and that Soledad has invented the whole thing (p. 64). Through Rosa's attempt at silencing Soledad, the writer ironizes the corrupt and repressive PRI. The writer uses Rosa's words to represent the official discourse which served to mask the truth behind the uprising and its aftermath. Clavel also draws attention to the enormous power exercised by the PRI over the Mexican media, and the official party's failed attempt to silence a national event on the scale of Tlatelolco.[6] It is interesting to note that when Soledad documents the event, she assumes the identity of an English journalist called Soledad Fryer (p. 62). The image of the English journalist painstakingly recording the testimonies of those caught up in the upheaval in her quest for truth (pp. 62–63) might be seen as an attempt by the author to ironize the British press's own distortion of truth following the massacre (Paz, p. 281). Soledad's account of the Tlatelolco uprising problematizes the concept of truth on various levels. The journalistic article she purports to write sways somewhat ambivalently between what would appear to be objective narration and imaginative reconstruction. The journalistic quality is reinforced by references to historical events such as the bombing of the Ciudad de los Palacios by the North Americans (*Los deseos*, p. 61) or by precise time-frames such as 2 October 1968 (p. 60). But the reliability of Soledad's account is questionable: first, because she fakes her real identity by assuming that of an English journalist; and second, because she has inserted into her objective narration imaginary characters such as her alter ego Lucía (p. 63).

The blurring of fact and fiction highlights the relative nature of truth, and the unreliability of language to convey monological truth, through various discourses — journalistic, political, historical — thus representing alternative visions to a single historical 'truth'. Clavel's emphasis on the imaginative aspect of her novel ultimately points to the literary foundation of the text, which may give an impression of historical veracity but ultimately boasts no greater claim to representing historical 'truth' than fiction itself. Ultimately, *Los deseos* serves to challenge the official (patriarchal) version of the events surrounding the Tlatelolco massacre by presenting a 'counter-discourse' to contradict the dominant discourse of the Mexican government. *Los deseos* plays out compellingly the clash between Soledad's efforts to recount the truth, echoing the desire of many Mexicans affected by these events but whose voices were often silenced, and the Mexican elite's stance on the event voiced through Rosa: 'aquí no hubo muertos ni heridos' [there were no dead or injured people here] (p. 64).

Soledad as 'sujet en procès'

In an attempt to reconstruct an alternative conception of national identity which is heterogeneous and divided, Clavel creates a non-patriarchal conception of female subjectivity by exploring the inner workings of the protagonist, who is presented as fragmented and contradictory and as a 'sujet en procès'. Clavel's construction of the self can be placed alongside contemporary notions of subjectivity and consciousness, which undermine the traditional view of the unitary self in favour of one which is inchoate and multiple. Soledad vacillates between negative and positive representations of selfhood, frequently portrayed in terms of female submission and the objectification of the male gaze, on the one hand, and alternative representations which go beyond the confining male constructions of gender, on the other. The text constantly vacillates between these two representations of this female subject, as will be examined throughout this chapter.

Soledad's fragmented self is seen in relation to the city trope which permeates Clavel's novel. Her journey of self-discovery and remapping of her own body in the megalopolis feminizes the traditional male quest in the Mexican urban novel. The notion of the city as a whore, which provides the space for male journeys over what is depicted as prostrate female terrain, continues to hold sway in Mexico's masculine literary (postcolonial) imagination.[7] In rather ambiguous fashion, Clavel appears to both challenge and reinstate this view of the city. The city as whore is symbolically portrayed in Soledad, who prostitutes her body in a building where she is subjected to sexual abuse by the 'Desconocido' (p. 31). Elsewhere Clavel alludes to the city's violent origins, and the link between men conquering and mapping the city and the vicious raping-mapping of the female/Soledad's body is powerfully depicted (p. 255). The foundation of the city is intimately connected to the cartography of male desire, where man writes the body of the female other and brutally inscribes upon it his own history. Yet the female city/body is also portrayed as eluding the male gaze and desire: 'la tomaban una y otra vez [...] y ellos en realidad no la poseían' [they raped her again and again [...] but in reality they did not possess her] (p. 255). This elusiveness may thus represent hope for a city/nation which has been ruled by a history of violence. The Soledad/City trope acquires positive meaning towards the end of the novel (p. 305) where Soledad's sense of being as independent of violent patriarchal domination and submission is reflected in the manner in which, as Clavel notes, 'la ciudad como un cuerpo amoroso reabsorbe a Soledad y que Soledad también posee' [the city as a symbol of a desiring body reabsorbs Soledad which she in turn also possesses].[8]

Soledad appears not as a defined being, but rather as a Kristevan 'sujet en procès', in continual flux, embodying opposing impulses and 'no-deseos'. For Kristeva the subject is constituted in language, and results from the contradictions between the semiotic — which refers to the drives of the body, the unconscious, the intuitive, the non-sense (the queer one might add) — and the symbolic order, that is the language, the law, and the order of the father.[9] The semiotic seeks to disrupt the symbolic, resulting in the destabilization of meaning and of the self. The self, which is divided between these two opposing forces, must seek a balance. For Kristeva, 'jouissance' [ecstasy] — which is 'sexual, physical, conceptual at one and the same time' (*Desire in Language*, p. 16) — follows from the challenge of this fundamental struggle. Soledad is torn between her (semiotic) private world of dreams, desires, and fears, and the public sphere which is dominated by the symbolic which is represented by patriarchal discourses. Soledad's mother, Soledad's lover Péter Nágy, and her male colleagues all represent the values of the symbolic as represented in particular in Mexican *desarrollismo*, *charrismo sindical* [trade union coercion], and patriarchal power structure.[10] The private world of Soledad, represented by the

Chinese vase, signifies the place of the semiotic, imagination, magic, 'non-desires', dark nightmares, and the unconscious.

Clavel's exploration of the mother-daughter relationship becomes a defining aspect in Soledad's process of becoming. The protagonist's search for identity and independence has been hampered by her family's traditional values, associated with the symbolic. Soledad's mother, Carmen, is a staunch defender of the patriarchal system, whose 'rules' relating to gender demand that both women and men alike conform to traditional gender stereotypes. Such a posture is specifically seen in the more privileged treatment Carmen gives her son Luis over Soledad, as Luzma Becerra notes.[11] Carmen hinders Soledad's development by imposing her own expectations on her daughter, presenting her with 'perfect' models that all women should follow 'las niñas no hablan [...] quietecita como una muñeca de porcelana: si se mueve se rompe' [little girls do not speak [...] still as a porcelain doll: if she moves, she breaks] (p. 21), thus reflecting the *machista* conservatism which assigns the female subject to the role of passive object.

Carmen is representative of the Kristevan notion of the abject, that dangerous border 'where meaning collapses' (*Powers of Horror*, p. 10). Kristeva discusses the way in which the abject element in humanity is controlled by society, with rituals such as the revulsion at disease, disfigurement, and the maternal. These rituals strive to maintain the boundaries between what is abject and what is not. The mother in this regard becomes the perfect representative of the abject. In psychoanalytic theory, for the subject-child to become a subject it must go through a series of stages to acquire a sense of self as differentiated from the other, including the need to go beyond the pre-Oedipal phase and ultimately to move away from being a part of its mother so that it is then able to enter into the symbolic order.[12] Therefore, the main threat to the child is its dependence upon the maternal presence, and it must reject the maternal as a way of achieving a boundary between self and m(other). According to Kristeva, the subject's initial move towards the expulsion of the m(other) is consolidated during the Mirror Stage, where the subject will acquire a sense of self, when it sees an image of its own body either through the gaze of others or reflected in a mirror, leading to the subject's identification with that image. The image creates a sense of wholeness as well as separateness of the self.[13] In *Los deseos* the process of rejection of the mother is connected to the symbol of the mirror, which is a recurring leitmotif throughout Clavel's text, suggesting some positive although mainly negative connotations in the construction of self. There is a curious ambivalence in one passage, where Soledad is standing in front of a mirror looking at herself. On the one hand, the passage suggests female narcissism and resistance to the m(other) who must be rejected; on the other, it also suggests female disempowerment, whereby the subject is engulfed by the mother. As Soledad looks into the mirror, her body becomes an object of desire for herself:

> Sus [...] labios carnosos que se parecían a los de su padre [...] A Soledad le gustaba tanto sus labios que [...] con la lengua [...] les dejaba un brillo de ciruela recién mordida [...] la imagen reflejada le fascinaba y [...] poco faltó para que la cubriera de besos, para que comiera aquella fruta carnosa y se consagrara en el culto de los que son fieles a sí mismos. (*Los deseos*, pp. 79–80)

> [Her [...] fleshy lips which looked liked her father's [...] Soledad liked her lips so much that [...] she would lick them with her tongue leaving them shiny like a newly eaten plum [...] the reflection of her image fascinated her so much [...] that she almost filled it with kisses, ate that fleshy fruit and gave herself to the cult of self love]

The association of the plum with lips has clear sexual connotations, where the glistening, fleshy fruit suggests female genitalia. Female narcissism and the autoerotic also become disturbingly suggestive of incestuous desire. Soledad conjures up the image of her dead father's lips in her reflection, signalling her identification with and desire for him. Soledad's narcissistic identification with the image of the body represents an important step in her psychic process as it allows her to acquire a sense of her own bodily boundaries and of a stable identity. But her desire for her own body is disturbed when her mother 'la sorprendió en el asombro y la seducción de contemplarse frente al espejo' [caught her in her state of awe and seduction of looking at herself in the mirror] (p. 79). Soledad's body now becomes the locus of shame and disgust (p. 80). Here she has lost the power of her own gaze and Carmen has seized power of representation, threatening to obliterate the borders between self and m(other). The mother inscribes in her daughter a negative image of her body as she makes her feel inadequate, and Soledad becomes a projected image moulded by her mother's own cultural values. Carmen has internalized society's repudiation of the female body and female sexual desire, transmitting these misogynistic attitudes to her daughter. Carmen perpetuates the myth of female genitalia as a shameful bodily organ which must be covered up: the daughter's fleshy, wet lips, which resemble female labia, must be suppressed. Soledad feels compelled to mimic her mother — 'una Soledad nueva la contempló con la boca empequeñecida' [a new Soledad looked at her with shrunken lips] (p. 80) — suggesting the daughter's recognition of her resemblance to her mother and, ultimately, Soledad's acknowledgement of both her own and woman's innate devalued and abject position in patriarchal society. Soledad is thus reduced to taking on an image which fragments rather than unifies her. The body she now sees reflected back towards her is grotesquely distorted: 'una línea por boca, sin labios. La boca de un simio o un pez' [a line for a lipless mouth. The lips of a monkey or a fish] (p. 80). Yet Soledad, finally, rejects the image she sees of her own body through the gaze of her mother: 'el labio no se le corrigió nunca porque se le cansaba y entonces se le levantaba más inflamado [...] y tal vez por eso no se volvió fantasma del todo' [her lip never corrected itself because it drooped and would become more inflamed [...] and that is why she never became entirely a ghost] (p. 80). Here Soledad resists being engulfed by her mother's gaze, thus creating a sense of separateness of the self from the abject (m)other.[14]

Elsewhere in the text, Kristeva's notion of matricide or the rejection of the maternal presence is further suggested through the verbal and textual expulsion of Carmen from the text.[15] In her desire to break away from Carmen's stifling authoritarianism which thwarts her self-realization, Soledad leaves the family home and engages in an affair with Péter Nágy, a Hungarian photographer. From this point onwards, references to Soledad's mother are virtually absent from the text, evincing a physical and textual expulsion of the castrating mother. Soledad's clear articulation of her desires and assertion of her identity hold the key to her power over herself. By engaging in an affair with Péter, Soledad is asserting her belief that her identity depends on her own desires and on fulfilling these, rather than on her place in a strictly controlled hierarchy. The encounter between Péter and Soledad and the ensuing expulsion of the mother figure from the text encourages an Oedipal reading of *Los deseos.* Indeed, the arrival of Péter (the 'father') and his sexual intercourse with Soledad seem effectively to contribute to Soledad's splitting up of the dyadic mother-child relationship. In line with Freudian Oedipal theory, Péter Nágy, who is described as having a 'mirada en el centro del universo' [gaze in the centre of the universe], (p. 75) represents the law of the father. But rather than having a positive impact on Soledad's psychosexual development, he reduces Soledad to absence and thus continues the ritual initiated by Soledad's mother of splintering her daughter's self, since he threatens to annihilate her being into an unfeeling nothingness. Furthermore, despite Soledad's apparent rejection of her overbearing mother in the context of her relationship with Péter, direct or indirect textual references to the mother figure throughout the text, though scarce, suggest Soledad's inability to reject the mother entirely. Although Soledad sees her mother as symbolizing all the traditions she refuses to adopt, paradoxically she also appears to identify with her mother elsewhere. In one passage, Soledad conjures up horrific images of a cannibalistic dragon which embodies, in Clavel's terms, 'una fuerza primordial del orden masculino'.[16] It is described in the novel as furiously devouring Soledad's alter ego Lucía while Soledad desperately tries to escape the dragon's fangs (pp. 38–39). These images are simultaneously enmeshed with images of Soledad's mother screaming wrathfully at her daughter whilst the mother also 'abrazaba a una muñeca del tamaño de Soledad' [hugged a doll the size of Soledad] (p. 39). This passage is rather ambivalent, as it suggests, on the one hand, Soledad's desire for unity with her mother, while, on the other, the dragon-mother threatens symbolically to engulf Soledad, thus posing a threat of psychic obliteration. While much psychoanalytical theory states that the mother needs to be rejected so that the child can separate itself from her, maternal cannibalism inverts this relationship (Kristeva, *Black Sun*, p. 27). Carmen is the devouring mother who refuses Soledad's borders, and thus her own existence, infecting her daughter with her own rejection. Yet Soledad's desire for unity with her mother suggests that she is unable entirely to reject Carmen while ultimately identifying with her as a woman. Soledad's inability to abject Carmen highlights the protagonist's struggle to enter into the symbolic realm where woman, from a Lacanian perspective, is perceived as a permanent outsider, as absence, as abject.[17] Soledad's identification with and rejection of her mother also suggests that the abject both repels and attracts because, ultimately, the borders between what is abject and what is not become blurred.[18]

Soledad then, whose physical borders become blurred in the text, comes to embody the abject itself, oscillating ambiguously between life and death, disease and cleanliness, visibility and invisibility, between the fully and partially formed subject, the semiotic and symbolic. As a subject in a continual state of becoming, Soledad's fragmented sense of (non-) self is linked to the idea of the ghostly, to invisibility, and to notions of (dis)embodiment. Invisibility is used to question the traditional barriers of fact and fiction, the possibility of a stable personal identity and of a unified reality or historical truth, reflecting the text's own structure, which similarly precludes closure and where there can be no end to the search for meanings. In line with magical realism, the ghostly in *Los deseos* also reconciles concepts which are normally considered as being opposed to each other: the real and the magical, for example, are presented on an equal footing. Amaryll Chanady observes that 'magical realism belongs neither entirely to the domain of fantasy (the creation of a world totally different from ours), nor to that of reality, our conventional everyday world'.[19] Magical realism thus has a dislocating effect on Clavel's reader, who is 'disconcerted not by the intrusion of the extraordinary into an otherwise normal world but rather by the blurring of boundaries between realities which he has been accustomed to keep apart'.[20] These slippages between fantasy and reality which inform the magical realism of Soledad's half-human, half-phantasmagoric existence mislead the reader, who is forced to question whether or not Soledad has committed suicide, whether she is alive or whether, in fact, she may be a ghost. Even Soledad, who understands that identity is in permanent flux, is unable to ascertain whether she is alive or dead: 'Ser y no estar ¿era esto la muerte, seguir mirando como si estuviéramos vivos? [being but not physically being. Was this death, still seeing things as if we were still alive?] (p. 298).

The uncertainty of Soledad's existence is further complicated as she engages in dialogue with dead historical figures, and thus the proximity of life and death creates a dialogue between them, recalling Juan Rulfo's notion of the 'diálogo de muertos' [dialogue of the dead] in *Pedro Páramo* (1955), whereby the barriers between life and death become indistinguishable.[21] Like the abject, Soledad's ghostliness threatens the borders between life and death by destabilizing the fixed boundaries which exist between the human and non-human. According to Kristeva, the most horrific example of the abject is the corpse, which is almost universally overcome by taboos and rituals which prevent it from threatening life: 'a border that has encroached upon everything. [...] The corpse seen without God, and outside of science, is the utmost of abjection. It is death infecting life. Abject' (*Powers of Horror*, pp. 3–4). Soledad's spectre and her deathliness become an intolerable 'presence' which remains 'outside of science' (*Powers of Horror*, pp.3–4), invoking not the miracles of science but more the possibilities of magic. Like the corpse, ghostliness provokes cultural, collective, and individual revulsion and fear, indicative of what Elizabeth Grosz sees as the 'cultural inability to accept the body's materiality, its limit [...] its mortality' (Kristeva, quoted in Grosz, *Sexual Subversions*, p. 91). Soledad's ghostliness/deathliness threatens to infect life and must be ultimately suppressed, as suggested in one humorous passage in which Clavel describes two government soldiers smoking marijuana while on duty (*Los deseos*, pp. 17–18). Invisible to both men, Soledad decides to play a prank on them by making coughing sounds and by placing her hand on one of the men's shoulders. The soldier is visibly frightened by the inexplicable occurrences, but dismisses the whole thing by finding a 'logical' explanation in the hallucinogenic effect the drug is having on them (p. 18). The soldiers' flippant attitude towards their duty might be seen as a gentle mockery of the general incompetence of the PRI and its official institutions such as the military. More pertinently, through the soldier's dismissive reaction to the supernatural, Clavel can be seen to attempt to verbalize the 'unsaid' of rationalism, which traditionally seeks to establish borders between the rational and irrational, life and death, the abject and non-abject, the symbolic and the semiotic.[22] Clavel appears to challenge patriarchal order and logic, which seeks to establish a kind of mental dictatorship as a way of banishing the deathly, the abject, the mad, and the other. Elsewhere Soledad is cast into the figure of a 'loca' [madwoman] (p. 190) and by being thus labelled, the abject element she comes to represent can be suppressed and ignored, adding further complexity to Soledad's already fraught process of self-definition.

Invisibility has a dual function in the construction of the self in process. Soledad's invisibility is celebrated as it offers her freedom from the strictures of patriarchal society, allowing her to construct a self-defined image of self. Invisibility is also associated with the semiotic, creativity, the magical, the intuitive, and the repressed. Paradoxically that same trope of invisibility is exploited by Clavel to show how in the world of the living, Soledad is defined symbolically as a 'sombra' [shadow], as abjection, and lack from a symbolic perspective. This oscillating perspective may be best understood by exploring the link between the body, the self, and desire. Clavel appears to recognize the body/self as a site fraught with complexities where the body is perceived as a subjective process which ultimately brings about a sense of self. The extensive references to body parts which pepper the text reinforce the view that the self is not perceived as a whole but rather as inchoate, relentlessly under threat of total annihilation.

Soledad's inability to recognize herself as a whole is particularly reinforced in the way Clavel resorts to metaphors of the female body as abject, disfigured, and grotesque to construct Soledad's bodily identity, drawing attention to the female character's spiritual and psychological predicament. While working as an assistant photographer to Péter she inadvertently spills a chemical on her hands, resulting in multiple burns. Following this incident, Soledad has a nightmare in which she visualizes herself as disfigured (p. 123). The skin is slowly peeling off her hands and she starts to wear white gloves to 'protect' them (p. 73). The polarities of dirt/disease (Soledad's hands) and cleanliness (white gloves) function as markers of cultural order and disorder in a way that again connects Soledad to the Kristevan concept of the abject.[23] Kristeva's view of the female body as the site of pollution in opposition to the notion of a clean and proper body are associated with Soledad's body as a site of shame and disfigurement. The gloves Soledad wears are linked to the notion of respectability, the colour white suggesting virginal purity and social propriety as well as signifying the subservient, self-conscious values of the feminine sphere. The pristine gloves are closely linked to the idea of containing threat and embarrassment: the overspilling of Soledad's bodily boundaries leads to a process of concealment designed to curtail her (women's/the abject's) threatening excesses.

Soledad's disfigurement becomes an expression for her lack and for her inability to recognize herself as a whole being because ultimately her existence is defined by the look and the desires of others. It is in this context that paradoxically the text seeks to create a more positive, non-patriarchal conception of female subjectivity and 'another measure of desire'.[24] Such an endeavour reveals, however, a dilemma in the female subject, who finds herself caught between a Lacanian 'desire to desire' and a 'desire to be desired', frequently unable to acquire a desire of her own.[25] On the one hand, Soledad strives to take control of her own life and actions and to desire on her own terms. On the other hand, she is controlled by the desires of others and by a need to be desired by others, threatening to reduce her to non-being. Soledad's body is frequently depicted as the (willing) construction of morbid male desire. When she prostitutes her body to the 'Desconocido' [Unknown Man] (p. 31), the nameless man fetishizes Soledad's body by subjecting her to sexual abuse, thus fragmenting her body into unfeeling pieces. Despite Soledad's harrowing experience, she is not portrayed in the text as a passive victim of sexual abuse. She freely accepts the sexual contract, which involves a commercial exchange conducted between her and the anonymous man: 'las monedas en mis manos son parte de un trato' [the coins in my hand are part of a deal] (p. 33). Although fetishization of the female body is linked to the notion of female disempowerment, Clavel also can be seen to suggest that it empowers the female subject in that the process of 'othering' brings about a re-evaluation of Soledad's sense of self, allowing her to experience desire for herself: '¿Quién no es juguete del deseo de los otros? Y sobre todo ¿quién no goza siéndolo?' [Who isn't the plaything of other people's desires? And more importantly, who doesn't enjoy being it?] (p. 31).

Elsewhere Soledad is portrayed as the object of male desire while also willingly playing to the 'rules of the game'. By agreeing to Péter's suggestion that she dress as a titillating nurse to look after his ailing friend Montero (p. 113), Soledad is conforming to male expectations by voluntarily objectifying herself in order to please men and make them desire her. Thus outfitted, Soledad provides sexual joy to both the ailing Montero and Péter Nágy (p. 115), while also providing herself with a sense of identity and purpose, despite the insidious effect on her: 'en una complicidad que la hacía sentir privilegiada [...] haciendo gala de esta identidad en préstamo' [in a complicity that made her feel privileged [...] and want to show off her borrowed identity] (p. 114). Yet Soledad's sartorial extravagance suggests her own fragile subjectivity, desperate to achieve a sense of completion by giving herself to others. Role-playing pushes Soledad to sexual excess, as she becomes part of a sordid orgy with Péter and Montero, whilst 'Péter la miraba como si estuviera haciendo el amor con aquella sombra' [Péter looked at her as if he were making love with that shadow] (p. 116). Here Péter's fantasizing male gaze reduces 'Sola'/Soledad's being to a 'sombra' and she ultimately becomes a site of lack.[26]

In her process of self-definition, Soledad yearns for the ideal unity of self (pp. 135–36). In her desire to complete her body/self, which she experiences as unfinished, she seeks to complement her lack with the other's completeness. On one occasion she observes Péter in the bedroom getting ready in front of a mirror (p. 127). Péter's image, which literally engulfs the entire mirror and suggests the Lacanian view (*Écrits*, pp. 1–7) that the mirror reflects men's world-view and women as other. As the mirror relegates Soledad, and by extension, all women to absence, so too it denies Soledad's/women's identity, rendering them unable to appropriate their own image. Soledad is suddenly overcome by a jealousy and hatred towards the 'completed' and 'unified' other (Péter). The protagonist's ability to recognize her own lack appears to be the initial step towards her ability to differentiate herself from the other, and ultimately to move towards freedom of the self. But in a moment of frenzied unthinking, she violently assaults Péter (p. 127). Her outburst could be seen as her attempt to subvert the opposition between her fragmented self/body and the unified body of the male other. But their relationship ends with violent abruptness, thus putting an end to the possibility of Soledad's reliance on her lover for self-definition. Later on, however, she recognizes and comes to accept that the self is a 'speculary' construction where the idea of a unitary self is based on imaginary relations (p. 197). This recognition of the speculary self is what ultimately allows Soledad to go 'beyond the mirror' where her image is no longer a 'reflection' of the masculine psyche but shaped by her own experiences and desires.[27]

The process of self-definition, which is determined by the contradictions inherent in the divided self between the semiotic and symbolic forces, is perhaps best illustrated in *Los deseos* in the symbol of the vase and in the construction of the self/double duality. Soledad's repressive family environment and the death of her father in particular, lead to her physical and psychic retreat into 'interior' spaces. Throughout the text there are references to a Chinese vase, which comes to symbolize the female character's psychological 'vase of one's own' of thoughts, memories, and fantasies. The vase, associated with the semiotic, becomes a site of pre-Oedipal *jouissance* where Soledad's irrational emotions, sexual non-desires, and subconscious thought-processes are played out. The vase is associated with nightmares: 'el oleaje de un mar comenzó a golpear las paredes del jarrón' [the waves of the sea started to crash against the walls of the vase] (p. 83). Here, the image of the sea threatening to engulf the vase suggests Soledad's subconscious fears of not being able to achieve unity of self with the other. The vase, where Soledad feels deeply shielded from the real world, also becomes associated with the maternal when Clavel refers to the 'interior del vientre del jarrón' [in the interior of the vase's womb] (p. 85), suggesting Soledad's repressed need for the archaic mother. Yet the womb-vase becomes an intra-uterine paradise and hell at the same time, where, as noted earlier, the mother/dragon is capable of devouring her own daughter by wielding total power over her life, as if she were still in her womb. The polarities which we encounter throughout the text (dark/light, Soledad/Lucía, self/other, man/woman, death/life) are continued through the metaphor of the vase. The vase figuratively is a space for liberation and creativity and a place of entrapment (pp. 24–27). There, Soledad seeks refuge in a world of fantasy where she makes up magical stories of mythic creatures and heroes in which she frequently appears as one of the characters. Stories not only engender creativity but also freedom to express one's non-desires (p. 22).

It is in the vase that Soledad creates her imaginary alter ego, Lucía. Soledad is held hostage by her fear of stepping into the real world, associated with the patriarchal, and living her life according to others' desires rather than her own. She finds, therefore, a sense of reprieve in sharing her afflictions with her stronger double. While Soledad can appear to be emotional and passive — attributes stereotypically associated with the feminine — Lucía emerges as aggressive, rational, and dominant, attributes stereotypically associated with the male. Yet when Clavel describes Soledad as being androgynous in appearance (p. 47), the opposition between male and female becomes blurred, thus suggesting a defiance of such rigid classification associated with patriarchal logic. Lucía represents both Soledad's opposite and her complement, metaphorically depicted in terms of light and dark. Whereas Soledad's various names denote loneliness (Soledad, Sola) and darkness/lack (Sombra), Lucía's name has positive associations: light (*luz*), lucidity (*lucidez*), to flaunt (*lucir*). Metaphors of darkness are associated with the semiotic, signalling Soledad's labyrinthine unconscious thought-processes and terrifying dreams, which reveal her anxieties and wishes. Paradoxically, metaphors of darkness also come to represent the symbolic repression of Soledad's desires as well as her lack. Soledad is the epitome of the passive woman who depends on others for her own fulfilment, and therefore the recurrent metaphors of darkness come to symbolize the anguish which she experiences at such dependence on others to give meaning to her existence.

Through the metaphors of darkness, Clavel weaves into the plot a subtle critique of the symbolic function, which excludes whatever it perceives as improper and insane, and therefore everything else stereotypically associated with the 'feminine' (intuition, sexual excess, nature, body). Lucía is a manifestation of primary drives, enacting Soledad's 'improper' unconscious desires and fantasies, which Soledad fears and desperately wants to repress. Lucía also embodies dark desires, even murderous instincts, pressing Soledad to fulfil her 'no-deseos' and her uninhibited sexual drives (e.g. pp. 49 and 57). Soledad's double prompts her to escape the imposition of the social and symbolic order by letting her imagination break through the dominant signifying practice. Thus through her engagement with a world of fantasy and the irrational, Soledad learns to reject the language of logic and sanity (p. 202) and listens to her bodily rhythms by immersing herself in a pre-Oedipal *jouissance*: 'ahora soy yo la imagen del espejo que remueve en ondas de placer acuoso' [I am now the image in the mirror, stirring in ripples of aqueous pleasure] (p. 82).

Soledad's expression of repressed sexual desire, which threatens to destabilize the symbolic order, is also linked to textual practice, where textual fragmentation and linguistic incoherence in *Los deseos* threaten the controlled narrative elsewhere, reflecting Elizabeth Grosz's contention that:

> Like the repressed, the semiotic can return in/as irruptions within the symbolic. It manifests itself as an interruption, a dissonance, a rhythm unsubsumable in the text's rational logic or controlled narrative. The semiotic is thus both the precondition of symbolic conditioning and its incontrollable excess. [28]

In the fantastical world which Soledad inhabits, meaning is exploded — 'las palabras chocaban unas con otras y le decían mensajes confusos' [the words collided one against the other and gave her confused messages] (p. 25) — by a 'non-sense', a rhythmical, sexual language, incomprehensible to the symbolic world (p. 39).

In her process of becoming, Soledad is torn between the alternative imperatives of rejecting Lucía and fusing with her so as to integrate her opposing selves: 'de no estar más separadamente. De fundirse' [of not being separated any longer and becoming fused] (p. 226). The fusion of the two selves is implied in the text's use of words and phrases which fuse opposites of dark and light, suggesting the blurring of consciousness and unconsciousness, life and death, desire and repression, self and other: 'su dualidad de luz y sombras le hablaba oscuramente de un tejido interno, la textura de un instante vivo detenido en un palpitar de muerte [...] algo que ya había percibido en el interior del vientre del jarrón' [her duality of light and shadows darkly spoke about an internal tissue, the texture of a living moment which had been detained by pulsating death [...] which was something she had already become aware of in the interior of the womb of the vase] (p. 85). Despite her duality of light and shadows, the internal conflict Soledad's split selves bring about, Soledad and Lucía mirror each other in many other respects. Clavel offers the reader barely any physical descriptions of both, thus making them almost impossible to tell apart. Towards the end of the novel, Soledad is faced with the choice of either rejecting her alter ego or fusing with Lucía, while also accepting the other's difference. In order to exist, Soledad must bridge the gaps between the contrasting semiotic/symbolic forces. *Jouissance* allows her to recognize both these unresolved divisions and her own provisional nature. The end suggests that Soledad has come to terms with her fragmented sense of self and that her split selves become reconciled: 'por fín parecían caminar juntas: como si su sombra y ella se dirigían hacia un mismo lugar' [at last they seemed to be walking together: as if she and her shadow were moving towards the same place] (p. 239). This fusion of selves towards the end of the novel suggests that Clavel's female character has been given the chance to go through a transforming experience that helps her regain a unique sense of identity. She is given the opportunity to enter the symbolic on her own terms, by coming to self-consciousness through a distinguishing of the self from others, but also the ability to go beyond the symbolic.

The end of the novel sheds a rather ambiguous light on Soledad's 'existence'. The epilogue suggests that Soledad chooses an existence as a (ghostly?) 'sombra' ('shadow'). Yet her literal and figural disembodiment is seen as representing potential for positive change, both at an individual level, pointing towards new spaces for Soledad's (women's) identity and expression, and at a national level.[29] The epilogue's final words 'Su cuerpo no la contiene' [her body cannot contain her] (p. 307), suggest that Soledad chooses to discard her old existence, associated with a staid social power structure and traditional familial traditions, in favour of living a life associated with Mexico's City's underground existence. The trope of invisibility reflects non-representation of women and women writers such as Clavel, while paradoxically also signalling hope for women's sexual, intellectual, and literary emancipation beyond male-dominated society. Clavel appears to be torn between a desire to remove all physical traces of femaleness through Soledad's invisibility and an attempt to inscribe the physical aspects of the corporeal.[30] Soledad's phantasmagoric state violates the integrity of the body, and therefore the potential for danger is unleashed: 'cuando Soledad salió del jarrón y descubrió que nadie podía verla, se le ocurrieron ideas disparatadas' [when Soledad came out of the vase and discovered that nobody could see her, she came up with insane ideas] (p. 13). Here, the female body is conceived as an obstacle to creativity, and thus by discarding its limitations Soledad is able to occupy an 'other' space where she is able to use her imagination. The text often emphasizes the importance of voice over the corporeal: 'la voz surge de dentro, atraviesa esa máscara que nos hemos fabricado [...] Si hay algo de auténtico en el hombre es su voz' [one's voice comes from within, it pierces though the mask which we have fabricated for ourselves [...] if there is something truly authentic in mankind, it is one's voice] (p. 272). Soledad's search for a voice of her own reflects Clavel's own search for recognition when, at an early point in her career, she was struggling to establish her voice in the Mexican literary establishment.

Clavel's apparent attempt to remove all physical traces of femaleness underlines the inversion of Cixous's call to 'write the body'.[31] Elsewhere there is the suggestion that she is alluding to *écriture féminine* (p. 283), thus emphasizing the importance of the female body.[32] The self-conscious aspect of *Los deseos* is strongly suggested since Soledad's fragmented identity/body becomes a symbol of the fragmented text itself. The materialization of Soledad's new inchoate self/ body (pp. 280–83) coincides with the materialization and completion of the book, but its own open-endedness precludes closure. Soledad's self-assertion, independent of patriarchal notions of feminine identity, coincides with Clavel's affirmation of her creative voice. This twofold process is suggested in the way in which Soledad's voice becomes merged with that of Clavel, as implied in the following free indirect style quotation, strongly intimating the inextricable link which exists between character, author, writing, self-expression, and desire:

> El cuerpo [...] había empezado a iluminarse [...] Los labios hablaron su lengua de piel e instinto, y yo me quedé sin tinta para escribir estas líneas. [...] La piel y el cuerpo se desataron y dejaron de obedecerme. Me convertí en una letra que estallaba, un signo que por fin encontraba su sentido. (*Los deseos*, pp. 281–83)
>
> [The [...] body had started to light up [...] her lips spoke to her about the language of the flesh and instinct, and I was left without ink to write these lines. [...] Flesh and body became unleashed and stopped obeying me. I was transformed into a letter which exploded, a sign which finally found its meaning]

'Poética de las sombras': Photography and Multimedia

The hitherto explored tropes of corporeality, (dis)embodiment, visbility and invisibity, being and non-being, light and shadow, and 'no-deseos', all of which define Soledad's inchoate being, are inexorably linked to Clavel's aesthetics of a 'poética de las sombras', which in turn is connected to the author's interest in photography. Clavel thus explains her notion of a poetics of shadows:

> Temáticamente, los canales más importantes que se me han ido abriendo son la indagación del deseo y su relación con el mundo de las sombras [...] se trata de dejarse ser una sombra en las manos de las sombras de uno mismo.[33]
>
> [Thematically the most important routes I have taken are those which have got to do with the exploration of desire and its relationship to the world of shadows [...] it is all about allowing oneself to become a shadow in one's own shadow]

Both in *Los deseos* and its multimedia dimension, Clavel's shadow poetics is informed in particular by Philippe Dubois's concept of photography as a luminous shadow or trace, which he develops in his seminal *L'Acte photographique et autres essais*.[34] Clavel describes the indelible mark which Dubois's notion of the 'empreinte lumineuse', that is, a trace or index of the real left by the existence of something physical and material (*L'Acte photographique*, pp. 40, 58), has left on *Los deseos* and her *oeuvre* as a whole:

> Philippe Dubois maneja el concepto de la fotografía como sombra luminosa, como huella luminosa; no como un mero reflejo [...] Ahí cuando se da el efecto fotográfico hay una irradiación de sales, está la luz; el cuerpo como un objeto opaco refleja esa luz y eso queda impreso en el papel fotográfico [...] Entonces hay una huella, ahí hay una sombra que se ilumina [...] la idea de que la fotografía no es una imagen sino la sombra, pues me permitió gestar esta idea de la poética de las sombras además que se ha ido definiendo mucho más a lo largo de los otros libros como en el caso de *Cuerpo náufrago* donde descubro la posibilidad de desarrollar la idea que las sombras son entidades deseantes.[35]
>
> [Philippe Dubois deals with the concept of photography as luminous shadow, as luminous trace; not merely as reflection [...] when the effect of the photographic irradiation of salts occurs, there is light there; the body as opaque object reflects that light which is captured on the photographic paper [...] There is therefore a trace, a shadow which lights up [...] the idea that photography is not an image but rather a shadow, thus permitted me to develop this idea of a shadow poetics which has taken much more shape in my other books such as *Cuerpo náufrago* where I discovered the possibility of developing the idea that shadows are desiring entities]

But Clavel's poetics of shadows also notably comprises a chiaroscuro dialectic of light and shadow whereby, as we have already seen in relation to Soledad's own clair-obscure existence, conventional associations of light (life, visibility, male, symbolic, rational, repression of drives) and dark/shadow (death, invisibility, magic, female, semiotic, primal drives) are both defied and reinforced. Clavel's 'poética de las sombras' in *Los deseos* has deep resonances with *El dibujante de sombras*, discussed in the final chapter of this study, particularly in the context of desire and photography, an artistic medium which relies as much on light as it does on darkness/shadows. Thus, in *El dibujante* the fundamental principle of using a negative and positive to produce the final image in analogue photography is encapsulated in the Huber twins, who are the negative and positive of one another, light and dark, complimentary and opposed. The same can be said of Soledad in relation to her (non-)being and her doppelgänger Lucía. Soledad also has parallels with the shadow artist Giotto of *El dibujante* in the context of the expression of repressed sexual desire and artistic freedom via the medium of photography and its early forms.

In Clavel's novel photography has both liberating and repressive implications for Soledad. Péter Nagy serves both as tutor to Soledad and obstacle to her photographic career. In this respect Emily Hind notes that the complexity of Clavel's 'thematic emerges as Péter plays a double role as inspiration and impediment for Soledad's art. Soledad may develop her skills, but only in subordination to the male photographer's ambitions'.[36] The intimate link between photography, artistic creativity, and sexual desire becomes apparent in the manner in which the tutor-tutee relationship between Soledad and Péter not only serves to develop Soledad's flourishing artistic talent but also her sexual experiences. Yet her artistic independence is curtailed as Péter uses Soledad as an object of his own creativity. Indeed, Péter's photography is driven by a desire to express 'una poética de las sombras' (*Los deseos*, p. 91). Soledad/Sombra becomes his ideal object of artistic inspiration for she embodies the shadow of photographic projection. Soledad's image and desirability become a function of Péter's photographic practices of imaging, such as framing, camera movement, angle, and lighting, thus denying Soledad's status as a desiring or speaking subject in her own right (pp. 75–76). Clavel's exploration of Soledad's shadow non-being in relation to Péter's artistry can be understood in the context of Roland Barthes's *Camera lucida* which informs the author's 'poética de las sombras'.[37] Here Barthes notes that 'whatever it grants to vision and whatever its manner, a photograph is always invisible: it is not it that we see' (p. 6). Hind notes that with this particular paradox, the photograph is always invisible, Soledad 'becomes the photograph, or the medium that cannot be seen but that acts upon others and that represents Péter's obsession' (*After Hours*, p. 434). This contradiction also suggests the ambiguous role of the shadow: it illustrates a duality in Soledad's being in terms of her lack, on the one hand, and, on the other, in terms of her position as both agent and Duboisean luminous desiring luminous presence.

Despite Soledad's status as a negative shadow in the context of her increasingly floundering relationship with Péter, her artistic talent and sense of self nevertheless flourish. Dogged by Soledad's infatuation with him, Péter tries to channel her obsession by encouraging her to develop her photographic portfolio. Entering a period of artistic creativity, Soledad now:

> switches places with Péter and he becomes muse to her role as photographer. Interestingly, Soledad fills a double function of subject and artist. The replacement of the masculine artist with a woman ambiguously resolves the problem of de-objectifying the female. (Hind, *After Hours*, p. 435)

Following Péter's abandonment of Soledad, she finds a second male master in the Mexican Martín Rueda. But like Nagy, 'this latter character acts as an equally ambiguous aid to Soledad's artistic growth' (*After Hours*, p. 430). Indeed, whilst Martín appears to encourage Soledad's creative endeavors he proves to be as harmful to her sense of creative independence as Nagy was. When Soledad shows photographs of Lola Álvarez to her employer Martín, he is dismissive of her work stating that it would be unlikely that they could be included in an exhibition.[38] Unbeknown to Soledad her photographs are finally published, but Martín fails to inform her about this achievement thus pushing her into permanent invisibility (*After Hours*, p. 440). The conflicting role of photography in *Los deseos*, as both empowering and disempowering, is particularly encapsulated in the conclusion of the novel when Soledad's image emerges in a group photograph. This passage reinforces, once again, the oscillating role of the shadow. Soledad embodies both negativity, from a patriarchal perspective, and positivity, in the Duboisean sense, whereby the shadow embodies a luminous desiring presence. Hind similarly remarks that this passage:

> illustrates her contradictory nature as invisible light that is apparent to the camera, which registers shadows. Of course, another interpretation for this oddity is to suppose that Soledad controls her visibility and that she intended for her face to appear on the film. (*After Hours*, p. 404)

Clavel's shadow poetics continues in the author's *Los deseos* multimedia endeavour. Following the publication of the novel, Clavel promoted the book at various press conferences in Mexico and six years later, in 2006, organized a small-scale photographic exhibition to accompany the promotion of the English translation of the book. During the writing process, Clavel had never envisaged creating a multimedia event to accompany her text. But it was thanks to both the success the previous year of the multimedia event for her novel *Cuerpo náufrago* and her friendship with the internationally acclaimed Mexican photographers Ricardo Vinós and Rogelio Cuéllar that the *Los deseos* exhibit came to fruition. The photography component of the *Cuerpo náufrago* exhibit is what cemented Clavel's artistic ideas about creating a photography exhibition for *Los deseos*. Upon reading Clavel's text, both Vinós and Cuéllar were astounded by the manner in which the author's 'poética de las sombras' had deep resonances with their own particular shadow poetics in their photographic *oeuvre*, and for Clavel and both artists the exhibition seemed a natural extension of the book. The event, held from 27 July to 31 August 2006 in the gallery of the Fondo Nacional para la Cultura y las Artes (FONCA) in Mexico City, comprised thirty two photographs accompanied by excerpts from *Los deseos y sus sombra*.[39] At first, Clavel had proposed for the exhibition that she, Vinós, and Cuéllar work together by taking photographs of locations in Mexico City which were referred to in *Los deseos* as a means of developing visually the notion of a 'poética de las sombras'. However due to the various professional commitments which Vinós and Cuéllar had at that time, they were unable to undertake the project. Clavel then simply decided that the exhibition would consist of thirty two (semi-) nudes which formed part of an existing corpus of black and white nudes taken individually by Vinós or Cuéllar between 1970 and 2006 which she personally chose, as well as a few black and white images of various locations in Mexico City taken by the photographers for the event. However one of the photographs displayed in the *Los deseos* exhibition was a black and white semi-nude photograph which Clavel commissioned Cuéllar to take as part of a series of photographs and which conceptually were hers. Indeed, she developed the idea for the photographs based on a photogram depicting a nude child lying amidst a bed of hydrangeas which appears in Catherine's Breillat's film *Anatomie de l'enfer* (2004). Clavel's and Cuéllar's image would eventually feature on the cover of Clavel's *Las Violetas son flores del deseo* (2007) and the series of photographs would be used for the multimedia event based on this novella. During one of our interviews, Clavel remarked that Vinós was so surprised by the synergies between her shadow poetics and his own, that he initially thought that *Los deseos* may have taken its inspiration from his *oeuvre*.[40] Cuéllar also remarks upon the striking similarities between Clavel's work and his own, and in particular how Péter Nagy could almost be an incarnation of himself: 'En el texto, Ana le da vida a un fotógrafo con una estética muy semejante a la mía, pues al igual que a mí, a su personaje lo seducen los desnudos' [In the text, Ana gives life to a male photographer whose aesthetic is very similar to my own, given that both I and her character are seduced by nudes].[41] Whilst Clavel was adamant that neither Vinós or Cuéllar was the source of her inspiration for the exploration of the 'poética de las sombras',[42] the manner in which both Vinós and Cuéllar coincide artistically, 'juegan con el deseo y sus propias técnicas, como son las sombras luminosas y la dualidad de los claroscuros' [play with desire and their own techniques, such as with luminous shadows and the duality of the claireobscure], has inexorable links to Clavel's literary piece (Velasco, 'Exhiben 32').

In *Los deseos*, the representation of Soledad as a Duboisean luminous shadow whose being oscillates between desiring agent and dehumanized object of desire, presence, and non-presence, is metonymically embodied in the female semi-nudes of Vinós, Cuéllar, and Clavel. The black and white images of the female semi-nudes, present woman-girl as disembodied and fragmented, as projections of the photographer's desire. What we see are not whole bodies but parts of them: torsos, legs, arms, pubic area, and the heads of the women/girls are cast into shadows or fall outside the frames of the images, thus occluding their identities. All of these images are untitled, poignantly reinforcing the women's/girls' anonymity and their status as immobilized fetish object set up for the delectation of the desiring (male) gaze. The frozen photographic subject links to Barthes's description of the photograph as a motionless image which does not mean 'only that the figures it represents do not move; it means that they do not *emerge*, do not *leave*: they are anesthetized and fastened down, like butterflies' (*Camera lucida*, p. 57). The idea of woman as object is reinforced via the juxtaposition of text and image. The photographs were accompanied by excerpts taken from the text as well as specifically Péter Nagy's 'Notas para el diseño de una sombra' [notes on the design of a shadow] in which he describes the subjection of the (female) body to the photographic process: 'Toma un cuerpo cualquiera y sométello a diferentes climas, temperaturas, intensidades, emociones [...] el resultado será una sombra iluminada, perfecta en obediencia y condición' [take any body and expose it to different temperatures, intensities, emotions [...] the result will be an illuminated body, perfect both in terms of its obedience and condition] (*Los deseos*, pp. 129–30). Yet even as Péter's reflections and the semi-nudes of the exhibition suggest female stasis and subjection, it is the presentation of woman as a chiaroscuro 'sombra iluminada', which paradoxically posits the female as agent of desire. Indeed Péter's reflections on his 'poética de las sombras', emphasize Dubois's notion of the shadow as desiring luminous presence:

> Al pensar con luz has de considerar las sombras y la penumbra: el contorno de un cuerpo se distingue de su fondo en la medida en que una voluntad íntima y secreta palpita en el objeto negándose a morir del todo, a ser visto — tocado — del todo. (*Les Deseos*, p. 130)
>
> [When one thinks in terms of light, you have to take into consideration both shadows and penumbra: the contours of a body are distinguished from the background to the extent in which an intimate and secret desire palpitates in the object, refusing to die totally or to be seen — or touched — in its entirety]

This ambiguous position of woman as agent or object is reinforced in the context of one of the exhibited images taken by Vinós (1989) through its ambiguous interplay

FIG. 2.1. Untitled. (1989). Photo: Ricardo Vinós.
Image used for front cover of *Desire and its Shadow* for English translation.
Courtesy of Ana Clavel.

of dark and light, text and image. It appeared on the poster used for the promotion of the multimedia exhibit as well as featuring on the front cover of the English translation of *Los deseos*, *Desire and its Shadow* (figure 2.1). It depicts the lower half of a female body set against a dark background lying on her side and, save for a pair of ruffle socks and underwear lowered to her knees, her bottom and legs are exposed.

Like this image, a number of others by Cuéllar, Clavel, and Vinós set up the female body for the consumption of the paedophilic gaze. This is reinforced by the manner in which the girls are often dressed in schoolgirl or Lolita-esque attire. Accompanying this and the other images is an excerpt taken from *Los deseos* which reads '¿Quién no es juguete del deseo de los otros? Y sobre todo ¿quién no goza siéndolo?' (p. 31). As we noted earlier in relation to this same passage, the process of 'othering' via the fetishization of the female body can paradoxically bring about an awareness of sense of self, allowing Soledad/women to experience desire for herself. The connections between text and image thus become apparent here as the illustrations harp back to the scene in which Soledad, still only a young girl clad in a short dress, is subjected to sexual abuse at the hands of the 'Desconocido' (p. 31). Even as Soledad is cast as the object of sexual abuse, so too does she experience sexual pleasure (disturbingly perhaps given the context of the paedophilic sexual encounter).

In another of Vinós's images (1983) the chiaroscuro interplay of light and dark also posits girl/woman as oscillating between empowerment and disempowerment. Here the girl, whose breasts, shoulders, and face are occluded in shadow, lies on an unmade bed, donning over-the-knee socks and underwear. Even as this photograph, to draw from Barthes, reduces her to a fetish object, so too does the image denote the female as a 'sombra deseante' [desiring shadow]. Next to her there is an ashtray with a cigarette, still alight, resting on it. The associated clichéd ritual of smoking a post-coital cigarette is unmistakable here. Thus, even as the girl/woman is presented as innocent victim of illicit sexual activity, so too does she become the voluntary co-participant who is in full control of her sexuality. Here her posture also implies a duality: though her legs are closed together, suggesting rejection of male penetration and untouchability, her posture is not at all tense but rather sensuously provocative inviting sexual intercourse, therefore adding to the overall feel which the picture conveys, that is, a sense of post-coital relaxation, mutual courtship, and sensuality. What draws us to this particular image, and the rest of the semi-nudes of Cuéllar, Ana Clavel, and Vinós, is that they nevertheless resist singular meaning through the mystery that their play of absence and presence, light and shadow evokes. Dubois's discussion of photographs as fetishized objects draws attention to their dual nature of presence and absence: 'the photograph is an object that can be touched [...] and embraced, yet it can only show us the untouchable, the inaccessible [...] an absence'.[43] Absence and presence are linked to the gaze. Vinós's image deeply disturbs the viewer precisely because we are unable to ascertain the gaze of the girl as her head remains outside of the frame. In relation to this and other female nudes of his own creation, Vinós notes that 'la mujer casi nunca mira de frente hacia la cámara con todo el cuerpo. Es como si escondiera algo. Es más, es como si las fotografías ocultaran algo a quien las observa' [the woman almost never looks straight ahead towards the camera with all her body. It is as if she were hiding something. What is more, it is as if the photographs were hiding something from the viewer].[44] Whilst the absent gaze can suggest self-empowerment, as Vinós suggests, so too can it suggest lack. Indeed, gaze often gives away signs of emotions, fears, and joy but in the case of Vinós' semi-nude, because of the absent gaze we are unable to ascertain the feelings of the photographic subject and therefore are unable to determine her 'true' position as either unwilling victim or desiring co-participant.

The same can be said of Ana Clavel's and Cuéllar's image (2006) displayed in the exhibition, in which a girl-child lies semi-clothed amongst a bed of hydrangeas and whose face is beyond the frame. As will be discussed in detail in Chapter 7, this particular image deeply perturbs the viewer because, through its duality of presence and absence, the image ambiguously plays upon a perceptible incongruity between (brutalized) innocent childhood and sexualized child-teenager and thus disturbs any possibility of offering a safe interpretation.[45]

The overall exhibition of *Los deseos* worked well as a visual proposition and extension of the written text. But the reason for its success was perhaps more to do with a set of coincidences than it being part of a truly well-thought out and integrated multimedia event. It just so happened that the art of Vinós and Cuéllar had many synergies with Clavel's work which complemented her shadow aesthetics. In this regard, the exhibit contrasts sharply with her bigger and more cohesive multimedia events for *Cuerpo náufrago*, *Las Violetas*, and *Las ninfas a veces sonríen*. Nevertheless, this multimedia endeavour, along with the literary text which inspired it, is a reflection of Clavel's versatile ability to work across various disciplines, which is perhaps even more powerfully encapsulated in both the textual and multimedia dimensions of *Cuerpo náufrago*, the focus of our attention of the next three chapters.

Notes to Chapter 2

1. Part of this chapter has been published previously in Finnegan and Lavery (eds.), *The Boom Femenino in Mexico* (published with permission of Cambridge Scholars Press).
2. Kristeva, 'Le sujet en procès', pp. 55–106, and *Powers of Horror.*
3. Edward W. Said, 'Foreword', in Ranajit Guha and Gavatri Chakravorty Spivak (eds.), *Selected Subaltern Studies* (New York and Oxford: Oxford University Press, 1988), p. vi, quoted in Dawn Slack, 'Cristina Pacheco's Narratives: Multimedia Chronicles', in Ignacio Corona and Beth E. Jörgensen (eds.), *The Contemporary Mexican Chronicle: Theoretical Perspectives on the Liminal Genre*, Suny Series in Latin American and Iberian Thought and Culture (Albany: State University of New York Press, 2002), pp. 221–39 (p. 223).
4. Michel de Certeau, *The Practice of Everyday Life*, trans. by S. F. Randall (Berkeley: California University Press, 1984), p. xvii.
5. Juan G. Gelpí, 'Walking in the Modern City: Subjectivity and Cultural Contacts in the Urban Crónicas of Salvador Novo and Carlos Monsisváis', in Corona and Jörgensen (eds.), *The Contemporary Mexican Chronicle*, pp. 201–20 (pp. 213–14).
6. In *Postdata* Octavio Paz's remarks: '¿Cúantos murieron? En México ningún periódico se ha atrevido a publicar cifras' [How many died? In Mexico no single paper has dared to publish the figures] (*El Laberinto de la soledad, Postdata y Vuelta a El laberinto de la soledad*, 2nd edn (Mexico City: Colección Popular, 1992), p. 281.
7. Cynthia Steele, *Politics, Gender and the Mexican Novel, 1968–1988: Beyond the Pyramid* (Austin: University of Texas Press, 1992), p. 23.
8. Clavel, email to Lavery, 8 March 2014, 16:29.
9. Julia Kristeva, *Desire in Language: A Semiotic Approach to Literature and Art*, ed. by Leon S. Roudiez, trans. by Thomas Gora and others (New York: Columbia University Press, 1980); and Elizabeth Grosz, *Sexual Subversions: Three French Feminists* (St Leonards, NSW: Allen and Unwin, 1989), p. 43.
10. *Charrismo sindical* refers to Mexico's tradition of political coercion prevalent in many Mexican trade unions, whose government-appointed leaders, or *charros*, exploit their political power to amass personal fortunes.

11. Becerra, 'Otra forma de estar en el mundo', p. 247.
12. Jacques Lacan views the Mirror Stage as the first step towards the acquisition of language and participation in the patriarchal symbolic order. *Écrits: A Selection*, trans. by Alan Sheridan (New York: W. W. Norton, 1977), pp. 1–7.
13. Julia Kristeva, *Powers of Horror*, and *Revolution in Poetic Language*, trans. by Margaret Waller (New York: Colombia University Press, 1984).
14. The contradictory representation of Carmen as abject and as embodying patriarchal values at the same time points to the paradoxical nature of the argument on abjection, whereby the symbolic order both denies and needs the abject as a way of establishing the very order which seeks to eliminate the abject. Kristeva argues that although the mother must be rendered abject, she too provides her infant with regulation that sets up paternal law, thus ensuring the child's entry into the symbolic order. John Lechte and Mary Zournazi, *The Kristeva Critical Reader* (Edinburgh: Edinburgh University Press, 2003), p. 45.
15. Julia Kristeva, *Black Sun*, trans. by L. S. Roudiez (New York: Columbia University Press, 1989), p. 27.
16. Clavel, email to Lavery, 8 March 2014, 16:29.
17. Kristeva challenges Lacan who views woman as lacking, and instead celebrates the possibilities latent in nothingness, thus offering woman an opportunity to become herself on her own terms.
18. The abject is 'the space of struggle against the mother, at the same time it is a desperate attempt to be her, to blur the divisions between the child's identity and the mother's' (Grosz, *Sexual Subversions*, p. 78).
19. Amaryll Beatrice Chanady, *Magical Realism and the Fantastic: Resolved Versus Unresolved Antinomies* (New York: Garland, 1985), p. ix.
20. Lloyd Hughes Davies, *Allende: La Casa de los espíritus*, ed. by Alan Deyremond and Stephen Hart, Critical Guides to Spanish Texts, 66 (London: Grant and Cutler, 2000), p. 61.
21. Violeta Peralta and Liliana Befumo Boschi, *Rulfo: la soledad creadora* (Buenos Aires: F. García Cambeiro, 1975), p. 62. When I asked Clavel during our interview if *Los deseos* had been influenced by Juan Rulfo's concept of the 'diálogo de muertos', the author mentioned the essay she had written called *La Deuda rulfiana* in which she states that her work had not drawn directly from his work but rather from other literary sources such as the work of Milan Kundera (Lavery, unpublished interview with Clavel, 2008). I would argue however that the parallels between Rulfo and Clavel in their exploration of the boundaries between life and death are compellingly strong.
22. Drawing from literary theorist Ana Rosa Domenella, Luzma Becerra places *Los deseos* within the tradition of *lo neofantástico*. Domenella uses the term 'neofantastic' to refer to a number of contemporary female writers such as García Bergua and Eudave 'porque la literatura fantástica tiene su apogeo en el siglo XIX y estas escritoras escriben desde una cultura globalizada y posmoderna' [because fantastic literature is at its height in the XIX century and these female writers write from the perspective of a globalized and postmodern culture] (quoted in Becerra, 'Otra forma de estar en el mundo', p. 257). Domenella notes that the fantastic 'se da como una ruptura de la coherencia universal' [represents a rupture with univeral coherence] (quoted in Becerra, p. 257). Becerra corroborates this view by remarking that in *Los deseos* the fantastic is used as a means of exploring how 'los acontecimientos [...] transgreden la lógica racional [...] La invisibilidad mediante la desaparición del cuerpo de Soledad, como consecuencia de sus deseos, se inscribe en lo extraño' [the events [...] transgress rational logic [...] Invisibility in the form of the disappearance of Soledad's body as a result of her desires, is inscribed in the bizarre] (p. 257). Becerra draws from Platas to conclude that in *Los deseos* these supernatural events ultimately 'parecen sobrenaturales durante una parte de la narración, (pero) tienen finalmente una explicación racional' [seem supernatural during some of the narration, (but) finally have a rational explanation] (quoted in Becerra, p. 257). In this sense the (neo)fantastic element of *Los deseos* as described by both Domenella and Becerra should be understood in the context of magical realism. Indeed a key feature of magical realism is authorial reticence: magical realism has overtones of the fantastic but is not unbelievable, the quotidian is not differentiated from the marvellous, and the supernatural is not seen as problematic. The fantastic or magical realist features of *Los deseos* and more generally Latin American magical realism thus differ from

European fantastic literature, since the latter 'lacks the ultimate reference to an objectively-existing reality', Peter Beardsell, *Europe and Latin America: Returning the Gaze* (Manchester: University of Manchester Press, 2000), p. 197. Leal makes an important distinction between these two modes: the magical realist writer 'does not need to justify the mysterious nature of events, as the writer of fantastic stories has to. In fantastic literature the supernatural invades a world ruled by reason', Luis Leal, 'Magical Realism in Spanish American literature', in Lois Parkinson Zamora and Wendy B. Faris (eds.), *Magical Realism: Theory, History, Community* (Durham, NC: Duke University Press, 1995), pp. 119–24 (p. 123). In the West rational mentality makes us think of the world as an objective phenomenon which can be tested and understood according to empirical criteria. Clavel, very much in the style of Isabel Allende and Gabriel García Márquez, uses the supernatural to ultimately subvert this faith in rational objectivity.

23. Kristeva, *Powers of Horror*. Clavel's interest in the abject and the polarities of dirt and cleanliness is an idea which I draw from Nuala Finnegan's examination of the works of Rosario Castellanos. See Nuala Finnegan, *Monstrous Projections of Femininity in the Fiction of Mexican Writer Rosario Castellanos* (Lewiston: Edwin Mellen, 2000), p. 102.
24. Teresa de Lauretis, *Alice Doesn't: Feminism, Semiotics, Cinema* (Bloomington: Indiana University Press, 1992), p. 68.
25. Quoted by Jeanne Vaughn, '¿En dónde van a florear? *La "Flor de Lis"*, and the Problematics of Identity', in Kristine Ibsen (ed.), *The Other Mirror: Women's Narrative in Mexico 1980–1995*, Contributions to the Study of World Literature, 80 (Westport, CT: Greenwood Press, 1997), pp. 41–56 (p. 41).
26. Soledad's names (Soledad, Sombra) act as a site of ambiguity as they suggest anonymity and lack as well as the failure of names to signify, to convey a unitary self. They suggest her elusive identity which resists appropriation by others.
27. The notion of the 'speculary' is explored by Luce Irigaray, *This Sex Which Is Not One*, trans. by Catherine Porter and Carolyn Burke (Ithaca: Cornell University Press, 1985), p. 77.
28. Elizabeth Grosz, *Jacques Lacan: A Feminist Introduction* (London: Routledge, 1990), p. 152.
29. Soledad's status as 'desaparecida' [disappeared] in June 1985, as advertised on the posters her mother has put up throughout Mexico City displaying Soledad's photograph and personal details, becomes a metaphor for Mexico's socio-political disasters and violence, all consequences of the rhetoric of *desarrollismo*. Her disappearance foreshadows the terrible events of the 1985 earthquake in which thousands of Mexicans died or were not accounted for. Clavel is pointing beyond the immediate problem of political injustice towards the social movements which followed the earthquake, movements representing the nation's refusal to continue participating in a corrupt system and its desire to reaffirm its integrity and social responsibility. For further details on these movements see Steele, *Politics, Gender and the Mexican Novel*, pp. 145–47.
30. Nuala Finnegan also examines this particular ambiguity in relation to the body in Rosario Castellano's work. See *Monstrous Projections*, p. 25.
31. Nuala Finnegan examines such an inversion in the context of Rosario Castellano's work. See *Monstrous Projections*, p. 65.
32. See Hélène Cixous, 'The Laugh of the Medusa', trans by Keith Cohen and Paula Cohen, *Signs*, 1:4 (1976), 875–93.
33. Herrera, 'Escritora de deseos y sombras: Entrevista con Ana Clavel'.
34. Philippe Dubois, *L'Acte photographique et autres essais* (Brussels: Médïa Editions Labor, 1990).
35. Lavery, unpublished interview with Clavel, 2008.
36. Emily Hind, 'After Hours: Six Mexican Women Writers on Borrowed Time', unpublished PhD dissertation, University of Virginia (2001), p. 430.
37. Becerra ('Otra forma') also analyzes *Los deseos* in the context of Barthes's work. Roland Barthes, *Camera lucida: Reflections on Photography* (New York: Hill and Wang, 1981).
38. In relation to these photographs, Ana Clavel comments that 'son fotos tomadas por la propia Soledad que antes le había mostrado a Lola Álvarez [Bravo], la famosa fotógrafa mexicana, esposa de Manuel Álvarez Bravo, cuyo nombre no pongo completo para jugar con una Lola Álvarez ficcional, pero quien conozca de fotografía mexicana sabe que me refería a ella' [they are photographs which have been taken by Soledad herself which she had beforehand shown to Lola Alvárez [Bravo], the famous Mexican photographer and wife of Manuel Álvarez Bravo.

I don't use her name in full in order to be able to play with a fictional Lola Álvarez, but for those who are familiar with Mexican photography they will know that I am referring to her], email to Lavery, 8 March 2014, 16:29.

39. The FONCA was at that time situated in calle Hamburgo, Zona Rosa, before it was moved to calle Argentina in the Cuauhtémoc district.
40. Lavery, unpublished interview with Clavel, 2008.
41. Karina Velasco, 'Exhiben 32 desnudos de Rogelio Cuéllar y Ricardo Vinós en galería del Fonca', *La Crónica*, 29 July 2006, <http://www.cronica.com.mx/nota.php?id_nota=253545> [accessed 21 May 2014].
42. Lavery, unpublished interview with Clavel, 2008.
43. Philippe Dubois, 'Photography Mise-en-Film: Autobiographical (Hi)stories and Psychic Apparatuses', in Patrice Petro (ed.), *Fugitive Images: From Photography to Video*, trans. by Lynne Kirby (Bloomington: Indiana University Press, 1995), pp. 152–72 (p. 167).
44. Tania Molina Ramírez, 'Explora artista el diálogo entre el cuerpo y el alma de la cámara', *La Jornada*, 8 September 2007, <http://www.jornada.unam.mx/2007/09/08/index.php?section=cultura&article=a04n1cul> [accessed 21 May 2014].
45. As will be also discussed in greater depth in Chapter 7, Clavel's and Rogelio Cuéllar's female lying amidst the hydrangeas is deeply influenced by Gustave Courbet's painting *L'Origine du monde* (1866), which depicts the close-up view of the pubic area and stomach of a naked woman with her legs spread open. Clavel, as will also be discussed, subsequently incorporated into *Cuerpo náufrago*, *Las Violetas son flores del deseo*, and *El dibujante de sombras* references to, or visual reworkings of, Courbet's work in order to explore woman's ambiguous position as object of the male gaze and agent of desire.

CHAPTER 3

❖

Cuerpo náufrago
Gender Troubling, Queer Desires, and Fantastical (Dis)embodiments

Whilst *Cuerpo náufrago* (2005) moves away from national-historical realities and their interrelationship with the individual as explored in Clavel's previous novel *Los deseos y su sombra*, both works share the same interest in the queer body in the form of bodily transcendence. Questions of the self, the corporeal, and desire in the context of broader issues relating to (trans)gender construction and sexual politics in Mexico are central in *Cuerpo náufrago*, thus countering the general tendency of the Mexican *boom femenino* to align the sexual with political crisis.[1] Though a comparatively more straightforward text than *Los deseos* both in terms of plot and narrative technique, the storyline of *Cuerpo náufrago* is even quirkier than that of Clavel's first novel: one morning Antonia wakes up transformed into a man, now called Antón, and is bestowed with hyper-masculine attributes including bulging muscles and a well-endowed penis. Antón/ia starts to live his/her new life according to the rules and rituals of masculinity, from conquering women to pursuing uninhibitedly his/her sexual exploits. More bizarrely perhaps, is Antón/ia's almost fetishist obsession with frequenting male public toilets and photographing urinals. The text has received some attention in the form of reviews in journals and newspapers and which attest to its overwhelmingly positive reception. It was listed as one of the best novels of 2005 in the cultural supplement of *Reforma* and a review of the book in the magazine *Siempre!* reads: 'con esta rara, inquietante novela, Ana se confirma como la gran narradora nacional viva' [with this bizarre, disturbing novel, Ana asserts herself as a great national contemporary Mexican woman writer].[2] Sergio Téllez-Pon praises *Cuerpo náufrago* as being Mexico's 'primera novela queer' [first queer novel] and recommends the text to readers based on its originality and contribution to Mexican letters.[3] If we are to understand Téllez-Pon's notion of queer in the sense of those identities and sexualities that do not conform with 'heteronormative' conceptions of gender and sexuality, then I disagree with his assertion that Clavel's novel is the first queer novel to be written in Mexico. *Cuerpo náufrago* must necessarily be included in an already extensive list of novels written by Mexican writers which explore queerness, often as a means of exploding the rigid binaries built on gender, sex, and sexuality alluded to by Kaminsky.[4] Clavel does not see *Cuerpo náufrago* as a novel which can be placed within the genre of Mexican 'gay-marked fiction'[5] because for the writer Antonia represents a character who embodies a 'fascination-envy of the penis'.[6] However as will be argued throughout this chapter, whilst *Cuerpo náufrago* provides a heteronormative reading so too is this same reading challenged as the novel displays a Kaminskian queer sensibility. 'The queer', Amy Kaminsky writes, 'is what is not straight, not normative. Gay and lesbian sexualities are two forms of queerness, but there are others'. She continues:

> Rubin wrote about outlaw sexualities from adultery to sadomasochism to pederasty, and more recent writers have focused on gender transgression that may or may not include sexual behavior but always implies sexual possibilities [...] With transgender, intersex, and bisexuality added to its categories, the queer undoes familiar binaries built around gender, sex, and sexuality — masculine-feminine, male-female, gay-straight.[7]

Márquez also identifies *Cuerpo náufrago* as a queer novel, in the Kaminskian sense of the word:

> Siguiendo las distintas rutas de la transmigración de género, la escritora llegó al movimiento Queer que se encumbró a partir de la década de los 90 del siglo XX para hablar de aquello que no se reduce a los cánones tradicionales de género o sexualidad, sino que responde a un cajón muy amplio en el que pueden entrar todas estas modalidades no tradicionales en sexualidad.[8]
>
> [Following the various transmigratory routes of genre, the writer embraced the Queer movement which came about during the decade of the 1990s in order to speak about those areas which cannot be boxed into traditional generic categories or sexual forms, and instead seeks to encompass a broad generic spectrum in which all kinds of non-traditional forms of sexuality are analyzed]

The exploration of queerness in *Cuerpo náufrago* is seen specifically within its scope of non-normative sexualities and desires, from non-reproductive, unmarried, or orgiastic sex, to gay, lesbian, bisexual, and, perhaps most significantly, hermaphroditic and transgender. Clavel's *Cuerpo náufrago* can thus also be seen as an example of 'outer-circle' sexualities.[9] The text ambivalently sways, in true postmodern fashion, between a desire to challenge gender narratives which espouse dominant and stereotypical gender/sex constructions, whilst also upholding such gender/sex constructions which maintain a strict binary division between male and female. My other reading of *Cuerpo náufrago* as a queer novel can be understood in the context of Kaminsky's and Halperin's understanding of the queer which not only refers to non-heteronormative sexuality but also to that which challenges notions of the normal.[10] *Cuerpo náufrago* has been heavily influenced by the queer fantastical works *Orlando: A Biography* (1928) by Virginia Woolf, Ovid's *Metamorphoses*, and the short story 'The Metamorphosis' (1915) by Franz Kafka, in all of which diverse kinds of metamorphoses occur.[11]I thus use the word queer as connected to the fantastical whereby Antonia's inexplicable transformation into a man, like Soledad's ghostliness in *Los deseos*, defies patriarchal logic as well as the borders between fact and fiction. *Cuerpo náufrago*, like *Los deseos*, oscillates ambiguously between fantasy, whereby the supernatural produces disbelief, and the magical realist, wherein apparently inexplicable events are presented in a matter-of-fact fashion. Finally, drawing from Judith Butler's examination of the role of fantasy, I suggest that Antonia's 'fantastical' transgender self also posits possibilities which lie beyond the norm, or even the real.

(Undoing) Gender Trouble

Antonia's gender confusion has caused some difficulties in my examination of *Cuerpo náufrago*, particularly when deciding which name to use when referring to Clavel's character. Thus the name Antón/ia will be used to reinforce the character's transgender character and the hermaphroditic amalgamation of alternating desires that at times match Antonia's 'original' gender and biological sex and at other times do not. I will use Antón when discussing the perception of others of him as a man and his active role as a man sexually. Finally, I shall refer to the character primarily as Antonia since the character's perspective of the male world she inhabits is principally, though not uniquely, that of a woman. This is reinforced in Antonia's view of herself as an intruder or 'contrabandista' [smuggler][12] in the world of male public toilets which is described as 'territorialmente masculino' [territorially male] (*Cuerpo*, p. 104). Clavel does not attack the territory of masculinist culture from the outside but from the inside by smuggling into that very space, through Antonia's body, her gendered gaze and voice. Antonia thus exposes the vulgar superficiality and prejudice of masculine values by incorporating (and ironizing) them into her own discourse as Antón. Clavel herself reinforces the fact that the *Weltanschauung* she explores is that of the female character: 'Antón, is apparently male although she preserves much of the time [...] a female perspective'.[13] Yet the words 'much of the time' belie the idea that the world view presented in *Cuerpo náufrago* represents a stable apprehension of the world from one singular standpoint, and instead suggests that there is also room for other perspectives, including that of the male Antón and the transgender Antón/ia.[14] The notion of a singular viewpoint is further complicated in the way that Clavel represents Antonia's male-female interstitial identity and world view with grammatically 'incorrect' transgendered language.

From the very outset of the novel Antón/ia's 'gender trouble' alerts the reader to Clavel's apparent concern with establishing the view that gender is to be viewed as a not altogether convincing masquerade. Antón/ia's hybrid gender thus represents a direct defiance of contemporary demarcations of sex, gender, and sexuality. Clavel can be seen as endorsing the notion of the constructedness of both sex and gender, and in this regard her vision of gender, sexuality, and identity can be aligned with Judith Butler's own discussions on the subject. In the prologue to *Cuerpo náufrago*, Clavel specifically cites Butler: '¿Cómo figura un cuerpo en su superficie la invisibilidad misma de su profundidad escondida?' [How does a body figure on its surface the very invisibility of its hidden depth?]. Butler explores in *Gender Trouble* how gendered identity is socially produced, and proposes to expose the postulations that confine the meaning of gender to conventional notions of masculinity and femininity by suggesting that nothing is innate, whether gender or sexual selfhood. Butler argues that anatomical differences are charted according to expectations about sexual desire, and specifically to society's 'compulsory heterosexuality',[15] which 'posits that there are two sexes and that desire runs from one sex to the other'.[16] Butler establishes important links between performativity and gender, where gender can be conceived of as a 'stylized repetition of acts [...] understood as the mundane way in which bodily gestures, movements, and styles of various kinds constitute the illusion of an abiding gendered self' and so ensuring the hegemony of heteronormative social ideologies (*Gender Trouble*, p. 140). Hegemonic masculinity and emphasized femininity refer to a set of cultural norms that shapes the presentation of the gendered self and bodily conduct such as gestures and movements which both men and women are expected to enact. The distinction made by feminists between the bodily sex (as a biological category) and gender (as a historical category) also becomes unhinged as Butler suggests that gender performance impacts upon us directly corporeally for sex is not 'a bodily given on which the construct of gender is artificially imposed, but [...] a cultural norm which governs the materialization of bodies'.[17]

Normative Sex and Gender

Despite her transformation, Antonia appears to accept unquestioningly normative conceptions of masculinity and femininity which influence her thinking about how she must 'do gender'. She readily embraces her newly found masculinity, by adopting the style, gestures, and behaviour of the opposite sex. Her enthusiasm for her new sex and gender change is intimately linked to the way in which she regards men as occupying a privileged status over women, both socially (*Cuerpo*, p. 13) and biologically (p. 29). Antonia's perception of men's privileged status brings to the reader's attention the unequal gender relations which still characterize contemporary Mexican society. Within Mexico, conventional gender (sexual) roles are deeply ingrained, whereby the idealized cultural expectations of appropriate male and female behaviour promote men to enact the *macho* role and women that of the passive female. In Latin America as a whole, the cultural emphasis on *machismo* translates into the perception that men must exemplify a number of characteristics such as dominance and sexual promiscuity, whereas *marianismo* emphasizes the view that women should embody certain traits such as submissiveness and chasteness.[18]

The idealized cultural expectations of appropriate male behaviour within Mexican society prompt Antonia to enact the *macho* role in her guise as Antón. Américo Paredes's definition of the quintessential Mexican *macho* matches in many ways the traits of *machismo* as exemplified in Antón and the various men she meets. Paredes notes that the 'characteristic traits of *machismo* are quite well known: the outrageous boast, a distinct phallic symbolism, the identification of the man with the male animal, and the ambivalence toward women — varying from an abject and tearful posture to brutal disdain'.[19] Physicality — which refers to bodily conduct and physical appearance — is an important feature of (Mexican) hegemonic masculinity, and becomes a key characteristic for the expression and performativity of Antón's maleness.[20] Physicality actively shapes Antón's presentation of self and bodily conduct, and influences his interaction with and perception of others. Mexican hegemonic masculinity privileges a particular kind of male body which is virile and the social significance of size and body shape encourages bodily awareness in men. Physicality also serves to symbolize the social power of men and to underline relations of domination and subordination between different groups of men (Howson, p. 54). Antón frequently comes across as an 'outrageous boast' (Paredes, p. 215), sizing his virile body up against other men. Once, whilst walking along a street, Antonia stops in front of a pharmacy window and begins to groom her hair. She suddenly becomes aware that another man has started to imitate him and in response to the other man's gesture, Antón puffs up his chest in defiance (*Cuerpo*, p. 20). The irony of course in this particular passage is that the other man Antonia sees is in fact her own image, or at least that of Antón's (p. 21). The 'punch line' of this scene is that Antonia in the guise of Antón is puffing herself up in defence against herself. This perhaps parodies the Lacanian view that the mirror reflects men's world-view and women as other, thus denying women's identity. Clavel humorously counters the idea of the mirror as lack by positing the view that there is ultimately no 'real' image reflected in it.

Penis size, or 'distinct phallic symbolism' (Paredes, p. 215), also becomes an important feature of masculinity: Antonia notices men in a sauna taking stock of each other's penises (*Cuerpo*, p. 65) or in men's toilets where 'por más que lo disimularan, los hombres siempre estaban viéndose el sexo propio y el de los otros en una perpetua comparación y competencia' [however much they tried to hide it, men were always looking at their own and other men's penises perpetually comparing themselves and competing against one another] (p. 65). This bizarre behaviour is part of a male ritual enacted by men in order to compete with one another as a way of satisfying their male ego and establishing their superiority over one another. Aware of the cultural value placed on organ size, Antonia is clearly pleased that she has a well-endowed penis (p. 104). These episodes humorously highlight the way in which hegemonic masculinity contributes to the internalization of the social and gendered meanings ascribed to the human body in ways that have a deep bearing on not only men's conduct but also on their sense of self (Howson, p. 54). The importance given to physicality and specifically penis size highlights Butler's perception that social gender constructions and behaviours have a direct influence on perceptions of corporeal sexes. These examples similarly play upon the anxieties that may afflict men in terms of how their own body shape and size compares to that of other men, and how their body shape and size may or may not conform to what is perceived as ideal by the standards of society.

The links between physicality, performance, and sexual violence are also highlighted in Clavel's text. Antonia is initially uncertain as to how she must perform masculinity, and finally resolves her predicament by turning, rather misguidedly, to antiquated models of masculinity based on *Amadis of Gaul,* a medieval chivalric romance prose, in which she hopes to find 'un modelo a seguir (claro que sin espada ni armadura ... por lo menos evidentes)' [a model to follow (of course without sword or armoury ... in appearance at least)] (*Cuerpo*, p. 17). She sets out to model herself on the eponymous Amadis of Gaul whom she perceives as the ideal embodiment of the chivalric code, as well as meeting all the prerequisite characteristics of hegemonic masculinity such as virility and sexual and physical prowess. Chivalric violence is suggested in images of conquest and domination (p. 18) which also become embroiled with images of sexual conquest. Antonia enthusiastically embraces the idea of performing chivalric masculinity since it implies an inversion of sexual roles (p. 27), where the active male, the conqueror, is sexually advantaged over the passive female, the conquered: 'siempre había esperado ser salvada [...] le correspondería ser el sujeto activo, el núcleo dominante de la oración amorosa, el potente caballero que embiste' [she had always hoped to be saved [...] it would now be her turn to be the active subject, the dominant one in command of amorous expression, the powerful thrusting knight] (p. 17). Antonia's misguided views about sexual roles bolster the now stereotyped cultural rules and ideals which shape or organize gendered constructions of male sexuality as 'active, aggressive, thrusting and powerful' and female sexuality as 'passive, powerless, submissive and receptive'.[21] Clavel describes the courting process as an inherently aggressive ritual and likens it to the tango danced between a man and a woman in which relations of domination and subordination are underlined, buttressing the heterosexual pact whereby the social and sexual power of men over women is reinforced (p. 20). Such a perception implicitly draws the reader's attention to the prerogative of Mexican society 'to prize the masculine role of the active *chingón* and denigrate the feminine *chingada*'.[22] Irwin explains that the verb *chingar* is a:

> multifaceted word whose primary definition is similar to "fuck" or "fuck over", signifies violent penetration, rape, power that takes advantage of weakness in others; the latter [*chingado*], by contrast, indicates a show of weakness and implies opening oneself up, allowing oneself to be violently penetrated. In relations between men and women, the man is traditionally the *chingón* and the woman the *chingada*, the fucker and the fucked.[23]

Antonia understands that as a woman she was the sexually 'fucked' insertee: 'cuando era mujer, había tenido sexo anal, así que sabía, doble, triplemente si sumamos vagina y boca, lo que era ser penetrada' [when she was a woman, she had anal sex, so she now knew doubly, triply even if we take into account both vagina and mouth, what it was like to be penetrated] (p. 122). Now, in her guise as Antón, Antonia sees it as appropriate to assume the role of the *chingón* particularly as she believes that all men are 'chingones' (p. 103). It would thus appear that Clavel is reducing the complex world of gender identity to the base level of an essentialist, phallic understanding of biological sex. The essentializing view of men's assumed innate conqueror-protector qualities are suggested in the text's proliferating references to medieval weaponry which become laden with sexual connotations. The idea that the knight is to protect the weaker sex with his sword also comes to signify the knight's desire to conquer and penetrate the weaker sex with his penis (p. 57), or the 'arma-dura' as Antonia calls it (p. 69).[24] This dual function of the sword draws attention firstly, as will be discussed below, how Antonia's obsession with her penis becomes enmeshed with male sexual performance anxiety which is translated into the fear of castration. Secondly, the other issue it raises relates to Antonia's apparent unquestioning acceptance of the sex and gender differentiation that society has established between men and women. Sex and gender categories become fused in *Cuerpo náufrago*. Antonia believes that now she is a man she must 'do masculinity' in a variety of ways by enacting the bodily gestures, movements, and styles which befit the prevailing cultural norms that men are expected to satisfy; and that since she is anatomically male, performing and desiring sexually as a man that is, she must by default desire and have sex with women only.

Society's 'compulsory heterosexuality' is also linked in *Cuerpo náufrago* to the undue pressures placed upon (Mexican) men to prove their sexual potency, which in turn is linked to performance anxieties about sexual failure. This double-edged sword is metaphorically suggested in the blade image: whilst it embodies a phallic prop which helps men to express their (reproductive) potency and domination, it also can wound, highlighting the vulnerability of the male organ and the threat of sexual failure. This view is bolstered in Antonia's comment that the penis is 'una arma-dura para guarecer una arma-blanda' [a hard weapon in order to shield a soft weapon] (p. 69). Clavel can thus be seen to be making an explicit statement about how men may feel vulnerable to criticism of their genital size or sexual performance. Clavel also appears to playing upon the anxieties men are bedeviled with in relation to how they feel obliged constantly to prove their sexual prowess, but are also compelled to hide any physical or emotional weakness which might be deemed as effeminate. These anxieties are signaled metaphorically in the fear of castration. Once, as Antonia is observing herself naked in the mirror, she suddenly drops a pair of scissors which she is holding in her hands and narrowly avoids getting injured. This incident leads her to reflect upon the vulnerability of the male organ which not only allows her to 'show it off' (p. 54) but also 'la hacía sentirse vulnerable [...] Cercenar, cortar, castrar [....] Se habían transformado en palabras [...] amenazantes' [made her feel vulnerable [...] slash, cut, castrate [...] these had become threatening words] (p. 54).

The references to sexual violence we have mentioned serve to reinforce the view that brutality between the sexes becomes instrumental in transforming gender difference into gender hierarchy. Moore suggests that oppositional gender discourses which emphasize the view that gender has only two forms, one male and one female, are also hierarchically dominant:

> It is a peculiar feature of gender discourses of this kind that the categories between woman and man are not just exclusive, but that the relationship between them is defined as one of hierarchical difference. Woman is man's other, what man is not, the lack and the object of man's desire and knowledge. ('The Problem of Explaining Violence in the Social Sciences', pp. 144–45)

Violence and domination appear to be at the heart of some of the sexual relations Clavel explores: Antonia views herself as the thrusting male and women as sexually receptive and subordinated to men (p. 20).[25] Gender hierarchy between men and women is also linked elsewhere in the text to other forms of hierarchical difference, specifically seen in Antonia's homosexual and bisexual relations. Whilst Clavel's exploration of homosexuality and bisexuality in the novel may suggest that she is celebrating possibilities which extend beyond the heterosexual norm, at times those same alternative expressions of sexuality frequently reflect heterosexual rituals of conquest and submission. Antonia's view about how men should perform masculinity become enmeshed with violence, homosexuality, and power relations. Antón engages in sexual activity with Raimundo which becomes a violent physical struggle of domination and submission: 'Antonia reconoció que nunca antes había sentido poder semejante: una plenitud victoriosa, el resplandor de una espada para someter y degollar al otro' [Antonia recognized that never before had she felt such power: a sense of victorious fulfillment with a splendorous sword used to subjugate and slit an other's throat] (p. 124).

Given Antonia's bisexual predilection for both sexes, this scene between Raimundo and Antón could be seen as an instance of bisexual rather than homosexual sex. If read as a bisexual encounter, Clavel can be seen to be underscoring the significance of bisexual practices between Mexican men, which, according to Carrier, are linked to specific roles rather than to whom one is having sex: '[a] Mexican male's masculine gender identity is not threatened by homosexual acts as long as he plays the insertor sex role; only the male insertee playing a female [sic] sex role, is considered homosexual'.[26] In Latin America as a whole, whereas the heterosexual *macho* who 'makes it both with men and women without ever yielding an iota of his masculine persona', Foster notes, 'the figure of the maricón (fag or queer, as understood in the most stereotypic terms) is reserved exclusively for the insertee' (*Sexual Textualities*, p. 3).[27] Richmond Ellis also reinforces the view that Latino-male sexual relations are characterized by unequal roles, which can similarly be broadly applied to a Mexican context:

> The so-called *activo* enacts a masculinity irreducible to homosexuality. The *pasivo*, in contrast, through his perceived passivity, is endowed with the essence of the feminine and [...] with the identity of homosexuality. In this way homoeroticism is subsumed within gender.[28]

Antón thus takes on the aggressive male insertor or *chingón* role whilst Raimundo is (un)willingly feminized in his male insertee or *chingado* role. The active/passive binaries suggested in the two male characters' roles of insertor/*chingón* and insertee/*chingado*, reinforce 'both sexual practice and power plays within a relationship' (Thornton, p. 152). Elsewhere in *Cuerpo náufrago*, references to homosexual rape also serve to reinforce the male/female gender hierarchy whereby the male aggressor or insertor feminizes the male victim, the insertee, who is reduced to lack. The fear of castration becomes unbearable when linked to male rape, since it implies a double threat to malehood 'tanto en la emasculación como en la violación el hombre dejaba de ser tal' [by being emasculated or raped, a man would no longer be a man] (p. 54). Whilst Antonia's stereotyped view that men and homosexuals are intrinsically violent may reinforce the view that the multifaceted and complicated question of identity has been reduced to an essentialist understanding of biological sex, Clavel can in fact be seen to be making a serious comment about Mexican society's views of homosexuality. *Cuerpo náufrago* reveals the way in which Mexican hegemonic masculinity gives emphasis to heterosexuality and subordinates, even stigmatizes, homosexuality, unmasking the deep-seated social anxiety felt by some Mexican men about the vulnerability to feminization or emasculation in male subjectivity through homosexual rape. An indirect observation is being made here about the way in which internalized homophobia is such an inexorable part of the conditioning of Mexican men that it has led to a very real threat in the form of physical violence to homosexuals across the nation.[29]

The textual references to homosexuality and male-to-male rape in *Cuerpo náufrago* with their specific emphasis on the sexual roles of the 'activo' insertor and 'pasivo' insertee, point to a central concern in Clavel's queer politics, namely, the function of performativity. In this respect, Clavel can be aligned with various Latino and Hispanic writers whose queer texts often emphasize the performative aspects, rather than those of identity, of queer sexualities so as to foreground 'the very constructedness of gender and how gender can be dissociated from the seeming fixity of biological sex' (Richmond Ellis, p. 6). Based on the preceding discussions, it would seem that Antonia accepts unquestioningly traditional heterosexual pacts whereby socially and culturally determined gender and sexual categories are deemed innate and immutable. However, through this character, Clavel can in fact be seen to be foregrounding the artifice of gender and attempts to denaturalize the correlation between man and masculinity and woman and femininity. Clavel appears to be suggesting that:

> If gender is constructed from a series of repeated actions learned within cultures, then there exists the possibility of breaking away from traditional performances of masculine and feminine. Subjects can be freed from restrictions associated with their sex and take on multiple gender identities.[30]

Performativity and 'Unintelligible' Gender Identities

Notwithstanding Antonia's ostensible acceptance of normative conceptions of masculinity and femininity, the disparity between gender and the performer and the role is constantly foregrounded, a technique which is deployed by Clavel in order to transgress gender norms. Antonia draws our attention to her performativity facilitated through a series of self-reflective comments. The duplicity of Antonia's asides frequently calls attention to the woman 'playing' a man and more generally to the precariousness of gender and identity. In such moments, Antonia now occupies the position of commentator, rather than that of participant in history. She underlines her performativity by mocking her own performances of masculinity (*Cuerpo*, p. 21). Antonia conceptualizes masculinity and femininity as an 'impostura de trajes estrechos' [imposture of tight-fitting outfits] (p. 64). She notes the facility with which she can perform her new gender (p. 14), although elsewhere she ponders over the trouble she has in 'doing' masculinity: '¿cómo se construye un disfraz de hombre?' Antonia deseó tener un manual que le diera instrucciones' [how does one construct the disguise of a man? Antonia wished she could have a manual with instructions] (p. 27). The humour implied here draws our attention to Antón/ia's liminal status in society as a transgender. Antón/ia falls outside society's gender rules which are set in stone, outlined in a kind of metaphoric manual of instructions which contains rigid ideas about how people should perform gender. But these rules are written only for those who slot into the established categories of masculinity and femininity and not for those who do not fit the bill, including LGTBQ peoples. The above quotation also underscores the artifice of gender. Gender is constituted through a series of practices which are associated with masculinity or femininity and are learned rather than inherent: 'estaba la opción de comportarse como un hombre. Pero eso ¿cómo se aprendía cuando una no había nacido así?' [there was the option of behaving like a man. But how did she learn how to be a man if she had not been born as one?] (p. 27). This quotation plays upon Simone de Beauvoir's celebrated saying 'One is not born, but rather becomes, a woman', suggesting that women are not born but are taught to become feminine.[31] Clavel appears to be critiquing this particular point of view by suggesting that Beauvoir's text fails to take into account the other side of the equation, that is, that men are not born as such but have to learn how to be masculine, an idea that Clavel explores and can be seen to be parodying through Antonia's own performance of masculinity. On the one hand, Antón's role as a 'macho chingón' [male fucker] underlines that certain Mexican male cultural traits of the archetypal *macho* are often more embedded in folklore than reality. On the other hand, Clavel appears not to be entirely dismissing the existence of *machismo* in Mexican society. She can be seen to be positing the view that the *macho* does not predominate as 'the' masculinity in Mexico and that a diversity of masculinities are in play in contemporary Mexican society. She also appears to be making a serious statement about how *machismo* is a very real fact of Mexican life and has important implications for how many Mexicans view homosexuality, which is characterized in the main by a deeply ingrained homophobia. The parodic treatment of 'doing' gender in *Cuerpo náufrago* ultimately also serves as a wider critique of the costs of gender's straitjacket both for men and women. It also serves to question Mexico's defined gender roles for both men and women, and to challenge the kind of rhetoric found in scholarly texts written by the likes of Ramos (1934), Paz (1950), and Mendoza (1962) which have served to perpetuate folkloric perceptions of masculinity and femininity.[32]

Throughout *Cuerpo náufrago* there are various allusions to cross-dressing. Cross-dressing, which disrupts normative conceptions of masculinity and femininity, serves to highlight the idea that gender is to be viewed as a kind of performance, and to emphasize the ways in which everyday bodily conduct fortifies a dichotomized view of gender. When Antonia is musing over how she should 'do' masculinity, she remembers the story of a valiant knight who turns out to be a woman (p. 18) and serves to emphasize the double function of cross-dressing. It acts as the standard-bearer of women's or transgenders' freedom against constricting social and gender-imposed identities. However, cross-dressing (from woman to man) and Antonia's transformation into a man suggest paradoxically that women are flawed and will only be able to express their identities by performing as men. This therefore implies that women are never able truly to express themselves on their own terms. More importantly Clavel appears to emphasize the way in which cultural practices of cross-dressing frequently rely on parody to challenge the notion of a primary gender identity, an idea also explored by Butler, who examines various examples of cross-dressing and drag as a means of drawing attention to gender parody and the artifice involved in 'doing gender'. Butler proposes that the performance of drag within gay culture is part of a self-consciously parodic performance and parade of femininity which rests on a demarcation between 'the anatomy of the performer and the gender that is being performed' (*Bodies that Matter*, p. 137). Her questioning of the traditional demarcation maintained between sex and gender indicates that 'there is nothing self-evidently gendered about either bodily conduct or the sexed body' (Howson, p. 61). According to Howson, Butler's examination of the drag-queen stems from her interest in the manner in which the drag-queen's 'exaggeration of what are recognized conventional displays of femininity encourages the audience to consider all gender displays as a kind of performance' (Howson, p. 61).

Butler's discussions on the interrelationship between gender and drag performance are illustrated in the episode in which Antonia goes to a 'table dance' bar where a transsexual is lap dancing. The drag-queen's self-consciously exaggerated performance and his/her over-emphasis of certain characteristics associated with the presentation of femininity are expressed in the 'sinuosidad deliberada de los movimientos al bailar' [the choreographed sinuousness of the movements as she danced] (*Cuerpo*, p. 116). The performer attempts to conceal his/her body parts that are 'construed as signs of the gender the cross-gender person seeks to elude' (Howson, p. 60). When the drag artist seeks to hide his/her pubic area, the men in the audience shout out: '¡ya quítatela, maricón!' [come on, take it off you faggot!] (*Cuerpo*, p. 116). It becomes clear from the men's mocking attitude that they are aware that the genital area of the performer is distinct from the gender being enacted, and that the act is ultimately a performance of femininity. The men's jeering serves to undermine any potential subversive element of cross-dressing. Their homophobic slur bolsters the view that heterosexuality's existence as a norm depends upon the 'othering' of what is not considered as fitting the norm, such as homosexuality or transvestism. The men's comment, which suggests that the drag artist is a kind of 'travesty' of natural law, reinforces implicitly the notion of lack. As already noted, the word *maricón* takes on a particular meaning in a Latin American sociocultural context whereby the bisexual *macho* assumes the role of the insertor, and the *maricón* that of the insertee. The *maricón* drag-queen in *Cuerpo náufrago* serves to sustain, but also challenge, the masculinist code. The *maricón*'s uncertain status threatens the masculinity of the *macho* jeering men in the audience, and this menace is countered in the form of verbal violence against the drag-queen as a way of reaffirming the male code. The abusive insult towards the performer becomes a metaphoric penile penetration of the *macho* insertor. However, the performer's response to the men's taunting — 'respondió con una señal obscena y, sin darles más importancia, continuó bailando para sí misma' [she answered back with an obscene gesture and, without paying any further attention to them, she carried on dancing for herself] (p. 116) — is significant. She identifies herself as a woman and her obscene gesticulation is a defiant riposte to normative conceptions that biological 'sex' is somehow the fixed marker of identity.

The drag-queen's cross-dressing has radical implications since the notion of an original identity is abandoned altogether. The drag act illustrates Butler's thesis that 'the parodic repetition of the 'original [...] reveals the original to be nothing other than a parody of the idea of the natural and the original' (*Gender Trouble*, p. 31). In *Cuerpo náufrago*, the performer's parodic imitation of femininity can be placed in opposition to Frederic Jameson's suggestion that the imitation that mocks the notion of an original is characteristic not of parody but rather pastiche.[33] In *Cuerpo náufrago* the loss of the sense of the normal can be seen 'as its own occasion for laughter, especially when the "normal", "the original" is revealed to be a copy, and an inevitably failed one, an ideal that no one can embody' (*Gender Trouble*, p. 138). Butler champions parody in general and drag performances in particular because both work to 'destabilize the naturalized categories of identity and desire' (*Gender Trouble*, p. 139). The drag performance episode in *Cuerpo náufrago* thus highlights powerfully 'a general troubling' in the double violation not only of received categories between male and female, normal and abnormal, natural and artificial, but also of those same categories which are deemed as lying outside the norm itself. The blurring of boundaries between the real and a performance of the real is suggested in the destabilization between the 'natural' and 'artificial' in *Cuerpo náufrago*. Antonia initially believes that the performer is a woman but is rather baffled by the artificiality of the performer's appearance: 'había algo artificial en los rasgos [...] la perfección de los senos y las nalgas' [there was something artificial about her traits [...] the perfection of her breasts and buttocks] (*Cuerpo*, p. 116). Following the men's derisory remarks, Antonia realizes that the performer is not a man, nor a drag-queen for that matter, but in fact a transsexual who has undergone plastic surgery. The performer is clearly neither a man nor a woman, but something ambiguously in between: a part of her suggests her femininity manifested in the (albeit constructed) breasts and certain (albeit stereotyped) characteristics associated with the presentation of the feminine as expressed in her provocative gestures. The other part of the performer reinforces his masculinity, as illustrated both in the reference to 'square shoulders' (p. 117) and in his attempt to conceal his genitals from the audience. Yet the division implied here between the 'naturally' male and 'constructed' female is questioned, as suggested in the performer's in-between identity which is described in terms of an 'incierto cruce de fronteras' [uncertain crossing of boundaries] (p. 117). This blurring of boundaries is reinforced in the assigned categories of drag and transsexual. Drag or transvestism are terms most typically used to describe male to female cross-dressing. They do not involve plastic surgery and concentrate 'on gender display through surface modification' (Howson, p. 64) such as the concealment of body parts linked with the 'real' sexual identity of the drag/transvestite and the display of certain 'behaviors, emotions and cognitions' socially and culturally associated with the feminine.[34] Transexualism on the other hand, involves specifically 'the transition from assigned sex to surgically reconstructed sex' (Howson, p. 64). The performer in *Cuerpo náufrago* ambiguously oscillates between both categories. The name-calling directed by the men to the performer ('maricón') leads the reader to believe that he is a man dressed in drag yet transexualism is made evident in the performer's sex change from male to female in certain body areas which suggest 'los vestigios del tránsito de un reino a otro por obra y gracia de la cirugía plástica y las hormonas' [the vestiges of the transition from one gender to the other by the grace and the work of plastic surgery and hormones] (*Cuerpo*, p. 117). Transexualism is also emphasized in the performer's aside to Antonia in which she implies that she is inhabiting the 'wrong' body: 'siempre fui mujer' [I was always a woman] (p. 118). Plastic surgery thus becomes the only viable means for the performer to achieve her desired gender as it offers a way of establishing a sense of feeling at home in her body and of making her body match her sense of self. Whilst references to plastic surgery serve to emphasize not only the trappings of femininity but also the repudiation of the notion of an original femininity linked to biology, cosmetic surgery in this example functions as a form of 'reinvention and self-empowerment' rather than a form of 'body modification in pursuit of cultural belonging (or 'fitting' in)' (Howson, p. 117). In possession of both a penis and breasts, the performer's hermaphroditic body comes to represent a fusion of different categories such as drag, cross-dresser, and transsexual, and thus suggests 'not just a category crisis of male and female, but the crisis of category itself'.[35] Although Antonia is visibly disturbed by the performer's 'gender confusion', she is also conscious that s/he mirrors her own uncertain identity (*Cuerpo*, p. 116). Antón/ia becomes sexually aroused at the sight of the performer's perfect pair of breasts which s/he is tempted to fondle, but from which she refrains hesitantly: '¿cómo enfrentar de sombra a sombra este otro cuerpo transformado?' [how to confront shadow to shadow this other transformed body?] (p. 117).[36] Antonia attempts to justify her hesitant gesture to the performer by explaining that she once was a woman (p. 117) to which the performer retorts 'yo también *ero* mujer' [I was also a wo/man] (p. 118). The anxiety Antonia expresses in engaging sexually with the performer may be linked to her unease which her transgender causes her, as it has opened up new ways of desiring which extend beyond the expression of 'natural' heterosexual desire which she had unquestioningly accepted prior to her transformation. The performer's play on words ('*ero* mujer') also points to a desire to foreground the arbitrariness of the rules governing language and to emphasize the view that gender and sexual categories, like desire itself, are not static, but rather permanently shifting. Antonia comes to understand that her identity is in continual flux, involving a transgendered or hermaphroditic intermix of alternating desires that may or may not correspond to her gender and biological sex. Following her transformation into a transgender, Antonia soon comes to embrace wholeheartedly that she is able to desire hermaphroditically, that is both men and women: 'siempre le habían atraído los cuerpos de otras mujeres. Entonces, ¿había sido lesbiana sin saberlo? Pero los hombres también le gustaban [...] El mundo era un vasto repertorio de posibilidades' [she had always been attracted to other women's bodies. So, had she therefore always been a lesbian without knowing it? But she also liked men [...] The world was a vast repertoire of possibilities] (p. 42). This predilection for both sexes is also suggested when Antonia reads Ovid's *Metamorphoses* (p. 151). She identifies with the figure of Tiresias who transforms into a woman: 'había conocido el placer en ambos sexos [...] su goce siempre había surgido en función de quien despertaba su deseo' [she had experienced the pleasure of both sexes [...] her pleasure had always been awakened according to whom it was who was stirring her desire] (p. 151). Antonia, who has an insatiable sexual drive, is keen to experiment with different sexual possibilities of various kinds including an orgy with Raimundo, Carlos, Tamara, and a nameless female stripper (pp. 109–10).

In *Cuerpo náufrago*, any notion of identity based on predetermined gender and sexual characteristics is exploded. Clavel can be seen to posit a view of (sexual) identity in line with postmodern perceptions of the (sexual) self, which is perceived as inchoate. Such meditations serve playfully, though not unproblematically, to propose a vision of identity that transcends the physical sex of the body and gender, as echoed in Antonia's suggestion that: 'más allá de los simulacros, las máscaras o los espejismos del género, seguía siendo quien era. ¿Entenderían estos burócratas que la identidad empieza por debajo de la piel?' [beyond the simulacrum, the masks and the mirages of gender, she continued to be whom she was. Would these bureaucrats understand that identity commences from beneath the skin?] (p. 179). Antonia expresses the view that people frequently misjudge others' personalities because of their physical appearance, and queries whether external appearance should be seen as an innate marker of identity at all: '¿La identidad empieza por lo que vemos?' [does identity start by what we can see?] (p. 12). What determines one's 'true' sexual selfhood and sense of identity are not the exterior markers of identity such as the sexed body, gender, clothes, or makeup, but rather human desire: 'más que en los cuerpos, es en el corazón donde reside el secreto y la diferencia, el verdadero sexo y la auténtica identidad se abren camino desde ahí adentro. Lo demás, son sólo ropajes, vestiduras, disfraces' [more so than in the body, it is in the heart where the secret resides and difference, one's true sex and authentic identity flourish from there] (pp. 174–75). In typical postmodern fashion, Clavel's ideas about the centrality of the body oscillate ambivalently: on the one hand, the author appears to be diminishing the importance of the material body, whilst on the other hand, physicality is posited as essential. Indeed, physicality actively moulds Antonia's presentation of self and bodily conduct as Antón and has an important bearing on his interaction with others. The centrality of the corporeal is foregrounded in particular in the sex scenes involving Antonia and other male and female characters in which the body becomes a vital means through which human desires and sexual fantasies can be expressed.

The opening paragraphs of *Cuerpo náufrago* immediately alert the reader to the protagonist's gender confusion:

> Ella — porque no cabía duda sobre su sexo, aunque las presiones de la época contribuyeran a que asumiera otros roles — [...] Ella misma, pero indudablemente un hombre: ahí entre sus piernas, plantado como una señal irreductible, su nuevo sexo. (*Cuerpo*, pp. 11–12)
>
> [She — because there was no doubt about her sex, although the pressure of those times made her take on other roles — [...] She was herself, but she was undoubtedly a man: there between her legs, like an irreducible sign, her new organ materialized]

This passage is pivotal in our understanding of Clavel's vision of identity: 'Ella — porque no cabía duda sobre su sexo' implies clear lines of sexual differentiation, yet the pronoun and noun slippage from 'Ella' to 'un hombre', immediately puts into question the singularity of Antonia's (sexual) identity. The opening lines are also important for their intertextual significance since these mirror almost literally the first sentence of Virginia Woolf's *Orlando*: 'He — for there could be no doubt about his sex, though the fashion of the time did something to disguise it'.[37] Whilst Woolf's name is cited in the acknowledgements of *Cuerpo náufrago*, explicit reference to *Orlando* is made on Clavel's website in which *Cuerpo náufrago* is described as 'una metamorfosis genérica inversa a la del *Orlando* de Virginia

Woolf' [a gender metamorphosis which reverses that of Virginia Woolf's *Orlando*].[38] Woolf's *Orlando* and its feminist reflections on gender and androgyny have left an indelible mark on Clavel's writing. Woolf's androgynous fusion of the masculine and the feminine has been critiqued in its attempt to transcend gender and the body altogether, as well as being perceived as the merging of the male and female sexes where differences ultimately dissolve.[39] Despite the fact that *Cuerpo náufrago* is written as a riposte to *Orlando*, it has much in common with Woolf's vision of androgyny which 'mixes gender qualities and sexual desires without attempting a new kind of idealized synthesis'.[40] Like Orlando, Antonia's transformation involves a spontaneous biological sex change and oscillation of sexual desires (Kaviola, pp. 235–36). In similar fashion to Orlando, Antonia's identity is in continual flux, involving a transgendered or hermaphroditic blend of alternating desires that sometimes match her 'original' gender and biological sex and sometimes do not (Kaviola, p. 252). Antonia's transgender, wherein various characteristics of gender and sexuality intermix, can thus be seen both as the hermaphroditic fusion of, rather than an androgynous absorption of, difference, wherein, Kaviola remarks, 'patriarchal notions of the radically unmarked feminine other are incorporated into the equally unmarked male self' (p. 256).

Antón/ia sees herself as a transgender, a 'tránsfuga' [transfugee] as she describes herself (*Cuerpo*, p. 63). Transgender is a fluid term encompassing an array of (sexual) identities, and Clavel can be said to explore Antonia's transgender sexuality specifically as a means of focusing on the issue 'of what it might mean to undo restrictively normative conceptions of sexual and gendered life' whereby the 'normative restriction becoming undone can undo a prior conception of one who is only to inaugurate a relatively newer one'.[41] Antonia is not a transgender in the sense of feeling trapped in the 'wrong' body, of feeling at odds with the gender one was assigned at birth, as transgenders often claim to experience: 'desde pequeña había deseado ser hombre. No porque se creyera un varón atrapado en el cuerpo de una mujer' [Ever since a child she had wanted to be a man. Not because she thought of herself as a man trapped in the body of a woman] (p. 13). Although Antonia in the main perceives the world from a woman's point of view, as already discussed, her hybrid intermix of the masculine and the feminine has certain elements of transgender. Antonia's transgender is perhaps best understood in the context of Kate Bornstein's own use of the term in *Gender Outlaw* (1995) in which the self-proclaimed transgender suggests that it does not imply a 'third gender', but rather 'a mode of passage between genders, an interstitial and transitional figure of gender that is not reducible to normative categories' (quoted in Butler, *Undoing Gender*, p. 43). Antonia, like Bornstein, lives a borderline life as neither a man nor a woman, but both. Antonia's interstitial and transitional gender is powerfully suggested in Clavel's description of Antonia as: 'doblemente tránsfuga, que patinaba en el terreno incierto de los tránsitos, deslizándose en los bordes, sin un lugar definido' [doubly transfugitive, slipping through the uncertain territory of transitions, sliding along borders, without a fixed location] (*Cuerpo*, p. 98). The idea that Antonia occupies a borderless in-between space is constantly accentuated in metaphors associated with the blurring of boundaries such as 'difuminaba los límites precisos de la vida [...]

donde la vida borraba sus límites' [the clear borders of life were blurred [...] where life blurred its own boundaries] (p. 139). The grey no-man's-land Antonia inhabits is also suggested in the metaphor of liminality, the 'liminal space' (p. 35) where 'se había mantenido en el borde de esa identidad limítrofe que según los ojos que miraran podían inclinar la balanza' [she had maintained herself at the limits of that liminal identity which, depending on who was looking, could tip the balance] (p. 179).[42] Ultimately this ambivalent in-between zone gives rise to fluid and hybrid (sexual) identities which serve to displace binary concepts (man/woman, male/female, fact/fiction) and predetermined sexual identity.

This interstitial space also foregrounds the role of language and its difficult relationship with representation, another central concern of postmodernism. Antonia's interstitial identity is represented in grammatically and logically 'impossible' sentences such as 'se sentía rígida e incómoda, pero al menos estaba protegido' [she felt rigid and uncomfortable, but at least he was protected] (p. 44), or 'Antonia se quedó mudo unos instantes' [Antonia, he remained silent for a few seconds] (p. 117). The character's transgender self-perception causes dislocations, not only at the level of the body and identity, but also at the level of language which is used to define new bodily possibilities. Language falls short in its endeavour to signify this unclassifiable body, as adjectives and nouns combine the feminine and the masculine in improbable ways, putting into question the traditional gendering of language and the conventional correspondence between the signifier and its signified. Generic confusion 'provokes a disjunction between language and its apparent referent, and this disruption of the gender binary signals the illusory status of gender identity'.[43] Antonia's body and actions thus 'appear to complicate these categories of sex, and, as the language employed to categorize him/her reveals, produce an 'unintelligible' gender (*Bodies and Texts*, p. 171). According to Butler, 'unintelligible' genders refer to:

> those which in some senses institute and maintain relations of coherence and continuity among sex, gender, sexual practice, and desire [...] The cultural matrix through which gender identity has become intelligible requires that certain kinds of "identities" cannot "exist" — that is those in which gender does not follow from sex, and those in which the practices of desire do not "follow" from either sex or gender. (*Undoing Gender*, p. 23)

Like the body-swapping character Azucena in Esquivel's *La Ley del amor* (*Bodies and Texts*, pp. 81–82), Antón/ia's body fits into the category of 'unintelligible' and therefore it seems appropriate for Clavel to use 'unintelligible' language to describe Antón/ia's unclassifiable gender.

Magical Realism and Fantasy

In *Cuerpo náufrago*, 'unintelligible' gender becomes enmeshed with Clavel's use of the fantastical and magical realism in order to question strict gender and sexual categories. Antonia's inexplicable transformation, like Soledad's phantasmagoric status in *Los deseos*, serves to blur borders between the rational and irrational, fact and fiction. In both novels the fantastical and the magical realist merge in their defiance of such boundaries. For Chanady, in fantastic literature apparently inexplicable events create incredulity or fear in the observer or narrator whereas, in 'contrast to the fantastic, the supernatural in magical realism does not disconcert the reader' and the 'same phenomena that are portrayed as problematical by the author of a fantastic narrative are presented in a matter-of-fact manner by the magical realist'.[44] Antonia's magical transformation produces both disbelief as well as unquestioning acceptance.[45] She wakes up one morning transformed into a man, not as a result of undergoing hormonal treatments or a sex reassignment operation, but as a result of an inexplicable act of magic: '¿hormonas? [...] No y tampoco me operé [...] De hecho, es increíble' [hormones? [...] No, and neither did I get operated on [...] The fact is that it is incredible] (*Cuerpo*, p. 24). These slippages between the unreal and 'reality', which inform Antonia's transgender existence, serve to reinforce Leal's definition of magical realism for whom the main events in magical realism 'have no logical or psychological explanation' and thus serve to emphasize 'the inadequacy and irrelevance of rational paradigms for the elucidation of fictional events' (Chanady, *Territorialization*, p. 131). Leal's perspective is best highlighted in the occasion when Antón confesses to Paula that 'antes fui mujer' [I used to be a woman] (*Cuerpo*, p. 161). Following her partner's admission, Paula, a trained biologist whose thinking is driven by scientific logic, seeks to find a rational explanation to Antón's transformation by reading about the nineteenth-century hermaphrodite Herculine Barbin whose story Michel Foucault brought to light in his book *Herculine Barbin, dite Alexine B* (1978). Another possible explanation Paula conjures up is that Antonia is a transgender who has undergone body modification by surgical intervention. Despite her attempts to rationalize Antonia's change Paula is left with an uncomfortable sense that her partner's transformation is in fact owed to an act of magic which cannot be explained logically. Paula finally opts to accept Antón/ia for who s/he is: 'a pesar del asombro, de lo incierto, balbuceos de una lógica que se descorría, guardó silencio y abrazó a Antonia' [in spite of the astonishment, the sense of unknowing and the mumblings about a logic that kept undoing itself, she kept quiet and hugged Antonia] (pp. 161–62). Paula's initial doubts foreground *Cuerpo náufrago* as an example of fantastic literature, whereby, to draw from Chanady, 'the apparently inexplicable events produce disbelief' (*Territorialization*, p. 140). However, Paula's gradual acceptance, and in particular that of Antonia's own unquestioning acceptance of her magically acquired male gender, reinforces *Cuerpo náufrago's* magical realist dimension.

Antonia's supernatural transformation could be read as an instance of madness or fantasy but elsewhere she herself challenges this view: 'la vida la había puesto ante la alternativa de la locura y podía creerse tan irreal como el personaje de una novela fantástica o aceptar que las reglas del juego sencillamente habían cambiado y afrontar las consecuencias' [life had offered her either the alternative of madness and for her to believe that she was as unreal as the character of a fantasy novel, or for her to accept that the rules of the game had simply changed and that she needed to confront these consequences] (*Cuerpo*, p. 29). This quotation recalls Leal's point about the inadequacy of rational paradigms to explain magical events in fiction, as well as to the way in which the text has been constructed, to its self-consciousness, by drawing our attention to Antonia as a character in a novel. It also foregrounds the way in which the text sways between the fantastical and the emphasis on disbelief, and the magical realist and the suspension of disbelief. Significantly though, the quotation also serves to explore how fantasy in its broadest sense should not be viewed as 'the opposite of reality' but rather, as Butler notes, as 'the articulation of the possible; it moves us beyond what is merely actual and present into a realm of possibility' (*Undoing Gender*, p. 28), and therefore to 'challenge the contingent limits of what will and will not be called reality' (p. 29).

Butler explicitly explores the notions of real versus fantasy in relation to transgender, transsexual, drag, butch, and femme persons who:

> make us not only question what is real, and what "must" be but they also show us how the norms that govern contemporary notions of reality can be questioned and how new modes of reality can become instituted. These practices of instituting new modes of reality take place through the scene of embodiment, where the body is not understood as a static and accomplished fact, but as [...] a mode of becoming that, in becoming otherwise, exceeds the norm, reworks the norm, and makes us see how realities to which we thought we were confined are not written in stone. (*Undoing Gender*, p. 29)

Clavel's representation of the 'fantastical' transgender self is used to disturb the notion of stable and unified sex and gender categories whereby Antón/ia's queer interstitial identity posits possibilities which lie beyond the norm, or even a different future for the standard itself. Such a prospect is also what forms 'part of the work of fantasy when we understand fantasy as taking the body as a point of departure for an articulation that is not always constrained by the body as it is' (*Undoing Gender*, p. 28). Transgender identities in *Cuerpo náufrago* thus serve to contest society's norms that govern the appearance of 'real' humanness and the compulsorily imposed ideals of what bodies should be like (*Undoing Gender*, p. 28). This is particularly reinforced in the ending of *Cuerpo náufrago* where Antonia is seen travelling to the Aeolian Islands in the Tyrrhenian Sea north of Sicily to join her lover Paula. On the island of Stromboli Antonia and Paula both go to a beach and swim naked in the sea. Though Clavel is providing a romantic ending, it is not in a traditional heterosexual sense. Whilst it appears that Clavel is attempting to reinscribe heternormativity through the monogamous coupling of Paula and Antón, it is clear that Antonia does not wish to renounce to her wide-ranging sexual desires for others in favour of a stable relationship. As Paula is kissing Antón on the island, Antonia is simultaneously thinking that 'she would need to share all this with Francisco' (*Cuerpo*, p. 183). The heterosexual romantic ending is also challenged in another way. The variance between Antonia's 'disguise' and her actual sex create 'sexual bivalency' which establishes concomitant heterosexual and lesbian readings. Antonia's 'disguise' as Antón offers a heterosexual reading, but our — and Paula's — knowledge of the character's actual identity offers a lesbian reading since Antonia and Paula are same-sexed. The ending similarly offers a transgendered reading in the sense that Paula comes to accept and love Antón/ia as a hermaphroditic intermix of both the masculine and feminine. The final paragraphs of the novel also imply that Antonia's trip has involved a coming to terms with who s/he is, as well as a recognition that she is able to love and/or desire both men and women hermaphroditically. Antonia sees herself as a Minotaur — the half man, half bull figure of Greek mythology — but her predicament is different from that of the Minotaur who, confined by King Minos to a dark labyrinth, was eventually killed at the hands of Theseus. As Antonia swims out of the sea: 'se supo minotauro superviviente [...] Un cuerpo náufrago, una sombra iluminada al fin' [she saw herself as a surviving minotaur [...] a shipwrecked body, a luminous shadow at last] (p. 185). Both the mythical — seen in the allusions to Greek and Roman mythological gods and figures — and the fantastical — in the form of Antonia's half woman, half man status — merge. Myth regresses to the genesis and innocence of humanity. Here again we note the ambivalence of Clavel's fiction: on the one hand the portrayal of myth as the return to origins and purity is a positive aspect, yet myth also suggests, on the other hand, the cyclical and resistance to change and progress. But Clavel can be seen to emphasize the principle of change rather than stasis and repetition. The author thus departs from the magical, mythic, and cyclical time of Elena Garro, Gabriel García Márquez, and Isabel Allende whose narrative worlds 'are structured by cyclic patterns which affect both characters and events'.[46] For Clavel, identity — as suggested in Antón/ia's transgender self — is a 'liquid treasure' (p. 184), fluid and in a constant process of metamorphosis, or, to draw from Halperin, 'in a state of becoming rather than as a referent for an existing form of life' (*Saint Foucault*, pp. 112–13).

One of the limitations that the reader may perceive in Clavel's queer positionality in *Cuerpo náufrago* is underscored in her depiction of non-heteronormative identities which are often reduced to sexual practices or desires, yet the author fails to acknowledge the often fraught complexities of queer identities which should necessarily take into account political, cultural, class, sexual, and racial differences. The fact that Antonia views the world from a woman's perspective and intrudes into a male, homosexual, transvestite, and transgender world as a 'contrabandista' points perhaps to the shortcomings of Clavel as an author in offering a deeper understanding of the real, felt, and wider-ranging (and not exclusively sexual) experiences of other (non-) heterosexual (sexual) identities. Antonia's change from female to male is a fantasy that may be seen to mock the hard reality of transitioning for many female to male or male to female transgender people. For Antonia, her transformation involves a simple event rather than an ongoing, difficult, and even painful transformation. The weaknesses we may locate in Clavel's queer politics are usefully understood in the context of the issues some critics take with queer theory and more generally with the use of the term 'queer'. Foster sees the term 'queer' as a privileged, dominant Western construct which has an 'imperfect and even distorting applicability to Latin America. Such misrepresentation is even greater if we take into account Latin America's enormously different regions, cultures, linguistic practices, classes and ethnic and racial traditions' (*Sexual Textualities*, p. 1). For her part, Suzanne Walters sees the all-inclusive thrust of queer theory as problematic in its attempt to join together different sexual identities under the heading of queer since it 'reduces queer politics to a banal (and potentially dangerous) politics of simple opposition, potentially affiliating groups, identities and practices that are explicitly and implicitly in opposition to each other' ('From Here to Queer', p. 8).[47] Another critique of queer theory is its attempt to go beyond gender. Whilst Walters praises queer theory's opening out of the concept of difference, the critic bemoans the fact that it neglects gender altogether and that in its challenge to the separation feminists have made between sex and gender, 'sex becomes the grand force of excess that can offer more possibilities for liberatory culture, and gender the constraint on that which would (naturally?) flow freely and polymorphously if left to its own devices' (p. 14). It often appears to be the case that Clavel is offering the view that gender, and by extension the female body, is associated with fixity and constraint whereas 'sexuality (typically thematized as male) becomes "the means of crossing" and "the figure of mobility"' (p. 14). Antón/ia represents a queer sexuality embodying the 'figural, performative, playful and fun' but in 'the process of making the female body the 'drag' on the (male) play of sexuality' (p. 14) the female body 'appears to become its own trap, and the operations of misogyny disappear from view'.[48] Going back to my earlier point, Antonia's transformation into a man therefore implies that women are lacking and are only able to articulate their identities by performing as men. The text could open itself up to further critique in its over-emphasis on the physical and material body and obsession with the male body as a perfect exemplar of mankind. The text seems at times to celebrate unapologetically *macho* excess and Antonia, who was not transformed into a wimp, but rather a stud who glories in all that being one implies, is a prime manifestation of this intemperance.

Despite these apparent 'shortcomings' in *Cuerpo náufrago*, Clavel offers a nuanced understanding of the inherent complexities surrounding issues of identity, gender, and sexuality. This is precisely why *Cuerpo náufrago* is notable for its ambiguity, for while Clavel's text expresses a desire to defy traditional gender and sex constructions and in particular a drive to transcend gender categories altogether, it paradoxically corroborates the normative gender/sex paradigm which maintains a rigid binary separation between male and female. Whilst Clavel's queer aesthetics expands the concept of difference by celebrating non-normative sexual identities, so too does it demonstrate the impossibility of simply ignoring or dismissing gender altogether.[49] Clavel's Butlerian queer politics must be applauded as it brings to light the view that compulsory heterosexuality cannot simply do away with all non-heterosexual desires or acts of those so-called 'deviants' such as bisexuals, hermaphrodites, transsexuals, homosexuals, lesbians, or other minority 'non-identities'. By exploring the shifting non-normative identities and desires she represents, Clavel can be seen as being driven by a desire to overturn the negative perception of 'queer as monstrous, queer as alien'.[50] In *Cuerpo náufrago* gender trouble serves as a Butlerian call 'for a loosening of the categories, a relaxation of our fixation on identity' (Leitch, p. 2487). Normative identity is challenged in the form of parody, various acts, and violations which serve to foreground identity's construction and to question any notion of an original gender identity. It must also be argued that Clavel's novel is not concerned with 'the expressions of sexuality as lived realities', but rather with foregrounding the 'relation between literary fantasies and the material world in which human exchanges take place'.[51] In particular, by offering the reader at least a glimmer of transgender, bisexual, male, and female homoerotic desires, Clavel can be seen to be revealing a world imbued with queer desires that provide a very real reflection of the emerging, and irrepressible, sexual dissidences of contemporary Mexican society. Whilst *Cuerpo náufrago* does not represent a collective queer consciousness, the novel could be seen as a powerful riposte to the silencing and repression which many, if not all, queer persons in a Mexican and non-Mexican context have experienced in various degrees.

Notes to Chapter 3

1. Diane E. Marting, 'Dangerous (To) Women: Sexual Fiction in Spanish America', in Sara Castro Glarén (ed.), *Narrativa femenina en América Latina: Prácticas y Perspectivas Teóricas/Latin American Women's Narrative: Practices and Theoretical Perspectives*, Theory and Criticism of Culture and Literature (Princeton: Markus Wiener, 2003), pp. 197–219 (p. 208).
2. Sergio Gonzalez Rodríguez, 'Mejores libros del 2005', Suplemento Cultural de Reforma, *Reforma*, 8 January 2006; Ignacio Trejo Fuentes, 'Ana Clavel: mujer con cuerpo de hombre', *Siempre!*, 22 January 2006.
3. Sergio Téllez-Pon, 'La Primera novela queer', *Tierra Adentro*, 139 (2006).
4. Novels dealing with homosexual themes written by Mexican writers comprise, for instance, *Vampiro en la colonia Roma* (1979) by Luis Zapata, *Utopía Gay* (1983) by José Rafael Calva, and more recently, *Púrpura* (1999) by Ana García Bergua. Whilst *Dos mujeres* (1990) by the Mexican-Jew Sara Levi Calderón explores lesbian love and identity, the topic of bisexuality is examined by Mexican Enrique Serna in *Fruta verde* (2006). If we are to include Gayle Rubin's ideas of outlaw sexualities and desires as an example of the queer, then Clavel's novella *Las Violetas son flores del deseo* (2007) can also be added to the category.
5. Foster, *Sexual Textualities*, p. 14.
6. Lavery, unpublished interview with Clavel, 2009.
7. Amy Kaminsky, 'The Queering of Latin American Literary Studies, p. 209. Definitions of the queer are diverse but they also have many commonalities since often 'they question such normal formulations as gender and sex [...] and they also question what it is to call oneself homosexual, a lesbian, a gay man, a transsexual and, indeed, a heterosexual', Stephen Farrier, 'Ga(y)zing at Soap: Representation and Reading-Queering Soap Opera', in Bruce Carson and Margaret Llewellyn-Jones (eds.), *Frames and Fictions on Television: The Politics of Identity Within Drama* (Exeter: Intellect Books, 2000), pp. 86–99 (p. 90). The queer is a controversial concept since it has a kind of in-built elusiveness, as Suzanna Walters notes in 'From Here to Queer: Radical Feminism, Postmodernism and the Lesbian Menace', in Iain Morland and Anabelle Wilcox (eds.), *Queer Theory* (Basingstoke: Palgrave, 2005), pp. 6–21 (p. 6). Whilst some praise the queer for its liberatory possibilities, others reject it outright for its reductionist approach of subsuming non-normative forms of sexuality and identity under a single umbrella term.
8. Carlos F. Márquez, 'El Cambio de género se ha dado para evadir las reglas del destino: Ana Clavel', *La Jornada Michoacán*, 10 November 2009, <http://www.lajornadamichoacan.com.mx/2009/11/10/index.php?section=cultura&article=012n1cul> [accessed 19 July 2014].
9. In 'Thinking Sex', Rubin provides a diagram depicting the sexual value system in the form of a large circle containing a smaller circle within it. The inner circle represents sanctioned sexual conduct: 'Sexuality that is to be viewed as 'good', 'normal' and 'natural' should ideally be heterosexual, marital, monogamous, reproductive, non-commercial...coupled, relational, within the same generation'. The outer limits of this circle reads: 'bad. Abnormal, unnatural, and damned sexuality: homosexual, unmarried, promiscuous, non-procreative, commercial, alone or in groups, casual, cross-generational, in public, pornography, with manufactured objects, sadomasochistic'. Gayle Rubin, 'Thinking Sex: Notes for a Radical Theory of the Politics of Sexuality', in *Pleasure and Danger: Exploring Female Sexuality*, ed. by Carole S. Vance (Boston: Routledge, 1984), 267–319 (p. 280; p. 281).
10. Kaminsky, 'The Queering of Latin American Literary Studies'; Halperin, *Saint Foucault: Towards a Gay Hagiography*.
11. Clavel also notes that Antón/ia is 'heredera de una tradición literaria (Ovidio, Apuleyo, Woolf, Kafka) que ve en el fenómeno de la metamorfosis una posibilidad ficcional de conocimiento,

exploración y aprendizaje' [part of a literary tradition (Ovid, Apuleius, Woolf, Kafka), which sees in the metamorphosis phenomenon the possibility of exploring via fiction diverse elements such as knowledge, discovery and psychological growth/development], email to Lavery, 11 March 2014, 01:33.

12. Joanna O'Connell, *Prospero's Daughter: The Prose of Rosario Castellanos*, Texas Pan American Series (Austin: University of Texas Press, 1995), p. 35.
13. Lavery, unpublished interview with Clavel, 2008.
14. The male perspective of the world is expressed in particular through the physiological transformation Antonia has undergone. Antón experiences penile urination, erections, and orgasms and assumes the insertor role during sexual intercourse with men and women as opposed to the female insertee role. The transgender perspective is emphasized by Antonia herself who becomes aware that she is able to desire men and women hermaphroditically, and whose heterogeneous sexual relations foreground a range of expressions of non-normative sexual desire.
15. Adrienne Rich coined the term 'compulsory heterosexuality' to indicate society's injunction against homosexual desires and acts, 'Compulsory Heterosexuality and Lesbian Existence', *Signs, Women: Sex and Sexuality*, 5:4 (1980), 631–60.
16. Vincent B. Leitch and others (eds.), *The Norton Anthology of Theory and Criticism* (New York: W. W. Norton, 2001), p. 2485.
17. Judith Butler, *Bodies that Matter: On the Discursive Limits of 'Sex'* (New York: Routledge, 1993), pp. 2–3.
18. See Evelyn P. Stevens, 'Marianismo: The Other Face of Machismo', in Ann Pescatello (ed.), *Female and Male in Latin America: Essays* (Pittsburgh, PA: University of Pittsburgh Press, 1973), pp. 89–103. According to Stevens, *marianismo* refers to the Latin American stereotype of the ideal woman as a counterpart to the *macho*. A 'real woman' (p. 94) is 'submissive to the demands of men' (p. 95), and sexually 'the ideal dictates not only premarital chastity for all women, but postnuptial frigidity. "Good" women do not enjoy coitus; they endure it when the duties of matrimony require it [...] "le hice el servicio", they may say' (p. 96). Moreover, for Stevens, not only are these prescriptions imposed by male-dominated society on women but women too uphold this arrangement and thus are 'not ready to relinquish their female chauvinism' (p. 100). Also see Marcela Raffaelli and Lenna L. Ontai, 'Gender Socialization in Latino/a Families: Results from Two Retrospective Studies', *Sex Roles: A Journal of Research*, 50: 5/6 (2004), 287–99.
19. Américo Paredes, 'The United States, Mexico, and Machismo', in Américo Paredes and Richard Bauman (eds.), *Folklore and Culture on the Texas-Mexican Border* (Austin: University of Texas Press, 1993), pp. 215–34 (p. 215).
20. Raewyn W. Connell, *Masculinities* (Cambridge, MA: Polity, 1995); and Alexandra Howson, *The Body in Society: An Introduction* (Cambridge, MA: Polity, 2005), pp. 53–55.
21. Henrietta Moore, 'The Problem of Explaining Violence in the Social Sciences', in Penelope Harvey and Peter Gow (eds.), *Sex and Violence: Issues of Representation and Experience* (London: Routledge, 1994), pp. 138–55 (p. 138).
22. Sandra Messinger Cypess, S., *La Malinche in Mexican Literature: From History to Myth* (Austin: University of Texas Press, 2000), p. 95.
23. Irwin, 'The Famous 41', p. 354.
24. This play on the word 'armoury' translates literally as 'hard weapon'.
25. This view of women as being subordinated to men is reversed in Raimundo's perception that men live in the shadow of women (*Cuerpo*, p. 87). This contrasts with the characterization of Soledad in *Los deseos* who, in the 'real' world at least, is defined as a 'shadow' or non-entity from a symbolic perspective. As in *Los deseos*, the proliferating references to shadows in *Cuerpo náufrago*, such as '¿Quién no es penumbra indefinida, deseo, sombra?' [who is not undefined penumbra, desire, shadow?] (p. 154), are inexorably linked to Clavel's 'shadow poetics' in which the shadow as desiring luminous presence is foregrounded.
26. Joseph M. Carrier, 'Mexican Male Bisexuality', in Fritz Klein and Timothy J. Wolf (eds.), *Bisexualities: Theory and Research* (New York: Haworth Press, 1985), pp. 75–85 (p. 75).
27. This disjunture between the bisexual insertor and the 'maricón' insertee might be usefully

understood in terms of the different perceptions which currently exist towards bisexualism and homosexuality in Mexico. Whereas Mexico's powerful cultural tradition of 'machismo' has fuelled the public stigmatization of homosexuality and led to violent reprisal against gays, male bisexuality, though a prevalent practice in the nation, 'is neither socially accepted nor stigmatized', Annick Prieur, 'Domination and Desire: Male Homosexuality and the Construction of Masculinity in Mexico', in Marit Melhuus and Kristi A. Stølen (eds.), *Machos, Mistresses, Madonnas* (London: Verso, 1996), p. 90. Prieur notes that, '[b]isexual practice, then, is kept secret rather than being accepted. Discretion is coupled with silence. The lack of verbalization is associated with the fact that this activity is not segregated from other activities and relegated to a ghetto' (p. 92). These sexual practices 'are private activities between individuals and, therefore, are not ascribed a marginal label [...] Two men can meet and have sex without either of them concluding that they are therefore homosexual, nor do they necessarily see themselves as being bisexual. There is a power in remaining silent', Niamh Thornton, 'Being Fruity in the Big City: Re-membering the Past in Enrique Serna's *Fruta verde*', in Victoria Carpenter (ed.), *(Re)Collecting the Past: History and Collective Memory in Latin American Narrative,* Hispanic Studies: Culture and Ideas, 31 (Oxford: Peter Lang, 2010), pp. 145–65 (p. 152).

28. Robert Richmond Ellis, 'Introduction', in Susana Chávez-Silverman and Librada Hernández (eds.), *Reading and Writing the Ambiente: Queer Sexualities in Latino, Latin American, and Spanish Culture* (Madison: University of Wisconsin Press, 2000), pp. 3–20 (p. 6).
29. Guillermo Núñez Norriega notes that homophobia is what characterizes Mexican heterosexuality. *Masculinidad e intimidad: identidad, sexualidad y sida* (Mexico City: UNAM y Miguel Ángel Porrúa, 2007), p. 70.
30. As discussed by Debra Shaw in relation to Pedro Almodóvar's *High Heels*, 'Men in High Heels: The Feminine Man and Performances of Femininity in *Tacones lejanos* by Pedro Almodóvar', *Journal of Iberian and Latin American Studies*, 6:1 (2000), 55–62 (p. 56).
31. Simone de Beauvoir, *The Second Sex*, ed. and trans. by Howard M. Parshley (London: Vintage, 1997), p. 295.
32. Samuel Ramos, *El Perfil del hombre y la cultura en México* (Mexico City: Imprenta Mundial, 1934); Octavio Paz, *El Laberinto de la soledad* (Mexico: Colección Popular, 1950); and Vicente T. Mendoza, 'El Machismo en México: a través de las canciones, corridos y cantares', *Cuadernos del Instituto Nacional de Antropología*, 3 (1962), 75–86.
33. Frederic Jameson, 'Postmodernism and Consumer Society', in Hal Foster (ed.), *The Anti-Aesthetic: Essays on Postmodern Culture* (Port Townsend, WA: Bay Press, 1983), pp. 111–25 (p. 114).
34. Richard Ekins and Dave King, 'Telling Body Transgendering Stories', in Kathryn Backett-Milburn and Linda McKie (eds.), *Constructing Gendered Bodies* (Basingstoke: Palgrave, 2001), pp. 179–203 (p. 363); Howson, p. 60.
35. Marjorie Garber, *Vested Interests: Cross-dressing and Cultural Anxiety* (London: Penguin Books, 1992), p. 17.
36. This particular quotation can be linked to Clavel's notion of 'shadow poetics' and specifically to the Duboisean notion that the shadow is a desiring luminous presence, as discussed in Chapter 2 in relation to *Los deseos*, and to *El dibujante*, in Chapter 9.
37. Virginia Woolf, *Orlando: A Biography* (London: Penguin, 1963), p. 9.
38. <www.anaclavel.com> [accessed July 2014].
39. Elaine Showalter, *A Literature of Their Own: British Women Novelists from Brönte to Lessing* (Princeton: Princeton University Press, 1997). Restucia remarks, however, that Woolf has commonalities with contemporary feminism in its attempt to valorize the idea of 'female difference' and to celebrate the 'feminine' and female experience, Frances L Restucia, '"Untying the Mother Tongue": Female Difference in Virginia Woolf's *A Room of One's Own*', *Tulsa Studies in Women's Literature*, 4:2 (1985), 253–64 (p. 263).
40. Karen Kaviola, 'Revisiting Woolf's Representations of Androgyny: Gender, Race, Sexuality, and Nation', *Tulsa Studies in Women's Literature*, 18:2 (1999), 235–61 (p. 236).
41. Judith Butler, *Undoing Gender* (New York: Routledge, 2004), p. 1.
42. I proposed to Clavel the view of Antonia as a transgender in the sense I have just elucidated, to which the author responded: 'Nunca me interesó desarrollar propiamente un tercer sexo de

manera deliberada aunque no obstante sí que explora la novela esta cuestión del transgénero en el sentido más abierto como tú lo planteas, en el sentido de que Antonia tiene una identidad intermedia' [I was never interested in purposefully developing a third sex although the novel does examine this question of transgender in its broad sense in the manner in which you are proposing, in the sense that Antonia possesses an interstitial identity], Lavery, unpublished interview with Clavel, 2008.

43. The idea of generic confusion examined here draws from Claire Taylor's analysis of the character of Azucena in Esquivel's *La Ley del amor* (1995), *Bodies and Texts*, p. 171.

44. Chanady, *Magical Realism and The Fantastic*, pp. 23–24, and 'The Territorialization of the Imaginary in Latin America: Self-Affirmation and Resistance to Metropolitian Paradigms', in Zamora and Faris (eds.), *Magical Realism*, pp. 125–44 (p. 140).

45. This particular point perhaps highlights the view held by a number of critics such as Angel Flores that fantasy and magical realism are two literary categories which cannot be easily separated, thus countering Luis Leal's attempt at rigid separation between both modes. Angel Flores, 'Magical Realism in Spanish America', in Zamora and Faris (eds.), *Magical Realism*, pp. 109–24. Luis Leal, 'Magical Realism in Spanish American Literature'. Magical realism is a highly problematic and widely disputed term. See bibliography for further references.

46. Davies, *Allende: La Casa de los espíritus*, p. 74.

47. My inclusion of the paedophilic as represented in Clavel's *Las Violetas son flores del deseo* under the banner of queer may be perceived as flawed. My intention however is not to suggest that outlaw sexuals of this kind are affiliated in any way, politically or morally, with gay identities and practices, but rather are an example of the queer in the Kaminskian sense of the word, that is, that it functions as a way of disturbing ideas of the normal.

48. Biddy Martin, 'Sexualities without Genders and Other Queer Utopias', *Diacritics*, Critical Crossings, 24 (2–3), 104–21, quoted in Walters, 'From Here to Queer', p. 15.

49. Elizabeth Weed notes that feminism and queer theory share many commonalities and affiliations, such as their critical perspectives regarding hegemonic discursive formations and practices, 'Introduction', in Elizabeth Weed and Naomi Schor (eds.), *Feminism Meets Queer Theory* (Bloomington: Indiana University Press, 1997), pp. vii–xiii. It is this particular shared counter-hegemonic positionality which allows us to read *Cuerpo náufrago* as representing the intermingling of both queer and feminist politics.

50. Sylvia Molloy and Robert McKee Irwin (eds.), *Hispanisms and Homosexualities*, Series Q (Durham, NC: Duke University Press, 1998), p. xiv.

51. Rosemary Geisdorfer Feal, 'Queer Cortázar and the Lectora Macho', in Chávez-Silverman and Hernández (eds.), *Reading and Writing the Ambiente*, pp. 239–56 (p. 241).

CHAPTER 4

❖

Cuerpo náufrago
Genre Troubling: Viscerality and Urinals as Textual and Visual Markers of Disruption

Gender trouble in *Cuerpo náufrago* translates into genre trouble. Just as Antón/ia's transgender defies rigid gender and sexual categorization, so too does Clavel's novel challenge rigid discursive and generic boundaries. This chapter will focus on the notion of discursive and genre trouble by examining the interrelationship between text and image. Such troubling will serve to explore reading experiences of *Cuerpo náufrago* in the context of the Barthesian notions of 'plaisir' [pleasurable reading] and 'jouissance' [erotics of reading][1] and Kristeva's abjection.[2] Both image and text work together as a means of bolstering and questioning conventional generic and disciplinary divides, challenging traditional discourses of bodily control and cleanliness which lie at the heart of the 'civilizing process' in Western and non-Western cultures, as well as gender and sexual categories. In the context of Clavel's exploration of the urinal and its social and practical function, both image and text serve to examine how public toilets are 'shaped by notions of propriety, hygiene, and the binary gender division'.[3] Troubling in *Cuerpo náufrago*, as text, visual proposition, and its multimedia dimension, becomes a prime instance of the queer in the Halperian meaning of the word.[4] In this sense, Clavel's queering ultimately stands for 'the disturbance of the status quo that requires a re-visioning [...] of all our categories'.[5]

As a multi-genre text *Cuerpo náufrago* is highly intertextual, deploying an array of visual and non-visual texts within its own complex textuality which ultimately challenge the reader's comfortable reading experience. Such disruption is richly illustrated by means of Barthes's concept of 'jouissance'. In Barthes's view of 'the erotics of reading', the writer must give pleasure to his reader who in turn will experience two types of sensation: 'plaisir' and 'jouissance'. 'Plaisir' relates to the reading experience typically produced by the conventional novel: 'the text that contents, fills, grants euphoria: the text that comes from culture and does not break with it, is linked to a comfortable practice of reading' (*The Pleasure of the Text*, p. 14). 'Jouissance' relates to the unexpected, to the:

> Text of bliss: the text that imposes a state of loss, the text that discomforts (perhaps to the point of a certain boredom), unsettles the reader's historical, cultural, psychological assumptions, the consistency of his tastes, values, memories, brings to a crisis his relation with language. (*The Pleasure of the Text*, p. 14)

Whilst there are ample examples of conventional texts (of *plaisir*) which incorporate images into their narratives, in *Cuerpo náufrago* the insertion of image into text causes commotion in the pleasurable reading experience because the images aim to parody such conventional forms. In other words, *Cuerpo náufrago* could be read as mock fiction in the sense that it purports to be fiction and yet it plays with non-literary genres including (digital) photography, sketches, and illustrations. The novel even contains an index. This intentional ridiculing of the conventional biographical mode of fiction and more generally of the traditional literary form — in the prescriptive sense of the word as purely printed text — has direct parallels with Virginia Woolf's *Orlando*. Even as Clavel appears to be mocking Woolf's novel, so too does she emulate Woolf's novel which is a 'mock biography complete with illustrations and an index, wittily mocking the form in which it is written in a manner Sandra Gilbert terms "metabiographical"'.[6] Where Clavel can be seen to queer and parody certain types of (fictional) biographical narratives which explore the lives of individuals accompanied by images of themselves, for instance, is by writing the fictional biography of an individual together with images not of her/ himself, but rather, of images of urinals, dissected vaginas, and (semi-) nudes. The inclusion of an array of photographs transforms the book into 'un libro-objeto, un catálogo de mingitorios en el que las fotografías sorprenden al lector tanto como a Antonia' [a book-object, a catalogue of urinals in which the photographs astound the reader as much as they do Antonia].[7] The readers, now turned viewers, can go from one image to the next as if browsing a catalogue or photography book. Yet these distinct forms are similarly parodied as they become imbued with *Cuerpo náufrago*'s inherently fictive discourse. The intermingling of text and image has therefore a dialogic function, 'a kind of dialogue between text and image' as Clavel notes.[8]

The use of photographs, illustrations, and paintings throughout the novel is linked to Antonia's obsession with anatomy and urinals, which is the basis of her quest for an understanding of her transgender self. The images are marked by their visceral quality which works to disturb the reader's 'plaisir'. The notions of 'plaisir' and 'jouissance' attributed to the reading experience can be understood by making reference to their analogous Barthesian terms, 'scriptible' [writerly] and 'lisible' [readerly].[9] Thus, while 'the comforts of *plaisir* are compatible with texts which are *lisible*', the 'comforts and surprises of *jouissance* arise from the *scriptible*'.[10] 'Writerly' texts are characterized by their narrative experimentation whereby the reader actively participates in the production of meaning (Barthes, *S/Z*, p. 5). 'Readerly' texts are uncomplicated in terms of structure and encourage passive consumption. Whilst *Cuerpo náufrago* is relatively uncomplicated structurally and therefore 'lisible', it is nevertheless also a 'writerly' text. With its exploration of queer themes — both in the sense of non-normative sexuality and the interest in urinals — and playful experimentation with an array of textual and non-textual genres, *Cuerpo náufrago* produces a heightened form of pleasure derived from 'a sense of interruption, a "breakdown" or gap, where, perhaps something unorthodox or unexpected occurs' (Cuddon, p. 672) and from the invitation to the reader to engage in the construction of meaning. Paradoxically, that same form of pleasure produced in one reader, may, in another, be experienced as a form of displeasure, whereby the queer in all its guises, abject viscerality, and narrative ruptures propel the reader into 'a state of loss' (Barthes, *The Pleasure of Reading*, p. 14).[11] The bizarre, grotesque, and pornographic subject matter of the images may illicit discomfort but may educe simultaneously, morbid fascination, and, in some instances, sexual arousal. These images thus cause abjection in the reader-viewer. The abject in the form of bodily functions (urine, faeces, and semen) and 'lower' bodily parts (vaginas and penises) alluded to or depicted in the images, create a Kristevan sense of horror and fascination at once. The text that accompanies these images serves to enhance these sensations produced in the reader. Yet, as the reader is compelled to move back and forth between text and image, both mediums have a reciprocal function: whilst images serve to fill in gaps which remain unexplained in the text, the text serves to fill in the gaps which remain unclear in the images. Their reciprocity is evinced in the way that the reader constructs meaning and serves to engage with the reader in ways that can be perceived as non-traditional in the act of reading literature. As readers we are transformed, unwittingly perhaps, into participant observers in the novel, firstly by reading and seeing what the character does and the world s/he inhabits, and then secondly by being encouraged to interact both mentally and physically with the text's construction.

Courbet's *L'Origine du monde* and the (Dis)Pleasure of Looking

The disruption of the 'pleasurable' reading experience is demonstrated in one instance when Antonia asks Paula to pose naked for a photographic shoot (*Cuerpo*, pp. 159–60), whereby text and image push the reader into the uneasy role of voyeuristic peeping Tom. The element of paedophilic desire emerges disturbingly through the sexual fantasies of both Antonia and Paula. Antonia reveals her lurid thoughts by remarking: 'Quiero tu pubis de niña' [I want your little girl pubis] (p. 159), and Paula, 'con la imagen de sí misma otra vez adolescente, casi púber' [with the image of herself as an almost pubescent adolescent once again], urges Antón to shave off her pubic hair for the shoot giving her the appearance 'como si hubiera vuelto a tener diez años' [as if I were again ten years old]. Antonia explains to Paula, 'nunca he violado a una niña' [I have never raped a little girl]. This passage is accompanied by an illustration which draws its inspiration from Courbet's *L'Origine du monde* (1866) which depicts the close-up view of the pubic area (pubic hair, labia, clitoris) and stomach of a naked woman with her legs spread open whilst lying on a bed. The original painting is framed to focus on the pubic area, whilst the lower legs, the torso, and the head fall beyond the edge of the composition. The text's illustration, created by Clavel and digital artist Paul Alarcón, is a reworking of Courbet's original and has been renamed *El origen rasurado* [The Shaved Origin].

Fig. 4.1. *El origen rasurado.*
Digital image. Ana Clavel and Paul Alarcón. Courtesy of Ana Clavel

Clavel and Alarcón's work is framed within what appears to be a wooden border with a hole in the centre in the form of a keyhole.[12] The gap also has an uncanny resemblance to a womb or, even more peculiarly, to a urinal. The womb-urinal association is explicitly made by Antonia who remarks that she has a predilection for photographing urinals which 'preservaban su forma original de matriz' [preserved their original shape of a womb] (p. 49). As our eyes look through the keyhole/womb/urinal we can see a black and white image of Courbet's naked woman, but whose pubic area has been shaven on one half (figure 4.1).

We assume that the woman is Paula, given that our imaginative reconstruction of the sex scene with Paula and Antón as recounted in the text is bolstered by the image presented to us. The juxtaposition of text and image can create in the reader two types of sensation: displeasure or 'jouissance', or perhaps both at once thus illiciting a form of abjection. Whatever the response, text and image are intended to compromise the comfort of the reader. The image puts into jeopardy the reader's 'plaisir' even more than the written passage, firstly, because it disrupts the narrative flow, and secondly, because the reader is turned into (un)willing spectator. We are encouraged not only to read about the pubis but also to look at it 'uncovered' (*Cuerpo*, p. 159) — both literally and metaphorically — from Antón/ia's perspective. Like Antón/ia, we become participants in the (dis)pleasure of looking. The pubis is utterly abject: we may be repulsed by it, but we cannot help but look at it. Whilst it horrifies us in all its graphicness, so too does it captivate us in a sexual sense of the titillating, drawing us in towards its hidden pleasures. The role of (dis)pleasure in looking can also be understood in the context of Laura Mulvey's perception that visual pleasure in mainstream cinema derives from and reproduces a structure of male looking and female 'to-be-looked-at-ness', wherein the spectator, whether male or female, is invited to identify with a 'male gaze' at an objectified female.[13] The determining male gaze which projects its fantasy onto the female figure is representative of a 'world ordered by sexual imbalance [in which] pleasure in looking has been split between active/male and passive/female' ('Visual Pleasure', p. 18). Spectatorship thus becomes inextricably intertwined with questions of sexual difference. Like Courbet's canvas, *El origen rasurado* appears to reproduce this male/female configuration of looking/being looked-at-ness. The gap in the centre of the wooden frame which resembles a womb (associated with the feminine) or possibly a urinal (associated with the male) could be seen as inviting both male and female spectators to look at the naked woman from a male, specifically Antón's, point of view. Both *L'Origine du monde* and *El origen rasurado* draw our gaze towards the pubic area, thus reducing woman to her sexual parts where the 'anonymous, faceless, amputated body does not so much suggest as flaunt the idea of a woman as a sexual object for the delectation and use of men'.[14]

Whilst the traditional male gaze paradigm is reinforced by Clavel, so too is it challenged, again causing another level of disruption in the reader-viewer's 'plaisir'. Image and writing become intertwined, aimed at subversive ends in order to embrace multiple ways of seeing and reading. When a text is placed alongside an image, the links between the written text and the visual image are often left for the reader to infer. Clavel's text explicates what is visually unstated in Courbet's canvas: the text erases the frames put around the naked woman/Paula by exploring the unspoken 'lacunae'. Clavel moves beyond what is inside the frame and tells us textually what might be outside, offering us another level of interpretation. Whilst the image may suggest that the female subject is the passive object of the male gaze, the text reveals that Paula willingly welcomes the male gaze and enjoys being gazed upon. She revels in seducing the onlooker and experiences pleasure actively. Indeed she encourages Antón to shave her pubic hair for the purpose of fulfilling their sexual fantasy. The analysis in Chapter 7 of the front cover image of *Las Violetas son flores del deseo* will suggest that the photograph of the splayed-legged girl/woman draws its inspiration from Courbet's *L'Origine du monde*. Whilst it may seem odd that Clavel uses Courbet's painting, given that she often contests the sort of female objectification the painter appears to be emphasizing, both writer and artist share more in common than may at first appear. They are contravening many of the heteronormative conventions which preside over the gendered gaze and the representations of gender, desire, and sexuality, whilst paradoxically bolstering those very same principles. Although the reclining nude in *L'Origine du monde* may intimate the idea of woman as passive object of male desire, her splayed-legged posture in fact suggests post-coital bliss. As Harrison notes, this is 'an image of the female in full command of her own sexual attribute'.[15] Clavel's reworking of Courbet's painting thus serves as a vehicle to promote 'women's right to be full sexual subjects belonging in the social and cultural mainstream and assuming their desire as freely as men have traditionally been able to' (Day, p. 218). Ultimately Clavel can be seen to use both text and image in synergy to break with trite clichés attached to women's lack of sexual initiative and inability to experience sexual pleasure.

The juxtaposition of text and image in *Cuerpo náufrago* continues to produce further dislocations in the context of the gaze, and thus the reader's 'plaisir'. Both in its textual and visual form, the heterosexual reading offered via the photo-shoot episode becomes simultaneously shattered as the reader/viewer is invited to 'transvestism', that is, to multiple gazes from the lesbian, bisexual, or transgender gazee who has not been accounted for in the (Mulvian) male paradigm of looking and desire.[16] *El origen rasurado* invites not only male heterosexual 'jouissance' but also other gazes and pleasures, thus providing viewers access to a multitude of spectator positions and desires. Narrative point of view and the reader's knowledge of Antonia's 'original' identity also contribute to the destabilization of a heterosexual interpretation which both text and image appear to be proposing. Taking my cue from Annette Kuhn's examination of cross-dressing films, '"true" gender is repeatedly made visible to the spectator, while the ignorance of certain of the film's characters — because unlike the spectator they are not in a position to see the truth — is constantly emphasized'.[17] The notion of privileged spectator positioning can be applied to the reader-spectators of *Cuerpo* who — unlike some of the unsuspecting characters in the novel, including Paula at least until sometime after the photo-shoot — know Antonia's 'true' sex because of their superior point of view or the narrative-visual 'view behind'.[18] It is this superior point of view that allows the reader-spectator the possibility of multiple readings and gazes. The conflict between Antonia's 'disguise' and her actual sex create 'sexual bivalency' (Straayer, p. 54) which establishes concurrent heterosexual and lesbian interactions: while on the one hand Antonia's 'disguise' as Antón offers a heterosexual reading, our knowledge of the character's actual identity, on the other hand, offers a lesbian reading since Antonia and Paula are same-sexed. Through the medium of Antón/ia's gaze, which is both male and female, the expression of both a male-female and female-female desire simultaneously reinforces and breaks with the conventional 'male' gaze paradigm which constructs heterosexual relations. In contrast to the photo-shoot, which collapses actual heterosexuality with implied lesbianism, the episode in which Antón and Raimundo have sex, explored in the previous chapter, 'collapses actual homosexuality' (Straayer, p. 55) with implied heterosexuality. Whilst in both scenes homosexual readings are possible, so too are heterosexual readings available to the reader-viewer. Indeed, whereas the heterosexual reading-viewing of the Antón-Paula episode requires the reader to suspend his or her disbelief and accept Antonia's disguise as Antón, the heterosexual reading implied in the Antón-

Raimundo scene requires the reader to disregard the disguise as Antón altogether. Ultimately heterosexual, lesbian, and homosexual readings, and ways of looking in these and other paradoxical episodes throughout *Cuerpo náufrago*, are not separable and thus require a queer reading, whether the reader-gazee finds it pleasurable, unpleasurable, or both. These readings can be experienced simultaneously though perhaps unequally since it depends on whether the reader-gazee has a 'predilection for opposition or similarity' or 'chooses to believe or disbelieve the disguise, which relates to her or his preference for certain sexual encounters vicariously available' (Straayer, p. 54). By reinforcing traditional conventions associated with the 'male gaze' and heterosexual desire, as well as subverting those very same conventions where a multitude of other gazes and desires are suggested, Clavel queers her text thus making the reader-spectator question the manner in which we look, read, and desire.

Urinals, The Scatological, and the Civilizing Process

The relevance of the images throughout *Cuerpo náufrago* can be understood in the context of the text's profound urge to discomfort and break boundaries. The illustrations of urinals may be seen as a possibly humorous riposte to the discourses of the (un)civilized body. They also serve both to foreground and to question the function of toilets as gendered spaces. Mary Douglas points out that notions of dirt and its management inform social arrangements in all cultures.[19] Clavel similarly can be seen to highlight how in all cultures, toilets become, as exemplars of the clean, civilized versus the dirty, improper body, 'windows onto the processes by which cultures define, separate, and manage dirt, and thus they contribute to the maintenance or violation of ideal order' (Gershenson and Penner (eds.), p. 13). In the context of gender binary roles, the toilet across the globe also works, on the whole, to segregate and maintain the gender divide between male and female.

One process involved in the civilization of society was the introduction of public health reforms in the nineteenth century. Clavel makes indirect allusion to these transformations via reference to general technological achievements of the nineteenth century in sanitary ware (*Cuerpo*, p. 101), as well as inclusion of a photograph depicting a semi-naked woman sitting on a bidet (p. 40). The image is by Gyula Halasz, better known as Brassäi, and is entitled 'La Toilette dans un hotel de passé. Rue Quincapoix' (ca. 1932). Sanitary developments in nineteenth-century Mexico are also alluded to when Clavel mentions the imported French bidet in 'casas porfirianas que conservan baños de la época' (p. 40). In nineteenth-century Mexico both sanitation and hygiene became part of nationalism, whereby Porfirian discourses encoded bathrooms, washhouses, and public baths in the language of class, morality, hygiene, progress and civilisation.[20] Sanitation was an inexorable part in promoting modern Mexico since 'a truly modern Mexico had to be necessarily a sanitary Mexico'.[21] The Porfirian modernizing endeavour was influenced in particular by imported (post-) colonial Western modernizing and civilizing discourses. Clavel's allusion to the imported French-pioneered bidet is significant in this respect. Mexico's adoption of this metaphorical 'seat' of Western civilization can be understood as the nation's attempt to rid itself of the filthy 'third world' image which 'first world' countries had formed of Mexico. Influenced by the prevailing view in the 1880s in European countries that there was a 'direct relationship between poor hygiene and national decline' (Tenorio-Trillo, p. 146), the Porfirian government's emphasis on sanitary aspects of Mexico's modern image was essential.

Whilst Clavel does not develop textually in any depth the manner in which Mexican or global governments have attempted and continue to attempt to civilize their nations via sanitation and health reforms, the author appears to be nevertheless keen to expose notions of the 'civilized body' which are intrinsic to such endeavours, as we shall see. Another point Clavel appears to be keen to raise is that despite the centrality of sanitation services in historical and contemporary political rhetoric and everyday human lives, both in Mexico and in many countries across the globe, the sanitary equipment itself and public toilets more generally appear to be an almost overlooked area in academic studies. When Antonia is doing research into the history of urinals in the Biblioteca Nacional in Mexico City, she remarks on the lack of critical attention urinals have received to date:

> Le parecía increíble que en los comienzos de un nuevo siglo y un nuevo milenio, cuando tantos objetos del mundo cotidiano habían sido sometidos a la mirada morbosa de los investigadores, los urinarios se mantuvieran escondidos en esa penumbra protectora de lo intencionalmente no visible. (*Cuerpo*, p. 101)
>
> [She thought that it was incredible that at the start of a new century and millennium, even when so many worldly objects had been subjected to the attention of the morbid gaze of researchers, urinals were hidden away in that penumbra which protects us from that which has been made intentionally invisible]

The underlying irony in this passage points to Antonia's own obsessive role as researcher into urinals which have become the subject of her own 'mirada morbosa', to which the reader of course is also an accomplice. Eveleigh similarly remarks on the lack of critical consideration devoted to the development of present-day sanitary appliances and notes that the fascination with the subject has long been mitigated by society's reluctance to probe the details of such a private and improper subject.[22] However both Gershenson and Penner remark that since the 1980s a critical strand of academic literature has been growing which examines toilets in relation to, for instance, sex segregation or the global water and sanitation crisis; they also mention a number of studies which take a sociological, psychoanalytical or architectural critical approach to the role of toilets (*Ladies and Gents: Public Toilets and Gender*, p. 11). This recent work is one of the first multidisciplinary studies to explore the cultural meanings, ideologies, and histories of public toilets. Whilst the toilet in academic criticism may still be relatively underexplored, it is a subject which, post-nineteenth century, has been widely used in literary, artistic, and film representations (Gershenson and Penner, p. 19). Although literary or visual references to personal habits and matters of hygiene are scarce in (pre-) nineteenth-century works (Eveleigh, p. xiv), references to the scatological, bodily functions, and sanitary appliances are significantly more abundant in twentieth- and twenty-first-century visual and written culture. Some such examples include, in the visual arts, Duchamp's urinal art-piece *Fountain* (1917), Sarah Lucas's toilet-base sculpture *Old In and Out Saggy* (1998), and Wim Delvoye's faeces-making digestive machine *Cloaca* (2000). Laura Esquivel's *Como agua para chocolate* (1985), which depicts Rosaura suffering from halitosis and flatulence, and of course, more recently, Antonia's fetishistic exploration of urinals in Clavel's *Cuerpo náufrago*, are two of the many existing examples of literary works which delve into scatological-related concerns. Toilet scenes abound in contemporary cinema too, including *El Fantasmsa de la libertad* (1974, dir. Luis Buñuel) and *Something about Mary* (1998, dir. Bobby and Peter Farrelly). In all these cases, the scatological functions as a humorous riposte to the social taboos surrounding the details of such a private subject.

The extensive visual examples of urinals and textual references to urination in *Cuerpo náufrago* can be understood as a parody of the taboo which surrounds the act of defecation and urination. Clavel offers the reader some very explicit accounts of urination: 'contempló el chisguete de orina que hacía bullir el fondo de agua mientras sopesaba la carga de su miembro en la mano' [he observed the stream of urine which made the bottom of the water bubble as she felt the weight of her organ in her hand] (*Cuerpo*, p. 104). The scatological also becomes enmeshed with penis jokes (p. 104) or sexual toilet humour (p. 64). Whilst Antonia is sitting in a sauna with a group of rambunctious men, one of them starts telling a rather crass joke about a daughter who asks her father permission to go to a party with her boyfriend (p. 64). The father agrees only on condition that the daughter performs fellatio on him. She assents, but when the father lowers his trousers the daughter remarks 'oye, papá, esta verga huele a mierda' [hey Dad, this dick stinks of shit] (p. 64). The father retorts: '¿pues qué querías? Tu hermano acababa de pedirme que le preste el coche' [well, what were thinking? Your brother has just asked me to lend him my car] (p. 64). This particular joke gains an added dimension in its allusion to 'closet' homosexuality, as will be discussed further on.

Despite the apparent lack of historical references to the urinal, during her research Antonia comes across the catalogue of an exhibition of urinals organized by the renowned North American Mott plumbing company in 1888: 'aparecieron formas estilizadas e innovadoras para la época, sistemas de desagüe que garantizaban la eliminación de impurezas y mal olor [...] los que más llamaron su atención fueron unos mingitorios plegables, "inofensivos a la vista"' [stylized forms appeared which were innovative for the period, waste systems which guaranteed the elimination of impurities and bad odours [...] the ones that most grabbed her attention were some foldable urinals which were 'easy on the eye'] (p. 101). Accompanying this passage is an image containing various illustrations of these foldable urinals, displayed in the Mott exhibition. The words 'eliminación de impurezas y mal olor' gain relevance in the context of the modern, civilized body. In *The Civilizing Process* (1939) Norbert Elias links the rise of the civilizing process to a growing control over corporeal excreta.[23] Elias explains that the civilizing process is part of an intricate alteration of human conduct from the 'grotesque' to the 'civilized', the latter term inexorably linked to notions of self-discipline, cleanliness, and concealment. According to Mikhail Bakhtin the grotesque refers to those forms of embodiment and conduct linked to pre-modern and impulsive forms of behaviour.[24] The grotesque, 'uncivilized' body is associated with dirtiness, bodily odour, uncontrolled body functions, and sexual activity which in Western and non-Western society have come to be associated with feelings of shame and exposure. The grotesque body is also linked to the broader context of Bakhtin's concept of 'Carnivalization'. Bakhtin argues that during carnival latent anarchic and pre-Oedipal energies led to the transgression of social and moral standards. Furthermore carnival exemplifies ritual inversions: 'it links the inversion of hierarchy [...] with a comic privileging of the bottom part of the body [...] over the rational and spiritual control of the head'.[25] The grotesque has a similar subversive function to carnival, and by extension the abject, as it serves to challenge pre-established conceptions of the controlled body. The frequently comic spirit of carnival, suggested in the proliferation of references to and images of urinals in *Cuerpo náufrago*, implies the triumph of the 'low' over the 'high' and of corporeal excess over corporeal control. The text seeks to give voice to the 'unsaid' of rationalism whose objective has been traditionally to impose a kind of mental dictatorship and eliminate the 'unreasonable other'.[26] *Cuerpo náufrago*'s 'privileging of the bottom part of the body' represents what Christine Büci-Glucksman terms a postmodern 'feminization' of culture and history: 'the metaphor of the feminine then rises up as an element in the break with a certain discredited rationality based upon the idea of a historical and symbolic continuum. It does this by designing heterogeneity, a new otherness'.[27] Patriarchal discourse frequently represses anything to do with the feminine (body (functions), the sexual, the queer) which it deems to be dangerous and potentially uncontrollable. Clavel can be seen to show that repressed female/queer discourses have their own particular validity and that they provide an important balance in a world of plural meanings.

Clavel's meticulous descriptions of bodily processes not considered acceptable in polite society also help to draw attention to the stifling emphasis placed by society on the control and management of body functions, rhythms, and smells, as suggested in the words 'eliminación de impurezas y mal olor'. In Laporte's *History of Shit*, the author seeks to demonstrate how 'the management of human waste is crucial to our identities as modern individuals; including the organization of the city, the rise of the nation-state, the development of capitalism, and the mandate for clean and proper language' (book blurb). For Laporte the civilizing process is linked to a devaluation of the senses whereby the containment of olfactory offences is key to bourgeois and emergent capitalist ideologies. Clavel's reference to foul smells such as 'los olores más transpirados y acres que le he olido a la orina. Un pedo de puercoespín' [the most acrid and transpiring stench that I have smelt emanating from urine. The fart of a porcupine] (*Cuerpo*, p. 39), serves to parody the need to control or eliminate olfactory offences and waste. Clavel's allusions to scatological odours and bodily functions find their counterpart in linguistic foulmouthedness. *Cuerpo náufrago* is notable for its grotesque language of excess seen in its occasional use of colloquialisms and expletives. Excessive, uncouth language is opposed to the precept of 'proper' linguistic norms. The presence of profanity can be perceived as an intentional form of 'consciousness' and as an act of agency, specifically used to 'reverse the deodorization of language by means of reeking syntax' (Rodolphe

El-Khoury, quoted in Gershenson and Penner (eds.), p. 27). Such language contrasts with the 'high' poetic and 'deodorized' academic language Clavel uses elsewhere.

Urine and its smell are also examples of the Kristevan abject. Kristeva discusses the way in which the abject element in humanity is controlled by society's expressions of revulsion at body waste and functions. These rituals strive to maintain the boundaries between what is abject and what is not, observed through the polarities of clean/unclean that function as markers of cultural and social order and disorder. As long as the body is clean and its bodily boundaries remain contained, then all threat to the social order is curbed. Kristeva draws from the anthropological perspective of Mary Douglas (*Purity and Danger*) who views the human body as a natural symbol used to express ideas about social disorder. Within a Kristevan framework, the abject is that which is 'radically excluded' (*Powers of Horror*, p. 2) but is 'what disturbs identity, system, order. What does not respect borders, positions, rules' (p. 4). Abjection thus threatens to destabilize the split between I and 'Other', inside and outside (p. 7). Aversion to fluids and corporeal waste underlines 'the fear of being absorbed into something which has no boundaries of its own', that something being characterized by excess.[28] In *Cuerpo náufrago* toilets are a site of abjection and the urinal in particular is an ambiguous object which mediates between the clean and dirty body. Urine — like other 'polluted' visceral fluids (e.g. faeces and semen) — embodies utmost abjection in the way that its visibility challenges bodily boundaries between clean and dirty, inside and outside:

> El olor reconcentrado de la orina, se alzó como una ola gigantesca que les quitó el aliento. La repugnancia, pero sobre todo el vértigo de descubrir en ese promiscuo mundo de olores una sordidez tumultuosa [...] aquello que nos es tan cercana, tan cálidamente, ajeno. (*Cuerpo*, p. 140)
>
> [The stench of concentrated urine which rose like a huge wave overwhelmed them. The revulsion but above all the wooziness it provoked in them came about from the discovery of a tumultuous sordidness in that promiscuous world of odours [...] that which is so close, yet so warmly foreign to us]

The smell of urine provokes a deep sense of abjection or 'repugnancia', whereby the boundaries between inside and outside are at risk of collapsing. Even though urine is intimately connected to the body and its processes, it is viewed as something alien ('tan cercano, tan cálidamente, ajeno'), improper ('sordidez tumultuosa'), provoking strong feelings of disgust in Antonia. The nausea she experiences caused by the stench of urine reinforces the Kristevan view that the abject must be controlled by society with rituals of revulsion. Scatology, a carnivalesque low bodily function, indicates the loss of social decorum and therefore must be contained at all costs. When Antón urinates he tries to be careful not to spill his urine on the toilet seat, but fails to do so (p. 104), suggesting the social pressure to control the excessive, leaking body. Clavel's exploration of the scatological serves as a reminder that despite the taboo of the scatological and society's public rejection of it because of the abjection it produces, waste nevertheless plays an important function in self-definition, as Laporte notes: 'To touch, even lightly, on the relationship of a subject to his shit, is to modify [...] that subject's relationship to the world and to those representations that he constructs of his situation in society' (*History of Shit*, p. 29).

This particular quotation underlines the ambiguous relationship between the abject, the body, and the self: despite the horror the abject produces in us, it also attracts, as Antonia remarks in relation to urinals: 'le habían provocado reacciones encontradas: una atracción aparejada con una violenta repulsión: el mundo secreto de los hombres desde la perspectiva de los desechos y lo prohibido' [they had provoked in her mixed reactions: fascination combined with violent repulsion: the secret world of men from the point of view of waste and the prohibited] (*Cuerpo*, p. 26).

Toilets and the Gender Divide

Just as toilets serve to dispose safely of abject bodily fluids and thus to contain the threat these pose to public life, so too do they function to maintain traditional gender divides. Indeed, public toilets are among the very few openly segregated spaces in contemporary (Western) culture and the 'physical differences between "gentlemen" and "ladies" remains central to (and is further naturalized by) their design' (Gershenson and Penner (eds.), p. 1). Antonia's physical and photographic exploration of male urinals underpins the view of toilets in general as highly gendered spaces. This is particularly reinforced in the context of her transgender male-female self. Her interstitial self comes into conflict when s/he is confronted with the uncertainty as to which toilets s/he must use: 'los símbolos damas/caballeros, como puertas ineludibles del destino, pero [...] ¿por cuál decidirse?' [the signs ladies/gentlemen, like inescapable doors of destiny, but [...] which should I go for?] (p. 25).

In his *Écrits*, Jacques Lacan examines how toilets specifically define us as gendered beings.[29] He shows the manner in which human beings enter the symbolic realm and are subjected to its arbitrary logic by making mention of a public toilet, accompanied by a drawing of two doors marked 'Ladies' and 'Gentlemen' (*Écrits*, p. 151). Such signs, which support the 'laws of urinary segregation' (p. 151), fix sexual difference in the public sphere. In a discussion relating to the principles of categorization, Paula affirms that: 'Las cosas sí son tajantes [...] al menos en un principio clasificatorio. ¿Sabían que la palabra latina "sexus" tiene el mismo origen que cortar, separar, seccionar? Por aquí el baño de mujeres, por allá los hombres' [things are categorical [...] at least in terms of principles of classification. Did you know that the Latin word 'sexus' has the same origin as the words to cut, to separate and to section? Women's toilets this way, men's that way] (*Cuerpo*, p. 149). In order to help toilet users determine which toilets they should enter, the distinction between male and female is often made by playing upon the differences between how masculinity and feminity is performed. Antonia alludes to various signs on toilet doors which denote Judith Butler's notion of 'doing gender', notably underpinned by the accessories or style of dress that are stereotypically associated with either men or women: 'un abanico y una pipa — o sus variantes' [a fan and a pipe — or their variations] (p. 179). Another way in which public toilets bolster the performance of gender is signaled in the act of urination. As a little girl, Antonia overheard her brothers discussing an incident in the boys' toilets at their school involving an urination competition (p. 103). A footnote accompanying this passage mentions that the standing up position is a uniquely Western practice: 'las formas y ritos de virilidad son cuestiones culturales [...] el narcisismo de orinar de pie se refiere a Occidente' [the behaviour and rituals of virility are cultural matters [...] the narcissism of urinating upright is a Western practice] (p. 103). These references to urination gain relevance in the context of Simone de Beauvoir's *The Second Sex* in which the feminist critic explores the impact of toilet behaviour and the social consequences of urinary control. Beauvoir argues that in the West toilet training for girls and boys indoctrinates men into a superior standing position and women into a subordinate squatting position, thus constituting 'for the little girl the most striking sexual differentiation' (p. 301). In Western society, whereas the erect position is reserved uniquely for a man, in order to urinate the woman is 'required to crouch, uncover herself, and therefore hide: a shameful and inconvenient procedure' (p. 301). This Western discourse which promotes unequal toilet practices between the sexes has been deeply ingrained in Antonia's brothers who perceive the standing position as a sign of male 'pride' and the crouching position as a 'disgrace' (*Cuerpo*, p. 103). The male loser in the urinating competition is humiliated by having to crouch down 'like a woman' (p. 103) and is thus divested of his masculinity. Given that women are stereotypically perceived as the negative other of men, being made to behave like a woman is tantamount to flawed masculinity. The winner of the urination contest is determined by the person who is able to direct his urine stream into the urinal from the farthest distance. At the heart of this male ritual is the notion of control and power. Beauvoir notes that one aspect which strongly contrasts in boys' and girls' toilet training is the way that boys are encouraged to control their urine stream by handling their own penis, whereas girls are taught that that their sexual organs are taboo (*The Second Sex*, pp. 301–02). As a man Antonia is able to urinate as men are taught to do by standing up, holding her genitals, and directing the flow of the fluid at her volition: 'con la mano, dirigió el chorro como si estuviera pintando el mingitorio capa por capa. Exhaló de placer ante este nuevo hallazgo' [with her hand she directed the flow as if she were painting the urinal layer by layer. She sighed with pleasure with this new discovery] (*Cuerpo*, p. 27). This suggests that men are privy to greater freedoms than women in particular in relation to the uninhibited access to, and control and power over, their genital area.

Whilst public toilets may be designed in such a way so as to manage human waste, to promote correct toilet protocol, and to segregate gender 'para simplificar, para evitar confusions e incertidumbres' [to simplify, to avoid confusion and uncertainty] (p. 180), so too do they become sites of ambiguous uncertainty, threatening boundaries between inner and outer, proper and improper, normal and odd, male and female. Clavel indicates that such uncertainty, which causes disruptions to the symbolic and spatial order associated with public toilets or toilet practices, creates a sense of abjection, that is, anxiety and disgust as well as fascination. Carlos tells Antón that however much he tries to keep the urine flowing directly into the urinal without over spilling 'siempre caerá una gota fuera de lugar' [a drop will always fall out of place] (p. 103). The 'fuera de lugar' recalls Douglas's notion of 'matter out of place', that is, dirt which involves a set of ordered relations and a contravention

FIG. 4.2. *Tod@s somos chingones.*
Digital image. Ana Clavel. Photo: Ana Clavel. Courtesy of Ana Clavel

of that order: 'Dirt is the by-product of a systematic ordering and classification of matter, in so far as ordering involves rejecting inappropriate elements. This idea of dirt takes us straight to the field of [...] symbolic systems of purity' (*Purity and Danger*, p. 36). Dirt can thus be seen as an example of the queer which works in contradistinction to what does not fit in neatly into the symbolic system of cleanliness. 'Matter out of place' threatens with formlessness whereby:

> Boundaries dissolve, a process in which the distinction between subjects and objects, as well as that between subjects, loses clarity. In public bathrooms the policing of formlessness creates distance from and borders between us and dirt

> (subject and object) as well as us and other users of the bathroom (subject and subject).[30]

In *Cuerpo náufrago* toilets are sites in which the policing of formlessness is constantly undermined. Even if toilets are designed to eliminate 'impurezas y mal olor', they become spaces in which bodies return to dirt. The allusions to semen and urine, for instance, are constant reminders that we are 'fleshy bodies contingent on a world that we cannot completely control. Within toilet stalls, we see our bodies leaking and the boundary between our bodies' insides and outside becoming unclear' and thus our bodies are permanently 'moving from a state of individuality toward undifferentiated form' (Schweder, p. 182). There is one photograph of a urinal taken in Museo del Chopo, Mexico City, and above the urinal the graffitied words *Tod@s somos chingones* can be read (*Cuerpo*, p. 100, and figure 4.2).

This graffiti embodies 'matter out of place', both physically and metaphorically, thus disturbing the viewer-reader and, even, one might argue, actual users. Lorens Holm suggests that the shock one feels when met with racist, sexist, or scatological toilet graffiti is caused by the fact that it is 'matter out of place'.[31] It is a form of displacement which is internal, threatening the representational border between inside and outside and therefore confronting us with the 'horror that simmers beneath any symbolic system' (Holm, p. 430), or, as Gershenson and Penner note, 'the Real which the Symbolic has repressed' (p. 430). By sullying the 'clean' toilet surfaces, the sexist and sexual allusions which the graffitied words 'Tod@s somos chingones' infer cause visual horror, yet the out of place graffiti equally causes viewers-readers-users to reflect upon wider social issues. It functions as a reflection of the issues relating to Mexico's pre-determined cultural discourses about gender which are characterized by a deeply ingrained sexism and homophobia, thus confronting us with the disavowed fears of Mexico's symbolic system. Intentionally aimed at the male user of the urinal, the graffitied words support the view of toilets as gendered spaces which promote gendered rituals and practices. As the male user of the urinal stands in front of the graffiti, the words remind him of his upright, omnipresent, and sexually active function as *chingón*, in contrast to the crouching, denigrated, and sexually passive *chingada*, thus perpetuating bigoted views about gender roles. At the same time, the possibility that women are also *chingonas* may be seen as having a humorous function foregrounding the view that women can also be sexually active, but in particular that the Mexican male cultural traits of the archetypal 'macho chingón' are often more embedded in folklore than reality. The graffiti is nevertheless also making a serious point about how *machismo* is a very real fact of Mexican life and has important implications not only in gender power relations but also for how many Mexicans view homosexuality which is characterized in the main by an embedded homophobia. The male perspective in the 'Tod@s somos chingones' bolsters Mexican men's 'proper' straight role as heterosexual and so underscores the way in which internalized homophobia is an inexorable element in the make-up of Mexican men. The graffiti reinforces the view that the heterosexual, 'macho chingón' predominates as 'the' masculinity of Mexico. The graffiti horrifies because it is 'matter-out-of-place' and plays upon an entrenched social anxiety felt by some Mexican males about their susceptibility to feminization, that is, to becoming a homosexual *chingada*. Ana Clavel reinforces this particular point when she notes in relation to this image:

> Como en los baños de hombres sólo entran hombres, el mensaje original debió de ser: Todos somos chingones, y la "a" dentro de la "o" en la foto que tomé del Museo del Chopo, la debió de escribir una segunda mano: la de un hombre gay que se burlaba así de la supuesta virilidad de los hombres puesto que los gay sostienen que todo hombre esconde a un gay en su interior.[32]
>
> [Given that men only go into male toilets, the original message will have been: 'We are all fuckers', the 'a' in the 'o' in the photo which I took in the Museo del Chopo, must have been inserted by someone else: a gay man who was taking the mick of the supposed virility of men given that homosexuals maintain that every man hides a homosexual in his interior]

The anxiety of emasculation triggers the need to express male-hood via a set of rituals and practices, and, in public conveniences, these translate into what Matt Houlbrook terms 'urinal etiquette',[33] the 'unwritten but tacitly understood behavioral codes that govern toilet use' (Gershenson and Penner, p. 18). Lee Edelman remarks that men's toilets are spaces that serve powerfully to assert heterosexual identity. There is an unspoken rule whereby even whilst men's genitals are uncovered at a urinal, other males must never look at them: 'The law of the men's room decrees that men's dicks be available for public contemplation at the urinal precisely to allow a correlative mandate: that such contemplation must never take place'.[34] In *Cuerpo náufrago* both male public conveniences and male single-sex saunas become areas of performance, governed by what Erving Goffman calls 'interpersonal rituals', at the heart of which the gaze and the aversion of the gaze play a central role.[35] This is exemplified in two instances, once when Antón is initially unable to urinate in the presence of Francisco whom she thinks is looking at him (p. 26). The other passage is set in a sauna where the nude Antonia is sat alongside a number of other naked men who obliquely observe each other in order to size up each other's organs (p. 65). Thus the ritual of looking and not looking — or at least not being seen to look — is significant. Given that penis size is a key feature of masculinity, discretely observing each others' penises is a male ritual enacted by men in order to compete with one another, to see how their own size compares to that of other men, and how their size may or may not conform to what is perceived as ideal by the standards of society. Not looking also plays a vital function in the assertion of heterosexual identity. One of the 'interpersonal rituals' which Goffman identifies is what the sociologist terms 'civil inattention', where one person acknowledges the other but instantly withdraws his or her attention before the other person starts to feel like 'a target of special curiosity' (Goffman, p. 84; Gershenson and Penner, p. 14). Goffman's study has particular resonance in queer studies whereby the performance that takes place in bathrooms — and male single-sex saunas I would add — 'is always charged with sexual meanings — and one withdraws one's attention to avoid being called queer' (Gershenson and Penner, p. 15). In *Cuerpo náufrago*, the aversion of the gaze and the expression of apparent indifference is a required performance in order for the male users of these shared public spaces to affirm their heterosexuality. Here the thought of being seen or getting caught watching is unbearable, revealing a pervasive male cultural anxiety about emasculation and 'about the capacities of gay men to transform or to queer' (Edelman, p. 154).

The joke told by one male sauna user alluded to earlier, in which a father has had anal sex with his son in exchange for the son borrowing his father's car (*Cuerpo*, p. 64), can also be interpreted as an affirmation of male heterosexuality. Despite its extreme crassness, the homophobic joke is received with laughter and such a response could be seen as a required performance by the men in order to bolster their masculinity, whose existence as the prevailing heteronormative standard relies on the denigration of that which is not perceived as being 'normal', such as homosexuality. Paradoxically the positive response to the gag reveals an ambiguous attitude towards homosexuality altogether. The father's bisexuality, suggested both in his sexual proposition to his daughter and concrete sexual act with his son, locates him as the heterosexual *macho* who 'makes it both with men and women without ever yielding an iota of his masculine persona'.[36] The men's positive response to the joke may be partly explained because it reaffirms heterosexuality, given that the father is portrayed as the *chingón* hailed in the graffitied words 'Tod@s somos chingones', that is, the 'active' one who 'remains unmarked by homosexuality'.[37] Yet their laughter could be seen as veiling a complicity amongst themselves about incest, closet bisexuality, and particularly homosexuality. It suggests that non-conventional sex, whether bisexual or homosexual, and regardless of whether one is the insertor or insertee, is condoned as long as it is kept under wraps. This reinforces the view that:

> Two men can meet and have sex without either of them concluding that they are therefore homosexual, nor do they necessarily see themselves as being bisexual. There is a power in remaining silent, that is not naming what has transpired.[38]

The graffiti 'Tod@s somos chingones' continues to produce further disruptions to our comfortable reading experience. The juxtaposition between the clean white surfaces of the urinal and its tiled surround, and the 'matter out of place' graffiti point to the way in which public toilets are abject spaces. These spaces are simultaneously:

> Hygienic and filthy, oppressive and liberating [...] while also constituting spaces of erotic fantasy. They are the setting for feelings of nausea, contamination, discomfort and panic [...] at the same time they hold associations of pleasure, safety, and the fulfillment of sexual desire.[39]

In *Cuerpo náufrago* such ambiguities serve to contest notions of 'proper relations' between people and the binary gender divide. Gender-segregated public conveniences are designed to keep men and women apart and prevent them from engaging in 'improper' sexual relations with one another. The stalls which serve as partitions between same-sexed toilets function to promote 'proper relations' between people of the same sex, to 'keep their occupants from crossing sexual boundaries' and as a form of policing sexual identity in order to 'keep bodies both discrete and discreet from others of the same sex and in line with sanctioned heterosexual behavior' (Schweder, pp. 182 & 184). Whilst toilets may have a utilitarian excretory purpose designed to remove filth, Clavel eroticizes these facilities. The words 'Tod@s somos chingones' shock since they give rise to the possibility that toilets are also sites for 'improper' sexual activity. The graffiti thus undermines the aim of public toilets to prevent 'sexual or subject-to-subject formlessness' (Schweder, p. 183). There is one passage within *Cuerpo náufrago* in which two nameless people have illicit sex in a public toilet. Here sexual formlessness becomes apparent in the literal mixing of bodies. One of the characters is a man and his assertion 'no sabía que las mujeres tuvieran pene' [he did not know that women had penises] (*Cuerpo*, p. 133) reveals that the other character is a trans-male. The nature of their sexual encounter is doubly illicit firstly because sex in public toilets is unlawful, and secondly because homosexuality, though not against the law in Mexico, is not widely endorsed in the country, often perceived as a morally indecent activity. This passage takes on an added dimension since the stereotypical association between male homosexuality and public conveniences as sites of cottaging (illicit sex between men in public lavatories) is reinforced. Cottaging has fomented a link between the dirt and defecation in the lavatory with the 'filthy' 'contaminating' homosexual, and this particular denigrating association has inexorably served to stigmatize homosexuals as abnormal (Andersson and Campkin, p. 210).

Sexual formlessness is expressed in other ways in *Cuerpo náufrago*. For Antonia, urinals represent a blurring of the boundaries between male and female, reflecting her own uncertain transgender self. The character believes that urinals are functional receptacles for male fluid but that they also provide erotic pleasure since their shape is strongly suggestive of the curvaceous female form: 'el mingitorio como las suaves caderas de una mujer [the urinal looking like the soft hips of a woman] (*Cuerpo*, p. 86). Elsewhere Antonia compares the urinal to the vaginal area of the woman (p. 136). There are a number of images of urinals which have been digitally manipulated in order to reinforce the correlation between male urinals and the female form, as well as the blurring of gender boundaries between male and female. One such image, entitled *El mingitorio es la sombra de una mujer* (*Cuerpo*, p. 86), is a reworking of Man Ray's *Untitled* (1926). Clavel and Alarcón's image depicts a female nude which, set against a black background, has been darkened from the waist upwards, whilst the stomach, pubic area, hips, and upper legs are visible. Through digital trickery of light and dark in *El mingitorio* the lower part of the female form takes on an uncanny resemblance to a urinal. The title of Clavel and Alarcón's image wittily reverses the stereotyped notion that women are men's shadows. This peculiar idea of correlating the urinal with the female form of course draws directly from the French conceptual artist Marcel Duchamp who saw a link between the female body and the sensuous quality of the urinal. Clavel is drawing here from Duchamp's seminal, albeit cryptic, statement which reinforces this link: 'one only has: for *female* the public urinal and one lives by it'.[40] Clavel includes the photograph taken by Alfred Stieglitz in 1917 of Duchamp's renowned ready-made *Fountain* which consisted of a mass-produced ceramic urinal mounted upside down on a pedestal, signed and dated by 'artist' R. Mutt. As Robin Lydenberg notes, Duchamp's urinal was used to disrupt systems of classification, including the binary opposition between the sexes.[41] William Camfield alludes to the fusion of genders in Duchamp's sculpture: 'a masculine association cannot be divorced from the object because the original identity and function of the urinal remain evident, yet the overriding image is one of some generic female form' (Camfield quoted in Lydenberg, p. 153).[42] The blurring between the male urinal and the female form in Duchamp's urinal and by extension *Cuerpo náufrago* supports Schweder's notion of formlessness whereby 'the distinction between subjects and objects [...] loses clarity' ('Stalls between Walls', p. 182). Despite the outright revulsion urinals produce in Antonia, so too do they attract her as they promise fulfillment of sexual desire, igniting a masturbatory impulse (*Cuerpo*, p. 33) and a desire to penetrate the object (p. 134). Whilst ejaculating into the urinal becomes a metonym for the sexual act of penetrating woman, the inanimate urinal represents woman as passive object of male desire. The 'Tod@s somos chingones' slogan graffitied on the toilet wall holds true once again: the male *chingón*, the active 'fucker', takes and subdues the female *chingada*, the passive 'fucked' one. Yet, as the '@' also suggests, the female urinal-vagina becomes an exemplar of formless ambiguity, oscillating between sexual tameness and threatening castration. As Carlos lists the different types of urinals he has encountered across the world, he mentions that they look like scary guillotines (p. 39), alluding to male anxiety in the face of female castration. The reader later comes across a bizarre image of a urinal shaped like a woman's wide-open mouth from which two sets of teeth are visible (p. 136). To either side of the image, two men are urinating into the adjacent urinals. Whereas the men are subsumed into relative darkness, the urinal and part of the surrounding tiles are clear to the eye. The dark contours of the men are presented in such a way that the light tiled area is made to resemble the curvaceous hips of a woman, and the urinal, at the centre, becomes the female vagina. The footnote accompanying this image informs the reader that the toilet, designed by the Dutch company Bathroom Mania!, was part of a set of toilets called *Kisses*, some of which were going to be installed at the John F. Kennedy International Airport in the USA. However, Virgin Airways abandoned plans to install the urinals after the National Organization for Women called them degrading to women. The urinal can be seen as horrifying on two fronts: firstly, it posits woman as denigrated passive object of male pleasure; secondly, the toothed vagina presents woman as castrator. The darkness surrounding the urinating men whose bodies fall out of the frame of the photograph suggests the idea of male fear of sexual inadequacy or of castration at the hands of voracious women. By casting the men into shadow, the stereotyped view of women as men's negative other is reversed: men are the negative other of (positive) women.

Sexual formlessness does not only suggest a literal mixing of bodies, but also the mixing of gender roles:

> Bathrooms are designed to be stages on which reductive gender roles are played out and reinforced. By going into separate rooms, we are choosing which role we will play in the performance of gender. A cross-dresser reveals the element of choice and performance when he or she makes the decision to enter either the 'ladies' or the 'gents'. The objections raised when people choose the 'wrong' door/identity reveal the widespread desire for a stable correlation between gender and sex. (Schweder, pp. 183–84)

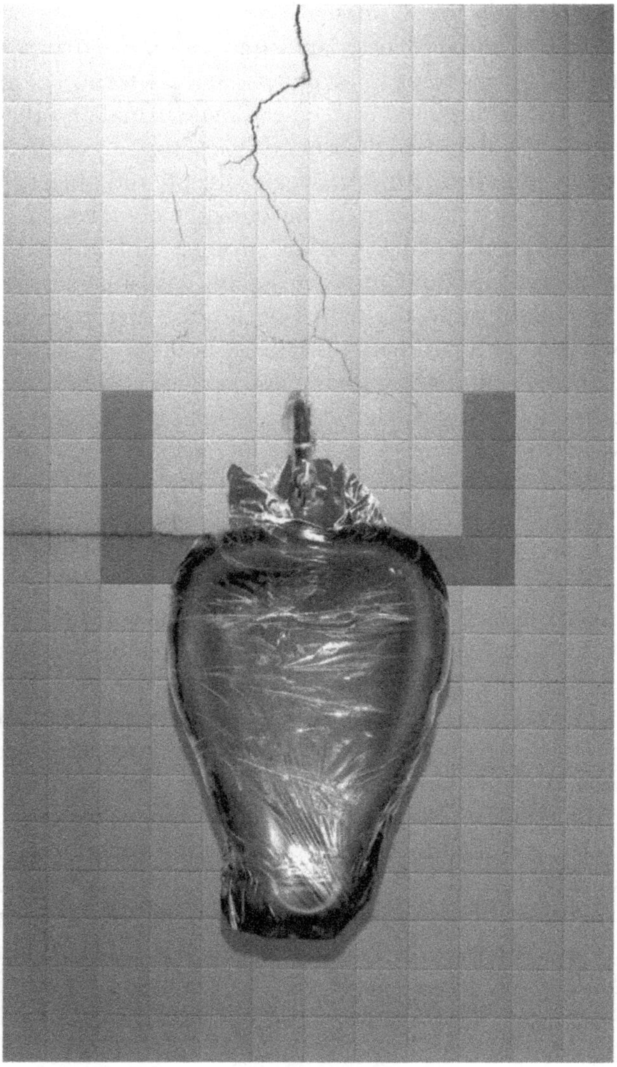

FIG. 4.3. *El mingitauro.*
Digital image. Ana Clavel and Paul Alarcón.

Earlier we noted how toilets force humans to define themselves as gendered beings and how certain toilet practices and toilet signs on doors underpin the notion of 'doing gender', accordingly promulgating an unwavering correspondence between gender and sex. The text demonstrates that this is a precarious construct constantly threatened by gender formlessness. The confusion of gender roles is suggested in particular in relation to one urinal which Antonia photographs and names 'mingitauro' [urinal-minotaur] (*Cuerpo*, pp. 98–99 & 122). It also features in *Cuerpo náufrago* (p. 167) and was included in the multimedia exhibit of the novel (figure 4.5).

The urinal, covered with a black plastic bin-bag which is gaffer-taped to the tiled wall, is bizarrely located in the female toilets in the Registro Civil in Mexico City

(*Cuerpo*, pp. 98–99). Antonia's description of the urinal as a 'mingitauro', which is a combination of the words *mingitorio* and *minotauro*, suggests linguistic formlessness.[43] 'El mingitauro' causes dislocations as it challenges 'rational' linguistic norms whilst it also foregrounds the arbitrariness of language in the sense that there is no logically inherent relationship between symbol and symbolized, and that instead meaning is constructed from specific conventions. As we mentioned in the previous chapter, Antonia's in-betweenness is denoted in grammatically 'impossible' sentences, and so the 'mingitauro' is, as an example of such 'unintelligible' language, a further instance of the character's 'unintelligible' gender. Antonia is moved at the sight of this object whose shape shifting between urinal, half animal, and half man reminds her of her own uncertain gender and sexual formlessness. The location of the 'mingitauro' disturbs as it is in the 'wrong' place. It challenges existing toilet arrangements which are designed to segregate male from female, as well as Western toilet practices which indoctrinate the view that the standing-up position is a uniquely male preserve. Uncovered, the urinal may invite women to urinate into the receptacle in a standing-up posture, and so the covered and monstrous urinal could be seen as warding women off in a move to promulgate proper toilet practices which maintain sexual difference. Indeed, 'pareciera como si el envoltorio fuera en realidad para impedir que alguna mujer — por curiosidad, ignorancia o perversión — lo utilice' [in fact it is as if the cover had been put on it as if to stop any woman who was trying to use it out of curiosity, ignorance or perversion] (p. 169). Whilst the idea of women urinating in an upright position is proscribed at a patriarchal discursive level, it is a material reality which the 'mingitauro' alerts us to indirectly. Paula draws our attention to the fact that women in England 'ya usan mingitorios [...] Se ponen un aparatejo y orinan de pie' [already use urinals [...] They put on a plastic apparatus and urinate whilst standing up] (p. 149), referring to the P-mate, a disposable device which allows women to urinate standing up. Whilst some perceive this prosthetic phallus as a sign of women's penis envy — thus corroborating the view of women as lacking —, others hail the P-mate's emancipatory quality for women.[44] The P-mate actively repudiates 'fixed ideas about what is 'proper' feminine behaviour and fosters an awareness of the acquired character of the conventions that govern toilet protocol' (Penner, p. 148). Like 'mingitauro', it foregrounds the view that the design of female toilets are a response to 'an ideologically dominant idea of femininity as modest, discreet, and hidden' (Penner, p. 149).

In *Cuerpo náufrago* the blurring of the gender divide is enhanced in particular through reference to unisex toilets (pp. 149 & 170) and seemingly confusing toilet signs (pp. 180–81) which have the effect of disturbing traditional gender divisions and 'toilet' protocols. Carlos notes that across the globe both women and men often share the same toilets (p. 149). When comparing different toilet protocols enacted in Europe and Chile, Raimundo explains that Parisian women's practice of using men's toilets, when unisex ones are not available, shock Latin Americans who are unaccustomed to this kind of gender-blurring behaviour (p. 170). The discomfort expressed at sharing toilets with the opposite sex reveals the prevalent fear of the natural order of things, that is the unfaltering correspondence between gender and sex, being shattered. In the context of Antonia's transgender self, unisex toilets acquire an added dimension. In the USA at least, the provision of unisex toilets has come about as a result of demands being made by 'previously invisible categories' (Gershenson and Penner, p. 7) such as gender-variant people. For transgenders, gender-assigned bathrooms are sites of discrimination as they are often at risk of being insulted or assaulted (Gershenson and Penner, p. 7). Although Antonia is not a transgender in the sense of 'being in the wrong body', her doubts about which toilets to use reflect the real-felt experiences of transgenders when faced with the ambiguity as to which toilets to use, in particular when unisex facilities are not available. Antonia, in her guise as Antón, is aware of 'correct' toilet etiquette and is weary of entering the 'wrong' toilet, fearful perhaps of upsetting female toilet users and being at the receiving end of their insults. But Antonia's choice to enter male toilets foregrounds 'the element of choice and performance' (Schweder, p. 183) that she is in full command of in her guise as Antón. Antonia, whose behaviour is influenced by gendered toilet protocols becomes baffled when she comes across a set of toilets in a café where the sign on the door of one reads 'Capuccino', and the other 'Espresso' (*Cuerpo*, pp. 179–81). By encouraging toilet users to enter one of either toilet not on the grounds of gender but rather based on one's preference for one type of coffee or another, gender-blurring unisex toilet practices are being promulgated. These signs with their confusing messages, also work as a humorous riposte to Western gender-prescriptive public toilet signage and practices which assure the certainty of sexual difference and segregation. Whilst the 'Capuccino'/'Espresso' signs make Antonia reflect upon the oppressive, yet precarious, nature of Western discourses which uphold the gender binary divide (p. 180), so too does she appreciate the comical dimension inherent in these door signs. Upon exiting the toilets, a waiter asks her '¿Un capuchino, un expreso?' [A cappuchino, an espresso?], to which she smiles and answers 'mejor un cortado ... para variar' [just for a change ... I'll have a black coffee with a bit of milk] (p. 181). Here she is contrasting playfully her male-female transgender self with the 'cortado', that is, a black espresso coffee 'cut' with a dash of milk that sits somewhere between the milky cappuccino and the black espresso.

The word 'cortado' similarly plays on the idea that Paula explains in relation to the etymological linguistic commonality between the Latin word 'sexus' and the Spanish words 'cortar, separar, seccionar' (pp. 149 & 180), which ultimately serve to underpin (Western) binary discourses relating to notions of gender and sexual differences. Paula's observation follows Antonia's finding of an illustration of a dissected vagina which appears in *Cuerpo náufrago* (pp. 48 & 148). The image entitled 'Corte transversal de matriz' was published in the book of anatomy *De humani corporis fabrica* (1543) by Andreas Vesalius, in which the anatomist's depiction of the genital areas of both men and women follow the Galenic theory of sexual isomorphism. The biased Galenic idea that (inferior) women were a kind of 'inside out sock of men' (p. 147) is reinforced in Vesalius's image of the dissected uterus. Clavel can be said to use this image ironically to highlight how isomorphism, and indirectly dimorphism, have been used at different stages in the history of anatomy as the basic principles guiding the understanding of the make-up of the body and how these often expose deeply-ingrained gender and sex inequalities. Whereas the former supported pre-Enlightenment social and political hierarchies which were rooted in male superiority and dominance, the latter, whilst positing the view of natural sex differences as unmediated by cultural constructions of gender, reflects similar gender biases.[45] Vesalius's image suggests sexual formlessness. The similarities between the male and female genital parts are quite striking: the labia — round with a small opening — look like the foreskin and curved, slit tip of the penis. The neck of the uterus or vagina also looks like a penis. Paula is struck by these remarkable resemblances (p. 147). Sexual formlessness is further reinforced when Antonia notes that Vesalius's penis-vagina has an uncanny resemblance to a urinal: 'aparte del increíble parecido que ese útero tiene con el mingitorio y con el pene, el grabado también podría leerse como una fantasía de la ambigüedad' [apart from the incredible resemblance that this uterus has with the urinal and the penis, the etching can be read as a fantasy of ambiguity] (p. 147). The ambiguity the dissected uterus conveys draws our attention to Antonia's own 'cortado(a)' in-betweenness which blurs strict sex and gender sociocultural differentiation. By drawing our attention to the sexual formlessness suggested in the illustration Clavel's novel exposes the biological and gender biases which often underlie medical discourses, which construct 'universalized models of sexed bodies' (Petersen, p. 2). *Cuerpo náufrago* is thus calling for a de-legitimization of the notion of a 'natural' sexed body or primary gender identity in order to 'open up some space for re-imagining the body' (Petersen, p. 14).

To conclude, Clavel's textual and in particular visual depiction of the abject in the form of (dissected) female genitalia, bodily functions, or urinals simultaneously horrifies and fascinates the viewer. The visual causes 'a crisis in viewing in much the same way as watching a horror film'.[46] In keeping with Kristevan theory, this crisis is produced because the reader-viewer is confronted with the abject body, fluids, and excreta which image and text elicit, thus threatening to collapse the boundary between self and other, inside and outside, male and female, clean and dirty, proper and improper. Barbara Creed considers the act of looking away as a mechanism for reconstructing the boundary between self and screen (Creed cited in Gear, p. 323). The reader-viewer of Clavel's work may well want to look away and re-establish the boundaries which have been disrupted in the presence of the abject, but is repeatedly compelled to return the gaze towards that which horrifies. This ambiguous feeling of fascination and repulsion thus points to the inability of any civilizing discourse to curtail, manage, or altogether banish anything that is queer, in all its multifaceted senses, or our inexorable connectedness with the functions and drives of our bodies.

Notes to Chapter 4

1. Barthes, *The Pleasure of the Text.*
2. Kristeva, *Powers of Horror.*
3. Gershenson and Penner (eds.), *Ladies and Gents*, p. 1.
4. The queer refers to that which is at variance with what is perceived as normal, Halperin, *Saint Foucault.*

5. Kaminsky, 'The Queering of Latin American Literary Studies', p. 210.
6. Sarah Annes Brown, *The Metamorphosis of Ovid: From Chaucer to Ted Hughes* (London: Duckworth, 1999), p. 201.
7. Ana García Bergua, 'Y ahora paso a retirarme, "Comida, Mingitorios y Zapatos"', *La Jornada Semanal*, 546, 21 August 2005, <http://anaclavel.com/jornada/anagarcia.htm> [accessed 10 March 2014].
8. Emilio Ebergenyi, 'Entrevista con Ana Clavel, quien habla de la instalación *Cuerpo náufrago* ready-made multimedia', 'Su casa y otros viajes', Radio Educación, 1060 AM, 19 September 2005, 9.35am, radio interview script, courtesy of Ana Clavel.
9. Roland Barthes, *S/Z,* trans. by Richard Miller (New York: Hill and Wang, 1974), p. 5.
10. John Anthony Cuddon, *A Dictionary of Literary Terms and Literary Theory*, rev. by Claire Preston (London: Blackwell, 1998), p. 672.
11. In her reading of this chapter, Claire Taylor noted that: 'presumably it is the uncomfortableness and shock of these images that jolt the reader out of a 'lisible' identification with Antonio's macho posturing'.
12. *El origen rasurado* draws from Marcel Duchamp's *Étant donnés* installation.
13. Mulvey, 'Visual Pleasure and Narrative Cinema', pp. 6–18.
14. Loraine Day, 'Annie Ernaux and Courbet's *L'Origine du monde*: The Maternal Body, Desire and Filial Identity in *Je ne suis pas sortie de ma nuit* and *Passion simple*', *French Forum*, 25:2 (2000), 205–26 (p. 218).
15. Charles Harrison, *Painting the Difference: Sex and Spectator in Modern Art* (Chicago: University of Chicago Press, 2005), p. 75.
16. Following the publication of Mulvey's 'Visual Pleasure and Narrative Cinema', the essay was the subject of much criticism. Her argument was seen as precluding women's enjoyment of classical Hollywood cinema because of the masculinization of the spectator. Mulvey addressed such issues in another essay, 'Afterthoughts on "Visual Pleasure and Narrative Cinema" inspired by King Vidor's *Duel in the Sun* (1946)', in *Visual and Other Pleasures*, 2nd edn (Basingstoke: Palgrave Macmillan, 2009), pp. 31–40, in which she develops her position by proposing the possibility of a kind of metaphoric 'transvestism' whereby the female viewer oscillates between a male-coded and female-coded viewing position. Mulvey's arguments have given rise to discussions and theoretical work relating to questions about the manner in which lesbian, gay, or bisexual spectatorship might also be negotiated.
17. Annette Kuhn, *The Power of the Image: Essays on Representation and Sexuality* (London: Routledge and Kegan Paul, 1985), p. 65.
18. Kuhn cited in Chris Straayer, *Deviant Eyes, Deviant Bodies: Sexual Re-Orientations in Film and Video* (New York: Columbia University Press, 1992), p. 56.
19. Douglas, *Purity and Danger.*
20. Victor M. Macías-González, 'Scrubbing the Queer Away, or Homosexuality and Mexico City Bathhouses, 1880–1920', unpublished paper presented at I Congreso Mexicano de la Comunidad Lésbica, Gay, Bisexual, Transgénero y Travestí, LGBTT, Memorias, Monterrey, N.L. México, 20–21 October 2001, 1–13, <http://lasa.international.pitt.edu/Lasa2001/MaciasGonzalezVictor.pdf> [accessed 10 March 2014].
21. Tenorio-Trillo, *Mexico at the World's Fairs*, p. 144.
22. David J. Eveleigh, *Boggs, Baths & Basins: The Story of Domestic Sanitation* (Stroud: Sutton Publishing, 2002), p. xiii.
23. Norbert Elias, *The Civilizing Process: Sociogenetic and Psychogenetic Investigations*, trans. by Edmond Jephcott (Oxford: Blackwell, 2000) (first published as *Über der Prozeß der Zivilisation*, vol. 1, in 1939).
24. Bakhtin, *Rabelais and his World.*
25. Peter Stalleybrass and Allon White, *The Politics and Poetics of Transgression* (London: Methuen, 1986), p. 183.
26. Lloyd Hughes Davies, *Allende: La Casa de los espíritus*, p. 63.
27. Christine Büci-Glucksmann, *Baroque Reason: The Aesthetics of Modernity*, transl. by Patrick Camiller (London: Sage, 1994), p. 49.
28. Elizabeth Grosz, *Volatile Bodies. Towards a Corporeal Feminism* (Bloomington and Indianapolis: Indiana University Press, 1994), p. 194.

29. Jacques Lacan, 'The Agency of the Letter in the Unconscious or Reason since Freud', in *Écrits: A Selection*, pp. 146–78.
30. Alex Schweder, 'Stalls Between Walls: Segregated Sexed Spaces', in *Ladies and Gents: Public Toilets and Gender* (Philadelphia: Temple University Press, 2009), pp. 182–88 (p. 182).
31. Lorens Holm, 'eS aitcH eYe Tee', *The Journal of Architecture*, 12:4 (2007), 423–36.
32. Clavel, email to Lavery, 11 March 2014, 04:19.
33. Matt Houlbrook, 'The Private World of Public Urinals: London 1918–1957', *London Journal*, 25: 1 (2000), 52–70 (p. 5).
34. Lee Edelman, 'Men's Room', in Joel Sanders (ed.), *Stud: Architectures of Masculinity* (New York: Princeton Architectural Press, 1996), pp. 152–61 (p. 153).
35. Erving Goffman, *The Presentation of Self in Everyday Life* (New York: Anchor Books, 1959).
36. Foster, *Sexual Textualities*, p. 3.
37. Irwin, 'The Famous 41', p. 355.
38. Thornton, 'Being Fruity in the Big City', p. 152.
39. Johan Andersson and Ben Campkin, '"White Tiles. Trickling Water. A Man!" Literary Representations of Cottaging in London', in Gershenson and Penner (eds.), *Ladies and Gents*, pp. 208–17 (pp. 211–12).
40. Michel Sanouillet and Elmer Peterson (eds.), *Salt Seller: The Writings of Marcel Duchamp* (New York: Oxford University Press, 1973), p. 23.
41. Robin Lydenberg, 'Marcel Duchamp's Legacy: Aesthetics, Gender, and National Identity in the Toilet', in Gershenson and Penner (eds.), *Ladies and Gents*, pp. 151–66 (p. 153).
42. Lydenberg also notes that Duchamp's urinal has been interpreted by a number of scholars from a queer perspective, whereby the focus on the anxiety caused by its destabilization of gender categories has shifted to the threatened collapse of the heterosexual/homosexual divide. The intentions of Duchamp's political and aesthetic manifestation were to link avant-garde artistic practice with repressed queer sexualities, particularly with those prohibited activities associated with public toilets, including voyeurism (p. 154).
43. During her reading of this chapter, Claire Taylor remarked on the way the urinal resembles a horned bull and that it may function as an oblique reference to bullfighting, a common pastime in Mexico, and by inference to male (violent) power and *machismo* explored throughout *Cuerpo náufrago*.
44. Barbara Penner, '(Re)Designing the "Unmentionable": Female Toilets in the Twentieth Century', in Gershenson and Penner (eds.), *Ladies and Gents*, pp. 141–50 (p. 141). Beauvoir notes (*The Second Sex*, pp. 301–04) that the freedom and apparent omnipotence boys display when urinating conduce to the penis envy of girls, but that 'normally reared' girls will not experience this kind of coveting. Sigmund Freud also mentions the cases of young girls urinating standing up as substantiation of their 'envy for the penis' (Freud quoted in Penner, p. 150). The website promoting the P-mate thus reads: 'P-MATE, allowing women to pee standing up without giving anything away!!! [...] NO MORE Squatting [...] NO MORE personal hygiene issues with public toilets', <http://www.pmate.co.uk/> [accessed 14 June 2014].
45. Alan Petersen, 'Sexing the Body: Representations of Sex Differences in Gray's Anatomy, 1858 to the Present', *Body & Society*, 4:1 (1998), 1–15 (pp. 1 & 14).
46. Rachel Gear, 'All Those Nasty Womanly Things: Women Artists, Technology and The Monstrous-Feminine', *Women's Studies International Forum*, 24:3–4, (2001), 321–33 (p. 323).

CHAPTER 5

❖

Cuerpo náufrago Beyond Text: Intermediality, Inter/Hypertextuality, and *Proyecto multimedia*

I will discuss in this chapter how both *Cuerpo náufrago* as text but in particular as multimedia endeavour elicits the idea of disciplinary and discursive troubling. In order to discuss such troubling, I will first analyze briefly the role of the novel's intertextuality in order then to highlight the manner in which the text's cyber dimension expands the notion of intertextuality through hypertextual and hypermedial readings. I then turn to an examination of the other multimedia elements of the novel. Because of the similarities between *Cuerpo náufrago* and *Las Violetas son flores del deseo* in terms of their hypertextual dimension, I will provide an analysis of hypertextuality in this chapter in relation to both works of fiction. I then focus on the other multimedia elements of Clavel's novel. *Cuerpo náufrago*, like *Las Violetas*, represented the starting point of a broader multimedia project called *Proyecto multimedia* spearheaded by Ana Clavel and the involvement of photographers, artists, and performers. It consisted of a mural and urban space intervention, a webpage and an exhibition which comprised a computer kiosk with access to the *Cuerpo náufrago* website, an art installation, a photographic display, and a performance. The overall multimedia elements were displayed in various locations in Mexico City following the novel's publication in 2005. *Proyecto multimedia* positions Clavel as both writer and artist, and in particular showcases the author's prowess in masterminding a unique artistic vision. It also suggests troubling, given that, as an extension of the novel, it disturbs, but equally complements, traditional conceptions of literature. Similarly, several of the multimedia elements serve, each in their own way, to bolster and to challenge traditional heteronormative gender roles and forms of desire. Finally, whilst the mural and urban space intervention functions to question the logic of commodity capitalism, the multimedia exhibition disturbs traditional notions of 'high' art by engaging audiences with 'low' quotidian-type experiences and fomenting their physical interaction with the artworks and the surrounding space.

Clavel the *Bricoleuse* and *Tres Veces Fuente*

In *Cuerpo náufrago* and its multimedia dimension, intertextuality, intermediality, and hypertextuality serve to disturb the category of the originary itself and, in particular, notions of 'authority', 'authenticity', and 'uniqueness' which traditional conceptions of art and literature support. Even as *Cuerpo náufrago*, both as text and *Proyecto multimedia*, is a calculated copy of works by other authors or artists, so is it a dialogic reworking through parody and digital manipulation. Through its transgression of textual boundaries in the form of diverse texts, media, and genres, it challenges the notion of authenticity of gender and identity, as well as concepts of authenticity, authority, and authorship attached to the work of art.[1]

In traversing the boundaries between different texts and the notions of high and low, it will be shown further on how the (multimedia) text valorizes the literary and artistic abject in the form of erotic or scatological art and literature and makes these central (Taylor, *Bodies and Texts*, p. 150). However it will be shown in the context of intertextuality that such abject art and literature, for all their threat to the status of the text or art as 'high' cultural production, they are often socially sanctioned forms of creativity (*Bodies and Texts*, p. 150). In my exploration of cultural recycling I will use the term intertext(uality) in the broad sense that Mary Orr proposes:

> 'Intertextuality' names a text's relation to other texts in the larger 'mosaic' of cultural practices and their expression. An 'intertext' is therefore a focalizing point within this network or system, while a text's 'intertextual' potential and status are derived from its relations with other texts.[2]

Whilst intertextuality is often seen as too loose a definition and an inadequate idea in an age in which new media are decentering the hegemony of print text (Orr, 'Intertextuality', p. 2), I use intertextuality as one of a number of useful terms to describe 'text within a text' or 'adaptation'. Although such concepts are of relevance to the multimedia dimension of *Cuerpo náufrago*, so too does it warrant terms such as hypertextuality and intermediality, as these expand the concept of intertextuality. The same can be said of the *Las Violetas* multimedia project. Unlike most print-based mediums, the hypertextual dimension of both the *Cuerpo náufrago* and *Las Violetas* websites encourages, for example, spontaneous, non-linear interactivity.[3] The broader multimedia *Cuerpo náufrago* endeavour and that of *Las Violetas*, with their intersection of different mediums such as art installation and photography, call for, in certain instances, an intermedial research perspective. Intermediality in its wide-ranging sense 'designates those configurations which have to do with a crossing of borders between media'.[4] Orr explains that the term 'describes how cultural productions are facilitated by their (re)interpretation and adaptation in a variety of media including text, performance, the plastic, and the visual arts' ('Intertextuality', p. 2).

Cuerpo náufrago's intertextuality has a number of critical functions, including to foreground literary constructedness and to dislodge the preconception of the work of literature as original product. Intertextual practice shows Clavel to be a true *bricoleuse*. The *bricoleur* is someone 'who works with his hands [...] uses devious means' and makes do 'with "whatever is at hand"', and therefore *bricolage* is a resourceful praxis which involves making new objects out of found material.[5] Clavel recombines the old and the new in order to produce something (un)radically different. Clavel's intertextuality rebuffs the Bloomian 'anxiety of influence' and by extension postmodernism's outright rejection of past sources, even though, paradoxically, she also challenges notions of origins and authority.[6] Whilst Clavel's work retains traces of previous voices, she does not absorb mimetically other texts. Instead, through recourse to devious means (both in the sense of artfulness and deviation), such as parody or (digital) reworkings of previous texts, *bricolage* is used to indicate a flexible creativity and dynamic adaptation.[7] The notion of flexible creativity ties into Kristeva's assertion that a text is a 'mosaic of quotations; any text is the absorption and transformation of another'.[8] This will be explored specifically in relation to Clavel's particular assimilation and transformation of Duchamp's *Fontaine* (1917) and Ingres's nude *La Source* (1856), both in *Cuerpo náufrago* and the *Proyecto multimedia* website. The tension between the concepts of the original and the copy thus comes into focus.

At the end of *Cuerpo náufrago*, the reader is encouraged to go beyond the textual boundaries of the novel and to enter into a hypertextual world: 'Conoce cómo surgió *Cuerpo náufrago* y su indagación en los baños públicos masculinos. Visita el portal <www.ana.clavel.com>' [Find out how *Cuerpo náufrago* came about and its exploration of male public toilets. Visit the website]. The sentence collapses the notion of 'originality' and of texts being self-contained spheres. Just as *Cuerpo náufrago* is a Kristevan mosaic of other texts, absorbed and transformed, so too does the hypermedial dimension imply that *Cuerpo náufrago* has been used as the inspiration for other 'texts', which will in turn motivate other (re)workings. When the website homepage is opened, the internet user is presented with the French painter Jean Auguste Dominique Ingres's nude *La Source* (1856), featuring a naked and demure-looking young woman holding a pitcher from which water is pouring out. It appears not only on the main website page but also both on the cover of *Cuerpo náufrago* and in the novel itself (p. 177), and so the intertextual connections are clear. Whilst all three images are almost exact reproductions of Ingres's 'original', they have been subjected to a number of digital manipulations both for the purposes of parody and artistic playfulness. In the novel, Raimundo gifts Antonia a folder containing a copy of Ingres's nude, but with a twist: 'en vez del cántaro que la muchacha solía cargar [...], aparecía [...] el prístino mingitorio de Duchamp' [instead of the pitcher which the young girl used to carry [...] there was now in its place Duchamp's original urinal] (p. 178). The description is accompanied by a digitally manipulated image entitled *Tres veces fuente* by Ana Clavel and digital artist and designer Paul Alarcón (p. 177). The same image which appears on the cover has been renamed as *La censura también es fuente* and, on the website, as *La censura también es fuente puesta al desnudo por sus mirones*. Both the image on the cover and the website have had an additional feature added, namely, a yellow ribbon which is wrapped strategically around the woman's private parts. On the ribbon, 'Zona de Riesgo' [Danger Zone] can be read on the bust area, and 'Prohibido Pasar' [No Entry] on the pubic area (figure 5.1).

Fig. 5.1. *La censura también es fuente.*
Digital image. Ana Clavel and Paul Alarcón. Courtesy of Ana Clavel

The convergence of both art and digital technology in the images posits *Cuerpo náufrago* (multimedia) as an intermedial locus which counters compartmentalization and thus cultivates a dynamic in-between space across the arts, humanities, and cybertechnology. The fusion of different media produces what Dick Higgins denotes as 'intermedia',[9] which refers to the 'crossovers and interrelations taking place between the arts and the media'.[10] The fusion of the Ingresian nude with the Duchampian urinal and the ribbon reflects the workings of intermedia, that is, the 'phenomena of crossing borders between traditional media (such as painting and photography) and contemporary media (such as cinema, television, video, computer and other hypermedia)'.[11] Such intermedial integration suggests Clavel's intentional blurring of 'high' established forms of art with new media such as digital art that have until recently 'not previously been considered art forms'.[12] The intermediality of the digitally manipulated semi-nude distinguishes it from the notion of multimedia. Both the *Cuerpo náufrago* and *Las Violetas* websites are examples of multimedia in the sense that different media — text, sound, image, and video — are 'presented together synchronously yet remain distinct' (Spielmann, p. 57) and they 'occur together, even interact, but do not structurally impact on each other' (Verstraete, p. 10). With intermediality, 'there is an interrelation of various — distinctly recognized — arts and media within one object but the interaction is such that they transform each other and a new form of art, or mediation, emerges' (Verstraete, p. 10). Spielmann also emphasizes this transformative element in both intermediality and intertextuality (p. 57). As we shall see, in the three *Fuentes* both the intermedial and the intertextual work to fuse a number of historically incongruous media, that is, the traditional (painting, the sculptural, and photography) with the new (cyber digital technology) in order to create a novel form of mediation which involves a self-reflective process. The transformative quality of Paul Alarcón's intermedial intervention in various images on the website is reinforced in the multimedia exhibition pamphlet which states that 'el sitio propone una sugestiva transfiguración iconográfica realizada por Paul Alarcón' [the website proposes a suggestive iconographic transformation carried out by Paul Alarcón].[13]

All three *Fuente* images are a prime exemplar of the Kristevan proclamation that 'any text is the absorption and transformation of another' (*The Kristeva Reader*, p. 37). Whilst the medley of intertextual references are a deferential nod to both Ingres and Duchamp, so too is the replacement of the nymph's pitcher with Duchamp's urinal an intertextual and intermedial parodic counterattack on notions of influence on, and authority and authenticity of, the work of art and, by extension, to established conceptions of 'proper' art. This humorous distortion of Ingres's nude exemplifies postmodern pastiche which has a number of sub-categories, including *capriccio*.[14] Clavel's three *Fuentes* can be seen emulating this notion which not only coalesces diverse pre-existing forms and styles like pastiche, but is also seen as anti-classical (Hoesterey, p. 10). Indeed: 'in visual art, music, or literary texts, a *capriccio* typically manifests itself as a flight of fantasy and sudden whim that surprises a conventional scene or setting' (Hoesterey, p. 10). Apart from their functional purpose, that is to contain and dispense fluids, the links between the pitcher and the urinal may at first seem tenuous and so the alteration of the classical image could appear as a game of sorts. But the replacement of one object with another is far from a random act of capriciousness and its critical purpose is unmistakable. On the *Cuerpo náufrago* website the alteration of the image is explained as a parodic, ironic take:

> Buceando en las frágiles fronteras de los géneros, había que [...] transgredir la imagen de la feminidad tan pródiga e inocente de la ninfa de Ingres y montarle al hombro una sutil ironía: el mingitorio de Duchamp, ese objeto de territorialidad de un mundo masculino tan celosamente resguardado [...] Y jugando mediante el poder de las palabras, retomar sus títulos originales, en un caso *La Source*, en el otro *Fontaine*, para concebir una tercera fuente: esta otra pródiga en perplejos significantes de alteridad.[15]
>
> [Whilst navigating the fragile boundaries of gender, it was necessary [...] to transgress Ingres's deeply prodigious and innocent image of femininity by placing on her shoulders a subtle irony: Duchamp's urinal, that earthly object belonging to the world of men which is so zealously shielded [...] and thus it was by playing with the power of language, by reworking the original titles, on the one hand *La Source* and on the other *Fontaine*, that a third source was conceived and one which revels in representing complex signifiers of alterity]

Clavel also explained that what she wanted to do with the manipulated image was to bring our attention to Duchamp's male-female urinal concept as a way of underpinning Antonia's transgender self in order to do away with traditional gender binaries.[16] Even though the imagery of fluids clearly connects *La Source* and *Fountain* (1917), Duchamp's 'ready-made' was not a direct response to Ingres's *La Source.* Nevertheless, Clavel makes explicit the connection between the two artists and their works via digital manipulation and intermediality: Duchamp's urinal came to epitomize an express assault on convention, the standardization of art and good taste, all of which characterize Ingres's *La Source.* It reflects the conceptions of beauty, taste, and, in particular, moral codes of its day with its expression of virginal chastity. The intermedial and desacratory thrust of the *Fuente* images underscores Duchamp's Dadaist contestatory art. As with his *Fountain* and *L.H.O.O.Q* (1919) pieces, this involved destruction as a creative act which was driven to negate painterly traditions represented by the 'Masters', such as Ingres, who embodied cultural reference points of origin for contemporary art. Clavel's substitution of the pitcher, a typically artisanal object, with a 'lowly' urinal, a mass-produced object, becomes symbolic of Duchamp's ready-made aesthetic.[17] Clavel's intermedial recreation of Ingres's classical nude has in some respects the same function as *L.H.O.O.Q* in that both writer and artist have chosen works which have been identified with 'all that is sacred and beautiful in art' in order to subvert prior canons.[18] By distorting these idealized images both Clavel and Duchamp can be said to be attacking the notions of taste and originality attached to these paintings which mechanical reproduction threatens to destroy (Judovitz, p. 139). The notion of replica is thus placed in counterpoint to what Walter Benjamin terms 'aura', that is the uniqueness of the work of art that gives it its 'authenticity'.[19] For Benjamin that which 'withers in the age of mechanical reproduction is the aura of a work of art [...] By making many reproductions it substitutes a plurality of copies for a unique existence' (p. 215).

Both Clavel's and Duchamp's ready-mades defy notions of 'aura' and traditional criteria defining a work of art, and draw our attention to the idea of in-authenticity. *Fountain* was not an original object in that it was a mould which was used to generate similar objects in bulk. Clavel's three *Fuentes* are also replicas of replicas. Both as text and website, *Cuerpo náufrago* itself is full of mass-reproduced urinals, and each of these objects is replaced with photographs which are replaced by copies of the 'original', and so, by reinforcing the postmodernist concept of reality ceaselessly replaced by its images, the author confounds concepts of origins and originality. Duchamp's urinal, signed with the fictitious 'R. MUTT', raises problems of attribution and contests the view of single authorship given that its reproduction involved other 'intermediaries' (Judovitz, pp. 127–28). Clavel's three *Fuentes* also resist single authorship and authority as well as notions of provenance. Like the 'original' *Fountain*, the superimposed urinal in the three *Fuentes* bears the signature 'R. Mutt', and since readers or web users of *Cuerpo náufrago* may not necessarily be familiar with either Duchamp's urinal or Ingres's *La Source*, they could well be led to believe that *Tres veces fuente* is the artistic creation of the signer. Conventionally the signature confers attribution and 'aura',[20] denoting 'the presence of the "author" as the "person who does the uttering," as the "origin," the source, in the production of the statement' (Derrida quoted in Allmer, p. 11). The title of both Ingres's nude and Duchamp's urinal figuratively connote the idea of the source of life or creativity. The signature in Clavel's three *Fuentes* thus links the work of art to a single authorial source but the reliability of the signature 'R. Mutt' is problematized. When the reader comes across the 'créditos de las imágenes' at the end of the novel, it becomes apparent that the image both in the novel and on the front cover is a reproduction of Ingres's and Duchamp's works which are fully acknowledged. But the image is not attributed to the 'R. MUTT' which appears on the urinal but rather to both Ana Clavel and Paul Alarcón. As a collaborative feat, *Tres veces fuente* resists the idea of attributing the work of art to one single author and so reproduces Duchamp's own playful intention in his replacement of his signature with a pseudonym. The website image *La censura también es fuente puesta...* does not even acknowledge Ingres or Duchamp and is simply accredited to Alarcón and Clavel whilst the R. MUTT signature is so blurred it is practically impossible to discern. The notion of reproduction is thus now replaced by the idea of 'creative' plagiarism. Whilst the attribution to both Clavel and Alarcón resists the concept of the work of art as a 'product of a mythical creative individual', their work is a '"collective invention" made out of plagiarism' (Allmer, p. 2), in the sense that they are passing off the website image as their own 'genuine' artistic production even though it is made out of other artworks. The notion of forgery stands in stark opposition to the copyright disclaimer at the end of the website. Whilst copyright laws confer authority and originality, so too does the language of the law, paradoxically, shroud in-authenticity.

The ribbon enveloping the nude looks like the tape typically used for cordoning off crime scenes and warding off onlookers. The image thus comes to represent the scene of a crime or forgery. If the web user clicks over the semi-nude the ribbon gently falls away and the female is revealed in her naked splendor. Alfaguara, the publisher of *Cuerpo náufrago*, requested that Clavel add the ribbon because the nude alone would be deemed inappropriate by the major book retailers in Mexico such as Sanborns, and therefore would affect sales of the book. Even as Clavel bowed to pressure, so too did the altered image parody puritanical criminalization of nudity. The semi-veiled nude also acts as an intertextual allusion to Courbet's *L'Origine du monde*, and the various coverings the painting was subjected to, as a way of (as discussed in Chapter 7) preventing instant access to the proscribed image of the bare female, whilst also enticing viewers to engage in an erotic peek-a-boo game. The interactive hypermedia element stretches the boundaries of 'creative flexibility' of text-based intertextuality, given that the web user is permitted not only to engage with the image at a metaphorical level and thus make intertextual connections, but also at the level of touch via the click of the mouse. Allowing users to unveil the nude plays to erotic fantasies and brings to the fore not only the role of the complicit *mirones* but also the *tocones* in the felony of looking at, and touching, that which is forbidden.[21]

The ribbon, like the various *L'Origine* screens, has deceptive functions as well as exposing deception itself. The veiling mechanism works in the way that Lacan proposes: 'if one wishes to deceive a man, what one presents to him is the painting of a veil, that is to say, something that incites him to ask what is behind it'.[22] Whilst the ribbon may be seen as a way of enticing the viewer to unveil the woman, so too does the exposed nude, which becomes a metonym for the source of life, knowledge and creativity, reveal 'woman as enigma'.[23] Clavel's use of digital trickery is noteworthy in relation to both Ingres's and Courbet's nudes, as it underscores the manner in which despite the artists' intended desire to provide realistic portrayals of woman, their works are nevertheless painterly representations. Trickery in the form of the unfurling ribbon is also an attention-grabbing gimmick purposefully drawing our attention to constructedness and technical ability. It, and indeed Clavel's Duchampian urinal, expose flagrant forgery not only as a way of demonstrating how the aura of a unique art object vanishes with repetition, but also as a means of upholding and parodying imitation and its processes. Cultural recycling in *La censura también es fuente puesta al desnudo por sus mirones* highlights an intertextual and intermedial process which involves not 'empty mimicry', but instead postmodern 'dynamic rejuvenation'.[24] Paradoxically Clavel's intermedial desecration of the Ingresian nude also puts such a concept into question. *Fountain* was a parodic attempt to destabilize traditional notions of what art is and Duchamp playfully juxtaposed 'high' with 'low' elements by seeking to raise the mass-produced lowly urinal to the status of an art object. The urinal served to parody bourgeois aesthetic sensibilities by questioning the manner in which certain cultural products come to be classified as 'high' art whilst others are classified as low 'art' by elite artistic establishments. The impossibility of maintaining a strict divide between 'high' and 'low' is humorously captured in Clavel's three *Fuentes* which bring together via intermediality 'the "high"-culture academic iconography' of Ingres' work[25] with the 'low' vulgar urinal of Duchamp.[26] Duchamp's mass-reproduced object challenged established notions attached to taste as the driving principle in the appreciation of art. *Fountain* proposes that an artwork's intrinsic 'worth' resides not at the level of aesthetic beauty, but rather at that of a conceptual and creative thought-process.

Ironically, even as Duchamp resisted the traditional ascriptions to art, such as notions of value and aesthetics, so too have his works come to epitomize some of these very attributions. Indeed, *Fountain* is often admired for its aesthetic qualities such as its sculpted curves. In a jeering gesture to Duchamp, Clavel praises the retinal, sculptural feminine beauty of the urinal (*Cuerpo*, p. 34). Even as Duchamp rebutted concepts of tradition and canonicity, his *Fountain* has come to be widely perceived as an icon of twentieth-century art and Duchamp himself, like Ingres, became canonized, an irony which *La censura también es fuente puesta al desnudo por sus mirones* humorously captures via intermediality. Clavel is thus reinforcing the view that Duchamp's abject art, despite its threat to the status of 'high' cultural production, has become itself a legitimized form of creativity.

The intertextual references to both Duchamp and Ingres may have a bearing on Clavel's own self-reflective comment on her status as novelist and on notions of literary legitimacy. Despite *Cuerpo náufrago*'s challenge to traditional ascriptions to 'high' taste with its exploration of the 'vulgar', so too is Clavel's art sanctioned like Duchamp's *Fountain.* Even though she is on the margins of the mainstream *boom femenino*, Clavel is becoming an increasingly nationally and internationally endorsed writer as evidenced in the various literary prizes she has received, the funding awarded to her for her writing by CONACULTA (the National Council for Culture and the Arts), and FONCA (the National Fund for Culture and Arts), the main funding bodies for cultural and artistic endeavours in Mexico,; and by being published by Alfaguara, the highly-respected big-player of the publishing industry in the Hispanic-speaking world. Such backing concedes to Clavel legitimacy as well as symbolic and financial capital. Women's writing, in particular the *boom femenino*, has often been deemed as an inferior form of 'literature', a perception which has beleaguered many women writers, including Clavel, with anxieties connected to issues of credibility and literary legitimacy. By intermedially and intertextually linking her work to highly regarded and authorized works, such as those of Duchamp, Ingres, and Courbet, Clavel is not only self-consciously playing the culture game to demonstrate her expansive 'cultural capital' but is also seeking to shield her work from the charge of banal literature, even though she is dealing with those same 'vulgar' topics which these consecrated artists themselves explore. The intellectualization of the 'improper' through reference to established texts is a defensive technique which allows Clavel to publish the kind of fiction she does with legitimacy. Ultimately whilst intertextual and intermedial practice allows for flexible creativity and innovation, as we have seen, so too does it contribute to Clavel's credibility as a writer of serious fiction.

Hypertextuality

Both the *Cuerpo náufrago* and *Las Violetas* websites have in their hypertext format many synergies with the notion of intertextuality.[27] Hypertext, a term coined by Ted Nelson in 1963, simply 'develops the status of "text" that is intertextuality's motor through digitalization' (Orr, *Intertextuality: Debates*, p. 49). The internet is often aligned with Barthes's notion of intertextuality as a tissue of texts because of their connective structures (*Intertextuality: Debates*, p. 49). Like postmodern intertextuality, digital media encompass all forms of 'text'. Both the *Cuerpo náufrago* and *Las Violetas* websites include 'texts' ranging from written-based material such as excerpts from the novel(la)s, descriptions of the (multimedia) works, links to other websites containing critical commentaries on Clavel's work, and audio-visual formats such as videos and images. In similar fashion to postmodern intertextuality, hypertext works to challenge concepts of origination and authority (*Intertextuality: Debates*, p. 50) as well as to celebrate concepts of replica. But, Orr notes, computer technologies with their 'electronic inclusiveness and facility with textual manipulation' outstrip both postmodern and Kristevan intertextuality (*Intertextuality: Debates*, p. 49). Unlike print-based intertextuality, what is innovative about digital hypertext 'is the speed of transfer from one node to another and the association, in the same medium, of texts, sounds and images in movement'.[28] The user can, for instance, read chapters from *Cuerpo náufrago* and *Las Violetas* which act as the springboard to other (inter)texts, and then, at a click of a mouse, can open other hypertextual links which offer instant inter- and contextual connectivity afforded by the web. These hypertexts include essays by Clavel reflecting on the writing process, articles examining Clavel's *oeuvre*, images and descriptions of the multimedia exhibitions, and video performances. Whilst all these 'texts' link back to Clavel's literary and multimedia works, so too do they provide the user with access to other 'texts'. Both websites offer extensive bio- and bibliographic details about the collaborators who participated in the multimedia exhibitions and links to their personal websites. Such references provide the users with possibilities to expand their knowledge of other forms of cultural production which are not directly linked to Clavel's work, and so the aim of the World Wide Web to maximize users' knowledge by linking information, data, and contexts is fulfilled.[29] Hypertext provides not merely an extension of, but rather a possible replacement of, as Orr suggests, intertextuality as a concept, given that the hypertext may be perceived as a 'less elitist and more inclusive (way) of describing cultural recycling than intertextuality' (*Intertextuality: Debates*, p. 21). One of the attractions of personal websites for authors like Clavel is the capacity to reach a wider audience. Even when access to the internet is not available to all in a specifically Latin American context where the middle class is small, websites such as Clavel's can 'be a way to reach audiences that would not normally buy copies of printed books'.[30] It would seem that Clavel's intended audience, in line with the World Wide Web's utopian drive of inclusivity, spans 'the whole gamut from ordinary to extraordinary users, from the computer as pastime or research tool' (*Intertextuality: Debates*, p. 49).

The websites are set up in a user-friendly way which provides easy navigation for all users. For instance, the book chapters on both websites have been built with Adobe Flash Player software which triggers each page to flick over to the next at the click of the mouse. Clavel thus uses digital technology to mimic the act of reading a printed book. The entertainment value which the interactive element confers on both websites is evinced in the sound emulating the noise of a page being flicked over on the *Las Violetas* website or the unfurling ribbon on the Ingresian nude on the *Cuerpo náufrago* website. Here, if the user clicks on another of the Ingresian nudes, the colour image turns into a black and white image which then gradually fades leaving only the stomach, vaginal area, and legs of the nude visible. This image also fades to reveal a white urinal. Whilst this may be seen as a gimmick flaunting expertise in digital manipulation, so too is the digital re-enactment of the Duchampian concept of the male-female urinal, which for many may be difficult to see in the mind's eye, brilliantly explicated visually through technological wizardry and intermediality. On the *Las Violetas* website, the entertainment element is also evident in the section under the 'Exposición' [Exhibition] sub-page where a video can be played in which we are given a tour of the exhibition of *Las Violetas.* Like the video performances on the *Las Violetas* and *Cuerpo náufrago* websites, this virtual tour enhances our understanding of the overall literary and multimedia endeavours. The idea of computer as pastime and user's interactivity is continued in the 'Exposición' sub-page where there are a number of Polaroid images of the various artists holding the papier mâché dolls they worked on. The words 'da clic en cualquiera de las imágenes' [click on any of the images] appear at the top of the page and when the user does so, another page pops up in which another series of jumbled-up Polaroid images come into sight featuring the worked on dolls. The user is able not only to maximize or minimize these images, but can also drag and drop them and place them in any configuration. This interactive component, as well as some of the other features detailed here such as the noise of pages turning or pages turning at a click of a mouse, does not appear to add anything to the meaning of the overall multimedia exhibitions and their artistic intent.[31] Such overall features in Clavel's websites are a deferential nod to her literary and multimedia postmodern aesthetics: whilst her work seeks to be intellectually challenging in terms of foregrounding the conceptual and creative thought-processes behind it, so too is it marked by its experimental hedonism. Indeed, the playful element is geared towards inviting interactivity by allowing the user to intervene both as a fun pastime but also to (de) construct meaning.

Even though Clavel's websites are not strictly forms of hyperfiction, her online creations have a number of features common with the print-medium and online hyperfictions of other writers. In Latin America, hyperfictions have existed even prior to the technological age of the World Wide Web. The Argentine writers Jorge Luis Borges and Julio Cortázar are perceived as the 'avatars of cyberliterature' both globally and in Latin America.[32] In the cyberculture age, Latin American hyperfiction writers include Blas Valdez and Doménico Chiappe. Cortázar's novel *Rayuela* (1963), considered as the prototype of the hypertext, is characterized by playfulness and improvization and is aimed at reader participation in the construction of meaning, characteristics which define Clavel's literary and multimedia endeavour.[33] The ability of the reader of Cortázar to skip randomly from one section to another in *Rayuela* pre-empts the 'structure' of hypertext which:

> challenges two key ordering principles in the logic of print and its theories: firstly, the (hierarchical) status of main text to note, forward, title or index is removed; secondly, the (authoritative) order of reading the page and manipulating what comes where in textual reception, is subverted. (Orr, *Intertextuality: Debates*, p. 50)

On both the *Cuerpo náufrago* and *Las Violetas* websites the home page setup seems to adhere to these ordering principles given that they contain a table of contents, thus encouraging a systematic reading. Yet here the act of reading and browsing is 'multilinear rather than linear' (Viegas, pp. 210 & 212). The user of both websites can read and use these sites as they see fit, abandon, or come back to them or physically recombine elements, as evidenced in the *La Violetas* doll reconfiguration game. Hypertext then is liberating for the dynamic reader. By selecting 'individualized paths', the reader can create temporal sequences of his or her own or change course when he or she chooses.[34] This notion of different reading paths which are propelled by interconnected groups of information items such as texts or images concurs with Roland Barthes's definition of the ideal text (1970) and later reinforced by Pierre Lévy (1993).[35]

The various levels of user and author participation on Clavel's websites serve to defy the traditional perception of cultural production as the artistic product of one single individual, which is what gives it its 'aura'. The websites are examples of popular culture or communal 'art' form inciting group intervention. Given the complexity of setting up the websites with their multimedia elements, it has involved a variety of disciplines and therefore the intervention of various 'authors', such as IT specialists and graphic designers.[36] The creation of the *Cuerpo náufrago* website represents a collective process in which both author(s) and readers intervene. Here everyone is (or can be) both author and reader. Whilst the reflective comments on *Cuerpo náufrago* as novel and multimedia event have been written by Clavel, users are invited to contribute by sending their views on the author's novel by email, all of which work to provide multilayered understandings. Clavel's website also becomes an example of the 'writerly' text which — to draw from Landow's theories on hypertext — 'blurs the boundaries between reader and writer and therefore instantiates another quality of Barthes's ideal text' (*Barthes and the Writerly Text*). When the user goes to the 'Reseñas y comentarios' sub-page on the *Cuerpo náufrago* website there are emails written by contributors. They appear to be set up in discussion group format aimed at fomenting a community around a common thread in order to engage in dialogue with Clavel. However, it becomes apparent that the emails have been sent to her private email address and have been simply cut and pasted onto the website. Thus, even as this website appears to be facilitating the path to participation, the site 'remains an object of static text with no opportunity for interactivity'.[37] Another problem that emerges with the email contribution on the *Cuerpo náufrago* website is the fact that it is limited to no more than three emails, thus raising issues of authorial intent. Even though Clavel's email address is visible in the sender field at the top of the pasted emails and thus could be seen as encouraging any user to contact her, the three emails inserted into the webpage suggest a premeditated selection of material, therefore challenging the idea of user inclusivity. None of the three senders — Cristina Peri Rossi, writer and essayist, José Carvajal, essayist, writer, and director of LIBRUSA, and Álvaro Enrigue, writer and literary critic — falls into the category of the casual reader. They correspond more to Riffaterre's model of the 'erudite' reader (Riffaterre cited in Orr, *Intertextuality: Debates*, p. 39). These emails point perhaps to the idea that Clavel does after all have an ideal reader in mind for her own work and thus is using these emails as springboards to attract a certain type of critical reader. They may also have a bearing on Clavel's anxieties relating to issues of literary legitimacy. All three contributors provide glowing comments on *Cuerpo náufrago,* as indeed do all the literary reviews which are made available on the website. The email contributors, the critics, as well as the newspapers where their reviews have been published, including *La Jornada* and *El Universal*, are highly esteemed and so all these consecrated intertextual sources contribute to establishing Clavel's standing as a respected writer of fiction.

Mural and Urban Space Intervention

To coincide with the book launch of *Cuerpo náufrago* Clavel organized the *Cuerpo náufrago proyecto multimedia* event, part of which was held in the Centro Cultural de España-México in Mexico City between 21 September and 30 October 2005. The event was heavily publicized in a number of established Mexican newspapers including *El Universal*, on the *Cuerpo náufrago* website, and in flyers. The most outstanding element of the marketing campaign was the mural and urban space intervention entitled *UrbEspectaculArt: Intervención pública. La censura también es fuente*, which involved 300 posters being placed on Eumex bus stop billboards in Mexico City's most prominent streets. A 10 x 6.5 metre canvas was also plastered over the exterior wall of the FONCA building which is located in the Zona Rosa district, a location which is of great significance in terms of issues relating to the commercialization of the (female) body, sexuality, gender, and prohibition, as will be discussed further on. Both posters and canvas feature the Ingresian semi-nude with the ribbon wrapped around the private parts. Whereas the poster image is accompanied by the words 'La identidad comienza con el deseo' [identity starts with desire], the words 'Quién decretó la prohibición? La identidad comienza con el deseo' [Who made prohibition law? Identity starts with desire] can be read on the canvas. With a high frequency of passers-by, these were prime locations for the media coverage of the event and such images were no doubt attention-grabbing. At the heart of Clavel's multimedia enterprise is a transgressive intent. Indeed, both the posters and the canvas have features characteristically used in shock advertisements to get spectator attention, including 'distinctiveness', 'ambiguity', and 'transgression of norms and taboos'.[38] An advertisement can elicit a sense of ambiguity in the way that it 'leaves room for various interpretations, if not of its content, at least of the intentions of the advertiser' (Vézina and Paul, p. 180). Clavel's urinal appears to have caused surprise in passers-by and whilst for some it was unclear what the actual object was, its very ambiguity seemed to ignite curiosity in others.[39] The '¿Quién decretó la prohibición?' on the ribbon also raises interpretative uncertainty and it is because of its rhetorical character that the onus to unravel meaning is placed on passers-by. Thus prohibition is defined in relation to the spectator. The ribbon with its 'Zona de Riesgo'/'Prohibido Pasar' establishes both a visual and metaphorical boundary between the spectator and sexual desire, the sanctioned and the unsanctioned. Prompted to think about the way in which 'La identidad comienza con el deseo', the spectator is left to ponder over where he or she places him- or herself in relation to Mexico's historical culture of censorship and self-censoring in the context of traditional heteronormative gender roles and forms of desire. Serving as a visual and textual threshold inviting us to cross from the outside world into the liminal zone of the multimedia exhibit, the posters and canvas will thus either tempt or dissuade passers-by, depending on their personal moral frameworks.

Clavel's Ingresian semi-nude was driven by an artistic and contestatory, rather than the purely commercial, impetus typical of many high-street advertisements. It was aimed, in part at least, at questioning contemporary media culture's promotion of insatiable consumption. Although *La censura también es fuente* appeals to the senses through its erotic content, it nevertheless works to contest commercial advertising sensory overload. The digitally imposed urinal parodies the manner in which the feminization of consumer culture has led to a surge in popularity of sensory communication in the media in which women, sex, and the senses are unproblematically conflated. Even as the Ingresian semi-nude may sexually arouse in the way that some contemporary sensory advertising does, so too does it seek to engage passers-by cognitively through intrigue and provocation, in order to think about broader questions relating to the overpowering effects of commercial advertising and in particular to proscriptive identity and gender roles. This artistic-intellectual purpose is underpinned on the *Cuerpo náufrago* website (<http://www.cuerponaufrago.com/fachada.htm>) on which the text is interspersed with sentences from the novel itself:

> En una ciudad como la nuestra, asolada por la prosa de la violencia visual cotidiana [...] *La censura también es fuente* intenta convertirse en un manantial de instantes de arte y perplejidad reflexiva en torno a las interrogantes: ¿Quién decreta la prohibición y el comportamiento de los cuerpos? ¿La identidad empieza por lo que vemos? [...] la identidad comienza por lo que deseamos [...] somos cuerpos encarcelados por nuestras mentes, y sólo cuando el deseo se abre paso, florecemos.
>
> [In a city like ours, ravaged by the language of quotidian visual violence [...] *La censura también es fuente* seeks to become a spring of various instances of art and complex reflexions on various questions: Who decreed prohibition and the behaviour of the body? Does identity arise out of what we see? [...] Does it arise from our desires [...] we are bodies which are trapped by our minds, and it is only when desire gives way, that we flourish.]

Mexican art critic José Manuel Springer notes that Clavel's mural and urban space intervention represents a public transgression in the way that it criticizes the manner in which media culture, as a product of late capitalism, simulates a schizoid experience.[40] *La censura también es fuente* probes passers-by to reflect on the links between the (semi-) explicit body and how desire is structured according to the logic of capitalism and the dominant sociopolitical ideology. Whilst Clavel's image proposes that desire is what defines one's identity, so too does it foreground critically the way in which that same desire, like a commodity, can be produced. Indeed, 'desire must appear unmarked, as "human nature". But, like commodities themselves, it is nature designed, packaged, and sold [...] where it is also marked for gender as if by some great accident of God: desire is masculinised; the desired, feminized'.[41] Late capitalism's instituting of desire as insatiable and endorsing endless accumulation has meant that the female body has become representative of the notion of impossibility: she is permanently out of reach and embodies that which can never be quite acquired (Schneider, pp. 5–6). Insatiable desire and paradigmatic lack are literally scripted across the Ingresian semi-nude as reinforced in the flirtatious words written on the ribbon 'Zona de Riesgo'/'Prohibido Pasar'. Whilst the first words keep us wanting that which is unknown, but desirable, the latter suggests the impossibility of attainment, thus reinforcing the mechanisms of capitalism.

The transgressive thrust of the Ingresian semi-nude becomes apparent on the *Cuerpo náufrago* website. Clavel's street artwork is placed in the context of the recent history of public art interventions and specifically those by internationally renowned artists Cuevas, Miralda, and Christo. The writer stresses the view that public intervention art is the most transgressive of all visual art forms. The appropriation of public spaces takes art out of traditional spaces such as museums and thus becomes 'un acto público-político, en la medida en que los cuerpos y el arte dialogan con los espectadores de manera inmediata' [a public-political act, in the manner in which both body and art are instantaneously in dialogue with the spectators].[42] By linking her work to the contestatory drive of street art, Clavel can be seen to underscore the way in which her multimedia and literary *oeuvre* is characterized by an impetus to breach taboos. The choice of location for the canvas — the Zona Rosa, or red-light district — is also imbued with transgressive intent. On the *Cuerpo náufrago* website the reader is made aware of the uniqueness of Clavel's intervention given that, since José Luis Cuevas's *Efímero* mural in 1967, very few murals have been painted in that area of Mexico City. The canvas's location in the Zona Rosa is particularly interesting, as the website emphasizes:

> El asunto de los géneros y la prohibición de los cuerpos [...] se potencializa al ubicarse en el espacio de un inmueble de la afamada Zona Rosa, donde a la fecha se verifica el cruce de discursos comerciales en torno a la erotización y el cuerpo como espectáculo.
>
> [the topic of gender and the prohibition of the body [...] is particularly enhanced given [its] location in a building in the famous Zona Rosa, where to date the crossing of commercial discourses relating to erotization and the body as spectacle become apparent]

This is an area where the commercialization of the (female) body is rife in the form of media advertisements and sex industry services. Even as the Zona Rosa 'connotes a permissive space',[43] and thus the possibility of flexible sexual identities and gender roles, sexist and dichotomized heterosexual gender roles feature heavily in mainstream media advertisements which litter the high streets of the entire city and the nation as a whole.[44] Feminist critics examining media representations of women have observed that female sexuality is frequently portrayed within the boundaries of two contrasting categories: one embodying woman as nurturing, and asexual, and the other as unprincipled and erotic.[45] These contrasting depictions of women can be compared to the Guadalupe and Malinche figures, both widely exploited in Mexican popular media from commercial advertising to cinema. These disparate views of women take on an added dimension in urban spaces whereby 'Woman is present in cities as temptress, as whore, as fallen woman [...] but also as virtuous womanhood'.[46] The intertwining of city space and the female body is reinforced in the Ingresian semi-nude canvas and its location, and functions to question dichotomized virgin-whore gender roles. Improper spaces (the Zona Rosa) become embroiled with woman who is presented as indecent or illicit as suggested in the words 'Zona de Riesgo', yet the woman's demure gaze, the veiling of her body, and the words 'Prohibido Pasar' all connote the idea of woman as chaste. The ribbon with its proscriptive wording similarly denotes the criminalization of the female body. Interestingly, by conflating the virgin-whore dyad, Clavel can be seen to confuse gender roles in order to propose that identity construction should not work according to unbending classifactory systems, but instead that 'La identidad comienza con el deseo'. Thus Clavel opens up possibilities not only for women, but also for men, and in particular for those forbidden non-heteronormative sexual identities which the Zona Rosa as queer space celebrates.[47] So, even as the Ingresian semi-nude canvas appears to bolster traditional binary constructs, image, text, and location work in synchrony to contest notions of fixed (sexual) identity and to assert the idea of sexuality and desire as the primary drivers of identity.

To coincide with the launch of the *Proyecto multimedia* the canvas was unveiled at noon to the public. Revealing the semi-nude at a time when the streets were at their busiest was an eye-grabbing publicity stunt to captivate the attention of passers-by. It also affirmed the unveiling as a self-conscious performative gesture. Given that a fundamental aspect of carnival is parody aimed at officialdom, the unveiling of the semi-nude functions as a humorous carnivalesque riposte to official ritual.[48] The visceral works to mock the ritual gesture of unveiling 'great' art and the solemnity which frequently surrounds such events, as well as, in a deferential nod to Duchamp, the cult value of art which such symbolic gestures reinforce. The revealing of the canvas similarly serves to provoke, both by startling passers-by with the image's eroticism and voyeurism and by provoking thought about matters relating to gender performativity and construction. The unveiling of the Ingresian semi-nude suggests erotic play in the form of striptease, an apposite description given that the Zona Rosa, as a place which revels in displaying 'el cuerpo como espectáculo' [body as spectacle] (<http://www.cuerdonaufrago.com/fachada.htm>), is renowned for its striptease bars in which not only women but also men, drag queens, and transgender people perform. Barthes notes that striptease is premised on incongruity:

> Woman is desexualized at the very moment when she is stripped naked [...] It is only the time taken in shedding clothes which makes voyeurs of the public [...] There will therefore be in striptease a whole series of coverings placed upon the body of the woman in proportion as she pretends to strip it bare [...] all aim at establishing the woman right from the start as an object in disguise. The end of the striptease is then no longer to drag into the light a hidden depth, but to signify, through the shedding of an incongruous and artificial clothing, nakedness as a natural vesture of woman, which amounts in the end to regaining a perfectly chaste state of the flesh.[49]

When the canvas was revealed, it was not the stripped naked Ingresian nymph but a female nude enveloped with a ribbon which bystanders were greeted with. Whereas Ingres intended to present his nymph as a desexualized virgin, it is paradoxically the semi-nakedness of *La censura también es fuente* which eroticizes the female. To draw from Freud, sexual curiosity is aroused and maintained by the visual concealment of the body since the 'covering of the body, which keeps abreast with civilization, continuously arouses sexual curiosity and serves to supplement the sexual object by uncovering the hidden parts'.[50] The revealing of the canvas only to reveal another layer which can be removed is significant as it functions as a form of erotic play which is intrinsic to striptease and emphasizes above all the *tease* in striptease. Indeed:

> the premise of the act is to imply what both the performer and the spectator know will never come — sexual fruition and exposure. A stripper's performance is all a tease. Wearing provocative clothing, or none at all, the stripper tantalizes her audience, implicitly promising a more satisfying degree of intimacy to come, which never arrives. (Schweitzer, p. 68)

The semi-nude's ribbon is reminiscent of the skimpy clothing a stripper wears and 'sexy clothing, which *implies* nudity, becomes more erotic than nudity itself' (Schweitzer, p. 68). Barthes mentions how the erotic is not so much about nakedness itself but rather about those zones where the clothes part and glimpses of the nude body are revealed and where 'knowing and unknowing begins'.[51] *La censura también es fuente* implies a knowing in the sense that, given that the semi-nude is visibly that of a female, most bystanders would most likely assume that the private parts hidden behind the ribbon are those of a woman. Yet so too does *La censura también es fuente* entail an unknowing. Given the queering of the Ingresian nude with its digitally imposed urinal, the Duchampian male-female urinal concept serves to put forward to passers-by the idea that they should not necessarily judge what they see based on appearance. Although the semi-nude may look like a woman, there is no reason why the concealed areas are of necessity occluding those attributes which are 'naturally' female. To bolster this perspective, the semi-nude can be intertextually linked to the drag-transsexual stripper in the novel *Cuerpo náufrago* (pp. 116–18). As we mentioned in Chapter 3, the performer's physique suggests an ambiguous blurring of male and female physical traits. Whilst she possesses feminine attributes manifested in her (notwithstanding surgically constructed) breasts and performance of femininity, his masculinity is implied in particular in his attempt to conceal his genitals from the audience. This intertextual allusion foregrounds the intention of the canvas which proposes that givens such as (sexual) identity are susceptible to unknowability and flux which the words 'Zona de Riesgo' powerfully connote. The unveiling of the semi-nude thus becomes a performative act to highlight the artifice of gender, whilst the semi-nude itself serves to propose that what ultimately establishes one's 'true' sexual selfhood and sense of identity are not exterior markers of identity (the sexed body, gender, clothes), but instead human desire and emotion, as captured in the sentence 'La identidad comienza con el deseo'.

The Multimedia Exhibition

The multimedia exhibition was displayed in a relatively small space, on the mezzanine. The first feature which visitors encountered as they came up the stairs were two pages from the *Cuerpo náufrago* novel displayed on a 1.80 x 1.10 metre panel and to the left there was a poster which included the Ingresian semi-nude and a blurb detailing the different parts of the multimedia project. To the right of the panel a computer kiosk had been set up from which visitors were able to browse the *Cuerpo náufrago* website. Above the panel there was a yellow clothes line which went along the entire wall, which was painted half in red and half in black, and continued onto the next wall, painted entirely in black. Fifty images of different types of urinals had been attached to the clothes line with wooden pegs. Against the black walls a set of photo-developing trays had been placed on a row of tables. The intention here was to give visitors the impression of being in a dark room. Above the trays featured Duchamp's celebrated saying 'No se tiene más que: por hembra al urinario y de eso vivimos' [one only has: for *female* the public urinal and one lives by it] and the words 'La identidad comienza con el deseo'. The opposite wall, painted entirely in red, had seven photographs, each 1m 20 x 70 cm and each of which was separated with toilet partitions. The final component of the exhibition was a performance which was initially performed live on the day of the book launch and then recorded onto a video which was projected onto a white wall. The fact that visitors were first greeted with the excerpts from the novel was intentional. Firstly, the two pages of the novel (pp. 50–51) displayed on the panel draw the visitor's attention to the central themes discussed both in the novel and the overall multimedia exhibition, such as the Duchampian notion of urinals as having erotic as well as male and female qualities, as well as Antón/ia's interstial gender. Secondly, the blurb to the left of the panel providing detail of the multimedia project was preceded by the statement that the novel 'is the origin of the project', and so established *Cuerpo náufrago* as a literary endeavour foremost. At the same time, the visitor's attention was constantly drawn to the inexorable links between the novel and the visual. The photographs were exhibited alongside fragments taken from Clavel's text and quotations from Marcel Duchamp on the fetishistic pleasure of the urinal. The photographic exhibition was based on the same collection of photographs of urinals found in *Cuerpo náufrago* as well as other photographs which do not feature in the text. Whilst the first sentence of the blurb on the panel stresses the notion of single authorship, the second emphasizes the idea of multi-authorship, thus throwing an interesting light onto the construction of the text and the multimedia exhibition. The photographs were taken by Clavel herself or by an array of friends, writers, artists, and professional photographers, including Érika Araiza and Mauricio Carrera. Consequently the text's construction, like the entire multimedia project, embodies cooperative practice.

The physical location of the text, photographs, and overall multimedia set-up also works to defy non-traditional modes of consumption of literary texts. Whilst *Cuerpo náufrago* mocks the literary form, it is nevertheless primarily to be read as a literary text which incorporates other media. The multimedia exhibition was aimed at integrating various disciplines to encourage new ways of conceptualizing the act of reading literature even as it foregrounds literariness. Thus the act of reading literature has been changed 'from a physically passive, solitary practice to a more active and shared experience'.[52] Whereas the reading of *Cuerpo náufrago* involves reader interaction at a visual-metaphoric level, the multimedia exhibitions of both *Cuerpo náufrago* and *Las Violetas* encouraged textual reading in conjunction with visual and physical participation. To make sense of the websites, (video) performances, images, art installations, and Clavel's literary works and their interrelationship, visitors were encouraged to move around the floor space by going backwards and forwards between the various (audio) visual and textual components of the multimedia exhibitions to (de)construct meaning(s) in order to reflect upon the main issues being raised in relation to, in the case of *Cuerpo náufrago*, urinals, desire, fetishism, and gender, and, in the case of *Las Violetas*, dolls, desire, fetishism, and gender. Both the *Cuerpo náufrago* and *Las Violetas* multimedia exhibitions have thus much in common with contemporary art installation aesthetics. Installation art is multivalent in character whereby the artist 'has total command of a space and might use any artistic means, including architecture, music, dance, and theatre, along with the visual arts, to create a synesthetic environment'.[53] The multivalent quality of the *Cuerpo náufrago* and *Las Violetas* multimedia projects, and their drive to engage audiences via quotidian-type experiences, queers traditional notions of high art.[54] As Rosenthal notes in relation to installation art:

> Because there is no frame separating this art from its viewing context, the work and the space having melded together into an approximation of a life experience, the sphere of art has effectively been compromised, even democratized [...] Installation art threatens to become the predominant mode of expression for the modern world [...] with its global character, desire for sensory overload, and demand for non-elitist practices. (*Understanding Installation Art*, p. 25)

In both multimedia projects, the focus on one individual work is abandoned 'in favor of a multiplicity of objects, images and experiences' (Rosenthal, p. 25). The lifelike experiences which the exhibitions seek to convey are achieved via two vital components of art installation, that is, space and time (Rosenthal, p. 27). The visitor in many respects becomes a kind of voyeur-participant moving around the bizarre world of male public toilets — like Antonia from *Cuerpo náufrago* — or dolls in the *Las Violetas* exhibition, and is thus encouraged to 'investigate the work of art much as he or she might explore some phenomenon in life, making one's way though actual space and time in order to gain knowledge' (Rosenthal, p. 27). In art installation the emphasis on time and space means that:

> Just as life consists of one perception followed by another, each fleeting, non-linear moment, an installation courts the same dense, ephemeral experience. Whereas painting and sculpture freeze time, installation abhors such an effect. The viewer is in the present, experiencing temporal flow and spatial awareness [...] life pervades this form of art. (Rosenthal, p. 27)

What also becomes apparent in both of Clavel's exhibitions is that 'the exalted status of art is undercut by the quotidian-type of experience — with its sights, smells and generally ephemeral character' which is key to installation as a whole (Rosenthal, p. 25). The worldly character of the *Cuerpo náufrago* and *Las Violetas* multimedia

FIG. 5.2. *Teseo/Deseo y el mingitauro en su laberinto.* Installation at Centro Cultural de España. 7 × 1.80 m. Concept: Ana Clavel. Photo: Ana Clavel. Courtesy of Ana Clavel

exhibitions is evinced in their focus on the visceral (desire, sex, and bodily functions) and the utilitarian (urinals and dolls). The installations also encourage the viewer's interaction with the setting where 'both the eye and the body became involved: physical and sensory recognitions/ interactions added to the viewer's awareness of the space and approached the viewer to experiences common to one's everyday emotions and experiences of life' (Rosenthal, p. 77). Sound, sight, and touch provided a synesthetic experience. Whereas music was being emitted from the *Cuerpo náufrago* video-performance, in the *Las Violetas* exhibition Arturo Buitrón's doll had loudspeakers inserted in it from which visitors could hear excerpts of the novella being read by Clavel. The synesthetic was extended to the olfactory in the *Las Violetas* exhibition given that Clavel had inserted in one doll an air freshener, and so every time visitors walked by it they could smell the scent of roses. Rocío Caballero's doll *Virginia Virginal* had a vagina made into the form of a miniature drawer which could be pulled out by visitors and from which potpourri wafted a faint scent of flowers. While some of the objects on display in both multimedia exhibitions afforded verbal-audio-visual stimulus such as the video-performances, others offered simultaneously physical interactive engagement such as the computer kiosks in which the viewer becomes a participant by activating and browsing the websites. In the *Las Violetas* exhibition the public could handle Caballero's doll as it had not only the aforementioned drawer, but also a wind-up mechanism on its back which emitted music.

Photography Installation: *Teseo/Deseo y el mingitauro en su laberinto*

The photographic art installation entitled *Teseo/Deseo y el mingitauro en su laberinto* in the *Cuerpo náufrago* exhibition also encouraged physical interaction between visitors and the art object on display. Visitors could stand in front of the photographs of urinals simulating the (male) standing urination posture whilst the wooden perpendicular dividers provided them with a sense of being bodily in a public toilet (figure 5.2).

Via its confusion of binaries such as public/private, male/female, proper/improper, the installation encouraged visitors to reflect on the way in which public spaces often promote gender binaries and specific performances of gender. Gender-segregated public conveniences and separate stalls work as a form of policing sexual identity and to ensure 'proper relations' either between men and women or between people of the same sex. The installation was in appearance designed uniquely for male users and so inviting only the male visitors to 'use' the urinals. Yet given the very public location of the installation, female visitors were equally invited to 'use' these facilities. Thus the installation purposefully confuses the gender dichotomies and segregation which public conveniences sustain.

Clavel reported to me in an informal conversation that visitors, whether female or male, often laughed in embarrassment when standing in front of the stalls. This response could be seen as a knee-jerk reaction to rules of social behaviour which deem certain acts, such as urination, as improper in public spaces. The fact that 'users' were being observed by others whilst 'urinating' may well have made them feel embarrassed as if they had been caught in the act of doing the 'unlawful' deed which should be done in private. By being located in an open space and thus blurring the boundaries between private and public, the installation functions to mock the absurdity of the taboo of urination and defecation which some Western and non-Western countries uphold. Bringing visitors together in an open space powerfully reinforces the idea that we all share this excretory human function despite it being publicly shunned. The fact that female visitors expressed feeling self-conscious could be explained in relation to the awkward feelings people sometimes have when they accidently choose the wrong toilet, which exposes the prevalent endorsement of the need for stable correlations between gender and sex. Such an attitude aligns these female visitors in many ways with Antonia as a 'contrabandista', in which she smuggles herself into a space officially assigned male. The urinals in the installation appear to promote the correct performance of toilet etiquette, specifically the standing position males are supposed to assume. This behaviour is purposely encouraged by the tags attached to the seven photographs on which the words 'Firme Aquí. R. MUTT' [Sign Here. R. MUTT] can be read (figure 5.2).[55] In the same interview, Clavel clarified to me that this was a joke relating to how when men 'van a los baños públicos usan la expresión: "Voy a firmar", para dar a entender que van a orinar' [go to public toilets they use the expression 'I'm going to sign' as a way of explaining that they are going to urinate]. She also explained that 'R. MUTT' was also meant as a light-hearted intertextual reference to Duchamp's fictitious signatory whose name appears on *Fountain*. It thus functions as a way of parodying the idea of single authorship typically attributed to the work of art, since multiple urinators can intervene with their own particular 'authorial' mark. My inability to 'get' the joke perhaps underpins that as a female I, along with some of the female visitors at the exhibition who might not have 'got' the joke either, was excluded from the space the installation appeared to be promoting for male 'users' only and who most probably would have understood the gag. However, the pamphlet accompanying the exhibition explains that the photographs of urinals exemplify 'the notion of a Western virility which takes pride in urinating in an upright position', and so the visitors who read this explanatory note as they looked at, and interacted with, the art installation were thus encouraged to ponder notions of 'doing gender' and how discourses of gender are often discriminatory. By foregrounding the 'Firme Aquí' as a male-only joke, its sheer exclusivity underscores the manner in which existing toilet arrangements, which are designed to segregate male from female, serve to promote, as discussed previously, unequal (Western) toilet practices which indoctrinate the view that the superior standing position is a uniquely male preserve, whilst the subordinate squatting position is uniquely female. Yet by having female visitors simulating the male urination position and thus feminizing male toilet practices, the installation rebuts notions about what is 'proper' feminine behaviour and encourages thought on the principles of toilet protocol.

The blurring between the male and the female is also suggested in the installation's images. Of the seven photographs on display, Paul Alarcón's *El mingitorio es el origen del mundo* (after Courbet) best captures this fusion. The image is of a white urinal mounted onto a white tiled wall which in places is splattered with grime. Clavel asked Alarcón to digitally impose the pubic area of a woman in the concave recess. The image is a replica of Courbet's *L'Origine du monde* nude. Amidst the black pubic hair the pudendal slit reveals shiny female genitalia from which digitally imposed yellow fluid emanates (figure 5.3). Clavel explains that with this image she sought to:

> Evidenciar la sexualización del mingitorio al imponer la imagen de Courbet en su interior, pero fue idea de Alarcón hacer que la vagina manara orina. Con una intención lúdica de homenaje a Courbet, yo decidí titularlo entonces *El mingitorio es el origen del mundo*.[56]
>
> [To give emphasis to the sexualization of the urinal by superimposing the image of Courbet in its interior, but it was Alarcón's idea to make the vagina excrete urine. It was with a playful intention to pay homage to Courbet, that I decided to give the image the title of *The Urinal is the Origin of the World*]

The intention is also to draw visitors' attention to the urinal as fetish object by replicating the Duchampian concept of the male-female urinal. Duchamp's 'no se tiene más que por hembra al urinario y de eso vivimos' splayed on the black wall of the exhibition acts as a textual aid to help visitors unravel the significance of Alarcón's blurring of the male urinal with the female form. As suggested earlier, for many Duchamp's conception may be complicated to grasp and so with the help of digital technology and intermediality, Alarcón's digital re-enactment of the Duchampian concept of the male-female urinal explicates visually what textually is not achieved as successfully. However, text, digital photography, painting, and

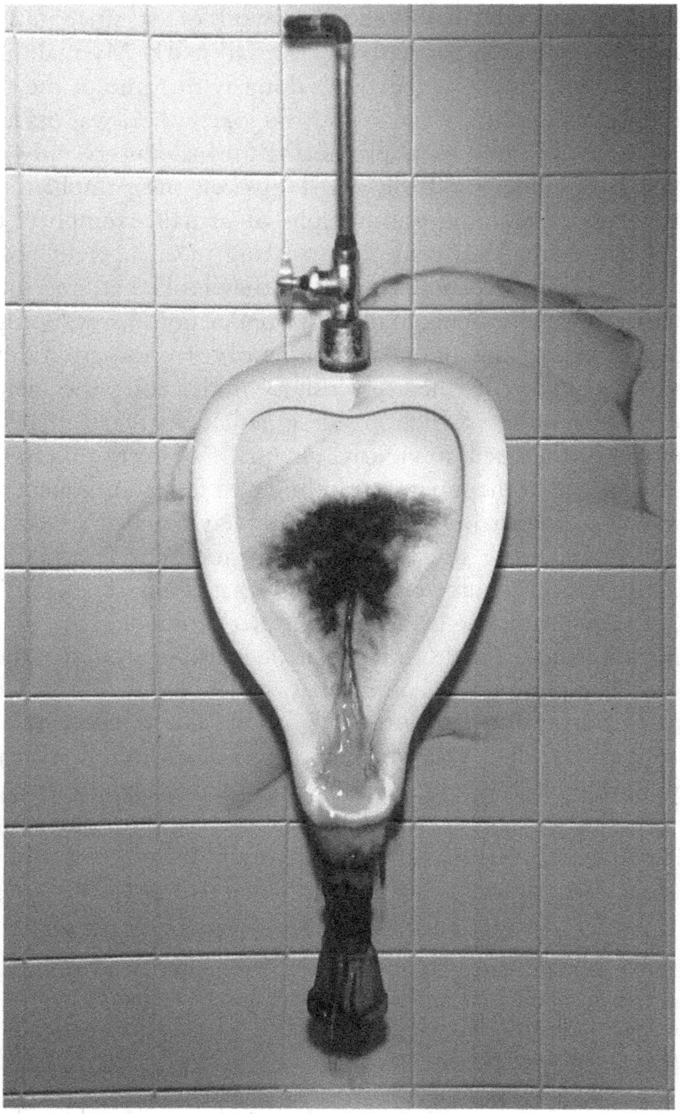

FIG. 5.3. *La censura también es fuente.*
Digital image. Ana Clavel and Paul Alarcón. Courtesy of Ana Clavel

art installation complement each other intermedially to produce variegated interpretations.

Visitor-participant responses to Alarcón's digitally altered image epitomize Kristevan abjection which produces a sense of horror and fascination at once. According to Clavel, visitors thought that Alarcón's image was powerful yet shocking in particular because of the yellow urine spurting out of the vaginal area.[57] Clavel was herself taken aback by Alarcón's idea of the simulated urine stream and mentioned to me that with the Ingresian semi-nude it would never have been her intention to replace the water emanating from the urinal with yellow urine, as this would have been too 'fuerte' [hardcore]. Nevertheless the urine jet, though visually grotesque, seems apt given that Alarcón is paying homage to the low brow humour implicit in the title of Duchamp's *Fountain*, which alludes to urine and the male act of urination. Alarcón's urinating female could be seen as an obsequious acknowledgement of the extensive history of what is popularly known as 'piss' art, including that of Duchamp, Carlos Luna, Andy Warhol, Yoshua Okón, and Helen Chadwick, which has been produced with the intention of flouting moral, social, and artistic conventions. For Chapman, images of urination in art can function 'as a sign of abjection, liberation, political resistance, eroticism [...] and gender difference'.[58] Via digital manipulation Alarcón's urination piece is contestatory. Both the title of Alarcón's work and the artwork itself teasingly play upon the title of Courbet's *L'Origine du monde* by suggesting that the source of male creativity is not located uniquely in the female, as Courbet's work proposes, but rather too in the male. Alarcón envisages male urination as a metaphor for the creative process and by inference the penis becomes the tool to create art. This recalls a passage in *Cuerpo náufrago* when Antonia is urinating and the act is compared to that of painting (p. 27). Paradoxically, Alarcón's depiction of a urinating female simultaneously parodies the idea of urination as 'a sign of maleness' (Chapman, 'Piss Art') and emblematic of artistic imagination as exclusively male. The urinating female defies the idea of women as objects and sources of male creativity, and proposes instead the view of women as subjects in their own right and as active agents of creativity. This could perhaps be interpreted as Alarcón's recognition, albeit in an unusual fashion, of Clavel's ingenuity and her role as architect of the overall literary and multimedia endeavour. Even as Alarcón appears to be mocking Courbet's work for its apparent depiction of woman as object of male pleasure, so too is the ambiguous portrayal of woman as oscillating between passive object and active subject a recognition of Courbet's own vacillating depiction of the female nude. As suggested in the previous chapter, even as Courbet's nude is reduced to her sexual parts, so too have critics noted that her unconstrained bearing in fact suggests post-coital enjoyment and thus a woman who is in full control of her own sexuality.

Flouting that which is 'proper' is seen in the manner in which the excreting urine, like the grime on the wall, abhors as it is abject 'matter out of place'.[59] Even though the correlation between urine and the urinal should be unproblematic, the depiction of a female urinating into a urinal shocks because it challenges the manner in which toilets are designed with their partitions to occlude people from seeing each other's private parts and waste. Genitalia and urine are abject because they contest inner and outer bodily boundaries. The splayed-legged 'pissing' woman disturbs because she defies the notion of contained femininity in line with Ingres's nymph and toilet protocols which, as mentioned previously, dictate that a woman crouch submissively when urinating. Female urination is similarly troubling for viewers because of its implied subtext of voyeurism and eroticism. The erotic is unequivocal given the intertextual allusions to Duchamp's male-female urinal idea and intermedially via the digitally imposed image of Courbet's nude. Clavel notes that 'la orina que mana de la vagina sugiere el famoso "orgasmo o eyaculación femenino"' [urine which emanates from the vagina suggests the famous phrase 'orgasm or female ejaculation'].[60] Furthermore, as viewers stand in the confined stalls, it is almost as if they are witnessing a peep show in which urination becomes an erotic fetishied act. The implied urophilia (popularly termed 'golden shower') perturbs because it is linked to 'improper' forms of sexual practice. The digitally imposed urine is spilling not only into the urinal but also overflowing it, dripping down the waste-pipe towards the floor. But the floor in the image has been cut out of the frame and, given the digitally realistic texturedness of the oozing fluid, it is almost as if the fluid were overflowing onto the actual floor of the exhibition where the visitors are standing. The spilling of fictive and artistic abjectness into the real world, not only reinforces the threat of the abject to boundaries between inner and outer, but moreover implicates the viewer standing between the stalls as voyeur and even as partaker in the unfolding illicit sex act. Thus, in uromasochistic fashion, the visitor-participant is being urinated on by the 'pissing' female. One final point to consider here is intention, that is, who the female is targeting with her urine stream. The overall installation appears to be intended for the male 'user' particularly because the female vagina is set up for penile penetration and the 'golden shower' is uniquely aimed at and for the pleasure of heterosexual men. Yet the fact that all visitors, whether male or female, heterosexual or not, were invited to interact with the art installation, both bolsters and queers this heteronormative reading. Thus the urinating woman not only solicits male heterosexual visual-physical enjoyment but also encourages other gazes and diverse spectator positions in relation to desire. The title of the installation *Teseo/Deseo y el mingitauro en su laberinto* with its reference to the 'mingitauro' urinal, which features both in Clavel's novel and in one of the seven images of the installation, is significant in this respect. The title of course is alluding to a passage in the novel in which Antonia compares her transgender self to the mythological Minotaur. The reference to the 'mingitauro' is significant as its shape-shifting fusion of the female, the male, animal, and urinal embodies Antonia's synthesis of genders and desires. *Cuerpo náufrago*, as literary and multimedia intervention, represents a site in which 'Teseo que le jos de matar a su Mingitauro, se deja seducir e indagar en sus propios laberintos' [Theseus, who, instead of killing his Minotaur, lets himself be seduced and to explore his personal labyrinths] (exhibition pamphlet), whereby the labyrinths of desire encourage Antonia, and indeed the visitors of the exhibition, to explore uninhibitedly the variegated paths of sexual desires.

(Video) Performance: *Somos cuerpos encarcelados por nuestras mentes*

Somos cuerpos encarcelados por nuestras mentes was originally presented as a live performance that took place in the auditorium in the Centro Cultural de España-México on the day of the book launch which was attended by around 300 visitors. The narrative of the performance (conceptualized by Clavel) is simple: a woman (performed by dancer Karol Jiménez) walks into some public conveniences and is met with a sculptural urinal which transforms into a man (dancer Isaac Hermosillo) and both woman and the urinal-man perform simulated sex acts. At the back of the stage on which the dancers are performing, images of urinals which feature in Clavel's novel and multimedia art exhibition, quotations from the novel, and Duchamp's words 'no se tiene más que: por hembra al urinario y de eso vivimos' are projected onto a screen at different points.[61] The performance is also accompanied by three songs from PJ Harvey's album *Is this Desire?* (1998) entitled 'Angeline', 'The Wind', and 'A Perfect Day Elise'.

From the outset we are alerted to the performance's intention which, like the rest of Clavel's literary and multimedia interventions, is driven to queer 'givens' and to challenge sexual, conceptual, and disciplinary boundaries, which this piece achieves via intertextuality and multimediality. Multimediality (Verstraete, p. 10) is reflected in the performance's use of the juxtaposition and interaction, but not fusion in the intermedial sense, of various media. As the female performer strolls into what is set up to look like public conveniences, a sign can be seen on the tiled floor depicting the simple stick-figure form of a woman and a man, both separated by a black line underneath which the word 'BAÑOS' [Toilets] is written. Whereas the male has a simple rectangular silhouette, the female is wearing a skirt. The toilet sign works here as an intertextual allusion to Clavel's novel in which toilet signs are perceived as underscoring the Butlerian concept of 'doing gender'.[62] The dancer drops her coat over the sign occluding the image altogether, a gesture which functions to mock pre-established gender construction. The costs of gender's straitjacket both for men and women is bolstered by the words 'Somos cuerpos encarcelados por nuestras mentes' [we are bodies which are trapped by our minds], taken from *Cuerpo náufrago,* which are projected onto the screen. The projected words which follow: 'Sólo cuando el deseo se abre, florecemos', also to be found in the novel, powerfully reinforce Clavel's adhesion to Hélène Cixous's proposition that personal identity stems inherently from the heart rather than sex: 'La identidad [...] más que en el sexo radica en el corazón humano' [Identity [...] arises more so from the human heart than sexuality].[63] The actress now approaches three urinals, two of them life-sized white porcelain urinals and the other, performed by the male dancer, positioned between the two real urinals. The performer's face is painted in white and he is wearing a white lycra all-in-one suit, simulating the porcelain surface of a urinal. The female dancer approaches one of the real urinals and caresses its borders hinting at the urinal as fetish. She then moves onto the other real urinal where she mimics removing her underwear and pretends to urinate into it in a semi-standing position as she faces towards the spectator. The performer's simulation of urination contravenes the idea that the standing position is reserved uniquely for men and that urinals are receptacles for the exclusive use of men. The female dancer finally moves onto the urinal-man. As she touches 'it' there is no response but soon the inanimate 'object' anthropomorphizes into a male who initially sexually takes control of the female performer as they simulate sex. While they mimic various erotic positions the dancers' bodies become enmeshed, oscillating between rough sex and tender caresses. At one point they appear to be dancing a tango, another clear intertextual reference to *Cuerpo náufrago* in which, as mentioned in Chapter 3, the courting process as an innately aggressive ritual is likened to the tango danced between a man and a woman. For Clavel the tango is the epitome of the workings of heterosexual sexual relations of domination and subordination whereby the social and sexual power of men over women is key. The Argentine 'tango' serves to bolster, in a specifically Mexican socio-cultural context, the view that men are the active *chingones* whereas women are the passive *chingadas*. Such a perspective is reinforced both performatively as the male dancer 'takes' the woman, but also visually as the image of the urinal with the words 'Tod@s somos chingones' written on its white surfaces appears on the screen as well as Clavel's/Alarcón's digitally manipulated *El origen rasurado* (after Courbet's *L'Origine du monde*). However, as our attention is drawn to the ambiguous '@' and to the stagedness of the performance through the enacting of the tango and the choreographed moves, we are also made aware that the performance itself is about the performance of gender and sex roles, which are not static but rather ever-changing. Thus even as the female performer is cast into the *chingada* role, so too is she cast into that of the female sexually active *chingona/castratrice*, whilst the male moves from his active 'fucker' role to that of *chingado*/submissive object of female pleasure. This duality in relation to the female performer is reinforced via the image projected onto the screen of one of the *Kisses* urinals produced by the Dutch company Bathroom Mania!, shaped like a woman's wide-open mouth with the contours of the urinal made to resemble lips from which two sets of teeth can be seen. As discussed in the previous chapter, even as the urinal suggests the view of woman as belittled passive object of the male gaze, so too does the toothed vagina represent Creed's notion of the 'vagina dentata'.[64] As the woman in the performance takes control of her male partner by forcing him aggressively into the positions she wants, this too foregrounds the perception that women can be in control of their, and others', sexuality. Interestingly, Duchamp's 'no se tiene más que: por hembra al urinario y de eso vivimos' is plastered over the *Kisses* image, and so the female performer both buttresses and rewrites the Duchampian concept of woman as fetish object as she moves between object of male desire and active desiring agent whereby the male becomes the object of that desire.

The heterosexual reading that has thus been offered is disturbed throughout the performance as a queer reading concurrently supplements the former. Playing the role of Antón/ia, the fe/male performer's uncertain gender becomes apparent at the start of the piece as she walks onto the stage wearing a skimpy white dress with killer white heels and a black, oversized man's coat. By not choosing to go either into a female or male lavatory as the toilet sign pre-empts, but rather stepping over the middle of it, that is over the line separating the male and female silhouettes, this points to the possibility of a transgender self that materializes towards the end of the performance. As the performance draws to a close, the female performer obliges her male partner rather brutally to sit on the step going up onto the stage. She stands in front of him and forces him to perform fellatio on her whilst, in male fashion, she jerks backwards and forwards roughly until she appears to ejaculate. In the spirit of the Duchampian male-female urinal concept, the ejaculation into the urinal becomes a metonym for the male sexual act of penetrating the passive woman. But the performance problematizes this notion as well as the association of certain sex acts with either male or female. Here, it is a woman who takes, and orgasms into, the urinal which does not suggest the female form, as Duchamp suggests, but rather the male one. The female performer, until this point at least, is visibly performing the role of a woman and is evidently female particularly given that the dress she is wearing is transparent and the pert breasts and nipples, a sign of 'natural' femininity, are clearly delineated. But the fellatio is typically a sexual act in which the male is given sexual pleasure by the female. There is thus a realization here that the 'female' character the performer is playing may in fact possess a penis, and so what was a heterosexual act now becomes imbued with queer homosexual or transgender readings. This problematic reading provides of course another intertextual allusion to Antón/ia's transgender identity, whose sexual activities with other characters, male or female, require an often simultaneous, heterosexual, lesbian, gay, bisexual, or transgender reading. Gender confusion is also reinforced during the performance in the various lines taken from the novel which are projected onto the screen such as '¿Quién es solamente hombre en el cuerpo de un hombre? ¿Y quién es únicamente mujer en el cuerpo de una mujer?' [Who is uniquely a man in the body of a man? And who is uniquely a woman in the body of a woman?].

Finally, the performance's queerness is further bolstered by the choice of musician and music. Rock singer PJ Harvey is notorious for her sartorial extravagance and quirky visual and acting performances on stage. What is particularly distinctive about her music is the way in which she queers distinct musical genres by mixing different styles to create innovative melodies.[65] This chameleonic feature of Harvey's music reflects Clavel's own drive to break generic and disciplinary boundaries by experimenting with different mediums. Harvey, an acknowledged bisexual, composes songs which blur traditional gender and traditional sexual/gender demarcations. Whilst many of her songs are about ex-girlfriends, others are marked by heterosexual relations. Interestingly, rather than selecting songs from the album *Is this Desire*? that overtly suggest gender blurring and deal with same-sex desire as a reflection of the gender bending in *Cuerpo náufrago*, performance and novel, Clavel has chosen songs which are focused on apparently heterosexual relations. In both 'Angeline' and 'The Wind' the women have worked in prostitution and are hoping to find a more fulfilled existence with a man who will care for them. 'A Perfect Day Elise' narrates the sexual relationship between Joe and Elise. The *Cuerpo náufrago* performance's multimedial dimension with its concurrent interaction of various media serves to underline its own gender blurring themes, serving thus to queer PJ Harvey's three apparently heterosexual melodies. This queering becomes apparent particularly in relation to 'A Perfect Day Elise'. In the performance, the fellatio the urinal-man is performing on the 'woman' culminates as s/he ejaculates, moments after which the song's words 'Said a prayer, pulled the trigger, and cried, "It's a perfect day, Elise"' can be heard. The gun as metonymic phallus is literalized in the performance and both gun and phallus are linked in the way that the relationship between Elise and the man in the song, and the urinal-man and 'woman' in the performance, is underpinned by brutality. However, whereas the culminating triumphant words entail death in Harvey's song, in the performance they serve as an expression of fe/male orgasmic pleasure. Where the queer subversion becomes most apparent is in the deconstruction of the clichéd view that a gun is a sign of heterosexual maleness, as the song suggests, since in the performance the phallus-gun connotes homo/transexuality instead. As the 'female' performer swaggers off the stage leaving a cowering urinal-man behind, the sentence 'somos cuerpos encarcelados por nuestras mentes' appears on the screen. These words reinforce the artificiality of sex and gender and, as social constructs, both function to constrain human instinct, an inexorable attribute which is what allows for a range of sexual and emotional expressions of desire. Even though Harvey's three songs chosen for the performance are underpinned by heterosexuality, taken in conjunction with the rest of the album these tracks are nevertheless obliquely queer. Jennifer Rycenga's comment that here 'Harvey's mediation on desire is filled with characters who slip and slide' suggests that the female characters (including those in 'Angeline' and 'The Wind') oscillate ambiguously between different hetero and non-heterosexual desires.[66] Thus, taking into account the album's overall reflection on the multifacetedness of desire, Harvey's music powerfully mirrors the meanderings of desire and the unfixity of gender as set forth both in the performance and the overall *Cuerpo náufrago* literary and multimedia intervention.

It is clear from the above analysis that Clavel is highly adept at exploiting an array of forms which go beyond the traditional literary print medium. She is able to highlight how multimedia can serve to queer the conventional perception that literature is the product of one single author or involves a solitary practice by encouraging, for instance, a more communal experience via the visual and physical (co-) participation in the various art forms which were created in response to a literary text. At the same time, Clavel also illustrates how the literary and the non-literary are inexorably interconnected and enrich one another through the exploration of common themes such as desire or the bodily and through variegated (inter)textual and multimedia experiences.

Notes to Chapter 5

1. I am taking my cue from Claire Taylor's analysis of Laura Esquivel's *Como agua para chocolate* in *Bodies and Texts*, p. 150.
2. Mary Orr, 'Intertextuality', in Michael Ryan (ed.), *The Encyclopedia of Literary and Cultural Theory. Volume II, Literary Theory from 1966 to the Present*, ed. by Robert Eaglestone, (Chichester: Blackwell, 2011), pp. 1–4, <http://www.literatureencyclopedia.com> [accessed 10 March 2014].
3. Theodor H. Nelson, *Literary Machines 93.1* (Sausalito, CA: Mindful Press, 1992), and 'Replacing the Printed Word', in Simon H. Lavington (ed.), *Information Processing* 80, *Proceedings of the IFIP Congress* (Amsterdam: North-Holland, 1980), pp. 1013–23.
4. Irina O. Rajewsky, 'Intermediality, Intertextuality, and Remediation: A Literary Perspective on Intermediality', *Intermedialites*, 6 (2005), 43–64 (p. 46).
5. Claude Lévi-Strauss, *The Savage Mind* (Chicago: University of Chicago Press, 1966), pp. 16–17.
6. Harold Bloom, *The Anxiety of Influence: A Theory of Poetry*, 2nd edn (New York: Oxford University Press, 1997).
7. Bettina E. Schmidt, *Caribbean Diaspora in the USA: Diversity of Caribbean Religions in New York City*, Vitality of Indigenous Religions Series (Hampshire: Ashgate, 2008), pp. 146–47.
8. Julia Kristeva, *The Kristeva Reader*, ed. by Toril Moi (New York: Columbia University Press, 1986), p. 37.
9. Dick Higgins, 'Intermedia', *Something Else Newsletter*, 1:1 (1966), 1–66.
10. Verstraete, 'Intermedialities', p. 7.
11. Spielmann, 'Synesthesia and Intersenses', p. 55.
12. Ken Friedman, 'Intermedia: Four Histories, Three Directions, Two Futures', in Hans Breder and Klaus-Peter Busse (eds.), *Intermedia: Enacting the Liminal* (Norderstedt: Dortmunder Schriften zur Kunst, 2005), pp. 51–62 (p. 51).

13. Although this blurb credits the digitally manipulated images and their creative thrust to Alarcón, both Alarcón and Clavel came up with the intermedial ideas. Alarcón was responsible for the technical aspect in the graphic design of the images.
14. Ingeborg Hoesterey, *Pastiche: Cultural Memory in Art, Film, Literature* (Bloomington: Indiana University Press, 2001), p. 14.
15. <http://www.cuerponaufrago.com/fachada.htm> [accessed 14 June 2014].
16. Lavery, unpublished interview Clavel, 2008.
17. Clavel has called her (literary) multimedia project 'readymade-multimedia' in recognition of the influence of Duchamp's ready-made aesthetic on her work.
18. Dalia Judovitz, *Unpacking Duchamp: Art in Transit* (Berkeley: University of California Press, 1995).
19. Benjamin, 'The Work of Art in the Age of Mechanical Reproduction'.
20. Patricia Allmer, 'La Reproduction interdite: René Magritte and Forgery', *Papers of Surrealism*, 5 (2007), 1–19 (p. 11), <http://www.surrealismcentre.ac.uk/papersofsurrealism/journal5/index.htm> [accessed 10 June 2014].
21. The role of the *mirones* and *tocones* is significant as Clavel's three *Fuente* images, and particularly *La censura también es fuente puesta al desnudo por sus mirones,* also draw from Duchamp's *Prière de toucher* [Please Touch] (1947) and *La Mariée mise à nu par ses célibataires même* [The Bride Stripped Bare by her Bachelors, Even] (1915–23), which is implicit in the title which Clavel chose for the image which appears on the *Cuerpo náufrago* homepage.
22. Jacques Lacan, *The Four Fundamental Concepts of Psycho-Analysis*, ed. by Jacques-Alain Miller and trans. by Alan Sheridan (Harmondsworth: Penguin, 1987), p. 112.
23. Lacan cited in Linda Clifton, 'Apropos Encore', in David Pereira (ed.), *Anguish & Erotics*, Papers of The Freudian School of Melbourne, *Lacanian Psychoanalytic Writings*, 22 (2004), 91–108 (p. 107).
24. Mary Orr, *Intertextuality: Debates and Contexts* (Cambridge: Polity, 2005), pp. 95 & 96.
25. David Bate, *Photography & Surrealism: Sexuality, Colonialism and Social Dissent* (London: I. B. Tauris, 2004), p. 122.
26. Clavel's intertextual references to Duchamp may have a bearing on the writer's own line of thinking regarding ideas surrounding high and low culture. The Mexican literary establishments have rejected much of women's writing because it has been perceived as catering to mass tastes by virtue of its 'lightness'. By foregrounding the 'lowly' urinal, Clavel parodies the literary establishment's practice of needing to make high/low distinctions as the basis of its criteria in the selection process which determines which texts can or cannot be included in the official national literary canon. Ironically, even as Clavel seeks to overcome high/low distinctions, so too does she reinforce these. As mentioned in the Introduction, Clavel has been keen to reassert the view of her writing as being different from certain strands of writing by *boom femenino* writers, in particular, the best-seller sort. In a newspaper article it is mentioned that Clavel 'nunca ha caído en las tentaciones del "best seller". ¿Cómo lo logra? Sencillo: "Me mantengo en mis niveles de exigencia"' [has never fallen into the temptation of the 'best-seller': How does she achieve this? It's simple: 'I adhere to my own personal levels of exigency'], 'Ana Clavel asegura que está al margen del "best seller"', no author, *Informador*, 8 March 2009, <http://www.informador.com.mx/cultura/2009/161631/6/ana-clavel-asegura-que-esta-al-margen-del-best-seller.htm> [accessed 8 June 2014]. This particular quotation raises issues of taste whereby the traditional ascription of best-sellers with poor quality is reinforced by Clavel. The 'niveles de exigencia' the writer adheres to are marked by 'writerly' qualities which she sees as central to her own writing and which stand in stark opposition to certain 'readerly' qualities of pre-packaged best-selling writing. This is a somewhat contradictory stance, given that even as Clavel's literary and multimedia work is marked by its intellectual and experimental thrust, so too is it characterized by its 'readerly' qualities, which include the focus on 'low' topics such as sex and urinals, as well as having an entertainment value which, for instance, the interactive dimension of the multimedia element confers.
27. The *Las Violetas* website, <http://www.violetasfloresdeldeseo.com> [accessed 14 June 2014], as indeed that of *Las ninfas*, was designed by website designer Alejandro Morales.
28. Cláudia A. Viegas, 'Contemporary Brazilian Fiction: Between Screens and Printed Pages', in Taylor and Pitman (eds.), *Latin American Cyberculture and Cyberliterature*, pp. 207–15 (p. 210).

29. Of course this is a more utopian view of the internet's function. Others view the web as a means for multinational media corporations to colonize online spaces.
30. Claire Taylor, 'Virtual Bodies in Cyberspace: Guzik Glantz's Weblog', in Taylor and Pitman (eds.), *Latin American Cyberculture and Cyberliterature* (2007), pp. 244–56 (p. 244).
31. However, in a comment made during her reading of this particular chapter, Niamh Thornton explained that sound, 'does have meaning: it is a reference to the real in a way that it is both an animation of the authentic and a simulacra (similar to Antón/ia's gender in some ways). Sound can draw attention to itself as construct or suggest an authenticity that is hyperreal'.
32. Taylor and Pitman (eds.), *Latin American Cyberculture and Cyberliterature*, p. 19.
33. Rob Rix, 'Julio Cortázar's Rayuela and the Challenges of Cyberliterature', in Taylor and Pitman (eds.), *Latin American Cyberculture and Cyberliterature*, pp. 194–206 (p. 195).
34. George P. Landow, *Barthes and the Writerly Text*, 'Hypertext' (1996), <http://www.cyberartsweb.org/cpace/ht/jhup/writerly.html> [accessed 10 March 2014].
35. João Canavilhas, 'Hypertext Newswriting Effects on Satisfaction, Comprehension and Attitudes', (2008), 1–17 (p. 3), <> [accessed 10 March 2014].
36. Doménico Chiappe, 'Creative Processes in Hypermedia Literature: Single Purpose, Multiple Authors', in *Latin American Cyberculture and Cyberliterature* (2007), pp. 216–26 (p. 216).
37. Shoshannah Holdom, 'Literary E-magazines in Latin America: From Textual Criticism to Virtual Communities', in Taylor and Pitman (eds.), *Latin American Cyberculture and Cyberliterature*, pp. 140–60 (p. 146). Clavel's *Cuerpo náufrago* multimedia project was built when web 2.0 was in its tentative beginnings and therefore 'interactive' sites using social media had not quite taken hold of the web.
38. Richard Vézina and Olivia Paul, 'Provocation in Advertising: A Conceptualization and an Empirical Assessment', *International Journal of Research in Marketing*, 14:2 (1997), 177–92 (p. 179).
39. Lavery, unpublished interview with Clavel, 2008.
40. José Manuel Springer, 'Imaginar el deseo masculino desde lo femenino y viceversa: Cuerpo naúfrago de Ana Clavel', *Réplica*, 17 October 2005, <http://www.replica21.com/archivo/articulos/s_t/384_springer_clavel.html> [accessed June 2014].
41. Rebecca Schneider, *The Explicit Body in Performance* (London: Routledge, 1997), p. 5.
42. 'Intervención artística de Ana Clavel en Zona Rosa: *La censura también es fuente* o como el arte público transgrede', CONACULTA, FONCA, unpublished material courtesy of Ana Clavel.
43. Emily Hind, 'Pita Amor, Sabina Berman, and Antonio Serrano: Camp in DF', in *Latin American Urban Cultural Production*, ed. and intro. by David William Foster, *Hispanic Issues On Line*, 3:7 (2008), 136–62 (p. 138), <http://spanport.cla.umn.edu/publications/HispanicIssues/pdfs/Hind.pdf> [accessed 10 June 2014]. Of course, as Nuala Finnegan perceptively commented during her reading of this chapter, the 'Zona de Riesgo' written on the ribbon covering the Ingresian nude is a clear wordplay on Zona Rosa.
44. [Anonymous] 'Prevalecen contenidos sexistas en medios: Segob', September 2010, <http://www.eluniversal.com.mx/notas/709542.html> [accessed 10 June 2014].
45. Leah M. Wyman and George N. Dionisopoulos, 'Transcending the Virgin/Whore Dichotomy: Telling Mina's Story in Bram Stoker's *Dracula*', *Women's Studies in Communication*, 23:2 (2000), 209–38 (p. 209).
46. Elizabeth Wilson, 'Into the Labyrinth', in Linda McDowell and Joanne P. Sharp (eds.), *Space, Gender and Knowledge: Feminist Readings* (London: Arnold, 1997), pp. 277–84 (p. 283).
47. During her reading of this chapter, Niamh Thornton remarked that the Zona Rosa is an 'interstitial space. Created as a zone for tourists that has been appropriated as a liminal space for Mexicans where the sex industry and queer clubs intersect: brothels, lap dancing clubs and sex shops, next door to gay discos. Usually gay and straight do not coincide in this way'.
48. Mikhail Bakhtin, *Problems of Dostoevsky's Poetics*, ed. and trans. by Caryl Emerson, Theory and History of Literature, 8 (Minneapolis: University of Minnesota Press, 1984), p. 127.
49. Roland Barthes, *Mythologies,* selected and trans. by Annette Lavers (New York: Hill and Wang, 1972), pp. 84–85.
50. Sigmund Freud cited in Dahlia Schweitzer, 'Striptease: The Art of Spectacle and Transgression', *The Journal of Popular Culture*, 34:1 (2000), 65–75 (p. 68).
51. Edward R. Haymes, 'The Sexual Stranger: The Sexual Quest in Wolfram's *Parzival*', in Frank

R. P. Akehurst and Stephanie Cain Van D'Elden (eds.), *The Stranger in Medieval Society*, Medieval Cultures, 12 (Minneapolis: University of Minnesota Press, 1997), pp. 80–91 (p. 80).

52. Ana María Rodríguez-Vivaldi, 'Shaking the Soul, the Mind, and the Reader: Laura Esquivel and the Multimedia Novel', *Pacific Coast Philology*, 38 (2003), 25–32 (p. 31).
53. Mark Rosenthal, *Understanding Installation Art: From Duchamp to Holzer* (Munich: Prestel, 2003), p. 25.
54. By encouraging the physical engagement of visitors with the multimedia art installation, Clavel challenges notions of the aesthetic distance of 'disinterestedness', to draw from Bourdieu, which the consumption of 'pure' art traditionally demands, Pierre Bourdieu, *Distinction: A Social Critique of the Judgement of Taste*, trans. by Richard Nice (London: Routledge & Kegan Paul, 1984). The 'barbarous' cultural mode of response Clavel's overall literary and multimedia works incite in the reader-viewer-participant could be seen in many ways as working to overcome the repressions of bourgeois 'high' culture, which require one to suppress physical and emotional expressions and to respond in a detached, intellectual manner. But for Clavel simultaneous high and low cultural modes of response are not incompatible. In the context of the *Cuerpo náufrago* performance, whilst the dancers simulate sexual positions which may lead to arousal in the public because of their 'real life' likeness, so too does the purposeful staginess of their act inscribe the performance as representation, which thus encourages viewers to respond in an intellectual manner in order to ponder over the wider issues which the performance raises in relation to sex, desire, and gender (performativity).
55. Clavel explains in relation to the tags that 'esta idea fue producto de la intervención del artista visual y diseñador mexicano Eric Olivares, quien visitó la exposición y decidió intervenirla pegando los cartelitos con masking-tape. Originalmente los cartelitos de "Firme aquí", con todo el sentido antropológico de "Orine aquí", usual en México, no existían' [this idea was the product of the artistic intervention of the Mexican visual artist and designer Eric Olivares, who visited the exhibition and decided to intervene artistically by sticking up the little signs with masking-tape. Originally the post-it notes with 'Sign here' written on them, in the anthropological sense of the word of 'Urinate here', which is typical in Mexico, had not been made for the exhibition], (Lavery, unpublished interview with Clavel, 2008).
56. Clavel, email to Lavery, 11 March 2014, 04:19.
57. Lavery, unpublished interview with Clavel, 2008
58. Christopher Chapman, 'Piss Art: Images of Urination in 20th Century Art' (1998), <http://ensemble.va.com.au/array/chap_00.html> [accessed 10 March 2011].
59. Douglas, *Purity and Danger*, p. 36.
60. Clavel, email to Lavery, 11 March 2014, 04:19.
61. Michel Sanouillet and Elmer Peterson (eds.), *Salt Seller: The Writings of Marcel Duchamp* (New York: Oxford University Press, 1973), p. 23.
62. Butler, *Gender Trouble*.
63. <http://www.cuerponaufrago.com/performance.htm> [accessed 2 December 2014].
64. Barbara Creed, *Monstrous-feminine: Film, Feminism, Psychoanalysis* (New York: Routledge, 1993), p. 106.
65. Jennifer J. Rycenga, 'Endless Caresses: Queer Exuberance in Large-Scale Form in Rock', in *Queering the Popular Pitch*, ed. by Sheila Whiteley and Jennifer J. Rycenga (New York: Routledge, 2006), pp. 235–47 (pp. 236–37).
66. Ibid., p. 243.

CHAPTER 6

Las Violetas son flores del deseo Outer-Circle 'Perversities', Hyperreal Golema Dolls, and Textuality

Whilst Ana Clavel's novella *Las Violetas son flores del* deseo (2007) has received critical acclaim, so too has it caused outrage for its queer Lolitaesque thematics of paedophilia, incest, and (implied) rape. The novella's plot is simple, yet deeply disturbing: Julián Mercader, the owner of a doll factory, becomes obsessed with his daughter Violeta. In his desperate attempt to sublimate his dark obsession, Julián resolves his dilemma by creating a set of dolls called Violetas, all of which bear an uncanny resemblance to his own daughter. Upon exhibiting the dolls at an international commerce fair in Amsterdam, Julián starts building a base of male clients who order from him dolls which are tailor-made to their sexual specifications. But the success of Julián's shady business backfires, making him the target of the 'Hermandad de la Luz Eterna' [The Brotherhood of the Eternal Light], which is hell-bent on cleansing the world of perversity through violent means. Perhaps more so than the novella's theme, it is the sexually explicit image of the book's front cover — to be analyzed in the next chapter — which caused greater agitation. It may be surprising that the novella and its front cover illustration cause the affront they do given that the direct or indirect exploration of the themes of rape, underage sex, and paedophilia are subjects which have been extensively examined in literature, films, and scholarly articles. Yet it is primarily those accounts which discuss the perspectives of the victims of abuse that are publicly sanctioned in contradistinction to those accounts which present the perpetrator's point of view and which, understandably, are demonized and largely perceived in the public eye as 'unspeakable'. In 2007 *Las Violetas* was the subject of some controversy in Mexico, causing mixed reactions in the public because of the sensitive nature of the topics it examined and in particular because of its treatment of these subjects from the perpetrator's perspective. For Clavel it would have been easy to tell the story from the victim's standpoint, but 'peligroso, porque es sencillo caer en el dramatismo y la victimización' [dangerous, because it is easy to fall into drama and victimization].[1] She did not set out to be deliberately provocative or:

> escribir una novela perturbadora [...] quise explorar literariamente el mundo de los deseos y en particular uno que me parece muy callado: el del incesto, pero no desde la perspectiva de la víctima, sino del padre [...] dar voz a un hombre

> que enfrentado a los límites bucea en sus zonas oscuras para no consumar el acto, para salvarse y salvar a su hija sin tampoco negar su deseo.[2]
>
> [to write a disturbing novel [...] I wanted to explore literarily the world of desire and in particular one which I believe is quite silenced: that of incest, but not from the perspective of the victim, but rather of the father's [...] to give voice to a man who confronts his own limits where he immerses himself in dark zones so as to not consummate the act, to save himself and his daughter, yet without negating his desire]

Clavel is unapologetic about her choice of subject since she perceives it as the task of the writer to explore the 'unutterable' and to challenge society's need to negate those forbidden areas of life which are perceived as posing a threat to the immutable order of things. Clavel thus emphasizes the responsibility both of the individual and society as a whole in recognizing that such matters, however disturbing, are an intrinsic aspect of contemporary society: 'esta es una época oscurantista para el deseo: se pretende uniformarlo, abolirlo, negarlo [...] reconocer que los deseos están ahí [...] puede ser purificador' [these are obscurantist times for desire: there are attempts to make it uniform, abolish it, negate it [...] recognizing that desires exist [...] can be purifying].[3] The Grupo Sanborns, Mexico's prestigious retail chain and cherished national institution, refused to sell *Las Violetas* on the grounds of the explicit content of both cover and book. Nevertheless, Clavel's novella is acclaimed by cultural critics, has been a sales success in Mexico and featured in 2007 in 'Los 10 libros más vendidos de la semana' 'The 10 most sold books of the week] list, coming in seventh place and notably preceding two bestseller writers, Ángeles Mastretta and Isabel Allende.[4] There are also a number of blog sites which feature readers' positive reactions to *Las Violetas*, evidencing the general success of the novella.[5] In 2005 it was awarded by Radio France International the Juan Rulfo Short Novel Prize in recognition of its literary merits, and was praised by the jury for its polished structure and style.[6] In his review of *Las Violetas*, Reyes remarks that 'Clavel alcanza una espléndida madurez. Se trata de una novela compleja, perturbadora, que deslumbra' [Clavel's voice has matured wonderfully. This is a complex and disturbing novel which dazzles].[7]

The overall positive reception of Clavel's novella has resonances with the critical acclaim Vladimir Nabokov's *Lolita* (1955) received, despite its controversial subject matter. Nabokov and Clavel share much in common in their novels. To suggest that under-age girls may be prematurely sexual, as both writers do, is received as culturally taboo.[8] Both texts are deplorable because of their focus on paedophilic desire but whereas the abuse of Dolores Haze is actually perpetrated by Humbert Humbert, the abuse against Julián's daughter Violeta is never realized, although it is inferred. As will be discussed here, Clavel's work — as Nabokov's novel — is told from the perpetrator's perspective and depicts its narrator Julián as unreliable. As in *Lolita*, the readers of *Las Violetas* are addressed directly by their narrator who seeks an empathetic connection between himself and his (prospective) reader. The reader's pleasurable reading is disturbed as he or she becomes implicated in the lurid thoughts of Julián. As will be examined, the reason why *Las Violetas* perturbs resides in the manner in which the narrative forces upon the reader the position of accomplice, even perpetrator of a (suggested) crime. *Las Violetas*, like *Lolita*, is as much about proscribed sexual desire as it is about the process of artistic creation. By foregrounding the role of the reader, as well as the manner in which fact and fiction blur indistinguishably, Clavel's novella highlights the mediated nature of the text and its constructedness. This chapter will also explore Julián's doll fetish, a prime example of the queer, which raises interesting questions about the role of substitution. Equally, sublimation underpins the key notions relating to the real and the simulacra which will be drawn from in my examination of Clavel's Violetas as avatars of the (female) Golem figure in Jewish Kabbalistic tradition. Given that *Las Violetas* draws from *Las Hortensias* (1949) by Felisberto Hernández, my discussion will be aided by Ksenija Bilbija's examination of the female Golem. Bilbija's work will also serve partly as the basis of my discussion of the (abject) female-maternal presence and the role of silence. *Las Hortensias* and *Las Violetas* also share the blurring of fact and fiction, the real and the simulacrum, the original and replica, and gain relevance in relation to notions of 'aura' (Benjamin, 'The Work of Art'), the post-human, the novella as work of artifice and its intertextuality. The outlandish idea of the dolls in *Las Violetas* draws its inspiration from two main sources: one visual, Hans Bellmer's *Les Jeux de la poupée* (1949); and the other textual, Felisberto Hernández's *Las Hortensias* (1949), Vladimir Nabokov's *Lolita* (1955), and Patrick Süskind's *Perfume: The Story of a Murderer* (1985). Here, intertextuality highlights literary constructedness and textual renovation via parody and literary reworkings. Ultimately, it will be shown that *Las Violetas*, like the rest of Clavel's *oeuvre*, is a truly postmodern text in the sense that is resists offering readers the comfort of one stable perspective whether it be in relation to reader complicity, Clavel's ambiguous feminist posturing in relation to (un)real women and their bodies, or in the context of her genre-bending experimentation and questions of the role of the author of fiction.

Reader Complicity

Julián's 'perversion' is a question of perception. Even if some believe that he is culpable of wrongdoing (*Las Violetas*, p. 25), the character does not perceive his incestuous desire as a crime because it is merely an unfulfilled craving. In his attempt to find an empathetic reader, Julián uses repetition as a tactic of persuasion: 'Quiero repetirlo una vez más: mi crimen no es del todo un crimen — aunque tampoco [...] inocente' [I want to state this again: my crime is not entirely a crime — although neither [...] innocent] (p. 35).[9] Julián seeks to make his reader a partner in crime in the metaphorical desire for rape, as a means of absolving his sense of guilt. He deliberately discomforts the reader, a tactic used to dislodge his or her position as incriminating reader and coerce him or her into the position of accomplice, and even perpetrator. This is seen in Julián's ruminations on the moral and philosophical nature of perversity. He notes that '"perverso" es aquello que lastimándonos no nos permite apartar la mirada. Remueve las tinieblas acalladas en nuestro interior y nos despierta apetitos urgentes' ['perverse' is that which is detrimental to us and does not allow us to look away. It stirs the dark core silenced in our inner selves and awakens desperate drives] (p. 25). Julián's ironic tone emphasizes his view that perversity is considered as such because of the historic medico-legal and religious discourses which have framed the perverse as that which is synonymous with abnormal sexuality and counters '"natural", "divinely sanctioned" and therefore "acceptable" sexuality'.[10] Julián remarks that when one is confronted with the 'perverse', one is confronted with the 'other' (p. 25), bringing to mind Julia Kristeva's notion of the uncanny. Whilst encounters with that which is different can lead to a sense of weirdness and threaten the boundaries of self and 'other', we do not, however, reject the uncanny outright because of the strange within ourselves whereby 'the sense of strangeness is a mainspring for identification with the other'.[11] Julián seeks to dispute the view that his lust is abnormal by suggesting that we all have an element of this 'perverse' otherness which we seek to repress because of societal pressures to conform to acceptable forms of sexual or moral behaviour (p. 36).

Julián challenges the readers' comfort zone by addressing them directly and by using a number of rhetorical devices such as the art of persuasion and insinuation to align the readers 'que lean estas palabras' [who read these words] (p. 36) with his viewpoint. The words 'La violación comienza con la mirada. Cualquiera que se haya asomado al pozo de sus deseos, lo sabe' [Rape begins with the gaze. Whoever has looked into the depths of their desires, knows this well] (p. 9) underpin Julián's strategy to make the reader his partner in crime. Through insinuation ('La violación comienza con la mirada') Julián proposes that the only brutality that his account suggests is one which is born of the reader's imagination because we all possess perverse desires. The early warnings of rape in *Las Violetas* are meant as a way of setting the reader's expectations of an impending rape for which he or she is (apparently) yearning. Julián teases his reader into believing that it will occur through repetition of the sentence 'La violación comienza con la mirada' (pp. 9 & 99) or variations of it (pp. 15 & 95). The rape of Violeta never assumes articulate form and therefore the repetition of this sentence forces the reader into 'a state of protracted sensitivity', thus providing 'the raw materials of violent description, while the reader's heightened anticipation of the event constructs those materials into a representation of violence'.[12] Julián ensnares his overeager reader in the web of his or her own dark desires and expectations. Denied an explicit account of violence, 'the reader is tempted and frustrated, tempted and frustrated, until the process of reading begins to assume the rhythm of desire' (Tanner, p. 564). When rape is finally committed in Julián's dream (*Las Violetas*, pp. 109–10), the prior implicit references to rape serve to 'rob the crime of its shock value' (Tanner, p. 564) and the 'reader's sympathy for the victim and the indignation inspired by the mere thought of the violent act become tinged with an impatience bred of familiarity' (Tanner, p. 565). The reader's 'horrified' response to the projected rape fades into 'numbed expectation' (Tanner, p. 565) and disappointment given that the rape only takes place at the level of the oneiric. However Julián's suggestion that he wakes up to find his 'amazona' [Amazon] — a name he uses to refer to Violeta — having intercourse with him implies his drive to trigger the workings of desire in his reader by provoking both a sense of frustrated disappointment and heightened sexual fulfilment. But the implication of an actual rape committed against Violeta is undermined since Julián uses the term 'amazona' not only to refer to Violeta but also to her aunt Isabel (p. 104) and one of his dolls (p. 133). The reader is thus left in a state of confused frustration as it is unclear with whom, or what, Julián is having intercourse.

The reader's anticipation of abuse which lends it imaginative form is also implied in the scene where Julián bounces twelve year old Violeta on his lap. It is insinuated, though not stated explicitly, that Violeta reaches climax: 'un rastro de sudor que le perlaba esa zona delicada [...] y que dispuesta entre la nariz y los labios, al excitarse es el botón de una flor a punto de prodigarse [...] Violeta [...] estaba absolutamente, inmaculadamente excitada' [a trace of sweat sparkled on that delicate zone [...] which lies between the nose and the lips and, and when it is excited it becomes the erect button of a flower which is about to flourish] (pp. 75–76). Julián thus uses rhetorical strategies which may prompt the reader to frame Violeta's experience as an orgasmic one. In the above quotation, when Julián describes the area between Violeta's nose and her mouth, the comparison of the area around the mouth with the erogenous genital zone is not made explicit but is implied, and thus it is left to the 'perverse' reader to tinge this scene with erotic meaning via the imagination. It must be borne in mind that Julián's implied ideal reader, that is, an empathetic reader who acknowledges (and perhaps revels in) his own 'tainted' 'otherness', is a fictional addressee who must not be necessarily confused with the reader of *Las Violetas*.

Like Humbert Humbert in *Lolita*, Julián is, in the reader's mind, ultimately an unreliable narrator and Clavel, who controls the narrative and is in control of rhetorical effects, reveals the lacunae in Julián's account.[13] The novel sets up an ambiguous relationship between us and Julián, by making us feel empathetic towards him, whilst also drawing our attention to his unreliable narration and therefore counteracting any sense of empathy. Our lack of empathy towards this character arises particularly in the context of his view that his crime is not a crime because he has not committed any brutality against Violeta. The novella's question of non-consensual sexual practice puts into question Julián's perspective. The first example emerges when Julián is playing the horsey game with Violeta. Violeta has been tricked into believing that she is playing with her father but Julián has strategically placed her there to experience *jouissance* (pp. 75–76). Her own insinuated orgasmic experience which he has orchestrated is non-consensual and therefore signals a form of indirect paedophilic abuse, even if it is not penetrative. The second example relates to Julián's dream of indirectly having sex with Violeta (pp. 109–10). This incident may not be condemned outright by the reader given that it is perpetrated at an oneiric level. However the reader is left with a very unsympathetic view of Julián given that the brutality of the scene, which involves non-consensual sexual practice, leaves us with a deep sense of unease as it opens up possibly involuntary thoughts of what the 'real' rape may be like if committed against an unwilling Violeta. The reader sees further cracks in Julián's defence of his 'crime'. Even as the two examples involve non-consent, Julián problematizes the view of abuse victims as 'victims' by suggesting that they 'enjoy' such treatment (pp. 76 & 110) and that victims can also be victimizers (pp. 108 & 109). Such fissures in Julián's account serve to critique his and the highly problematic conventional patriarchal ploy of encoding abuse victims as taking pleasure from rape, thus relieving the perpetrator from responsibility for the crime. When Julián wakes up after his dream to find that he is having sex with his 'amazona' (p. 110), the implication that it could be Violeta converts his 'innocent' lust for his daughter into an incestuous offence. However the suggestion that she is enjoying intercourse with him (p. 110) once again deflects the perpetrator's accountability. For Julián, it is almost as if Violeta deserves such treatment because her sexual precociousness makes the nymphet as 'irremediable violada' [irremediably raped] (p. 47).

At the same time, there appears to be an ambiguous reversal in relation to the victim/victimizer dyad. Indeed, whilst under the effects of the sedative which Isabel and Violeta have administered to him, it is suggested that Julián is raped by his daughter or possibly even by her aunt (pp. 108 & 109). This positioning of Julián as a victim of sexual abuse reinforces both his own previous point about the relative nature of 'perversity' and the text's ambiguous representation of victimhood. As Clavel clarifies:

> Yo quería sugerir la idea de que era Julián quien era subyugado, 'violado' por Isabel o Violeta, porque desde muy al principio a mí me pareció importante por lo menos mantener la ambigüedad del 'victimario'. Desde el final del capítulo I quise sugerir que la inocencia también puede ultrajar a quien la mira, invertir la premisa inicial: si la violación comienza con la mirada, habría que ver entonces quién viola a quién.[14]
>
> [I wanted to suggest the idea that Julián was subjugated: 'raped' by Isabel or Violeta, because from the outset I thought it was important to at least maintain the ambiguity of the 'victimizer'. From the end of chapter 1 I wanted to suggest that innocence can also cause affront to the gazer, invert the initial premise: if rape starts with the gaze, then we have to deal with the question of who rapes who]

Thus, even as our sympathy for Julián may be waning, Clavel appears to be throwing her character a lifeline which saves him from becoming entirely deplorable, both by casting him as the victim and by suggesting that he is both remorseful and mad. Although Julián does not believe his crime to be an offence, there are nevertheless rumblings of remorse (pp. 80 & 126). Julián's culpability is insinuated elsewhere as he seeks forgiveness from his reader as in his allusion at the start of the novella to the Greek myth of the king of Sipylus, Tantalus: 'Tántalo contempla la clemencia de los dioses en la mano de la Sacerdotisa que ha de prodigar la expiación y el término de la condena' [Tantalus observes the mercy of the gods in the hands of the Priestess who will determine the atonement and the terms of the sentence] (p. 17). The 'Sacerdotisa' could be interpreted as his view of the reader's role in determining what the terms are of his or her final judgement of Julián. The 'Sacerdotista' symbolically rematerializes towards the end of the novella when Julián calls upon the reader to be lenient in the judgement of him (p. 132). The reader starts almost to pity Julián because of the realization that the narrator-character has fallen into psychosis (pp. 95, 97, 81, 101, 117, & 120–21), which becomes apparent in his demented flights of fantasy in the form of obsessive doll-making, and in his belief that historical persons or fictional characters from other texts inhabit his world or that inquisitorial sects are persecuting him. It must be noted that the narrator is recounting the events from a retrospective position. The narrator in the present views himself as having been one of the lucky ones to escape becoming the victim of the 'Brotherhood of Light'. When Julián comments towards the end of the novella that 'no fue una noche permanente' [the night was not permanent] (p. 131), this highlights his perception that he has not only escaped the talons of death but also those of madness. But even as he is writing his account he lets slip that he is suffering from delusions of persecution, fearing that his dolls will be confiscated by some kind of 'Council of Decency and Justice', as happened with Horacio's Hortensia dolls (p. 45). Julián perceives his account as a cohesive narrative recounting the events of the past relating to his doll-making obsession and the 'Brotherhood' saga which, in his mind, only momentarily affected his mental health (p. 112). But the narrative belies the view that the Julián of the present has recovered from his short-lived insanity. A number of rhetorical devices serve to underpin to his unstable mind. The narrator is unable to piece together a totally cohesive narrative, occasionally drip-feeding information in pell-mell fashion to his reader who can only make sense of such information retrospectively. Traditional perceptions of the real and the unreal become confusingly blurred since the 'real' world is tainted with absurdity as it becomes inhabited with life-sized dolls who replace real human beings or characters who claim to be 'real' writers. In this regards the novella can be linked to magical realism as explored earlier in relation to *Los deseos y su sombra* and *Cuerpo náufrago*. In *Las Violetas* the fantastical has a similar function to these two texts in the sense that it serves to question traditional divisions maintained between, for instance, sanity and insanity or fact and fiction. In the context of Julián's insane narrative, the character also jumps incoherently from one discussion to another (p. 17) and finds it difficult to structure his thoughts in a coherent manner (p. 80). The repetition of the words 'Las Violetas comenzaron a florecer' (pp. 79–80) signal circularity, the hallmark of Julián's lunatic narrative and mental insanity. Just as the dolls are beginning to multiply, so too does he increasingly lose control over his mind and his literary and mechanic creations. The repetition of other words such as 'afuera diluviaba' [it was pouring outside] or its variants (pp. 64, 65, 69, & 113), endless rhetorical questions (p. 101), textual fragmentation, and blanks on the page (p. 64), all underscore Julián's increased disconnection from the real world as he ventures progressively towards psychosis, as well as the text's own schizophrenia.[15] Ultimately, Julián's 'crime' may well be condemned by some readers but others may feel nevertheless an element, however insignificant, of empathy towards this tortured character, given that his psychotic episodes are reflections perhaps of a man whose unfulfilled sexual desire, as well as the (un)conscious guilt that those feelings produce in him, have driven him to insanity. He compares his own predicament to the rape victim tied to a tree that he dreams of and to Tantalus, eternally condemned to a constant state of unquenched desire (pp. 109, & 101–02).

Golema Dolls

Instead of committing incest with Violeta, Julián sublimates his sexual desire by writing a confession of his 'crime' and creating the dolls. Freudian sublimation is defined as 'working off frustrated desires (especially sexual drives) through socially acceptable activities' whereby 'art, music [...] and other creative activities (can) serve to rechannel sexual energies into productive behaviour'.[16] Whilst artistic creation is perceived as a socially sanctioned activity, Julián's sexual inspiration for such creativity — an underage child — is putatively condemned. However, given that Julián commits the crime of incest only in his hyperreal world of dreams, the reader may be inclined to tolerate his doll products particularly as the novella's central theme of substitution can be situated in a long history of consecrated visual and literary production. Whilst discussing the creative writing process of *Las Violetas*, Clavel alludes to the Greek legend recounted by Pliny the Elder in which the daughter of Butades, a potter of Sicyon, drew the outline of her beloved's face which was projected onto a wall by the light of a lamp. Her father then pressed clay onto this silhouette 'creando así el primer simulacro sustitutivo del deseo del que se tiene noticia en Occidente' [thus creating in this way the first replacement simulacra of desire which the Western world received news of].[17] Since this story's inception, 'la creación de sucedáneos humanizados ha estado asociada a la restitución de un placer original que busca en la sustitución una satisfacción compensatoria' [the creation of human-like substitutions has been associated with the return to an originary pleasure which seeks in the replacement object a compensatory fulfilment] ('Los caballeros', p. 61). The author cites various examples of visual and literary production which encompass such a thrust, including the story of the artist Pygmalion, Jacques Offenbach's opera *The Tales of Hoffmann* (1881), the film *Tamaño natural* (1973) by Luis García Berlanga, and Juan José Arreola's short story 'Anuncio' (1961). Clavel's Violetas draw their inspiration from Hernández's *Las Hortensias* (1949), in which the protagonist Horacio enlists a doll-manufacturer to make a life-like doll called Hortensia made in the image of his own wife, María Hortensia.

In the examples cited above, all of the creations are female and their owners and/or creators are male. In some of these accounts there 'is the symbolic desire of (the) male master to avoid the female role in the process of procreation and, therefore, the urgency to prove that men have the sole power in creation'.[18] These female creations can thus be compared to the figure of the Golem, which, according to Kabbalistic tradition, is an 'artificial anthropoid', created by mystical mediation.[19] The formation of the simulacrum of a human being is linked to the medieval Kabbalist's aspiration to possess his god's divine knowledge and sole power of creation. The female Golem is:

> a simulacrum whose purpose is to substitute for the 'real' woman and offer the fulfilment of sexual desire (often as an evasion of some kind of societal censorship) to the creator [...] the female presence is clearly suppressed [...] external features of the female body have been replicated in a simulacrum which, in turn, is expected to be obedient, silent [...] and willing to accept established hierarchies.[20]

Whilst Clavel's Violetas 'fit' into the features of the prototypical *Golema* outlined here, so too does the text simultaneously deconstruct the female Golem myth given that the unruly maternal/female presence in the process of (pro)creation cannot be eradicated. Julián's desire to inscribe his fatherly signature on his daughter and Golem products is challenged as both the maternal constantly encroaches and the original elides the demiurge's grasp. Julián's drive to exclude the maternal from the fatherly (pro)creative process can be understood in relation to his gradual move from the real world (associated with the maternal) towards the hyperreal world (associated with the paternal) which is inhabited by replicas. Notions of the real, the hyperreal, and the replica are central motifs in *Las Violetas* — as indeed in Clavel's *Cuerpo náufrago* and *El dibujante de sombras* — and can be framed within Jean Baudrillard's discussion of the role of simulacrum.[21] For Baudrillard the real has been erased and the hyperrreal has substituted the original with its numerous concurrent representations which problematize the referent. Therefore postmodern reality 'is no longer a question of imitation, nor of reduplication, nor even parody' but rather 'a question of substituting signs of the real for the real itself' (*Simulations*, p. 4). This entails the replacement of the real by its 'operational double' as well as a conscious acknowledgement of a proxy reality, or hyperreality. The creation of the Golem Hortensia presupposes a loss and is fatal for the creator Horacio in *Las Hortensias* (Bilbija, 'Las Hortensias', p. 249). The same can be said of Julián given that, although he is not literally erased from the text itself as Horacio finally is, he falls into hyperreal madness. In *Las Hortensias*, the real and the hyperreal coexist (Bilbija, 'The Youngest Doll', p. 881), whereas the imaginary and hyperreal world take over the human living world of Julián from the beginning of the novella, thus reinforcing Baudrillard's notion of the 'liquidation of referentials'.[22] The character's increased contact with 'artificial anthropoids' (Idel, p. 3) and decreased interaction with real human beings starts at an early age. Julián's early experiences of being in his father's doll factory stands for a duality, as we shall see, which will mark the rest of Julián's real and unreal existence, underscored by the present and absent 'real' female or maternal, and the sense of loss that this (non-)existence entails.

(Un)real Female-Maternal Presence/Absence Dyad

The maternal presence/absence duality becomes apparent during Helena's conception of Violeta, which marks the beginning of the end of the relationship between Julián and his wife. Julián describes the breakdown in their marriage as 'a rift' and blames it on Violeta (p. 31). This event causes him to distance himself from the living world (p. 57). Immersed now in hyperreality, Julián's life is overtaken by mechanical reproduction: 'me refugié en la fábrica y en las muñecas [....] en las películas silentes [...] libros de fotografía, de pintura y de anatomía' [I took refuge in the factory and dolls [...] in silent movies [...] in books of photography, painting and anatomy] (p. 32). The strengthening bond between mother and daughter makes Julián feel jealous as well as emotionally and sexually superfluous (pp. 27 & 31). His marginalization in the family triad, Helena's eventual departure from the marital home (p. 55), and his increasing obsession with his child-daughter nymphet drive him to centre his creative and sexual energies on creating his 'prohibited' Violetas. Helena is not the only absent figure in Julián's life. Although the real Violeta, together with Julián's obsession and eventual psychosis, is what drives the entire novella, she is almost never physically present (pp. 33 & 48). The only Violeta that thus inhabits Julián's world are copies of copies of his daughter. The female-maternal presence continues nevertheless to be inexorable. Helena is obsessed with becoming pregnant but, unable to conceive immediately, she vests her attention in 'mothering' the first series of 'inofensiva' Violeta dolls as if they were her own daughters (p. 28). This has resonances with Horacio's wife's interaction with the doll Hortensia which she mothers. Yet Helena knows that the Violetas are not the real daughter, but simulacrums of one. For Helena, like María Hortensia (Bilbija, 'Las Hortensias', p. 259), playing with the dolls is part of a conscious role-play performance: 'como si siempre jugara a ser una madre entregada en esa mezcla de verdad y simulacro que tienen los juegos de niños' [as if she were pretending to be a doting mother in that game of truth and make-believe which is typical of children's games] (*Las Violetas*, p. 29). Thus, whilst both Helena and María Hortensia denote reality, both Julián and Horacio connote the quest for the hyperreal ('Las Hortensias', p. 259). Although Helena's doll obsession reflects her sense of lack, when she falls pregnant with Violeta her lacking turns to actual maternal fulfilment.

The inevitable female-maternal presence is similarly underpinned by Julián's sexualization. His 'normal' heternonormative sexualization process as an adolescent is compromised as his sexual awakening is ignited not by female human beings, but rather by representations of the real, that is, by the ready-to-assemble dolls in the factory, as well as by Hans Bellmer's photography of contortioned mannequins (p. 19). Julián's 'abnormal' sexualization is prompted in particular by an encounter when he is a child with Naty. Upon entering one of the store rooms, Naty undresses and sits next to the nude dolls. Julián discovers the female child's pudendal slit, the marker of sexual difference between the penis-possessing male and the 'lacking' female-mother, and remarks '(e)stás rota' [you're broken] (p. 22). Following this incident, Julián hides amidst a box filled with dolls and as he gazes towards one doll, 'me sentí seguro junto al universo perfecto de su cuerpo cerrado y sin cicatriz' [I felt secure next to that perfect universe of her sealed and scarless body] (p. 23). This passage reveals many of the issues which are central to our understanding of Julián's psychosexual complexities. In this encounter between Naty, Julián, and the dolls, the real and unreal interact uncomfortably given that it is 'the artificial resurrection' (Baudrillard, *Simulacra*, p. 2) that has a 'perfect' body to which Julián pays emotional and erotic attention, whereas the real Naty is imperfect and repulsive.[23] Even though both the simulacrum and Naty share innocent purity, unlike the dolls whose childhood has been frozen, Naty's broken pudenda suggests the impermanence of childhood and impending motherhood. Here the conflict between the real/unreal, pure/sullied, child/maternal, is linked to the conflict between the father and mother role in procreation. Bilbija explains that:

> Golems are not born: they are made in a solitary act that denies the role of the woman in the creation of 'real' life. The role of the mother is subsumed by the father who simulates conception by literary means. ('The Youngest Doll', p. 882)

In his desire to establish his sole power in (pro)creation, Julián sees himself as the 'progenitor' (p. 74) of the Violeta dolls and thus assumes the role of the mother by simulating conception of his Violetas by imaginary, literary, artistic, and mechanic means At the heart of Julián's rejection of 'the monstrous power of the maternal imagination and desire' there lies 'the recurring fantasy of a child born from man alone'.[24] Julián's horror of the maternal is accompanied nevertheless by a sense of awe at the power the maternal figure and her reproductive capabilities, as evidenced in his pre-Oedipal yearning to return to the safe womb (p. 107). Clavel provides us with a feminist rebuttal of the patriarchal construction of the Golem figure by its creator in which the mother figure is redundant, given that the maternal presence is a constant threat as embodied in the recurrent metaphor of the 'herida' [wound]. According to Bilbija, the prototypical female Golem 'does not grow and age, but is created as an already attractive, physically mature female' ('Las Hortensias', p. 249). Julián's dolls, however, age, gradually grow in dimension, and mature sexually. Whilst the initial series of Violeta dolls are sexually precocious (p. 27), they are nevertheless child-like and contrast sharply with the later life-sized Violetas which are perverse (p. 27) in their uncertain status between child, adolescent, and woman. Ironically, despite the apparent lack of maternal traces in the 'harmless ones' (pp. 71 & 93), these are nevertheless unwittingly inscribed in them by their creator since 'harían las delicias maternales de niñas anónimas y distantes' [they would fulfil the maternal pleasures of anonymous and distant little girls] (p. 19). Playing with dolls is a sterotypically female activity, the dolls serving as simulacrums of 'babies' which help to prime their female 'mothers' to become 'good' nurturing mothers in real life.[25]

The Female-Maternal Wound

What differentiates the fabricated Violetas from the real humans Violeta and Naty, is that the latter have pudenal slits from which they can menstruate, a sign of maternal capability. When Julián describes Naty's pudenda as 'rota' in contrast to the doll 'sin cicatriz', and therefore states his preference for the unreal body over the real, this underscores his deep fear of the real, abject 'wounded' female body and its reproductive abilities. Whilst the unsullied pre-pubescent female body of Violeta and the innocent doll replicas provokes in Julián fascination and desire, Violeta's human body horrifies because of the threat of its latent monstrosity which pubescence will trigger. The mixture of attraction and repulsion that Julián feels renders Violeta monstrous. Thus:

> Woman, as a sign of difference, is monstrous. If we define the monster as a bodily entity that is anomalous and deviant vis-à-vis the norm, then we can argue that the female body shares with the monster the privilege of bringing out a unique blend of fascination and horror. (Braidotti, p. 81)

The view of the maturing 'wounded' female body is linked to 'the power and danger perceived to be inherent in woman's fecund flesh, her seeping, leaking, bleeding womb standing as site of pollution and source of dread'.[26] The vaginal 'herida' is the locus of menstrual blood which, like birth, has been identified as a taboo subject and associated with the 'abject' as well as the carnivalesque grotesque.[27] Menstruation is associated with a dangerous 'entry into the reproductive reality that is presumed to be women's primary domain'.[28] This presumption has made many feminists such as Simone de Beauvoir regard the ability of women's bodies to reproduce as a negative capability. The text seems ambiguous in terms of how childbearing, which menstruation connotes, is positioned as it portrays it via its abject quality as both a negative capability as well as a life-affirming capacity.[29] The idea of threat which is associated with abject menstruation and the dread it produces, is apparent when Julián discovers that Violeta has begun to menstruate (pp. 69–71). Julián seems not to know what is happening to her, as reinforced in Isabel's grievance that men 'nunca saben nada' [never know anything] (p. 70). But Julián's apparent unknowing may in fact be masking his desire to suppress the knowledge of the inevitable physiological changes Violeta is undergoing in her process of becoming a woman. Unlike the prepubescent original Violeta and her replicas, whom he finds unthreatening, the pubescent Violeta threatens because she becomes 'positioned as powerful [...] [a] source of moral and physical contamination' (Ussher, p. 1). Following Julián's discovery, he now views Violeta as 'rota'. Ironically, even as he perceives her as imperfect because of her maternal capabilities, he decides to manufacture a new set of 'perversa' Violeta dolls which replicate Violeta's flourishing womanhood (p. 71). He gives these dolls a 'grieta esencial' [essential crack] from which blood can emanate. But unlike in the case of Violeta and Naty, from whose 'wound' maternal blood flows, the blood emanating from the dolls' vaginas is a reference to their virginal deflowerment via rape. As Clavel notes:

> Las Violetas sangran porque son vírgenes, porque tienen un himen que puede ser rasgado, no porque puedan menstruar (eso cibernéticamente sería muy complicado). La menstruación conlleva el asunto del embarazo, y si Julián las ve como inofensivas y fascinantes es porque puede consumar con ellas una violación sin consecuencias, sin embarazo posible [...] por lo que investigué, es lo que temen los violadores, dejar huellas de su delito.[30]
>
> [The Violetas bleed because they are virgins, because then have a hymen that can be torn, not because they can menstruate (cibernetically that would be very complicated). Menstruation is linked to the question of pregnancy, and if Julián sees them as inoffensive and fascinating it is because he can rape them without consequences, without them being able to get pregnant [...] from what I have researched, that is precisely what rapists fear, that is leaving traces of their crime]

Creating pubescent dolls can be understood as Julián's desire to capture Violeta's 'true' essence, but such attempt proves futile perhaps in part because he is denying the 'monstrous' maternal capabilities in his doll replicas. Furthermore, Violeta constantly evades his grasp. Julián's aggressive desire to smash his perverse dolls (p. 71) suggests his anger at the impossibility of possessing Violeta and his frustrated ambition to freeze his daughter in a permanent state of unthreatening prepubescent innocence. But Violeta is in permanent flux and therefore the menace of the feminine, with its association of material time and bodily ageing, challenges the 'male realm of eternal unchanged forms'.[31] Julián's aggression is therefore a response to the knowledge that Violeta's immobility as inanimate purified object will be neutralized by 'feminine mutability' (Davies, *Allende*, p. 419). Just as the brutality denotes Julián's desire to inscribe the fatherly signature on his doll products without female intervention, so too does it denote, with its incising quality, the brutal penetrative act of rape which he fantasizes about committing against his daughter, thus reinforcing the view that the demiurge cannot (pro)create without female or maternal presence. The real and unreal Violetas' 'grieta esencial' and their susceptibility to rape thus reminds Julián of his own vulnerability as demiurge who seeks in vain to control (pro)creation without maternal or female participation.

Violeta's 'grieta' also reminds Julián of his 'origins, of having been born of woman'.[32] The 'wound' both fascinates and terrifies Julián because whilst it provides orgasmic pleasure, so too is it linked to the 'maternal body as site of the origin of life [...] We are all of woman born, and the mother's body as threshold of existence is both sacred and soiled, holy and hellish' (Braidotti, p. 81). The dread that the wound-possessing female causes in Julián because of her links to maternal origins, also becomes apparent when he discovers that Helena is pregnant with Violeta. The changing body of the mother (p. 29) reminds us of the 'morphologically dubious' (Braidotti, p. 81) qualities of the wounded and abject maternal body which challenges male unmutability. The foetus in the maternal vessel also terrifies. The sadistic imagery of Julián killing the monstrous foetus (p. 29) is connected to his perception that Violeta's demonic nymphomania is to blame for his succumbing to perversity. The abject fear which the foetus provokes in Julián can be linked to Kristeva's notion of the uncanny, discussed earlier, which the word 'ajeno' suggests. Even as Julián attempts to eradicate the 'strange' monster foetus, this act of destruction is only one which he imagines and does not carry out in 'reality' because he recognizes in the unborn Violeta that part of his 'other' self driven by irrepressible desires. Grosz observes that men see it as part of their '"function" [...] to extend bodily interests beyond the male body's skin through its proprietorial role, its "extended corporeality" in the mother whom he has impregnated and the child thereby produced, making them *his* products, possessions, responsibilities' (*Volatile Bodies*, p. 199). Whilst by 'killing' the foetus Julián is asserting his proprietal role in relation to Helena, Violeta, and their bodies, so too is that same objective thwarted. After Helena gives birth to Violeta, Julián resentfully remarks that Helena 'se olvidó de mí y de las Violetas, como si sólo hubiéramos sido el ensayo, el pretexto para su maternidad unívoca' [forgot about me and the Violetas, as if we had simply been used as a rehearsal, a pretext for her univocal motherhood] (p. 31). The words 'ensayo' [essay, or rehearsal] and 'pretexto' point to the idea of literary creativity, and the 'uni' in 'univoca' is the Latin prefix for 'one'. Helena poses a menace to Julián in that she usurps his role as demiurge and his objective to create without female participation. She instead assumes the role of demiurge who creates without male involvement since she has sole responsibility for the formation of Violeta *in utero*. Although male sperm is an essential element in the conception of a child, the creation of the unborn child from the moment of conception depends on many other elements which are attributed *univocally* to the mother: it relies on the mother for nourishment and a supply of hormones, on maternal tissue and blood, all necessary for the normal foetal formation of 'piel, sangre y tejidos' [skin, blood and tissue] (p. 29).

In Kabbalistic tradition the demiurge seeks to replicate the power of creation of their god in order to make the simulacrum of a human being. This process is twofold as it involves, firstly, the physical formation of the body via the assembling of organic and inorganic materials, and, secondly, the body's animation whereby 'a magical word — the name of God — is uttered, or some kind of spark — either electrical or emotional — can be used to 'vivify' the body' (Bilbija, 'The Youngest Doll', pp. 878–79). Helena's power to create a human life aligns her with God's power to create an ideal human original, and thus surpasses Julián's own ability to form imperfect replicas of the real. Whereas Julián structures his dolls out of primarily synthetic materials, Helena forms her daughter solely out of organic material. Both have the power of animation, but the tools they have at their disposal are different. Helena's 'knowledge' to create human beings is biologically innate passed down via the female generational line. However Julián's knowledge of how to make the 'muñecas prohibidas' [prohibited dolls] (p. 26) is one which has been acquired through many years of 'entrenamiento e iniciación' [training and initiation] (p. 19) passed down the patriarchal line from grandfather to father to son and from his father's German associate Klaus, another paternal figure to Julián (p. 94). Julián's allusion to the 'genio del mal' [evil genie] (p. 29) in Helena's stomach suggests that Helena has magical abilities to animate her daughter. However, her ability to 'vivify' Violeta is inherent, unlike Julián's talent to bring his dolls to life which is fabricated.

The Double Encoding of Silence and Feminist Contestatory (Im)possibilities

Given that the real Violeta is a reminder of Julián's frustrated 'fantasy of a child born from man alone' (Braidotti, p. 87) and that she will never be possessed by him, the Violetas embody the demiurge's desire to have utter control over his female creations and possessions, on whose bodies he seeks to stamp the sign of the master. In his quest to reproduce his daughter in his simulacra he seeks to replicate 'ideal' woman/childhood, whereby woman/child is the embodiment of men's desires which require her to be subordinate and silent. Even though the dolls are anthropomorphized ('que sangraran, entre otras propiedades físicas como el calor corporal y la textura aduraznada de la piel' [can bleed, amongst other physical characteristics, such as corporeal heat or suppleness of skin texture], p. 37), they are divested of human autonomy and have been created to be exploited sexually in a socially consequence-free manner by their abusing owners. The male clients to whom Julián sells the dolls can cross into rape fantasy without repercussions: 'encontraron en las Violetas la esperanza de consumar una violación silenciosa [...] sin consecuencias' [discovered in the Violetas the hope of carrying out a silent rape [...] without consequences] (p. 37). Thus *jouissance* — that is, in Kristeva's conception of the term, the bliss of sexual enjoyment without fear of the costs — is what fuels in Julián and his clients the unrepressed pursuit of paedophilic, sado-masochistic, and sexually violent pleasures.[33] The word 'silenciosa' is of particular significance as it underlines how Clavel's fictive dolls appeal to men because of their subservient quality (p. 82). Julián promotes his dolls commercially with the promise of 'silent love', in the sense that they are unable to tell of the sexual crime committed against them. Their silence is of importance as it is anchored in gender-based power relations and the dynamics of control and submission. Julián's and his male clients' 'relationship' with the dolls reinforces an image of the powerless female self, as well as women's historical voicelessness and the denial of their authority to articulate their own lives and desires in the face of patriarchy. Sexual role-playing is one example in particular which permits men to render women muted objects. Role-playing is one fantasy Julián indulges in by enacting perverse sadomasochistic and bondage-like scenarios in which the dolls are hit and physically restrained by him (pp. 98–99).[34]

Clavel's description of the dolls as 'herméticas' (p. 99) is significant as it highlights the double function which silence plays. Whilst it perpetuates female powerlessness, so too is it a will not to speak imbued with transgressive and feminist potentiality. Debra Castillo sees silence as a subversive tool and quotes Trinh T Minh-ha: 'Silence is so commonly set in opposition to speech. Silence as a will to say or a will to unsay and as a language of its own has barely been explored'.[35] Clavel's dolls use silence (p. 99) as a weapon of resistance against male abuse. But Castillo also points to the limitations of silence, particularly as a political strategy (*Talking Back*, p. 40). *Las Violetas* offers diverse possibilities for resistance with the playful shuffling of different levels of hitherto silenced realities such as the unspeakable topic of rape and paedophilia where women are the objects of that abuse, and which imply a powerful feminist questioning of male structures of knowledge, gender, and power. Speaking (out) is thus an important element here and is set up against the notion of speechlessness. The Violeta dolls are apparently speechless. According to Bilbija, the Golem is not mute by nature but rather because of the '(socially) "impure" tendencies of her creator, such as sexual exploitation, it is understandable why the female Golem does not have a chance (nor is it in the interest of their demiurge) to possess the power of speech' ('Las Hortensias', p. 257). Whilst it is not Julián's intention to bestow such a power on his dolls, they do nevertheless speak out against his 'impure' tendencies: 'eran también esfinges del destino cuyos labios inmóviles parecían murmurar: "Sabemos mucho mejor que tú mismo lo que estás pensando detrás"' [they were also sphinxes of destiny whose immobile lips seemed to be whispering: 'we know much more than you do what you are really thinking deep down'] (p. 74). It is unclear if the dolls' vivification is a result of Julián's imagination or their wilful selves, but their outspokenness confronts Julián's sense of imperviousness and inner fears of losing control over his creations and his own mind (p. 74). Another instance in which voice denotes the dolls' assertiveness is seen when Julián is haunted by their silent thoughts of becoming human: '¿Qué piensa una muñeca cuando le haces el amor? ¿Acaso su carne dormida no soñará que es en verdad una muchacha?' [What is a doll thinking when you make love to her? Will her dormant flesh in fact be dreaming that she is a real girl?] (p. 94). Julián's terror of losing control over his products also resides in the dolls' desires to become real women: 'Alguna feminista me acusará de equiparar a las mujeres con muñecas, de reducirlas a su esencia de objeto ritual. Por lo contrario. Las Violetas siempre aspiraron a convertirse en mujeres' [Some feminist will criticize me for comparing women to dolls, of reducing them essence to ritual object. On the contrary. The Violetas were always aspired to transform themselves into women] (p. 37). The dolls' vivification leads them to become increasingly unwieldy and they refuse to 'participate in the rituals and games' Julián fashions for them (p. 95). His inability to control his Golemas presupposes a loss which is indicated in his decline towards hyperreal madness. Julián's inability to control his artificial creations becomes a metonym for his frustrated desire to possess his daughter in the flesh. Central to Julián's doll-making process is his desire to capture the 'truth' of his daughter in her replicas, and therefore an apparent tension between the 'original' and the replica emerges whereby his daughter is designated as 'el modelo original' [the original model] (p. 34). *Las Violetas* can be understood within the context of postmodernism whereby the original/replica tension serves to challenge traditional notions of immutable subjectivity. In order to capture Violeta's essence, Julián creates dolls which replicate physiological characteristics of his daughter such as her virginal odour (pp. 34, & 90–91). He seeks to perfect the replicas in order to produce a model which most closely resembles his daughter (p. 94). Yet the closer Julián attempts to replicate the original, the more removed the 'real' Violeta is. The dolls, with their 'extraordinary resemblance' to Violeta, are only a copy of a copy of the real, given that they are based on a photograph of Violeta (p. 94). Towards the end of the novella the Violeta copies and original become confused (p. 110). In the final passage of the novella, Julián has a dream in which his 'amazona', mistaken for the doll 'Desnombrada' [Nameless], one of Julián's artificial humanoids, emasculates him and he becomes pregnant 'por fin ha de sembrarme en el vientre un nombre y un rostro verdaderos' [and finally to plant in my womb an authentic name and face].[36] Through his emasculation and impregnation, this passage powerfully marks the Golem demiurge's loss of control over Violeta and his replicas, as well as a shift in power. It evinces a role reversal indicating the female/Violeta/Desnombrada's inscription on the male as a means of marking him as her sexual and procreative possession. It also reinforces, in a parodic fashion of sorts, the inevitable maternal presence which Julián so vehemently has attempted to deny, as previously explored.

The blending of Violeta with the artificial 'Desnombrada' points to the ultimate power they have to evade the grip of patriarchy. *Las Violetas* follows the tradition of the Golem myth whereby the production of the male Golem typically ends in the destruction of the demiurge (Bilbija, 'Las Hortensias', p. 263). But *Las Violetas* also breaks with the traditional Golem structure whereby the fall of the demiurge typically coincides with the end of his creation ('Las Hortensias', p. 247). In a world in which the female is inscribed in destructive patriarchal values, *Las Violetas* appears to give the female reader little hope for feminist contestatory possibilities. However, the fusion of the real and hyperreal at the end of the novella signals the resistance of both the flesh and blood Violeta and her artificial humanoid copies to the impression of the fatherly inscription. Such opposition also points to a 'powerful cultural deconstruction of an everlasting patriarchal yearning to appropriate the female body and its reproductive function' (Bilbija, 'The Youngest Doll', p. 887). Taking my cue from the cyborg and cyber theories of Donna Haraway and Rosi

Braidotti, the fusion of the real and unreal provides feminist renewal as it highlights the possibilities latent in the post-human whereby the tension between the human and the artificial serves to disrupt traditional patriarchal understandings of reality, selfhood, identity, and the body. Clavel thus can be seen as proposing in the real female Violeta and the 'Desnombrada' doll — whose identity is composed of both the female and the male (pp. 98–99) — a newly combined self in the form of the cyborg whose fluid characteristics do away with the law of the father and distinctions such as human/machine or male/female differences. Drawing from Donna Haraway's 'A Cyborg Manifesto', Braidotti comments that the cyborg 'aims at reconceptualizing the human being as an embodied and yet nonunified, and therefore non-Cartesian, entity' (*Nomadic Subjects*, p. 106). Ultimately the cyborg-doll allows for a new space, certainly more utopian, where 'speechlessness will be voluntary, where masters will vanish, and where values will be human. There, the doll would be only a doll' ('The Youngest Doll', p. 887).

Textual Constructedness and Authorial Intent

In a text in which the simulacrum has taken the place of the referent, *Las Violetas* points to the immanence of the hyperreal, underlines notions of 'aura' (Benjamin, 'The Work of Art'), the text's constructedness, as well as its rich intertextuality which calls for a search for the novella's literary sources. Such postmodern characteristics challenge the manner in which 'authoritative' literature and art champion such concepts as uniqueness, authenticity, and authority, and uphold jurisdictions and boundaries between individual authors, eras, texts, and genres (Davies, *Allende,* p. 415). The Violeta doll replicas as primers of imperfect (human) reality signal the view that 'art is a powerful though partial and imperfect copy of life that often replaces the real' (*Allende*, p. 422), whereby 'reality and its artistic representation become fused as reality [...] packaged as art' (*Allende*, p. 422). This fusion exemplifies how Clavel's novella is more about the work of artifice than the story of one man's sexual lust for his daughter. For Julián the desire to capture the essence of his daughter is less about the 'real' Violeta, and more about a languishing for aesthetic beauty. Julián's doll-making starts out as a Freudian subliminal labour aimed at substituting his passion for the inaccessible 'object' of his desire: 'busqué consumar en las Violetas una pasión que me abrazaba las entrañas, en vez de dirigirla hacia el objeto real' [I sought to consume in the Violetas, instead of in the real object, a passion which had taken over my entire being] (p. 47). Yet art as a sublimation of sexuality is challenged, given that for Julián sex gradually becomes 'the ancilla of art'.[37] Julián's doll-making and his narrative are inspired by his wish to capture the elusive beauty of the 'nymphet' Violeta which he summons in his mind, verbally, and through his Golema creations. For Julián his Violetas are inspired more by the creative imagination rather than his actual daughter: 'brotaron como capullos desde el fermento de mis fantasias y mis entrañas [...] me consolaba imaginar el tacto inmóvil y reverente de sus hermanas' [flourished like buds from within my brewing fantasies and my inner being [...] I took solace by imagining the immobile and reverent touch of her sisters] (p. 81). Julián perceives his dolls not as mass-produced objects (p. 44), but rather as unique beautiful works of art of the creative genius. When Julián is overtaken by creative fervour fuelled by his lust, he makes a number of sketches of the dolls on a blank canvas (p. 81). Etching on the virginal canvas connotes Julián's desire to leave his fatherly (reproductive) imprint on his doll creations.[38] It also becomes a platform upon which ideas are born from the artist whose creative genius is marked by his desire to overcome the perennial challenge of making something out of nothing. Julián's drive to encapsulate aesthetic beauty in his 'original' creations becomes an affirmation of their auratic quality.[39] But by being sold to paedophilic clients, they become inexorably linked to monetary value and market forces, and therefore their aura invariably diminishes. Another aspect which threatens the dolls' uniqueness, and therefore their aura, is that they have been mechanically reproduced. By populating her text with mass-produced dolls, replicas of a mould which has been inspired by photographs of the 'original', Clavel can be seen to celebrate the disappearance of aura and inauthenticity in order to confound concepts of origins and originiality. Whilst Julián sees his mass-produced dolls as artistic creations, they explode the notion of artistic creation as being devoid of utilitarian use. Julián is no artist as such but rather 'a self-made man whose ownership and management of a doll shop have made him wealthy. His artwork consists not in what he makes, but what he does with what is made for him through modern technology'.[40]

Even Julián's surname 'Merchant' serves to bolster his role as a money-making businessman. Even though Julián asserts that it was not his idea to commercialize the prohibited Violetas (p. 94), his products are 'subject to all the effects of mechanical reproduction: serialization, commercialization, marketing' (Sucre, p. 485). The idea of attributing the work of art to one single author is also undermined as the creation of the dolls is part of a collaborative feat. Julián states that he was the one who conceived them (p. 126), reinforcing his role as architect of the dolls, but various other 'authors' are involved in their production including Klaus Wagner, Clara, and various master turners (p. 82). The idea that Julián's dolls are not authorially unique is illustrated in the manner in which they have been inspired by Hans Bellmer's mannequins in *Les Jeux de la poupée*. Furthermore, although Julián asserts that his creations are not inspired by the Hortensias (p. 38), the reader is alerted to the significance of intertextuality in the making of *Las Violetas*.

Intertextuality in *Las Violetas* serves to underscore literary constructedness and the notion that all texts, both literary and non-literary, are intertextual. Similarly, Irma López notes that Clavel's intertextual novella serves creatively to engage with the dynamic participation of the reader (*Confluencias y demarcaciones*, p. 182). The doll replica and her simulated human functions, such as virginal odour 'of forest and honey' (p. 90), represent parodic tropes for, firstly, Julián's obsessive yet frustrated quest for core identity, and secondly, the impossibility of a singular authorial identity attached to works of art or literature. The significance of the tropes can be usefully placed in the context of the role of the intertext in Patrick Süskind's *Perfume: The Story of a Murderer*, a novel which has left its odorous imprint on *Las Violetas*. In Süskind's novel, the recurring metaphor of the perfume is an appropriate trope for this self-constructing text which is comprised of 'a parodic blend of the tradition's master codes', whereby 'the myth of singular voice [...] is abandoned and the dead ancestors return in citational clusters'.[41] Jean-Baptiste Grenouille's perfume-making process as analogy of intertextual alchemy (Adams, p. 273), echoes Julián's alchemical doll-making which in turn parallels the intertextual process of *Las Violetas*. As with Süskind's text, *Las Violetas* is a prime example of postmodern pastiche, in which the intertextual literary allusions serve to underpin the novella's status as a work of art. Yet even as the novella retains traces of previous voices, these texts are not mimetically absorbed but rather transformed through recourse to parody and literary reworkings. The chapter in which Julián commissions Clara to produce a perfume to replicate his daughter's virginal odour reeks of Süskind's text, yet subtle parody becomes apparent. In the original text the knowledge of perfume making is held by men and is passed down patrilineally, and thus by replacing the male alchemist with a female one, *Las Violetas* can be seen to mock the common association of scientific knowledge and expertise with maleness.

The contestation of imitation similarly emerges in the references to Hans Bellmer's *Les Jeux de poupée*, such as in the role-playing scenes of tortured dolls which Julián sets up and are referred to by him as 'The games of the Violetas' (p. 97). Whilst this suggests Julián's blind adaptation of the 'original' text, the creative thrust in *Las Violetas* resides in its intertextual 'creative plagiarism'. This becomes most apparent in the manner in which literary characters associated with other texts transform into other literary characters from other texts. As Horacio — the protagonist of Henández's *Las Hortensias* — narrates his deluded story about the 'Brotherhood', Julián is reminded of the White Rabbit in *Alice in Wonderland* (1866) (*Las Violetas*, pp. 117–18). Historical artists and writers and their creative products or characters also populate Clavel's novella. Whilst their histories are provided with a new lease of life, so too are they queered given that they are different from those linked to the original texts. Thus, Hans Bellmer himself is made a character of the novella whose fate is clouded by uncertainty. The fusion of historical facts about his life with fictional embellishment (pp. 101, 124, & 125) becomes a metonym for 'creative plagiarism' and multivoicedness of postmodern texts, in which the boundaries between individual authors or artists and their work are exploded. References to Felisberto Hernández's 'real' step-brother, Horacio Hernández, who claims to be the author himself and to have written *Las Hortensias*, mock these particular delimitations. Giving the character the first name of the *Las Hortensias* protagonist and the surname of the text's creator, as well as including a number of biographical details attributed to the historical Felisberto Hernández, demonstrates the manner in which intertextuality can lead to alchemical innovation. Julián becomes uncertain if HH is who he claims to be or is in fact the author of *Las Hortensias*, a member of the 'Brotherhood' sect claiming to be HH, or even FH. Julián's uncertainty (or deluded mind) becomes apparent as the initials of HH and FH merge to create a new fictive character who bears the initials of FHH (p. 129). The shapeshifting HH (whose initials could also be a play on Nabokov's Humbert Humbert) reveals to Julián: 'Soy Horacio Hernández, soy Felisberto Hernández, puedo ser Klaus Wagner o Julián Mercader [...] Yo no soy nadie, soy muchos' [I am Horacio Hernández, I am Felisberto Hernández, I could be Klaus Wagner or

Julián Mercader [...] I am nobody, I am many] (p. 131). Like the doll replicas, HH's multiple identities bolster the postmodern view of subjectivity as unfixed. But this particular ambiguity has a jarring, yet humorous, effect aimed at drawing our attention to Clavel's self-consciousness. The blurring of fact and fiction underscores the manner in with the real and imaginary cannot be kept apart. As Julián notes in relation to the hazy story surrounding the Hortensias and their 'authors': 'ignoro si el arte siguió a la vida, o si fue la vida la que se obstinó en parecerse al arte' [I don't know if art followed life, or if it was life that insisted on appearing like art itself] (p. 38). Ironically, Julián's own life and his doll replicas which are imbued with the hyper(real) also exemplify the view that life can imitate art and vice versa.

HH's morphing identities similarly point to the omnipotence of the author of fiction. An author can determine the fate of characters, and it becomes apparent that the all-powerful 'Sacerdotista' mentioned at the start and end of the novella could in fact be the demiurge Ana Clavel, the author-figure who determines the destinies of Julián and others. The novella is an example of polyphony in the sense that the author's voice appears to have no more authority than the voices of the other characters, who have diverse opinions, and the reader produces meaning(s) and interpretations which the author cannot predict or control. For Barthes such polyphony evinces the death of the author and the birth of the reader.[42] Yet Clavel's novella also gives emphasis to the presence of the 'mother' of the work and in particular to the unequal relationship between author and character. Clavel, the author, confers on her reader a privileged narrative point of view in which we are given, as already mentioned, an insight into the inconsistent account of an unreliable narrator who is not conferred a position to see truth. Julián is aware that his life is spiralling out of control but is not granted the ability to comprehend that he is the Golem-like product of the 'original' author-creator intent on making him part of her 'crazed' plot. Violeta notes that Julián has become like one of his doll creations (p. 77), alluding indirectly to Clavel's own particular mode of ownership of her puppet-like Julián. Clavel provides dramatic (un)structure in his life in order to assert her hold of the narrator-character. From an existence of relative stability, reflected in Julián's inheritance of the doll factory, marriage to a wife, and conception of a daughter, Clavel immediately plunges her character into an existence of crazed erotic obsession. She occasionally presents the object of desire bodily to him but always keeps it just out of reach and thus, like Tantalus, Julián is left in a constant state of yearning. Clavel's punishment of her character is signalled by his position of demented unknowing. From his initial self-assured moral position relating to his 'harmless crime' and clarity of objective in creating the dolls, he is henceforth thrown into uncertainty. As HH's presence becomes ever more visible in his life, Julián is plunged into doubt about the 'Worshippers' and his fate at their hands. Whilst the reader is equally thrust into unknowing, so too do we become aware that Julián's uncertainty is propelled not by the 'Brotherhood' but rather by Clavel, in whose hands her character's fate lies. Clavel almost kills off her character, who suffers a heart attack because of the strain his muddled existence causes him, but instead of dying he survives only then to be plunged into hyperreal madness and a reclusive existence tainted with delusions of persecution (pp. 17 & 133).

Perhaps the clearest sign of Clavel's manipulation of her unknowing character is seen in the manner in which she makes him victim of her demented genre-bending experimentation. Julián's mad-scientist role using incongruous techniques in his laboratory to develop his dolls has its analogy with Clavel as demented writer piecing together her narrative with different genres. Julián, the laboratory guinea-pig, bears the brunt of Clavel's alchemy. The novella's 'mad' quality is marked by its unexpected fusion and parody of different genres, which confuse both reader and character alike. Whilst the broad erotic literary genre of the novella is constantly foregrounded, so too is the reader's expectation of the sexual constantly frustrated. This is made apparent as the sexual content of the novella is bombarded by the presence of other genres which have no apparent congruity with the former. Thus the novella shifts from a plot driven by sexual intent to one which fuses a mad-scientist-as-creator plot and the fantastical. The latter is underpinned in the form of speaking dolls, the fusion of fictional characters with real living subjects, and the ominous 'Hermandad'.

But even then the novella undergoes an abrupt transformation as yet another genre emerges, namely, a pseudo-detective or mystery drama in which Julián is trying to unravel the mysterious death of Klaus, who HH is, what the role of the sect is, and what his own fate may be at their hands. Julián at one point notes that Felisberto Hernández's *Las Hortensias* is an 'abysmal account' (p. 111) failing to see that his own abysmal experiences are part of a metafictive existence subject, not to the laws of science or religion, but to those of literariness as he is haphazardly tumbled around in a demented jumble of genres. As a novella which can be placed in the generic genre of the fantastic, readers are expected to suspend their belief and not to question the illogical occurrences in the novella. But Clavel parodies this assumption, as she draws our attention to its incredibility. As HH recounts his 'outrageous story', Julián is described as being in a state of 'dumbfounded immobility' (p. 119). His stupefaction reflects our own sense of disbelief which the plotline elicits. Equally, Julián's stupefaction relates to his own lack of awareness countered by our awareness of his existence as the character of a 'maudit' [cursed] plotline in which he is no more than a verbal construct. Julián's and our incredulity is bolstered as the pseudo-detectivesque plotline becomes a parody of itself. The police get involved in the Klaus murder case and although a number of people are made suspects, including Julián himself, the case is closed following a botched operation (p. 113). HH subsequently materializes in Julián's doll factory and informs Julián that he knows who has killed Klaus (p. 113). The setting in which this exchange takes place provides a comical take on 'serious' suspense-type fiction. A number of rhetorical devices are used to exaggerate the increasing sense of tension, such as repeated references to the stormy weather and torrential downpours (pp. 113, 115, 117, 121, & 127), and to Julián's and HH's increasingly paranoid state of mind. When HH finally reveals that it is the 'Brotherhood of Eternal Light' who is guilty of Klaus's death (p. 121) the reader is far from horrified given all the diversionary tactics that have been used, from the repeated meteorological references to the larger-than-life accounts HH provides about his 'real' identity (p. 38). After HH reveals that he is FH, he leaves Julián the only surviving copy of the

Las Hortensias which has been written in an invented stenography (p. 38). The only words that Julián can make out are: 'Obras póstumas (Mi vida como muerto) por Felisberto H. Hernández' [Posthumous Work (My life as a dead man) by Felisberto H. Hernández] (p. 128). The intrigue surrounding HH's character deepens as the reader — as indeed Julián — is left baffled as to whether this posthumous work has been written by the character who goes by the name of HH, FH, or the merged FHH. But intrigue turns to laughter as the narrator notes that he should express amusement at Horacio's 'outrageous story' (p. 120). Laughter serves to undermine the 'seriousness' of certain types of 'historias de detectives' [detective stories] (p. 118) and highlights a self-conscious statement by Clavel that her own manic invention, like that of HH, can be subject to the reader's amusement. At the same time, Clavel revels in madness, an intrinsic element of the queer, and serves to question, as we have seen, perceptions of the normal or perverse, the boundaries between the real and the unreal, and, finally, patriarchal or literary conventions. As in Lewis Carroll's *Alice in Wonderland*, madness deviates from the norm in *Las Violetas* and thus offers liberating possibilities. In the context of literary history:

> Madness has turned out to be a rich and many-layered concept. Insanity not only affects (mental) action and communication in the fictional world; it also brings in fundamental concepts such as the creative imagination, genius [...] [and] considerations of artistic and literary production.[43]

Clavel described to me the writing process of *Las Violetas* as frenzied, partially mirroring Julián's own demented state with his doll production.[44] The writing process for her was troublesome, both because of the edgy thematic and the demented narrative threads she had to bring together, reflecting the narrator's own difficulty in structuring his thoughts. Yet whilst lunacy leads to Julián's demise as he submerges himself in hyperreal realms, madness is a rejuvenating force for Ana Clavel, the creative genius of *Las Violetas*. In this respect the Golem myth is reworked, as the female demiurge survives and her product in the form of a book is completed, whilst the male Golem by-product is destroyed.

Notes to Chapter 6

1. Yanet Aguilar Sosa, 'Le da voz propia al incesto y sus abismos', *El Universal*, 7 November 2007, <http://www.eluniversal.com.mx/cultura/54563.html> [accessed 22 June 2014].
2. Unpublished document supplied to me by Clavel in 2008.
3. Clavel, unpublished material.
4. 'Los 10 libros más vendidos de la semana', <http://espanol.news.yahoo.com/s/ap/071116/entretenimiento/esp_lib_los_diez_libros> [accessed 22 June 2014]. For an incisive analysis of *Las Violetas*, see López, *Confluencias y demarcaciones*, pp. 143–75, and Graciela Martínez-Alce, 'La apropiación y sus formas: las violetas de Ana Clavel', in Miguel Rodríguez Lozano (ed.), *Nada es lo que parece: Estudios sobre la novela Mexicana 2000–2009* (Mexico City: Universidad Nacional Autónoma de México, Instituto de Investigaciones Filológicas, Centro de Estudios Literarios), pp. 107–21.
5. <www.tiempolibre.com.mx/blog/> and <http://mx.answers.yahoo.com/question/index?qid=20080610112612AAwHMdo> [accessed 22 June 2014].
6. 'Ganan mexicanos Premio Internacional Juan Rulfo', <http://www.terra.com.mx/articulo.aspx?articuloId=177386> [accessed 22 June 2014].
7. Juan José Reyes, 'Seducciones múltiples de Ana Clavel', *Siempre!*, LIV: 2858 (2007), 70–71 (p. 70).

8. Victoria Best, 'The Uses and Abuses of Children: Fairy Tales and The Pornographic', in Anna Fahraeus and Annakatrin Jonsson (eds.), *Textual Ethos Studies, or Locating Ethics*, 26, Critical Studies: Critical Theory, Literature & Culture (Amsterdam: Rodopi: 2005), pp. 229–44 (p. 230). Julián believes that the nymphatic quality of his daughter Violeta was already brewing *in utero* (p. 30). The demonic qualities of Humbert Humbert's 'girl-children nymphets' (Nabokov, *Lolita* (London: Penguin, 1980), p. 17) is echoed in Julián's description of his daughter doll replicas as 'flores del mal' [flowers of evil] (*Las Violetas*, p. 111).
9. Humbert Humbert similarly perceives his sexual interest in underage girls as 'practically harmless' (*Lolita*, p. 87).
10. Dany Nobus and Lisa Downing (eds.), *Perversion: Psychoanalytic Perspectives/Perspectives on Psychoanalysis* (London: Karnac Books, 2006), pp. 5 & 8.
11. Kristeva, *Strangers to Ourselves*, pp. 189 & 192.
12. Laura E. Tanner, 'Reading Rape: *Sanctuary* and *The Women of Brewster Place*', *American Literature*, 62:4 (1990), 559–82 (p. 564).
13. Nomi Tamir-Ghez, 'The Art of Persuasion in Nabokov's *Lolita*', *Poetics Today*, 11:2 (1979), 65–83 (p. 68).
14. Clavel, email to Lavery, 11 March 2014, 01:33
15. The fragmentation also suggests *jouissance*, thus emphasizing Julián's frustrated sexual desire for Violeta.
16. Dennis Coon and John O. Mitterer, *Introduction to Psychology: Gateways to Mind and Behavior*, 12th edn (Belmont, CA: Wadsworth, Cengage, 2010), p. 442.
17. Ana Clavel, 'Los Caballeros las prefieren mudas', *Nexos* (March 2008), 61–65 (p. 61).
18. Ksenija Bilbija, '"The Youngest Doll" by Rosario Ferré: On Women, Dolls, Golems and Cyborgs', *Callaloo: A Journal of African American and African Arts and Letters*, 17:3 (1994), 878–88 (p. 878).
19. Moshe Idel, *Golem: Jewish Magical and Mystical Traditions on the Artificial Anthropoid* (Albany: State University of New York Press, 1990), p. 3.
20. Ksenija Bilbija, '"Las Hortensias" by Felisberto Hernández: The Fabrication of Desire', in Giovanna Covi (ed.), *Critical Studies on the Feminist Subject* (Trento: University of Trento Press, 1997), pp. 245–63 (p. 249).
21. Baudrillard, *Simulations*.
22. Jean Baudrillard, *Simulacra and Simulation*, trans. by Sheila Faria Glaser (Ann Arbor: University of Michigan Press, 1994), p. 167.
23. Julián's horror at the sight of Naty's vaginal area is the trigger that leads to his obsession with the doll as fetish object.
24. Braidotti, *Nomadic Subjects*, p. 87.
25. Hernández's Hortensia doll also has signs of the maternal. Bilbija, 'Las Hortensias', p. 254.
26. Jane M. Ussher, *Managing the Monstrous Feminine: Regulating the Reproductive Body* (London: Routledge, 2006), p. 1.
27. Within a Kristevan framework, the abject is that which is 'radically excluded' but which 'from its place of banishment [...] does not cease challenging its master', Kristeva, *Powers of Horror*, p. 2. Abjection is caused by 'what disturbs identity, system, order. What does not respect borders, positions, rules' (*Powers of Horror*, p. 4). The abject threatens to destabilize the split between I and 'other', inside and outside (*Powers of Horror*, p. 7). In patriarchal society, 'woman' and the female body have come to be closely associated with the abject because they are cast as the negative 'other' to the male body, particularly when pregnant. Femininity is associated with 'the fluid, the viscous, the half-formed, or the indeterminate' in opposition to the masculine unified whole, Grosz, *Volatile Bodies*, p. 195. Aversion to fluids such as blood or vaginal secretions is related to the 'the horror of femininity' which Grosz in turn connects with 'the fear of being absorbed into something which has no boundaries of its own' (p. 194). In line with the Kristevan concept of the abject, for Bakhtin the grotesque 'means to concern oneself with the lower stratum of the body, the life of the belly and the reproductive organs; it therefore relates to acts of defecation and copulation, conception, pregnancy, and birth', *Rabelais and his World*, p. 21. In *Las Violetas* with its association with the inversion of hierarchy, the grotesque has a similar subversive function to carnival, and by extension the abject, as it serves to challenge pre-

established conceptions of the controlled (female) body. Yet also in Clavel's novella, as with the carnivalesque and the abject, the grotesque can also be linked to the notion of disempowerment and lacking female body.

28. Barbara Brook, *Feminist Perspectives on the Body*, Feminist Perspectives (London: Longman, 1990), p. 53; Grosz, *Volatile Bodies*, p. 205.
29. This particular ambiguity in relation to childbearing and motherhood is also seen in the short story 'Cuando María mire el mar', as discussed in Chapter 1.
30. Clavel, email to Lavery, 11 March (2014), 01:33.
31. I take my cue here from Lloyd Hughes Davies's analysis of Isabel Allende's *La Casa de los espíritus*. See *Allende: La Casa de los espíritus*, p. 419.
32. Creed, *Monstrous-feminine*, p. 48.
33. Ann Rosalind Jones, 'Writing the Body: Towards an Understanding of *L'Écriture féminine*', in Elaine Showalter (ed.), *The New Feminist Criticism: Essays on Women, Literature and Theory* (London: Virago Press, 1986), pp. 361–77 (p. 375).
34. This scene is reminiscent of Bellmer's haunting images of distorted and abused mannequins. Julián sees his own sadistic desires towards his dolls (and indirectly the real Violeta), which reduces them to unfeeling body parts, as a mirror image of those same impious desires articulated in Bellmer's photography collection (pp. 58–59).
35. Debra Castillo, *Talking Back: Toward a Latin American Feminist Literary Criticism* (Ithaca, NY: Cornell University Press, 1992), p. 40.
36. Clavel notes that the 'Desnombrada' could equally be seen as 'una emisaria de la demencial Hermandad de la Luz que lo va a convertir en hembra, como antes a Klaus' [an emissary of the demented Brotherhood of Light which is going to convert him into a woman, as happened with Klaus], email to Lavery, 11 March 2014, 01:33.
37. Nabokov cited in Ellen Pifer, 'The Lolita Phenomenon from Paris to Tehran', in Julian W. Connolly (ed.), *The Cambridge Companion to Nabokov* (Cambridge: Cambridge University Press, 2005), pp. 185–99 (p. 191).
38. Whereas the dolls epitomize Julián's ideal of procreation and creativity without maternal intervention, Clavel's short story 'Cuando María mire el mar' entails, as examined in Chapter 1, an inexorable link between procreation, creativity in the form of self-expression, and motherhood.
39. Benjamin, 'The Work of Art in the Age of Mechanical Reproduction'.
40. Natalia Sucre, 'Distracting Art: Reading Shock in Felisberto Hernández's "Las Hortensias"', *Hispania*, 86:3 (2003), 482–92 (p. 485).
41. Jeffrey Adams, 'Narcissism and Creativity in the Postmodern Era: The Case of Patrick Süskind's *Das Parfum*', *The Germanic Review*, 75:4 (2000), 259–79 (p. 271).
42. Roland Barthes, 'From Work to Text', in Josue V. Harari (ed.), *Textual Strategies* (New York: Cornell University Press, 1979), pp. 73–81 (p. 78).
43. Lars Bernaerts, Luc Herman, and Bart Vervacek, 'Narrative Threads of Madness', *Style*, 43:3 (2009), 283–90 (p. 285).
44. Informal discussion between Lavery and Clavel, Mexico, 2008.

CHAPTER 7

Las Violetas son flores del deseo
Peritextuality and Reader-Spectator Complicities

Perhaps more than the Lolitaesque thematics of *Las Violetas son flores del deseo*, it is the sexually explicit image of the book's front cover which caused greater shock.[1] It is this image which is the focus of the present chapter.[2] It will be argued that the negative reception of the book cover's explicit image may be understood as a reflection of a general discomfort that is often felt towards public displays of (semi-) nudity, despite the apparent relaxation of attitudes towards (semi-) nakedness in contemporary society. It will also be suggested that the erotic content of the image, which implies both a knowing and an unknowing, perturbs the viewer-reader's comfort zone. The image ambiguously plays upon a perceptible incongruity between innocent childhood and sexualized child-teenager and thus disturbs any possibility of offering a safe interpretation. Drawing from Gérard Genette's notion of paratextuality and specifically peritextuality, as well as from Pauline Harris and Barbara McKenzie's ideas on this concept, I will analyse the text's front cover image and other visual or peritextual elements including the title of the book and the blurb, in order to suggest that these serve as visual and textual hooks to entice the reader to cross, and equally to dissuade the reader from crossing, the threshold of the book. Thus, 'more than a boundary [...], the paratext is, rather, a threshold, or [...] a "vestibule" that offers the world at large the possibility of either stepping inside or turning away'.[3] Paratextuality refers to those literary and printerly 'thresholds' which mediate between book, author, publisher, and reader and comprises liminal devices and conventions which lie within the book, the so-called 'peritext', and outside it, the 'epitext' (Genette, p. 5). Book covers, back cover blurbs, epigraphs, titles of books, font styles, layout, and visual media are all examples of the peritext. Those elements which reside outside the text and form part of the private and public history of the book, such as marketing campaigns or interviews, are referred to as the epitext. Whilst both features are equally important in relation to the book's overall paratextual dimension, this chapter will focus, for reasons of space, on the peritextual devices surrounding the presentation of Clavel's novella.

Peritextuality might appear to have little bearing on one's interpretation of the text in hand, yet it is a 'fringe' of 'the printed text which in reality controls one's whole reading of the text' (Philippe Lejeune quoted in Genette, p. 2). For Genette, this edge represents:

> the conveyor of a commentary that is authorial or more or less legitimated by the author, constitutes a zone between text and off-text, a zone not only of transition but also of *transaction*: a privileged place of pragmatics and a strategy, of an influence on the public, an influence that [...] is at the service of a better reception for the text and a more pertinent reading of it (more pertinent, of course, in the eyes of the author and his allies). (*Paratexts*, p. 2)

Peritextuality, which acts as the interface between (potential) reader and text, is important for framing our expectations and interpretations of the text in hand as well as prompting us to step into the text itself.[4] Ultimately peritextuality is as significant as the text itself in how it mediates between the reader and the text (Harris, p. 2). Although peritextual elements are frequently intended by authors, illustrators, and publishers to frame the reader's expectations and interpretations, the way in which a reader decodes the peritext of the book is an individual affair. Whilst peritextuality can serve to anchor our interpretation, it also serves to disrupt interpretations, to create ambiguity or sense of dislocation (Harris, p. 6). Each time more information is revealed through the peritext, the (prospective) reader finds him- or herself having to modify his or her predictions about what the book might be about and to accommodate multiple perspectives.[5] The strong reactions that the image of *Las Violetas* has prompted in some can be explained in the context of the peritextual which functions to foreground the sensitive themes of paedophilia and rape as well as issues of reader-viewer complicity. I also propose that peritextuality has an ambiguous function, as it serves to anchor the reader's understanding on the one hand, yet also disrupts interpretations on the other hand, thus generating a sense of dislocation. Similarly whilst peritextual elements are presented in such a way in order to force upon the reader-viewer the position of accomplice, so too does our awareness of their constructedness serve to detach us from becoming implicated in the actual crime-scene the image intimates. Similarly however, the peritextual underlines the idea that the only violence the image hints at is fundamentally born of the reader's imagination and desire for that violence.

The illustration of the book cover of *Las Violetas* (figure 7.1) is a black and white photograph which was conceptualized by Ana Clavel and taken by Rogelio Cuéllar. It depicts a girl/woman lying amongst a bed of hydrangeas wearing school uniform, ballerina shoes, and white ruffle ankle socks. Her skirt is hitched up around her stomach and her legs, which are bent at the knees, are spread wide open, revealing her flowery underwear.

In an interview with Clavel, she mentioned that many had described her and Cuéllar's image as being 'muy fuerte' [hardcore] and the reason for which prospective readers may have been put off reading the book.[6] Such negative reaction to the female semi-nude may in part be understood in the context of the generalized 'fear' of (semi-) nudity. The naked body has been present since the earliest examples of Greek art, yet the creation and display of this kind of art continues to inflame opinions: 'today, even with our supposed relaxation of the codes of behaviour surrounding nudity, such images are considered provocative, dangerous, and are often

FIG. 7.1. Front cover of *Las Violetas son flores del deseo.* Digital image. Concept: Ana Clavel. Photo: Rogelio Cuéllar. Courtesy of Ana Clavel.

unwelcome in the public sphere'.[7] In many ways semi-nudity can be considered as more 'dangerous' than nudity itself because where glimpses of the nude body are revealed a 'knowing and unknowing begins'.[8] In relation to the book cover image of *Las Violetas,* Clavel reveals her surprise at the intense reactions expressed towards the image:

> Para muchos resultó escandalosa la imagen [...] yo traía la tradición de la mirada como punto de deslumbramiento ante el cuerpo femenino, una tradición que tiene hitos ejemplares en Courbet y *El origen del mundo; Étant donnés* de Duchamp, y las muñecas de Bellmer. Le hice la propuesta al fotógrafo Rogelio

Cuéllar que trabajáramos una serie entorno a esta temática. Así resultó la imagen de la portada pero nunca se me ocurrió que pudiera despertar tantos alegatos y reacciones.[9]

[For many the image was scandalous [...] I was drawing from a tradition of the admiring gaze towards the female body, a tradition which is exemplary in Courbet's *The Origin of the World*, *Étant donnés* by Duchamp and Bellmer's dolls. I proposed to the photographer Rogelio Cuéllar that we work on a series which revolved around such a theme. It is thus that the image came about but I never thought that this young girl on the front cover would unleash such diatribe and reactions]

As previously mentioned, Sanborns refused to sell *Las Violetas* on the grounds of the cover's explicit content. The chain promotes itself as a family store and therefore most likely would have perceived it as entirely inappropriate for them to stock this kind of book which appears to deal with underage pornographic material. Clavel candidly conveys her annoyance at Sanborns outdated puritanism:

Es una cuestión muy delicada pues Sanborns se está convirtiendo entonces en una especie de papá moral para decir qué es lo que está bien y qué es lo que no, y nos convierte al público en general en una suerte de minusválidos morales y mentales. (Aranda, 'El Centinela')

[This is a very delicate question given that Sanborns is becoming a kind of father of morality who determines what is correct and what isn't, and is converting us the general public into moral and mental handicaps of sorts]

It is not the first time that Clavel has had to contend with 'papá moral' regarding the content of her book covers. Indeed, back in 2005, just before *Cuerpo* was published with Alfaguara, the publishers suggested to the writer that she should rethink the image on the cover since the Ingresian female nude was too explicit and that Sanborns would possibly refuse to sell it:

Cuando propuse mi novela con el desnudo original en la portada, que es una obra considerada como un icono de la feminidad, mis editores me dijeron: es posible que Sanborns no la quiera distribuir por tratarse de un desnudo. Entonces, en lugar de pelear, le busqué una salida y la salida fue ponerle yo misma estas cintas de precaución, aprovechar la censura para volver la imagen más seductora y sugestiva.[10]

[When I proposed that my novel contain on its front cover the original nude, an art piece in itself which is considered as an icon of femininity, my editors said to me: it is quite possible that Sanborns will not want to distribute the book because it contains a nude. So, instead of fighting my corner, I found a way round things which involved me personally adding the barrier tapes and I thus took advantage of that censorship in order to make the image more seductive and suggestive]

As discussed in Chapter 5, in response to Alfaguara's recommendation, both Clavel and digital artist Paul Alarcón digitally manipulated the original and added a ribbon to the nude. This served to parody both censorship and social taboos surrounding sex and desire, as well as to attack Sanborn's posturing as guardian of social propriety. This particular episode can be understood in the wider context of the Mexican publishing industry and the problems which have hampered the Mexican book trade since the 1980s. In 1982, with the oil crisis, the devaluation of the peso and the nationalization of the Mexican banking system, the publishing industry underwent a major crisis whereby published output declined and publishers collapsed or merged with large multinational publishing corporations.[11] Since then, the literary publishing industry in Mexico has been monopolized by a number of major publishers, mainly foreign. The big players in the Mexican publishing industry preside over the production and distribution of books and are responsible for giving subsidies and discounts to those bookshops which sell their books to customers at a discount. The market position of independent bookshops in Mexico is effectively fettered by chains such as Gandhi and major retail stores like Sams, Palacio de Hierro, Wal Mart or Sanborns. With the increasingly competitive Mexican book industry at a near standstill because of unfair competition, the absence of reading habits, and soaring production and distribution costs, publishers like Alfaguara are very aware of the buying and selling power of the likes of Sanborns or Gandhi. Publishers are therefore frequently forced to bow to demands made by these major conglomerates by offering higher discount rates on the books they sell to them or, for instance, by feeling obliged to design their book covers to accord with the companies' ethical and business standards and practices.[12] In this respect, Alberto Aranda laments the monopoly that certain chain stores have:

> Además de influir en el precio al público, cadenas como Sanborns determinan de una u otra manera el diseño de las portadas de los libros, ya que una imagen, al no cubrir sus estándares, simplemente no tendrá cabida en sus establecimientos. ('El Centinela')
>
> [Apart from influencing book prices for the public, chains such as Sanborns determine one way or the other the design of book covers, since if a particular image does not fit its standards, it will simply not have a place in its establishments]

Traditional book publishing companies usually have all rights and creative control over the design and text of a book, meaning that authors usually have no involvement in decisions about how the book is designed, edited, or marketed. In this respect, Ana Clavel's experience with Alfaguara has been unusual as she has had a significant degree of involvement in the publishing process. With both *Cuerpo náufrago* and *Las Violetas son flores del deseo*, she had direct input in their editing, layout, cover design, and marketing.[13] Whilst Alfaguara encouraged Clavel to tone down the original *Cuerpo náufrago* image of the female nude, the publishers were nevertheless entirely happy with the choice of image for *Las Violetas son flores del deseo* despite its explicit content, and did not ask Clavel to alter the image in any way. By the time *Las Violetas* was published, Ana Clavel was already an established writer in Mexico with both *Los deseos y su sombra* and *Cuerpo náufrago* having been national sales successes. It appears that Alfaguara might have been willing to take a gamble with *Las Violetas*, regardless of the retail giant Sanborn's possible response, confident perhaps that the novella would sell on the author's name alone and be another hit with readers.[14]

Vexed responses to the cover contrast with some of the more positive reactions by the general reader of *Las Violetas* as seen in various blog entries in which the readers make frequent reference to the attention-grabbing cover.[15] Unless a reader is specifically looking for a particular book by a certain author, the illustration on the book cover is often the single most important factor in convincing him or her to buy and read that text. Having picked up the book and read the title and the back cover copy, there is of course no assurance that the reader will necessarily buy it. Yet frequently it is the case that not only image but title and back cover copy alike are all important peritextual devices which serve the purpose of hooking the reader.[16]

More crucially, though, peritexuality provides the reader with a point of entry into the fictive world contained within the book covers. The peritextual elements on the book jacket of *Las Violetas* encourage the reader to engage in a code-breaking process in order to decipher these devices and identify the possible relationship among them. As code breaker, the reader will not only have to make sense of the information that these paratextual devices communicate but also of the ways in which that information is constructed. As the reader of *Las Violetas* engages in making interpretations which are conveyed through the peritextual devices, he or she might be encouraged to consider a series of questions such as how peritextuality may confirm or disrupt his or her predictions about the content of the text, and how the peritext highlights ambiguity. Peritextual elements will also help readers to establish the genre of the book, to ascertain the purpose/s of the text in hand and to frame their reading focus. *Las Violetas*'s peritextuality thus prompts the reader to consider another set of questions such as what kind of text this may be, how the peritext helps him or her know what information about genre is being offered or how this particular information shapes his or her expectations about the text (Harris, p. 12). The title of *Las Violetas*, its cover copy and image all prompt the reader to frame the text within the broad genre of sexual fiction.[17] The word 'desire' appears both in the title of the book and then in the blurb, serving peritextually to anchor the reader's likely interpretation of the book's genre as sexual fiction.[18] This reading is further corroborated by the sexually explicit image on the cover, which we shall examine further on. Sexual fiction is meant here in the broadest sense of the term, encompassing any (sub-)genre such as erotic, soft/hard porn, or romantic fiction and, whilst each of these are different (sub-)genres in their own right with their own set of assumptions and expectations, they all share an interest in sexual themes. Thus, readers expect certain elements to be included in sexual fiction: it must deal substantively with 'narrative material that makes important and open use of sexual activity as its subject matter' and can encompass erotically stimulating descriptions which can, but not necessarily, lead to arousal in the reader.[19] Although sexual fiction can be predictable and pre-packaged according to popular formulas, it has no rules in terms of form and content, other than the fact that it should focus on erotic themes, and thus defies strict categorization (Charney, p. 164). Traditional sexual fiction such as the romance genre focuses almost invariably on tales of forbidden passion which are exclusively heterosexual, but sexual fiction on the whole is in its various manifestations extremely rich in its exploration of multiple points of view on sexual experiences, ranging from non-heterosexual sexualities including transgender to lesbianism. More vitally perhaps, the writer of sexual fiction pushes us into realms of 'reality' which frequently lie beyond our comfort zone by exposing us to what may be perceived of as deeply disturbing sexual manifestations such as sadomasochism, rape, or paedophilia. Although sexual fiction explores a range of sexual experiences, it frequently concentrates on adult sexual activity, and so when it deviates from this norm by focusing on paedophilia, child sexualisation, or abuse, the impact on the reader is to a large extent much greater. The peritextual in *Las Violetas* serves to forewarn the reader not only of the erotic nature of the text but also of its inquiry into the 'unspeakable' side of sexuality focusing on paedophilia, child sexualisation, and sexual violence. Rather than serving to anchor one preferred interpretation, the peritextual devices exploited on the book cover and epigraph of *Las Violetas* create in the main disruptions to our understanding. Far from conjuring up safe interpretations in the reader's mind, the peritext provokes questions and raises possibilities which threaten, incite discomfort, and thus produce, to draw from Haymes (p. 80), an 'unknowing'. Each time information is revealed through each peritextual device, we find that our interpretations are subjected to modification, disruption, or disquieting ambiguity. It is perhaps precisely because of the unease elicited through these peritextaul elements that the book cover caused the tumult it has following its publication.

The photograph on the cover of *Las Violetas* draws its inspiration from a photogram in Catherine Breillat's film *Anatomie de l'infer* [Anatomy of Hell] (2004) and Jean Désiré Gustave Courbet's painting *L'Origine du monde* (1866). Courbet's work portrays the close-up view of the pubic area and stomach of a naked woman with her legs spread open whilst lying on a bed. The *Las Violetas* photograph is also influenced by Duchamp's framed artwork *Étant donnés* (1946–66) a hybrid art piece which combines photography and art installation as well as Hans Bellmer's collection of photographs of mannequins *Les Jeux de la poupée* (1949). In *Étant donnés* we are presented with a wooden door with two peep holes through which we can see a three-dimensional diorama depicting an autumn landscape. In the midst of this scenery is a life-size model of a naked woman lying on her back, with her face obscured, legs spread wide open, and vagina fully exposed to the viewer. She is holding a gas lamp in one hand in the air and in the background a *trompe l'oeil* waterfall can be observed. The peritextual element of *Las Violetas* is clearly significant here to making intertextual associations that help shape our assumptions of the novella's erotic nature.[20] Whilst Courbet's and Duchamp's works are ambiguous in their own way and may perturb the viewer because of their unabashed exposure of nudity, the shock factor is lessened precisely because little or nothing is left to the imagination. In contrast, the illustration on the cover of *Las Violetas*, whilst brazenly sexual, is far more provocative in its suggestiveness, thus allowing for multiple, even incongruous, readings. The peritextual elements on the book cover deliberately draw our attention towards the sexual. The photograph is framed to focus on the pubic area, whilst the girl's head falls beyond the edge of the composition. The hydrangeas to the left of the girl are slightly out of focus whereas the hydrangeas to the right of her are obscured by the title of the text which is framed within a purple rectangle. The girl's left leg carries over onto the purple rectangle in almost collage fashion. Thus both the composition of the photograph and the position of the title of the book on the cover work strategically, drawing the spectator's gaze in a kind of funnel effect towards the girl's pubic area. The anonymous, faceless body does not so much suggest as flaunt the idea of a girl-child as a sexual object for the delectation and use of the (male) gazee.

The photograph may have caused the stir it has because of the way in which it draws attention to that which is not supposed to be looked at or imagined: a sexualized, under-aged schoolgirl whose panties are so tight-fitting that the spectator can almost make out (or imagine?) the shape of her genitalia. By luring our gaze towards the illicit, the image also confronts us with feelings — whether conscious or unconscious — of shame, guilt, lust, or desire. The image purposefully creates discomfort in the viewer through its apparent contradiction between innocent childhood and sexualized child-teenager. The blurring of the lines between childhood and womanhood — which are suggested in the girl's school uniform with its connotations in the main of innocence and the non-sexual, on the one hand, and her brazen, self-assured sexualized pose, on the other — has a jarring effect on the viewer, disturbing any possibility of offering a safe interpretation. Clavel's intention may well have been to reveal what some may perceive as an uncomfortable truth: that young under-aged girls are increasingly experienced with many forms of sexuality in today's society. Thus the photograph works here as a means of mocking commonplace postulations about sexual propriety and an ideology of 'natural' female self-control and modesty. Paradoxically, the image reflects society's awareness of young women's increased sexual self-assertiveness, whilst also revealing its reactive desire to see these young women as disempowered, infantilized, and objectified, in other words, rendered 'unthreatening'. The image also may signal the photographer's taunting awareness of the (male) eroticization of the schoolgirl in uniform, a sexual fetish prevalent in both Western and especially Japanese popular culture. Such a fixation is associated with the so-called 'Lolita' complex, a term derived from Nabokov's novel *Lolita*, which refers to adult men's sexual predilection for prepubescent or under-age girls. Clavel and Cuéllar's photograph points towards the underlying irony of society's fickle morality: whilst paedophilic sexual perversion of this kind is putatively condemned, the promotion in visual culture of 'barely-legals' and the adultification of under-aged girls mimicking adult-like sexualized poses are sanctioned by the media and the consumer alike.

As we observe the image on the front cover of *Las Violetas*, we feel the urge to try to make sense of what we see, yet the photograph itself resists providing us with any concrete answers. Our compunction to ascertain the identity of the girl on the cover proves futile since her face is obscured from sight. As the subtle photographic techniques of focus and framing devices force the viewer's eyes towards the girl's pubic area, we are compelled to consider why it is that she is laying amidst the hydrangeas with her legs splayed: is this an open invitation to sexual intercourse? Or are we about to witness something much more sinister altogether? Since the image itself denies us any kind of satisfactory resolution, we look for clues in other peritextual elements presented to us on the book cover as well as the epigraph. As the reader's attention moves away from the image on the book cover, to the epigraph and then to the back cover copy, so too is the reader compelled to rethink his or her understanding of the image and expectations about the content of *Las Violetas* as a whole.

The *Las Violetas* epigraph reads: '...por mucho menos se muere' [one dies for much less]. In a work of fiction the epigraph is frequently allographic, that is, a quotation which is 'attributed to an author who is not the author of the work' (Genette, p. 151). In *Las Violetas* the 'epigraphed' (Genette, p. 151) author is not acknowledged and given that the sentence is not within quotation marks it would not make it immediately apparent that it is an allographic epigraph (Genette, p. 153). Genette notes that in such instances of anonymous epigraphs:

> thanks to common knowledge or patient scholarship, the name of the epigraphed may be unearthed. The ordinary reader, when not helped by some editorial note, most often remains in a state of uncertainty as the epigrapher intended, and is left to his conjectures or his indifference. (*Paratexts*, p. 153)

The *Las Violetas* reader may well not be able to identify the quotation or its source, and the words may not help him or her in trying to unearth the meanings of the image on the front cover of Clavel's novella. At the same time, its anonymity can be seen as fulfilling the typical use of the epigraph by authors as a 'mute gesture whose interpretation is left up to the reader' (Genette, p. 156). In an informal email exchange, Clavel explained that she did not want to attribute the epigraph to its author because it would frame the potential reader's understanding. She explained to me that the quotation was taken from *Les Chants de Maldoror* by the Count of Lautréamont (aka Isidor Lucien Ducasse):

> El epígrafe en francés dice así: '... on meurt à moins'. Yo no quise poner el origen de la cita porque me parecía predisponer la novela demasiado hacia una literatura "maldita". En la edición francesa sí apareció el nombre de Lautréamont porque el traductor me convenció de amparar la novela bajo la sombra de Ducasse.[21]

> [The epigraph in French says the following: '... on meurt à moins'. I did not want to insert a reference to where the quotation originated from because I thought that this would frame the novella too much within a 'maudit' [cursed] literature. In the French edition the name of Lautréamont did appear because the translator convinced me that I should shelter the novella under the shadow of Ducasse]

If the reader identifies the quotation and its source, then the epigraph could be seen as working peritextually to pre-empt his or her understanding of the cover's image. Given that Ducasse's work contains an array of expressions of outlawed sexuality such as pederasty, coprophilia, and bestiality, the reader is alerted to the front cover's own exploration of forbidden forms of sexual desire. Epigraphs work in the main to comment on a text 'whose meaning it indirectly specifies or emphasises' (Genette, p. 156) and so Ducasse's quotation could be seen as having a *mise en abyme* function. Clavel explained to me that:

> el contexto de la cita de Ducasse, es la exaltación de la muerte como algo sublime. Un éxtasis, un encuentro con una belleza que nos trasciende. Cuando

> no es así, Lautréamont lo lamenta: por motivos banales también se muere [...] Y mi idea de la muerte y lo sublime es uno de los ejes que se desprenden de la lectura toda de los Cantos.[22]
>
> [Ducasse's quotation relates to the exaltation of death as something which is sublime. It involves a rapture and the encounter with beauty which transcends us. Lautréamont laments when this is not the case: for banal reasons he too dies [...] My idea of death and the sublime is one of the key areas which emerges from my reading of the Songs]

Lautrémont's death can be seen as a reference to Julián's own metaphoric 'death' in the sense that he is unable to sublimate his dark desires for Violeta.[23]

Even if epigraphs function to provide an interpretation of the text in question, the *Las Violetas* epigraph on its own does not really help in bringing to light 'truth' about the novella's front cover image and so the reader is compelled to look at other peritextual features which might help him or her to decipher meaning(s). The cover copy functions to both reveal but also confuse signification. Written to a formula, the blurb contains all the right ingredients to hook the reader's interest. Indeed, like many well-written book blurbs, whilst not giving too much away about the content of the text, it is sufficiently provocative and engaging to tempt us to cross the threshold of the book. It might, however, also very well discourage a prospective reader altogether. Indeed, incited to navigate through 'las tinieblas de los deseos clandestinos' [the dark depths of clandestine desires], we are immediately alerted to the text's exploration of incest and paedophilia which become disturbingly enmeshed with the theme of rape. The rather startling words 'La Violación comienza con la mirada' [Rape starts with the gaze] have an important bearing on our role as readers and spectators and points to the centrality of gaze in pre-empting the act before the actual crime itself has been committed. Whilst often the visual precedes and anticipates the written form, in the case of the book cover copy of *Las Violetas*, the written form frames the visual. Indeed, the sentence brings awareness to the reader of his or her own active role in looking. Specifically, the words 'violación' and 'mirada' prompt us to turn the book over and to look at the image once again and to reassess its meanings based upon the new interpretations these words confer upon it. Even whilst the book cover blurb informs the reader that Julián does not commit the act of incest with his daughter ('evitar la catástrofe de la culpa' [avoid the catastrophe of guilt]), the word 'violación' in a sense contaminates our reading of this image as it foregrounds the possibility that we are now in fact witnessing a crime scene, specifically the possible rape of a young teenage girl. This new layer of meaning forces us to look for further clues to provide clarity or even closure, this time by examining the book's title on the front cover.[24]

Yet the title *Las Violetas son flores del deseo* itself has a puzzling effect on the reader, thus fulfilling Umberto Eco's view that a title 'must muddle the reader's ideas, not regiment them' (Eco quoted in Genette, p. 4). Clavel's title caters to 'the mouth-watering powers of a certain amount of obscurity or ambiguity: a good title would say enough about the subject matter to stimulate curiosity and not enough to sate it' (Genette, p. 4). Both in popular culture and historically in the Humanities violets are often perceived as representing modesty and chastity, but the connotation of (sexual) innocence which these flowers denote is instantly undermined by the words 'son flores del deseo' [are flowers of desire], signifying the sexual arousal that innocence can stimulate or the sexual lust felt towards that which is pure or sexually unsullied.[25] Just as Clavel cleverly plays here upon notions of innocence and the perverse at a textual level, so do she and Cuéllar at the level of image, thus both mediums complement each other. Ultimately, the juxtaposition of image and text on the front cover creates dislocations in our reading and viewing experience. The word 'violación' in the back cover blurb serves to further pollute our interpretation of the text's overall possible meanings as the associative link between the words 'violetas' [violets] in the book title and 'violas (viol(et)as)' becomes apparent. The association between the book's title and the statement 'La violación comienza con la mirada' in the blurb also becomes ever more apparent as they both merge to form yet another layer of meaning suggested in the words 'violas' 'con la mirada'. There is soon the realization that the second person singular 'tú violas' is directly referring to the reader-viewer and that 'la mirada' is the reader-viewer's own gaze. Ultimately, 'violas' 'con la mirada' suggest that the reader-spectator's 'presence is not that merely of observer but participant' in the violence the girl's/woman's body has or is about to, bear testimony.[26] Thus here the peritextual elements — image and text — work strategically to lock, even if momentarily, the reader 'into a position of a voyeur or even worse an accomplice' (Tanner, p. 560). This position of colluder also means that the reader-viewer assumes a 'knowing' (Haymes, p. 80), whether voluntary or involuntary.

Paradoxically, whilst the peritextual elements of *Las Violetas* oblige the reader's participation as accomplice in the implied violence of the image, they also underline the book cover's own constructedness, to its artificiality and thus offer us the comfort of aesthetic distance. Readers are not 'distracted' '"cultural dopes" but active, critical users' of culture and know that book covers with their different peritextual features are intended by authors, illustrators, and publishers to frame the reader's expectations and interpretations.[27] In the example of *Las Violetas*, this knowledge allows them to resist passive absorption and thus to engage critically with the material presented on the cover by deciphering how the peritextual devices have been presented in order to force upon the reader the position of accomplice. The reader-viewer is aware that the image on the book cover does not offer a direct representation of rape, and yet the textual references to rape both in the blurb and title are skilfully compelling us to link these words to the illustration and forcing us to imagine the possibility that a rape may have taken, or is about to take, place. The awareness of the book cover's constructedness and therefore the aesthetic distance that this knowledge gives us ultimately 'allows the reader or viewer to accept the work's invitation to titillation without appearing to become implicated in its trafficking with violence' (Tanner, p. 560). Yet even whilst aesthetic distance provides us with a sense of separation upon which voyeurism depends, the reader-spectator is still left with a feeling of unease bolstered by the words 'deseos' in the title and 'deseos clandestinos' in the blurb. Since the peritextual devices have served to force the reader into the position not of observer but that of partner in crime, then it is quite plausible to assume that these dark desires are referring not only to those of Julián and his paedophilic clients, but also to those of the reader-spectator. The reader-spectator may justify his or her reading of rape in the photograph as the result of peritextual devices skilfully and strategically working together to draw us towards this interpretation. Yet the references to desire on the book cover also raise an uncomfortable question, namely, whether our reading of violence is not so much or uniquely the product of artistry but rather the product of our own desire for violence enacted in our minds. Ultimately the reason why the cover of *Las Violetas* so deeply terrifies, yet also, oddly perhaps, attracts, is because the only brutality that the image suggests — an interpretation bolstered by the other peritextual devices thus discussed — is one which is born of the reader-viewer's imagination and (dark) desires.

Peritextuality is an almost entirely overlooked area in literary studies perhaps because those elements which are attached to the main text in its material form, such as its illustration or the cover copy, are perceived as superfluous to the narrative and the reader's understanding of it. However, the analysis here of the peritext can be seen perhaps as a call to literary critics to give greater attention to this neglected field given that it helps us to appreciate, for instance, why a reader may or may not want to cross the threshold of the book or how it functions in pre-empting the reader's understanding of an overall work. The peritextual elements of *Las Violetas* serve textually, visually, and physically not so much to pre-establish his or her understanding of the narrative but more so to complement, and enrich, one of the many readings that Clavel's novella offers. Indeed, just as the peritextual devices force upon the reader-viewer the position of accomplice, which provokes utter discomfort, so too does the narrative itself of *Las Violetas* work strategically to lock the reader into the position of accomplice, as previously discussed.[28] Like the image on the cover, the novel horrifies because, through insinuation, it proposes that any inherent violence originates in the reader's imagination because ultimately we all possess perverse desires. In this respect, the reader's reaction to the cover image after reading the novel remains unaltered given that the text of the novella confirms the latent meaning of the image on its cover.

Notes to Chapter 7

1. This chapter has been published previously as 'Ana Clavel's *Las Violetas son flores del deseo* and Peritextuality', *Hispanic Research Journal*, 14:2 (2013), 159–74.
2. The image was displayed throughout the *Las Violetas* multimedia exhibition, including on the website's front page and various banners, as well as featuring in the photographic installation and on one of the cardboard dolls.
3. Genette, *Paratexts*, p. 2.
4. Harris, 'At the Interface Between Reader and Text', p. 2.
5. Harris and McKenzie, 'Inviting Dissent'.
6. Lavery, unpublished interview with Clavel, 2008.
7. Mahon, *Eroticism and Art*, cover blurb.
8. Haymes, 'The Sexual Stranger', p. 80.
9. Alberto Aranda, 'El centinela de las buenas conciencias', 2 May 2008, http://www.noticias.canal22.org.mx/noticia.html?n=12283 [accessed 14 June 2014].
10. Unpublished document supplied to Lavery by Clavel in 2008.
11. Jesús Anaya Rosique, 'Estadísticas del sector editorial: problemas y perspectivas — I', *Libros*

de México, 19 (1996), 63–70; Danny Anderson, 'Creating Cultural Prestige: Editorial Joaquín Mortiz', *Latin American Research Review*, 31:2 (1996), 3–41; Jean Franco, *The Decline and Fall of the Lettered City: Latin America After the Cold War* (Cambridge, MA: Harvard University Press, 2002); Finnegan, *Ambivalence, Modernity, Power.*

12. David Sánchez Montiel, 2008, <http://www.cfc.gob.mx/index.php?option=com_content&task=view&id=2447&Itemid=206> [accessed 20 June 2014], [Anonymous], 'Sobre la Ley de fomento para la lectura y el libro', <http://www.leydellibro.org.mx/Ley_de_Fomento_para_la_Lectura_y_el_Libro.pdf> [accessed 20 June 2014].
13. Whilst both publisher and author teamed up to promote the books, Clavel had control over the format of both book launches by introducing the multimedia events. It has mostly been the author's ongoing initiatives in the form of interviews (press and television), book fairs, writing articles, readings, and (multimedia) book launch events, which has enabled her to sustain the public's continuing interest in the books.
14. It appears that Clavel has sold *Las Violetas* thanks, in part at least, to a devoted fan base and name recognition, as evidenced on one blogsite where various bloggers explain that they purchased or are intending to purchase *Las Violetas* either because they have already read and enjoy her work, she is well-known, or because the text has been awarded a prestigious prize. <http://www.tiempolibre.com.mx/blog/> [accessed 14 June 2014].
15. On the blog site <www.tiempolibre.com.mx/blog/>, featuring readers' reviews of *Las Violetas*, there is one entry in which the reader, Ingrid Jovana Lepe Sánchez, explains that she was compelled to read Clavel's text because of the suggestive image of the book cover: 'porque [...] la portada llamó mi atención, es diferente a la de otras obras, además por que me gustan mucho los libros de Ana Clavel' [because [...] the front cover caught my attention. It is different from other works and what is more I like Ana Clavel's books very much].
16. On the blog site <www.tiempolibre.com.mx/blog/> one entry highlights specifically the way in which the title of Clavel's novella was one of the reasons the reader wanted to buy the book.
17. Genette notes that 'genre indication is an appendage of the title [...] its purpose is to announce the genre status decided on for the work that follows the title. This status is official in the sense that it is the one the author and publisher want to attribute to the text and in the sense that no reader can justifiably be unaware of or disregard this attribution, even if he does not feel bound to agree with it' (p. 94).
18. It was not however Clavel's intention to frame *Las Violetas* in this genre as she informed me in an email exchange (Clavel, email to Lavery, 20 April 2011, 16:29). Here she mentions that she envisioned the front cover as a reflection of the manner in which Julián perceives Violeta in his desire and fantasies. For Clavel the image is simply another aspect which adds to the novella and relates specifically to Julián's fascinated gaze for Violeta and to how some may be stirred by the beauty of an adolescent body. Clavel similarly states that if she had known that the cover on the book of the Mexican edition was going to cause such controversy, she would have used another one, like the one on the French edition which features one of the dolls she worked on for the multimedia event. During her reading of my chapter, Sarah Bowskill remarked that the image may also serve to frame the novella within the genre of crime fiction given that the girl/woman lying in the flowerbed looks like a dead body that has been abandoned, a very perceptive comment given that the novella is significant for its ambiguous oscillation between erotic, fantasy, and detective/mystery fiction.
19. Maurice Charney, *Sexual Fiction* (Routledge: London, 2003), p. 5.
20. Although intertextuality is important to the meanings a reader constructs with the text in hand (Harris, p. 12), readers of *Las Violetas* may not necessarily make these intertextual connections since it all depends on whether they are familiar with the art of Bellmer, Courbet, or Duchamp, or with Clavel's *Cuerpo náufrago* and *Las Violetas* in which the author draws from all three artists.
21. Clavel, email to Lavery, 20 April 2011, 16:29.
22. Clavel, email to Lavery, 21 April 2011, 14:24.
23. Clavel also provided another interpretation of the epigraph's reference to death: 'Al introducir el elemento de la Hermandad de la Luz Eterna, llegué a considerar que Julián era cercado por esas

fuerzas del mal y al final de la novela, estaba a punto de sucumbir como antes Klaus' [When I introduced the aspect relating to the Brotherhood of Eternal Light, I came to consider the idea that Julián was being hounded by those evils forces and that at the end of the novella, he was about to succumb as Klaus had done previously], Clavel, email to Lavery, 22 April 2011, 14:52.

24. A book's title is a vital peritextual feature given that it designates the book and describes the text in hand, 'depending on which feature or features the sender chooses as the bearer(s) of this description — inevitably partial and therefore selective — and depending also on the addressee's interpretation, which appears most often as a hypothesis about the motives of the sender, who, for the addressee, is the author' (Genette, p. 93). The other purposes of the title include its connotative function 'attached (whether or not by authorial intent) to the descriptive function' and the temptation function which 'is always present but may prove positive, negative, or nil depending on the receiver, who does not always conform to the sender's own idea of his addressee' (p. 93).

25. In Renaissance and Baroque Spanish poetry, violets also represent death (because of their black colour). Luis de Góngora has black violets rain down upon the love bed of Acis and Galatea in his mythological poem *Fábula de Polifemo y Galatea* (1612), Luis de Góngora, *Obras completas*, ed. by Antonio Carreira, 2 vols (Madrid: Biblioteca Castro, 2000), I, 346–47 (ll. 333–36). Death, of course, is often linked to sex in literature and art.

26. Tanner, 'Reading Rape', p. 560.

27. Meaghan Morris, 'Banality in Cultural Studies', in John Storey (ed.), *What Is Cultural Studies? A Reader* (London: Arnold, 1996), pp. 147–67 (pp. 156–57).

28. A number of blogs written by readers of Clavel's novella have commented on how the text made them feel like Julián's partner in crime. One says that *Las Violetas* 'me obligó perpetrar un crimen [...] Clavel me obligó a repasar mi manual de perversiones [...] Cómplice' [it forced me to perpetrate a crime [...] Clavel forced me to revise my personal manual of perversions], Agustín Galván, <http://duendecallejeroelemental.blogspot.com/2008_11_01_archive.html> [accessed 22 June 2011]. Another mentions that when taking into account Clavel's statement that: '"La violación inicia con la mirada" ... Todos somos unos violadores en potencia' ['Rape starts with the gaze' ... we are all potential rapists], Martha Avelina Rojas, 'Periodismo', 27 April 2008, <http://avelina-tropos.blogspot.com/2008/04/ana-clavel-me-dej-atnita-con-su-novela.html> [accessed 26 June 2014].

CHAPTER 8

❖

Las Violetas son flores del deseo
Multitextuality: (Cyber) Art Installation, (Performing) Dolls, and (Multi)authorship

When Ana Clavel finished *Cuerpo náufrago proyecto multimedia* in 2005 the author swore to herself that she would never embark upon another multimedia book launch venture of this kind as she found it 'exhausting'.[1] But during our interview Clavel commented that 'me dan verdadera flojera las presentaciones tradicionales. Entonces ya me volví a meter en todo el asunto multimedia de nuevo' [I really cannot be bothered with traditional book presentations. And that is why I got myself involved again with the whole multimedia business]. In the style of the *Cuerpo náufrago* and *Las ninfas a veces sonríen* multimedia presentations, the *Las Violetas* multimedia project confirms Clavel's status as multimedia writer-artist. It also illustrates her desire to queer the conventional by invigorating the concept of what book launches are conventionally known to be. Whilst it can be argued that today no book launches are mono-media in the sense that they are promoted in multimedia fashion through for instance interviews, blogs, Twitter, or F2F book signings, the scope of the multimedia intervention for Clavel's book launches is unprecedented, in Mexico at least. For the *Las Violetas* book launch, as for those for *Cuerpo náufrago* and *Las ninfas*, Clavel combined the more traditional promotional elements, such as printed fliers, press conferences, Q&A sessions, book signings, and interviews, with a full-blown exhibition based on the novella. The exhibition was held in the Casa Refugio Citlaltépetl in Condesa, Mexico City, and was open to the public for a month between 2 April and 2 May 2008.[2] The multimedia project, masterminded by Clavel, consisted of four distinct, but interrelated, areas: an exhibition of fourteen cardboard dolls, a performance, an installation, and a website (<http://www.violetasfloresdeldeseo.com/>). The four multimedia areas were interlinked by the queer themes of doll fetish, desire, and incest, which are all central to the novella. What also made Clavel's event different from 'run-of-the-mill' book launches was its interactive dimension whereby visitors were able to touch, even smell, some of the exhibited objects and were encouraged to explore the history of the show by browsing the *Las Violetas* website.

This chapter examines the photographic art installation which also features the image on the front cover of *Las Violetas*. It will explore the role of the exhibition's website and how it serves to enhance our understanding of the overall installation's variegated meanings. The installation, which is called *El origen del juego: Dados Courbet, Duchamp, Bellmer*, draws its inspiration from the three artists featured in the title. Here Clavel explores all three artists' work in relation to their often ambiguous depiction of the female (nude) which she both reproduces and reworks. Whilst the installation and various paratextual elements draw the spectator's attention to the manner in which the signifier does not educe one meaning but rather manifold and often perplexing interpretations, paradoxically the viewer-participant's frame of reference is also in a sense pre-empted, thus forcing the viewer-participant not only to observe but also to participate metaphorically in the act of rape. It will be argued that by encouraging the viewer's optical and physical participation, the overall installation is set up in such a way that aesthetic violence and actual violence become blurred, thus compelling the viewer to become the actual perpetrator of the crime.

Following this study's analysis of the photographic art installation, I turn my focus to the doll exhibition and the performance. Whilst Clavel's multimedia dolls were inspired by literature and the visual arts, they were also influenced by the Mexican Lupita dolls. I also discuss how there is an uncanny resemblance between Julián's Violetas and the 'real' sex dolls created by the likes of Abyss Creations and Orient Industry. They share, for instance, their anthropomorphism, yet equally ambiguous oscillation between both the human and non-human, real and unreal, their status as fetish objects of paedophilic desire, or their manufacturedness which renders both childhood and womanhood muted. Following their reading of *Las Violetas*, thirteen artists worked artistically on a papier-mâché doll which Clavel had given to each of them. Far from offering visitors at the exhibition comforting interpretations which dolls typically elicit via their connection to childhood innocence and play, their artistic renditions were unanimously horrifying. The themes which are explored in these dolls, such as menstrual and virginal blood, abjection, paedophilic sexual violence, perversity, the notion of the nymphatic child, the role of the maternal reproductive function, and reader-viewer complicity, all work, each in their own way, as clear intertextual allusions to Clavel's novella. Finally, I will examine briefly the performance *Quisiera ser mujer .... Quisiera ser persona*, discussing how the concomitant interaction of the performance's multimedia components, including voice, music, text, image, and performance, serve to underpin *Las Violetas*'s own literary and non-literary intertextual constructedness, as well as emphasizing various issues including (paedophilic) sexual violence, reader-spectator complicity, and the ambiguous position of girl-woman as sexually passive or active, as object of (male) pleasure, or as complicit with the patriarchal gaze. I will also discuss in the context of the exhibition ideas relating to authorial self-reference and (multi)authorship.

Installation

The front cover image of Clavel's novella was taken as part of a series of photographs of (semi-) nudes which draw their inspiration from Courbet's seminal nude *L'Origine du monde* (1886) and were exclusively produced for the *Las Violetas* multimedia project. These photographs formed the basis of the art installation for the book launch exhibition, involving the collaborative input of both Ana Clavel and Rogelio Cuéllar. Clavel explains on her website that she had come up with the idea of the overall installation and specifically proposed the photograph series to Cuéllar 'quien, también acostumbrado a indagaciones personales en torno a la obra clásica de Courbet, hizo variantes de desnudos [...] que simulaban el trabajo alquímico de los daguerrotipos' [who, also used to drawing from the classical work of Courbet, reworked a number of nudes [...] which simulated alchemical daguerreotypes].[3] It is no coincidence that the installation's title *El origen del juego: Dados Courbet, Duchamp, Bellmer* features all three artists. Like Clavel and Cuéllar, both Bellmer and Duchamp were strongly informed by Courbet's *L'Origine du monde*, partially referred to in the installation's modified title.[4]

In the style of *L'Origine du monde* (and by inference the female mannequins of Bellmer and Duchamp), Clavel's installation draws the viewer's gaze in towards the female pubic area. The *El origen del juego* installation consists of a 1.45 x 1m black rectangular panel from which two mannequin legs protrude before the viewer's eyes and between them an adjustable aperture of a camera lens can be seen (figure 8.1).

The installation, which resembles the exterior of a traditional camera with its diaphragm, endorses the traditional ascription of femininity to photography. The camera is a 'hand-maiden', a box with an aperture that passively receives the imprint of an image — but only in negative'.[5] The analogy of negative to female serves to underscore the view of woman 'as less than, more incomplete; possessing, perhaps, only a negative capacity' (McGrath, p. 331). The diaphragm brings to mind the female vagina, an association Clavel clearly wanted to elicit in the viewer:

> Imaginar la vagina como un diafragma fotográfico, o la mirilla para ver otra realidad [...] me seducía crear un artefacto en el que las piernas abiertas de un maniquí se abrieran para atisbar una serie de imágenes como los fotogramas de una película antigua.[6]
>
> [To imagine the vagina as a photographic diaphragm, or the peephole through which to see another reality [...] I was seduced by the idea of creating an artefact in which the splayed legs of a mannequin would allow spectators to see the series of images presented in the form of the photograms typically used in a vintage film strip]

There is a button just above the diaphragm acting as a prompting device to invite audience participation and for the viewer to peer through the peephole. The image of the installation on the *Las Violetas* website makes use of, with the help of IT techniques and digital manipulation, a number of prompting devices which are in many ways more effective than the prompting device used in the original installation in encouraging — but also, as we shall discuss further on, warding off — the viewer to look beyond the diaphragm. In the website image, users can see at the centre of the diaphragm a bright flickering light coming on and off. Above the image, the words 'Da clic en el diafragma para ver las fotos' [to see the photos, click on the diaphragm] can be read and as the user moves the cursor over the diaphragm the words 'Da clic aquí' [Click here] pop up. These words and the flickering light work together strategically to entice the viewer to see what may

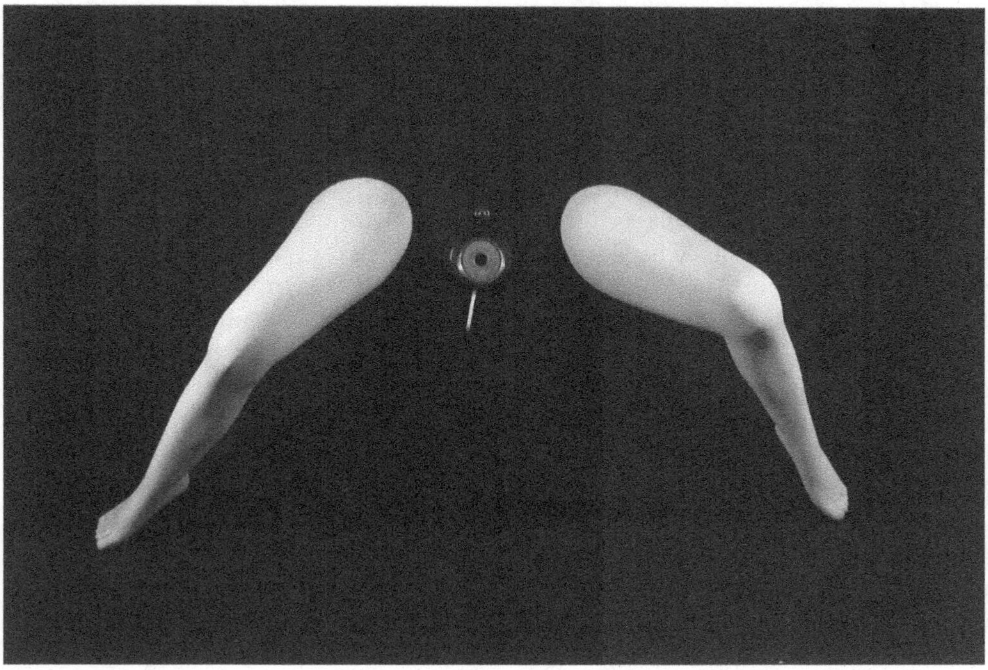

FIG. 8.1. *El origen del juego: Dados Courbet, Duchamp, Bellmer.*
Ana Clavel. Installation. Photo: Ana Clavel. Courtesy of Ana Clavel

lie beyond the diaphragm. The emanating, flickering light could be interpreted metaphorically as the vagina as source of convulsive orgasmic pleasure. The words 'Da clic aquí' also become sexually loaded. They only appear if the viewer puts the cursor over the area of the diaphragm/vagina and the only way to enter it is by pressing the cursor. The cursor appears in the form of a human hand. The pressing of the cursor brings to mind the hand which presses the vaginal erogenous zone, stimulating the clitoris to reach orgasm. The user is left perplexed wondering if the orgasmic light source is an invitation for him or her to give pleasure to this object in the form of a camera-as-woman by pressing on the hand icon, or if the camera-as-woman is in fact offering to give the viewer (virtual) sexual pleasure. The viewer thus has two available options: either to penetrate the diaphragm/vagina or to choose not to enter at all. Whilst the sparkling light serves to welcome the viewer in, the overlapping metal blades surrounding the aperture opening of the diaphragm could be seen as serving to ward off intruders. The blades look like the teeth in a mouth opening and closing in a threatening manner. This vagina-mouth may serve to deter the male participant in particular as the vagina-mouth becomes a kind of toothed vagina, the now stereotyped symbol of the male fear of castration at the hands of predatory women during heterosexual intercourse. The myth of the woman as castrator points to the:

> male fears and fantasies about the female genitals as a trap, a black hole which threatens to swallow them up and cut them into pieces. The *vagina dentata* is the mouth of hell — a terrifying symbol of woman as the devil's gateway.[7]

The toothed vagina also works to challenge traditional patriarchal conceptions of submissive female sexuality. This point is particularly reinforced in the way the camera's diaphragm becomes a metaphor for the vaginal contraceptive diaphragm which, after its invention in the 1980s, came to be perceived as the embodiment of women's sexual agency and liberation.

The problem with this particular psychoanalytical feminist reading of the castrating diaphragm-vagina is that it assumes that the spectator-participant of the installation is male. This interpretation is at risk of becoming unhinged if we take into account questions of audience. The installation and the works of Bellmer, Courbet, and Duchamp appear to reproduce a Mulvian male/female configuration of looking/being looked-at-ness whereby the pleasure of viewing has been constructed for heterosexual male spectators.[8] But the installation's appeal to a presumed male viewer comes into question since the exhibition was open to both genders, and, undoubtedly, to people of diverse sexual orientations. Thus Mulvey's assumption that the gaze is male is both reinforced but likewise shattered as *El origen del juego* not only invites male heterosexual visual enjoyment but also solicits other gazes, so giving viewers access to 'a plenitude of spectator positions rather than binary codes of gazing',[9] as well as to 'different positions in relation to desire'.[10] Nonetheless, the installation *is* strongly encoded in terms of penetration and with the vagina as the target for the implied male 'member'. So, even if the viewers include women, gays, or lesbians it could be argued that the installation encoded the viewer's response beforehand. The installation is, on the whole, far from the multiple, non-hierarchical, non-penetrative lesbian sexuality as envisioned by Hélène Cixous or Luce Irigaray. Indeed, we do not see here a multiplicity of various parts of the female body, but one particular part set up for penetration.

Having been tempted to go beyond the threshold of the diaphragm-vagina — whose entrance via the gaze suggests the idea of the 'body of a woman available for imaginative penetration' (Taylor, *Marcel Duchamp*, p. 113) —, the unwary male or female viewer encounters the image of the front cover of *Las Violetas*. This image forms part of a series of twelve photographs which appear on a vintage film strip. The subsequent photographs depict the girl/woman in uniform with her underwear removed, and the camera directs the gaze towards the pubic area. As with the first image, the head has been cropped out of the frame, which has the effect of reducing the woman to body parts and to object of (male) desire. In some of these images, the pudenda are clearly visible whereas in others they are difficult to discern as they are covered in a swathe of autumnal leaves.[11] The daguerreotype vintage finish of the sepia-coloured photos also serves on occasion to obscure the image. Every fourth photograph is taken in *bokeh* style achieved by motion blur. These out-of-focus images are punctuated by an explosion of colour of purples, whites, and greens merging hazily. In the real-life size installation the photographs rotate on a carousel slide projector and in order to view the photographs the spectator must press the button above the diaphragm. In the virtual installation, the photographs are all presented on the film strip on a single webpage and the viewer can click on each image in order to maximize and minimize it. The action of clicking on the installation's 'botón-timbre-clitoris' [button-bell-clitoris] and mouse/cursor suggests the masturbatory process culminating in ecstasies.[12] The clicking of the button/mouse/cursor emulates the movement of the hand masturbating the genital area, building up sexual excitement culminating in the final orgasmic eruption the *bokeh* style images convey.

The overall installation is set up to encourage the viewer to participate in a process of revealing and concealing. The installation's panel — which serves to conceal the female (semi-) nudes in the photographs — can be compared to the numerous coverings which were used historically to hide *L'Origine du monde* by its various private owners in order 'to prevent immediate access to the taboo image of exposed female genitalia' (Taylor, *Marcel Duchamp*, p. 112). The work's last owner was the psychoanalyst Jacques Lacan and he too continued the tradition of concealing this erotic painting. André Masson produced a painting entitled *Terre érotique* (1943) on a sliding panel that would cover Courbet's work. Having seen Masson's painting at the Lacans in the late 1950s, Duchamp was inspired by it to use an ancient wooden door to conceal his *Étant donnés* female nude. But, as Linda Clifton surmises, 'a covering, a screening also allows, of course, a revealing. Concealing and revealing, that game of hide and seek so integral to erotic play'.[13] Lacan used the *Terre érotique* panel as part of a peek-a-boo or striptease game theatrically revealing and hiding Courbet's painting to the startled surprise of visitors (Taylor, *Marcel Duchamp*, p. 113; Sayer, p. 15). In the style of *Terre érotique*, *L'Origine du monde*, and *Étant donnés,* the spectators of Clavel's *El origen del juego* are encouraged to engage in metaphoric erotic play by interacting in peek-a-boo fashion with the installation. Having looked beyond the panel, the viewer can press the button which reveals a photograph of the woman and with every click of the button, items of clothing are removed leading towards the images of exposed female genitalia. As with Courbet's nude, this gradual revealing of the female sexual organs is in line with traditional artistic representation of the female body where 'the last veil to be lifted is that which conceals the genitals' (Clifton, 'The Gaze', p. 40).

The viewer-participant may find it bizarre that Clavel has chosen to refer to the works of Courbet, Bellmer, and Duchamp as the source of inspiration for her installation since she has been influenced by feminist thinking which challenges the type of female objectification these male artists appear to be reinforcing. The works of Courbet, Bellmer, and Duchamp have been created by men for (one presupposes at least) men, whereby the pleasure of viewing has been constructed for heterosexual masculine spectators. Yet all these artists have more in common with Clavel's literary and multimedia works than may at first appear, since they break with many of the heteronormative conventions which normally govern the gendered gaze, desire, and sexuality, whilst, paradoxically, reinforcing those very same standards. The word *juego* in the installation's title is significant in this respect as it refers to the playful, but also simultaneously to the ambiguous, nature of the works of Courbet, Bellmer, and Duchamp which Clavel seeks to both replicate and rework. James Rubin examines the links between Courbet's subject and the title he chose by suggesting that:

> while the composition's brutal and ultimate example of metynomy represents woman as pure object of dominance and possession, its title points to her quite

> differently as an absolute necessity to which the male is subject and on whom he is dependent.[14]

Courbet's female body is thus identified as the source of life, knowledge, and creativity. Although she is seen as a sexual object, woman becomes indispensable to man's self-knowledge and artistic inspiration. The monopoly of power traditionally exercised by the male gaze is linked to men's need for knowledge. Both looking and possessing woman via the penetration of the vagina therefore becomes the key to masculine self-knowledge. Yet simultaneously, the 'obsession with the female nude (whether as creative artists, producers of pornography or consumers of visual image) [is] frequently linked to man's anxiety in the face of female difference, and the desire to fathom the mystery of female sexuality', for which Courbet's *L'Origine* — and by extension Clavel's installation — becomes a metaphor.[15] Lacan linked the terrifying — yet irresistible[16] — eroticism that made the screening of Courbet's nude necessary not only to the 'horror of castration, the void conveyed by a woman's genitals' but also to the enigmas of feminine sexuality.[17] The screening 'suggests something of Woman as enigma' (Clifton, 'Apropos Encore', p. 107), as does the screening of the female nude in *El origen del juego*. Both in Courbet's painting and Clavel's installation the idea of hidden truth is also connected to the unknowability of women and their desire to exclude men from their 'inner' being. Thus Courbet's and Clavel's work suggest that even if the female body is often mutilated by the aestheticizing and eroticizing (male) gaze, it ultimately evades all attempts to circumscribe it. Clavel's use of a camera as a vagina is significant in relation to Courbet's painting, as it highlights that Courbet's proposed 'return-to-nature' and 'showing-the-female-for-what-it-is' is ultimately a representation. The camera-as-vagina represents precisely representation and therefore Clavel can be seen to be reminding us that we should not take Courbet's work at face value.

Critics, usually feminist, have often protested against Bellmer and Duchamp as eliciting 'charges of irredeemable misogyny and sexual violence',[18] but Sayer notes that the problem with this particular view is that the signifier is collapsed into the signified ('Doll Parts', p. 17). Drawing from Jacques Lacan, Sayer remarks that Bellmer's work lays bare the 'illusion' that 'the signifier answers to the function of representing the signified, or better, that the signifier has to answer for its existence in the name of any signification whatsoever' ('Doll Parts', p. 18). Bellmer's works do not seek to represent reality faithfully but rather to emphasize the dolls' artificiality, which ultimately serves to disrupt the 'male gaze' and lay bare the constructedness of all sexual identities (Sayer, p. 28). Both Susan Rubin Suleiman and Rosalind Krauss similarly allude to the often contradictory and myriad meanings Bellmer's signifiers evoke.[19] In the *El origen del juego* (semi-) nude series, Clavel can be seen to underscore the inherent instability between signifier and signified, whereby the signifier does not elicit one static meaning but rather multiple and confusing interpretations, thus serving 'to create meaning itself as blurred' (Krauss, p. 156). Whilst it appears that Clavel may have wanted to elicit a single meaning by resorting to subtle paratextual techniques, it becomes evident that her installation defies fixity and so the viewer is unable to draw any one specific conclusion. The three *bokeh* photographs in particular make it difficult for us to draw a single meaning as they lend themselves to ambiguous interpretation. Both the blurriness of the images and the sense of movement captured in them underpin the view that meaning is unstable. Though it is difficult to know what these images are actually depicting, given that all we see is a swathe of confused colour, the viewer, influenced by notions of common sense and order, presupposes that the *bokeh* images are representing the nudes — albeit in some kind of abstract manner — since they are part of the series of photographs. But it is our imagination, rather than a concrete represented reality, which drives us to fill in the *lacunae*, thus inviting our active participation in the construction of meaning(s).

The images of the (semi-) nude may be construed as an intimate scene of a woman in a state of post-coital bliss or even the moment preceding auto-eroticism which the viewer-voyeur has been allowed momentarily to observe. The *bokeh* images convey perhaps the masturbatory orgasmic explosion which the woman is experiencing. This particular reading of Clavel's and Cuéllar's (semi-) nudes as an instance of female masturbation is supported by interpretations of Courbet's *L'Origine du monde* as portraying an image of auto-eroticism.[20] Whilst Clavel's and Cuéllar's nudes invite the voyeuristic gaze, the female depicted here resists the notion of passive female. The allusion to the woman's self-pleasure is not aimed exclusively at male pleasure but also at stimulating the fantasy of the female viewer, yet the male and female viewer's direct exclusion from the scene suggests that women do not need to rely on sexual intervention by others, whether female or male, to achieve pleasure. Auto-eroticism particularly challenges heteronormative conceptions of female sexuality. Masturbation defies 'normal' feminine sexuality which in its 'natural' form depends on masculine intervention: the male 'completes' the female, making up her 'lack'. Thus masturbation permits women to express their sexual selves for themselves independently of any oppressive male conception of female sexuality. By inviting male and female viewers to observe the woman's exposed sex and implied autoeroticism, Clavel appears to seek to 'demystify woman's body, to destroy the notion of her having a phallic 'lack', and to make visible her potential and desire for sexual pleasure' (Mahon, p. 243).

The other interpretations the series of photographs elicit involve the more 'direct' participation of the viewer. Here the woman/school girl's self-assured sexualized pose, splayed legs and fully exposed vaginal area could be perceived as an incitement to (metaphoric) sexual intercourse with her. The *bokeh* images denote the frantic final moments leading to climatic orgasm as part of consensual sex between the viewer-participant and the girl/woman. There is a darker interpretation which these *bokeh* images incite, that is that we are not only the spectators, but also the perpetrators, of a violent crime. It could be suggested that this particular understanding had already been framed in the viewer's mind even before he or she had participated in the actual installation itself.[21] Throughout the exhibition there were excerpts of the novella *Las Violetas* which formed part of a number of the objects there on display. As the viewers came into Casa Refugio, they were met with artist Gabriel Macotela's doll *Mujer con luz interna* propped up on a fake stone plinth from which a vertical panel emerged. On this panel the viewers could read the first few paragraphs of Clavel's novella commencing with the assertion that 'La violación comienza con la mirada'. These same paragraphs were also part of an audio recording read by Ana Clavel installed in the doll *Empiernada Violeta* by Arturo Buitrón and which the viewers could hear as they walked by. The paragraphs also appeared on the banner which featured the front cover of the novella with its title and image depicting the girl/woman in school uniform that we also see in the installation. Thus, by the time the viewer had reached the installation on the landing at the top of the stairs in Casa Refugio, the audio, textual, and visual elements peppered throughout the exhibition had served as paratextual hooks to frame the viewer's understanding of the installation's photographs. With the 'la violación comienza con la mirada' sentence firmly in the viewer's mind, the spectator is led to believe that he or she may be the witness of a rape scene which has already or is about to take place. The sentence, combined with the title of the novella, also strewn throughout the exhibition written on, or in relation to, the various objects displayed there, serves to draw attention to the spectator that his or her presence is not that of observer any longer but rather of perpetrator. As suggested earlier, the associative link between the words 'violetas' in the book title and 'violas (viol(et)as)' directly implicates the spectator in the unfolding rape scene. This perspective is particularly reinforced in the *bokeh* images. Given that they defy a fixed positionality, the viewer must try actively to unravel what these images mean. The viewer, trying to make sense of the fuzziness, strings together a number of clues found in the paratextual elements that preceded his or her physical engagement with the installation. The repeated references to the book title as well as to 'la violación comienza con la mirada' in the audio, textual, and visual components of the exhibition, help the viewer to begin to peel away the haze of the *bokeh* images. The jarred motion effect of the *bokeh* images conjure up the idea of the brutal act of rape, a sexual struggle culminating in the *jouissance* of the perpetrator on account of the involuntary submission of the victim. Yet this scene is not articulated in the images themselves but rather in the spectator's mind, ultimately reinforcing the point in relation to the book cover image of *Las Violetas*, that is, that the only sadism that the images infer is one which originates in the spectator's imagination and (dark) desire rather than as a result of the the skilful use of peritextual elements.

The book cover image of *Las Violetas* and its peritextual elements have a different effect on the reader-viewer compared to the installation and its particular function in relation to the viewer-participant. Earlier on, it was suggested that whilst the peritextual elements on the *Las Violetas* book cover force us to assume the position of accomplice, the peritextual also serves to foreground our aesthetic distance and therefore reaffirms the merely literary nature of the violence enacted in the reader/viewer's mind. In *El origen del juego*, however, even whilst the overall installation pre-empts the artistic interest on the viewer's part by foregrounding its formal and other aspects, the boundaries between art and life, aesthetic violence and actual violence are far more blurred. This may be due, in part at least, to the fact that, as the viewer mentally recreates this rape scene, he or she also becomes aware via the physical interaction with the installation of his/her role not only as voyeur, but also as perpetrator. The viewers of Clavel's installation experienced similar physical constraints as those of Duchamp's *Étant donnés* and in both cases served to reinforce their role as active participants. The holes in Duchamp's wooden door and the diaphragm in Clavel's installation align the viewer's glance with the nude's pubic area. The viewer's gaze which is directed at the pubic area becomes a metaphor for the physical penetration of the vagina, and thus the viewer becomes the violator 'whose gaze perpetuates the violence of a crime that reduces woman to object'.[22] This physical alignment is a 'concrete limitation of sight, that is as effective as a strong pair of hands that jerk the viewer's head into position' (Tanner, p. 560). This enforced physical restriction in many ways parallels the dynamics of sexual violence. Just as sexual violence is about domination, so too does *El origen del juego* force the viewer to observe and participate in the act of rape, even while the viewer has chosen voluntarily to peek through the diaphragm. In turn, the gaze of the viewer also becomes symbolic of the dynamics of power whereby s/he is in control of the gaze over the objectified female whose gaze has been denied since her head has been cropped out of the frame. Physically locked into the position of author of the crime, the viewer becomes directly engaged with the crime scene not only at the level of sight but also at the physical level of touch. Indeed the finger convulsively pressing on the button mimics the paroxysmal physical penetration of the woman's vagina. Ultimately Clavel's installation has a similar function to Duchamp's work, that is, to upset the 'justification of aesthetic convention by undercutting the viewer's sense of distinction between studying a scene of artistic violence and participating in an act of literal violation' (Tanner, p. 560). Both *Étant donnés* and *El origen del juego* are outrageous, not because they contravene 'the boundaries that separate violence from the artistic representation of violence' but because they oblige their 'viewers to recognize that transgression' (Tanner, p. 560).

What remains clear is that underlying the playful ambiguities and interpretations of the *Las Violetas*'s book cover and installation is Clavel's desire to challenge and stir her readers-viewers-participants. The multimedia author seeks to explore how sexual desire is controlled by social custom and by taboos that deem certain acts as illicit or unlawful, such as incest, autoeroticism, and nakedness (Mahon, p. 13), and the essence of her work is precisely to confront those taboos. In this sense, Clavel's literary and multimedia *oeuvre* brings us, as Mahon notes in relation to erotic art:

> Face to face with love and sexual desire, titillation and carnal attraction, as well as the desires of others which we may find repulsive. It tests our individual and collective idea not only of what is 'pleasing' but also of what is 'decent' or 'proper'. (*Eroticism and Art*, p. 11)

During the *Las Violetas* exhibition, a visitor commented to me that the (semi-) nudes of the photographic installation could be perceived by some as tasteless pornography. The Violetas (semi-) nude images do not sit easily within popular notions of good taste nor within the 'comfortable' boundaries of the unacceptable. Notions of good taste are not merely the reflection of individual preferences alone but also include those standards of taste which are often shared by the majority if not all members of society.[23] Good taste typically encompasses our sense of beauty and reflects the 'prevailing morality' in society.[24] While increasingly liberal attitudes towards the pornographic, sex, and nudity are apparent in many Western and non-Western societies regardless of the existing puritanical ideologies concerning moral conduct and behaviours, the depiction or reference to sexual violence, rape, incest, and child abuse in the mainstream media and erotic art is still understandably often seen as tasteless and as an affront to public morality, propriety, and human dignity. Prevailing attitudes towards these unlawful actions have become harder in recent times even though 'evidence of their pervasiveness has become more available and taboos on their discussion have become more difficult to maintain' (Shaw, p. 3). Pornography is tolerated to an extent as long as it is of an adult heterosexual orientation and does not stray into more 'abnormal' or non-heteronormative versions such as the autoerotic, lesbian, homosexual, transgender, or paedophilic. *Las Violetas* as text and as multimedia endeavour breaks boundaries precisely because of its exploration of non-heteronormative forms of sexuality relating to women's autoeroticism or morally objectionable forms of sexuality such as incest, paedophilia, and sexual violence, which have provoked a deep sense of unease in the reader and spectator of Clavel's work. Clavel thus defies the notion of 'contained' eroticism — that is the erotic which is deemed acceptable in relation to the dominant tastes and moral and sexual codes of society. Here the boundaries of the visually and aesthetically acceptable are confronted:

> Purity gives way to danger, beauty is replaced with obscenity, grace with abjection, and modesty with the explicit. Sexual desire is no longer simply staged between the viewer and the object in the image so that the former may be elevated, his/her mind raised above the flesh to ponder on the spirit. The viewer is no longer seduced, he/she is shocked, the eye affronted and moral certainty disturbed. (Mahon, p.19)

As mentioned in Chapter 6, Clavel is not apologetic about the topic of her work since she perceives it as the task of the writer to explore those realms which are 'unspeakable' in society. By dealing with the unutterable, Clavel can be seen to be emphasizing the responsibility both of the individual and society as a whole in recognizing that issues of sexual violence, child abuse, paedophilia, or incest are part of our reality. Yet Clavel's variegated representations of 'unspeakable' forms of sexuality in both her *oeuvre* and multimedia work were not produced as forms of perversion or pornography nor written to be deliberately provocative. This former point is corroborated by Rogelio Cuéllar who perceives his own photographic work as having many synergies with Clavel's own literary/multimedia work in the way that both are neither pornographic nor perverse, but rather examples of erotic art:

> Entre la pornografía y lo erótico, el erotismo es una línea muy delgadita, y me gusta tocar esas fibras, hacer fotografía de desnudos con fuerza erótica sin llegar a la pornografía o a la perversidad. Cuando Ana y yo nos encontramos profesionalmente, leí y leo sus obras. Hay paralelas concordancias aquí entre transgredir lo bien hecho y tocar fibras del erotismo.[25]
>
> [Between pornography and the erotic and eroticism, there is a very fine line and which is one that I like to explore by taking photographs of nudes with erotic force but do not fall into pornography or perversity. When Ana and I met professionally, I read and continue to read her works. There are many synergies here in terms of transgressing that which is correct and exploring the erotic]

The difference between the erotic and the pornographic is explained by Jerrold

Levinson who notes that whilst both pornography and erotic art aim to stimulate sexual thoughts and feelings, erotic art also:

> Aims in some measure to draw the viewer's attention to the vehicle, inviting the viewer to contemplate the relationship between the stimulation achieved and the means employed to achieve it, and more broadly, the relationship between the erotic content of the image and its other contents.[26]

Whilst the textual and visual elements of *Las Violetas* as text and multimedia work potentially generate sexual arousal, our attention is constantly drawn towards the work's constructedness and thus to 'dwell in and on our state of stimulation without going beyond it, appreciating instead its relation to and interaction with the other aspects — formal, expressive, social, political — of the representation that occasions it' (Levinson, p. 238). Yet even as the attention of the reader-viewer-participant is steered towards the 'vehicle', Clavel's erotic work has a contradictory hold on our senses as well as our imaginations: it both repels and fascinates. Back in its day, *L'Origine du monde* produced horror in its spectators yet its shock factor, it could be argued, has been dulled by the endless reproduction of this image by artists and writers such as Bellmer, Duchamp, Cuéllar, and Clavel. Yet even as replicas, the Violetas (semi-) nudes are able to repel their viewers, and the reason why they horrify can be explained in the context of the Bataillean understanding of eroticism, that is, 'that man's erotic urges terrify him' (Georges Bataille quoted in Mahon, p. 13). Clavel's multimedia and literary works challenge the reader and viewer because:

> It is the frisson of the narrow divide between erotic desire and erotic excess, between the acceptable representations of eroticism and ones that cause outrage, that exposes not just the true nature of eroticism but our human trepidation when the erotic is given representational form. (Mahon, p. 13)

Whilst the act of looking away functions as a mechanism to keep at bay the dread which the erotic produces, we are constantly compelled to look again at the Violetas (semi-) nudes because of our innate (even morbid?) curiosity about eroticism and inherent need for sexual feelings, in whatever way, shape, or form these may manifest themselves. The pleasure we get from these erotic works can be in a sense explained as a 'tension — one between life and art [...] — [...] that generates an edgy pleasure akin to, if not identical with, that of the sublime' (Levinson, p. 238). This tension is heightened in the way that the image on the *Las Violetas* book cover and the photographic installation not only ambiguously oscillate between encouraging aesthetic detachment and visceral pleasure but also elicit in the viewer a sense of repulsion and shock.

Doll Exhibition

Perhaps the queerest element of the overall *Las Violetas* multimedia exhibition were the fourteen cardboard dolls on display. When discussing the writing process of *Las Violetas*, Clavel notes that the novella's outlandish doll idea was inspired by fiction and the visual arts and remarks in relation to these dolls: 'creía yo que solo existían en la imaginación y en la fantasía' [I thought that they only existed in the imagination and in fantasy].[27] However, during a trip to Los Angeles following the publication of *Las Violetas* in 2007, Clavel went to an erotica exhibition where she came across the '"muñecas reales", hermosas mujeres de silicón que para nada tienen que ver con las grotescas muñecas inflables' ['real dolls', beautiful silicon women which have nothing to do with those grotesque air dolls] ('Los Caballeros', p. 65). She came across a stand full of dolls sold by the company Abyss Creations, the creator of the RealDoll brand, and was shocked by their human qualities ('Los Caballeros', p. 65). Clavel was given an Abyss Creations catalogue at the exhibition and what stands out in particular in this leaflet are the testimonials of clients who had purchased a doll. In all the cases the clients express their satisfaction with the dolls, both at the level of sexual pleasure they provide ('My wife isn't as good') and their human-likeness ('I cannot get over how REAL she looks and feels').[28] The Abyss Creations Company manufacture realistic custom-made dolls which have human attributes thanks to their durable posable PVC skeletons made with silicone flesh.[29] Clavel was surprised how similar the 'real' dolls were to her 'fictive' Violetas and to Felisberto Hernández's Hortensias in terms of their human attributes, but notes that it would be unlikely that any of the 'real' dolls would be called 'Violeta' 'porque la tecnología aún no ha hecho possible que las muñecas puedan ser vírgenes y sangrar' [because technology has not made it possible yet for the dolls to be virgins and to bleed] ('Los Caballeros', p. 65). Though Clavel's novella's sinister otherworldliness is very much embedded in the realms of fiction, the power of *Las Violetas* to shock the reader lies in its ability to capture the often surreal and frequently horrifying quality of actual lived reality. Like the RealDolls, those created by Julián are grotesque in their humanness. Julián's description of the character traits of his Violetas has disquieting similarities to those accounts given in the online testimonials of clients on the Abyss Creations company website who allude not only to the dolls' perfect human physical attributes but also to their personalities. Like children playing with dolls, the sex doll owners, like Julián, make up personalities for their life-sized toys. For instance 'Arnaud' comments that 'Jenny' has a 'soulful face'[30] and another client says the dolls have a 'presence'.[31]

In my interview with Clavel, the author cited the example of Japan where men buy dolls as an alternative to developing meaningful real-life relationships, and provided the case of a Japanese manufacturer called The Orient Industry which produces life-sized and anatomically accurate sex dolls. Hideo Tsuchiya, president of Orient Industry claims that the dolls are made to console men who have not been successful in finding love particularly as 'nowadays, women are sometimes more dominant than men in the real world, and they don't always pay attention to men'.[32] David Levy discusses the gendered use of sex dolls in Japan and the United States, and comments in relation to the popularity of such dolls:

> The marketing of RealDolls and their cousins from other manufacturers tends to be based on the idea that they are 'the perfect woman' [...] because they provide all the benefits of a human female partner without any of the complications involved with human relationships, and because they make no demands of their owners, with no conversation and no foreplay required.[33]

As O'Neill remarks, the perception of the 'real' dolls as both human and non-human is significant for even if these dolls are not alive, they assume human form and can be 'animated through sexual fantasy, even if this animation occurs only in the perception of their male partners [...] the power of fantasy in creating satisfying interactions, both sexual and non-sexual, is a primary element of the human/doll relationship'.[34] This is compellingly exemplified not only in the context of the relationships which men have developed with the 'real' RealDolls as underpinned in the testimonies discussed above, but also in the relationship Julián has with the Violetas, as discussed in Chapter 6. The male owners of the RealDolls and Orient Industry dolls often claim in their testimonies that their silent companions are more than mere sex toys and play a significant role in their day-to-day lives. One anonymous Abyss Creations client claims that his life has improved vastly as his doll is like a companion and provides emotional support.[35] The emotional bond is so powerful that some men claim to be in love with their dolls, as is the case of Julián who is infatuated with his Violeta creations mirroring Horacio's obsession with his Hortensia in Hernández's novel. Whilst doll ownership may be perceived as a perverse pastime and delusional, for the majority of doll owners — who acknowledge that their dolls are not real human beings — it is no more than a hobby. In contrast, the Violetas have consumed Julián's and Horacio's entire lives to the point of madness.

Many of the dolls manufactured by companies such as Orient Industry and Abyss Creations are made to look like underage nymphets, and the men who buy them often seek to fulfil their repressed paedophilic desires. They can act out their fantasies of forbidden sex in consequence-free and legal ways facilitated via the sex industry. This particular point is reminiscent of *Las Violetas* in which, as discussed in Chapter 6, Julián's prohibited dolls have been manufactured in order to be misused sexually in a socially consequence-free manner by their owners who can cross into rape fantasy without ramifications. Both in the real world and in the fictive world of *Las Violetas*, doll fetish has a similar role of substitution — where the real is replaced by the unreal fetish object. In fetishism theory, which has been extensively studied by Lacan and Freud in their essays on psychoanalytical theory, the fetish object serves to disavow the threat to castration or acts as a means of over-coming castration anxiety. Ultimately fetishism is understood as compensating for that which is lacking. Whilst the intention here is not to expand upon this perspective, it is nevertheless this psychoanalytical viewpoint which helps us partially to understand the behaviour of some of the 'real' owners of sex dolls and in particular Julián's own actions, for whom his Violeta replicas, which become a substitute for his daughter Violeta, compensate for his sense of lack. Another characteristic which the 'real' and Clavel's 'unreal' dolls share in common is the manner in which they attract men because of their malleable quality. The title of Clavel's article 'Los caballeros las prefieren mudas' [Gentlemen prefer them mute] forcefully suggests this point and here Clavel notes that a number of male friends she spoke to said of the 'real' dolls that 'el hecho de que sean calladas, los seduce aún más' [the fact that they are silent, seduces them even more] ('Los caballeros', p. 65). This silent characteristic underpins the idea that whilst both the 'fictive' and 'real' dolls are grotesque for their fabrication, it is their manufactured-ness that renders 'real' womanhood — and by extension childhood — unthreatening and muted. Sexual role-playing is one instance which allows men to render the dolls mindlessly obedient objects. A substantial number of the RealDoll testimonials discuss sexual role-playing involving the clients creating sex scenes and dressing the dolls up in different outfits, even replacing their heads with different ones. In *Las Violetas*, role-playing is one fantasy Julián takes pleasure in by enacting sadomasochistic and bondage-like scenarios in which the dolls are brutalized and physically restrained by him (*Las Violetas*, pp. 98–99). Julián shares with the owners of the 'real' sex dolls the ability to compose these sex scenes in keeping with their own imperatives with no demands made by the yielding dolls.

Clavel explains that her discovery of the 'real' dolls, reinforces the universal law that 'la realidad siempre supera a la fantasía' [fantasy always takes the place of fantasy] ('Los Caballeros', p. 65). Yet the opposite also holds true, that is, that fiction or fantasy often supersede reality, but ultimately, as the human-like dolls attest in both the world of the living and the imaginary realms of fiction, the boundaries between the real and the unreal blur in disturbing, and often indistinguishable, ways. The overlapping of fiction and the real and vice versa is poignantly captured in Clavel's multimedia exhibition. The multimedia project reveals the way in which fiction can spill into the real, living world which in turn imbues the unreal with the real, and yet where simultaneously other multiple (intertextual) layers of fictions and fantasies emerge. For Clavel, the intertextual and visual references to Hernández's *Las Hortensias* and Bellmer's *Les Jeux de la poupée* in *Las Violetas*, made the multimedia project a logical extension of the text. Clavel's exposure to the Abyss Creations and Orient Industry dolls also partially motivated her exhibition endeavour. Yet the actual dolls Clavel displayed in the exhibition were not silicon mannequins in the style of the 'real' dolls, instead they drew direct inspiration from a Mexican tradition. Indeed, it was Clavel's friend, the poet and journalist Rosa María Villarreal, who suggested that the dolls could be moulded in the shape of the artisanal handcrafted Lupita dolls which are made out of papier-mâché. Villarreal believed that this would add 'un toque como más artesanal [...] como un juego, una vuelta de tuerca más popular' [a more artisanal touch [...] like a game, it gives it a more popular twist].[36] Given that the exhibition was more of a creative, witty, rather than solely intellectual, exercise, Clavel agreed to this idea as she thought that the Lupitas would add a touch of humour. Clavel diverged in one significant way though from Villarreal's proposal, namely, rather than having dolls created the size of the traditional Lupita which is typically up to 30 cm long, Clavel proposed human-sized dolls of 1.5 m for the exhibition for the simple reason 'porque si no, no tiene chiste' [because if not it won't be funny], the 'chiste' being that Clavel herself is 1.5 m tall.[37] This particular example clearly highlights Clavel's self-referential humour and this is one of a number of areas within the exhibition which demonstrated a calculated display of authorial self-reference.[38] Clavel's dolls also suggest a queering of both the 'real' dolls and of the Lupita tradition via the intersection of the sexual and the folkloric. Clavel commissioned fourteen blank dolls from different 'cartoneros' [papier-mâché artisans] who are based in Sonora

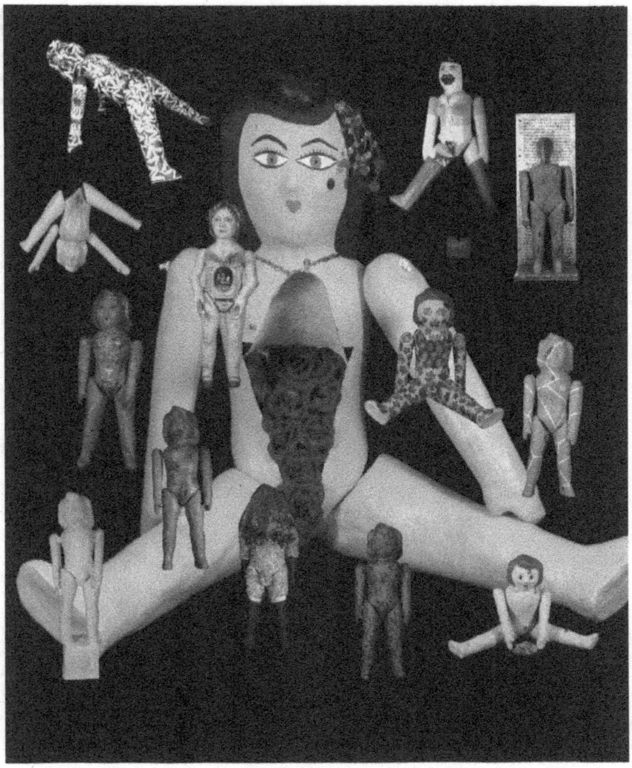

FIG. 8.2. Photo-collage of 14 dolls exhibited at Casa Refugio. Digital image. Arturo Buitrón and Gabriel Macotela. Courtesy of Ana Clavel.

Market in Mexico City and who specialize in making 'piñatas' or papier-mâché figures. Clavel then asked thirteen artists to intervene artistically on the blank cardboard doll, seen in the illustration below (figure 8.2), based on their reading and interpretation of *Las Violetas*. To each artist she said: 'Haz con ella lo que quieras. Destázala, adórnala, píntala' [Do whatever you want with her. Disembowel her, adorn her, paint her].[39]

The thirteen artists, some of whom are of international repute, ranged from painters and plastic artists to sculptors. They were: Arturo Rivera, Gabriel Macotela, Rocío Caballero, Saúl Kaminer, Alejandro Escalante, Maribel Portela, Rubén Maya Moreno, Gustavo Monroy, Claire Becker, Jocelyne Marmottan, Luis Manuel Serrano, Arturo Buitrón, and Tarsicio Padilla. Ana Clavel also worked on one of the dolls. I interviewed the majority of these artists and what is particularly striking is the almost unanimous disgust they expressed towards the doll. A number of them commented that in the text, Clavel's dolls were very sensuous, even desirable. The 'real' blank version however horrified them. Some said that they found the task of initiating the whole project very daunting particularly given that the presence of this doll in their art studios had become disruptive to their day-to-day work. Some hid them from sight and purposefully tried to ignore this bothersome presence all together. Saúl Kaminer was the only artist to actually find the doll sensuous and explained to me that the whole process of artistically working on his doll was similar to a courtship between lovers.[40] Interestingly, all these artists gradually developed an emotional relationship of sorts with these dolls, reminiscent, to an

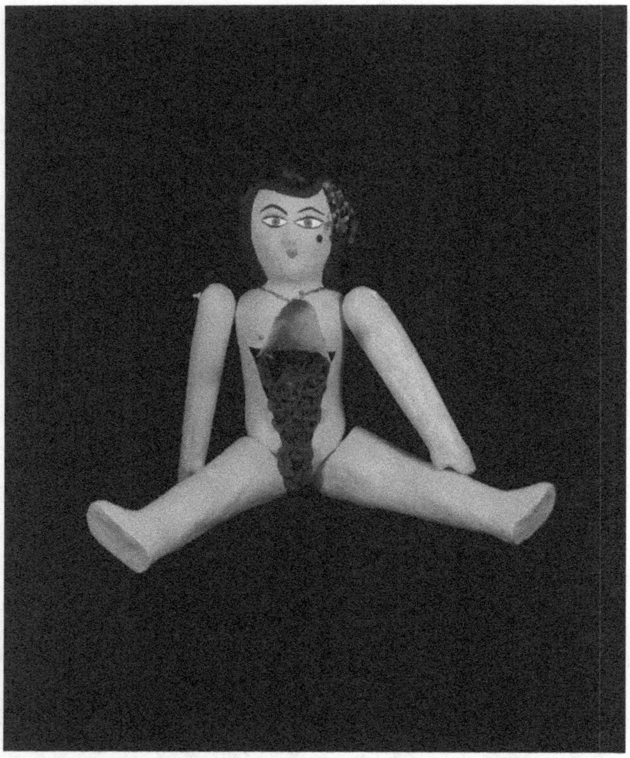

FIG. 8.3. *Ábreme y tu vida se teñirá de violeta.* Ana Clavel. Doll size: 1.5 m. Photo: Rogelio Cuéllar and Arturo Buitrón. Courtesy of Ana Clavel.

extent, of Julian's own emotional connection to the 'unreal' Violetas. Yet again this particular example provides a fascinating example of where the boundaries between the real and unreal blur.

Whilst each of the worked on dolls represents a unique artistic vision and adds new and multiple layers to our understanding of *Las Violetas*, they all share a disturbing quality. These dolls are not like the primarily anodyne-looking Lupita dolls. On the contrary, they are haunting renditions of this folkloric doll. The torso of Clavel's doll *Ábreme y tu vida se teñirá de violeta* (figure 8.3) has been cut open and in the centre roses are bunched together and gently spill over the vaginal area. Whilst the roses — which are an allusion to the virginal odour of Julián's manufactured Violetas — suggest romance and romantic sensuality, the sea of red also has a jarring effect on the spectator as it and the title accompanying the doll conjure up images of a brutalized body from which blood pours out. The blood theme also connects intertextually back to Clavel's text recalling the real Violeta's menstrual blood, as well as her replica's virginal blood.

The blood theme is continued in Gustavo Monroy's doll *Violeta frutal* which was suspended from the ceiling, blood pouring down from the vagina. Arturo Rivera's *Violeta violenta (divertimento)* suggests the playfulness of the artist's sadistic imagination and alerts us to the horror this doll embodies. Here Rivera toys with common stereotypes of the female as sexual predator, combining late nineteenth-century ideas of the *femme fatale* with twentieth-century fears of the vamp. Dressed in 'sexy' underwear, blood is gushing out from her vagina. Her face is demented, mouth gaping open revealing razor sharp, almost vampire-like teeth. Rivera is clearly drawing here from the traditional image of woman as monster, an enduring trope in visual culture in which 'the monstrous woman is represented as out of control, threatening, and all-consuming'.[41] *Violeta violenta* epitomizes the multifarious characteristics of Creed's monstrous-feminine. The doll's 'mouth of hell' (Creed, p. 106) becomes a kind of sexual threat to men, the castrating *vagina dentata* mentioned earlier in this chapter. Drawing from Creed's monstrous-feminine Gear notes that the female monster is:

> The *vagina dentata*, the monstrous womb, the castrator, and the possessed monster, driven by her desire to kill men. But she is also, in psychoanalytic terms at least, castrated, which brings us to the notion of the spectacle of woman as bleeding wound. Our encounter with the monstrous-feminine [...] reinforces Creed's observation that at the heart of the female monster lie the deadly female genitals. ('All Those Nasty Womanly Things', p. 321)

By embodying the notion of woman as monstrous 'other', that is 'anomalous and deviant vis-á-vis the norm', the multimedia exhibition dolls, as indeed Julián's versions, produce fascination and horror in the spectator-reader.[42] Gear stresses that the abject body is the source of this ambiguity (p. 322). Monroy's and Rivera's dolls may be perceived by some as more shocking than fascinating because of their flagrant exposure of abject bodily fluids. The blood seeping out of the vaginas of the dolls is a clear reference to Clavel's Violetas' virginity, the 'mark' of childhood innocence. Thus the blood pouring down the exhibited dolls' legs disturbingly suggests a deflowering. Viewers may be particularly perturbed by this interpretation since the possibility of defilement is reinforced as it becomes enmeshed with the exhibition's paratextual references to paedophilia, incest, and rape. Blood is also an allusion to the the real Violeta's human-like capacity to menstruate. As mentioned in Chapter 2, Kristeva examines the way in which the abject aspect in humanity is kept under control by society with rituals such as the disgust of bodily fluids or the maternal.[43] These rituals seek to preserve the boundaries between what is abject and what is not. Violeta's menstruating body highlights Kristeva's view of the female body as the site of pollution in opposition to the notion of a 'clean' and 'proper' body. The polarities of dirt/disease and cleanliness function as indicators of cultural order and disorder in a way that links menstrual blood and other bodily wastes to the Kristevan idea of the abject.[44] The abject is ultimately that 'which arouses fear and disgust as fluidity threatens to overcome fixity' (Gear, p. 322) and by extension order being supplanted by disorder and chaos. However, even as the viewers' attention is drawn to the 'improper' menstrual blood, so too is the myth of the 'proper' body and menstruation as a shameful bodily function which must be contained as well as the more general ideological containment of woman's gendered and sexual identity flagrantly exploded by Kaminer and Rivera. As we saw in our examination of *Las Violetas* previously, menstrual blood is also associated with woman's maternal reproductive function, which, according to Creed is what makes woman, and her sexual difference, especially monstrous (p. 48). Monroy's and Rivera's dolls present woman as monstrous in her indeterminate status as both child and woman, oscillating between her virginal innocence, associated with the notion

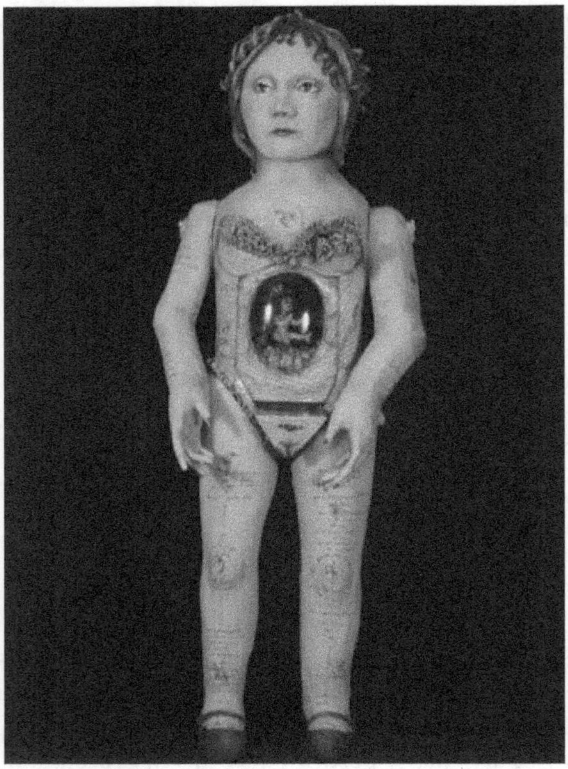

FIG. 8.4. *Virginia Virginal.* Rocío Caballero. Doll size: 1.5 m. Photo: Rogelio Cuéllar and Arturo Buitrón. Courtesy of Ana Clavel.

of the 'natural' human state', and her sexualized, reproductive capabilities.[45]

Nowhere is this ambiguity better captured than in Rocío Caballero's doll *Virginia virginal.*[46] Of all the dolls, *Virginia virginal* is perhaps the one which closet mirrors and best explicates visually the spirit of Clavel's novella. This doll is also one of the most artistically accomplished of the fourteen dolls on display in terms of attention to detail and also the most disturbing in its proposition that children may be prematurely sexual, which of course closely mirrors Julián's view of Violeta and her replicas as sexually precocious. *Virginia Virginal*'s tight corkscrew curls give her a child-like innocence and the virginal is clearly connoted in the name which Caballero has chosen for her. Paradoxically that same innocence becomes tainted via the doll's sexualization as underscored by the full body frilly boned corset she is wearing and her matching red lips and nails. In the centre of *Virginia virginal*'s corset there is a glass pane through which one can observe a naked, plastic doll rotating on an axis and this is by far the most perturbing example of the notion of a child as sexually precocious (figure 8.4).

The intertextual references to Clavel's novella cannot go unnoticed here. Julián's suggestion that the monstrous foetus of Violeta is prematurely nymphatic (*Las Violetas*, p. 30) is replicated in Caballero's rendition whereby the sexualization of the miniature plastic doll is suggested in her painted red lips, a feature which also signals her child-mother's own nymphatic qualities. Another intertextual feature which links *Virginia virginal* to the real and unreal Violetas, is Caballero's inclusion in her version of a realistic pudendal slit. In the examination of *Las Violetas* in Chapter 6, it was suggested that the pubic 'herida' [wound] of the real Violeta signals her maternal and reproductive qualities, a feature which Julián finds particularly horrifying. By presenting *Virginia virginal* as 'rota', Caballero underscores woman's monstrous quality: on the one hand, the slit attracts because of the promise of orgasmic *jouissance*, on the other hand, it repulses as it is a reminder of the 'maternal body as site of the origin of life [...] We are all of woman born, and the mother's body as threshold of existence is both sacred and soiled, holy and hellish' (Braidotti paraphrasing Kristeva, p. 81).

Emblazoned all over the naked flesh of *Virginia virginal* are excerpts taken from Clavel's book. The sentences along with various images of hearts and flowers resemble tattoos and have a rather jarring visual effect as they contrast sharply with the otherwise smooth, porcelain-like quality of the doll's skin. The words, which are those uttered and written by Julián, are etched onto the skin and thus represent the brutal impression of the fatherly inscription of the female. Readers who have read the text will be familiar with the excerpts Caballero has added to her doll, including the words in which Julián ponders over the moral and philosophical nature of perversity: '"perverso" es aquello que lastimándonos no nos permite apartar la mirada' ['perverse' is that which is detrimental to us and does not allow us to look away] (*Las Violetas*, p. 25). What also becomes apparent is that a number of these sentences have been repeated (e.g. '"perverso" es aquello que lastimándonos no nos permite' or 'La violación comienza con la mirada') and various words have been circled again and again in red ink pen by the artist, such as 'Violetas', 'Perverso' and 'Violación'. In the previous chapter it was suggested that Julián uses a number of rhetorical strategies including repetition of key sentences such as those found on Caballero's doll in order to coerce the reader into the position of partner in crime. It is via the reiteration of allusions to rape and to humankind's innate perversity that Julián proposes that the only violence that his account suggests is one which is born of the reader's imagination because we all possess perverse desires. It is uncanny how Caballero's doll achieves the same effect. It was noted earlier that a number of paratextual features of the exhibition which contain the assertion that 'La violación comienza con la mirada' served to frame the spectator's interpretation of the photographs, specifically that the anonymous female depicted in the images is the victim of rape. These same paratextual elements combined with the repeated sentences and circled words on the doll pre-empt in the viewer a similar interpretation, that is, that before us stands a virgin deflowered through rape but with an added twist, namely, that she has been impregnated by the perpetrator. Whilst the repeated words etched on the doll's skin implicate the 'perverse' viewer as voyeuristic participant observer, it is the physical interaction required of the viewer which pushes him or her into position of perpetrator. Given the small font of the words, visitors were prompted to get closer to *Virginia virginal* in order to read the text, to the point that their faces were almost pressed against her. Such proximity meant that they often ended up holding the doll in a rather awkward manner with their hands. The wind-up mechanism which visitors were able to use worked jerkily and the miniature drawer from which pot-pourri wafted out had to be yanked open. Viewers were also often seen sticking their hands into the drawer and extracting the material. The ungraciousness with which visitors fondled the doll is evocative of the dynamics of rape which involves violent manhandling and manipulation during intercourse between perpetrator and victim, who, like the doll, is cast as the unfeeling object of (male) desire.

The striking similarities between Caballero's *Virginia virginal* doll and Clavel's novella not only suggest Caballero's sensitive reading of *Las Violetas* but also the overlapping interests that both artist and writer share in their respective talents. Indeed, Caballero's own doll-making and painterly work bears a strong resemblance to Clavel's thematics, seen for instance, in Caballero's fascination with innocence and ideas of the perverse, powerfully captured in her creation of angel-like figures. The Violetas exhibition dolls as exemplars of the fusion of artistic voices and creative synergy, that of Clavel on the one hand, and that of the various artists on the other, as we see for instance in Arturo Rivera's gothic *Violeta violenta* which draws from a number of thematics explored in Clavel's novella such as female menstrual or virginal blood, as discussed. So too is his rendition embedded in his fascination with the beauty of horror, violence, and madness in his own work, as we see for instance in his daunting collection of paintings entitled *La Belleza de lo terrible* (2007). Another notable doll which embodies this creative synergy is *Violeta Nahuala* by painter, installation artist, and graphic artist Rubén Maya Moreno (figure 8.5).

It is interesting to note that it was Clavel, and not Maya Moreno, who decided what name to give *Violeta Nahuala* and indeed what to call many of the other dolls after they had been artistically realized. This particular aspect points to Clavel's desire to assert her authority in the overall exhibition. The names she gave the dolls were based on her interpretation of the artists' visual interpretation of *Las Violetas*, and so this added another interesting layer to the whole doll-creating and creative processes. In the case of *Violeta Nahuala* — a monstrous rendition with a set of four eyes, painted head to toe in 'Mexican' pink, and covered with vaginas — I asked Clavel why she had chosen that name:

> Porque cuando la vi me pareció un ser dual, un ser de dos mundos, pero no me remitió ni a un discurso religioso budista, ni esotérico, aunque Rubén me había mencionado algo de los masones, de signos masónicos que tiene atrás. A mí me hacía pensar en esa imagen mítica de las leyendas prehispánicas del Nahual. Y por el hecho del color, este colorido como rosa mexicano, no la podía pensar más que como una suerte de alebrije muy bizarro y muy de influencia prehispánica. Entonces ésa fue una lectura que hice yo.[47]
>
> [Because when I saw her I thought that she was like a dual being, a being from two worlds, but she did not suggest to me a Buddhist religious or esoteric discourse, although Rubén had mentioned to me something about masons, and masonic signs which she has on her back. The doll reminded me of that mythical image of the pre-Hispanic legends about the Nahual. And because of the colour, that sort of Mexican pink, I could only think that she was some kind of very bizarre pre-Hispanic style folk art sculpture]

Whilst Maya Moreno's own work is partially influenced by pre-Hispanic culture, he did not agree with Clavel's idea of the Nahuala and explained to me that the doll was inspired by Buddhism, another strand which runs deeply through this

FIG. 8.5. *Violeta Nahuala.* Rubén Maya Moreno. Doll size: 1.5 m. Photo: Rogelio Cuéllar and Arturo Buitrón. Courtesy of Ana Clavel.

oeuvre.[48] In the context of the *Nahuala* doll, he mentioned that the double eyes in fact related to the Buddhist double vision of the world in which mind and body form an integral part of it. Despite these apparent differences, both Maya Moreno's and Clavel's viewpoints added a new subtext to *Las Violetas* suggesting the power of literature and art to evoke a multiplicity of interpretations. More so than a divergence of ideas, the doll in fact merges a number of commonalities which exist between Maya Moreno's and Clavel's creative thinking. Maya Moreno thus discusses his interpretation of the text as embodied in his doll:

> Las vaginas pueden interpretarse como heridas, y al mismo tiempo se convierten en ventanas hacia la sensualidad de la mujer. La sensibilidad del cuerpo, de las vaginas, es un punto importante en la doble visión. Traté de darle un equilibrio al personaje real de Violeta y remarcar que el poder del deseo es vital, es un detonante para lograr algo, llámese enamoramiento o deseo carnal.[49]
>
> [The vaginas can be interpreted as wounds, as well as becoming windows into the sensuality of woman. The sensitivity of the body, of vaginas, is an important aspect in this double vision. I tried to provide a sense of balance in the character of the real Violeta and to underscore how the power of desire is vital, it is the trigger to fulfil something such as falling in love or carnal lust]

This interpretation closely mirrors the view expressed in Clavel's *Las Violetas* of the vaginal slit as providing immensurable pleasure on the one hand, and as a horrifying 'herida' on the other, as it becomes associated with women's sexual reproductive capability. In this sense Clavel's novella also has parallels with Maya Moreno's own artistic work in the manner in which a mixture of attraction and repulsion positions woman as monstrous 'other'.

Performance

The performance entitled *Quisiera ser mujer ... Quisiera ser persona* was acted out during the exhibition by choreographer and ballet dancer Lourdes Fernández. It was later recorded and uploaded onto the *Las Violetas* website. Whilst Fernández had some input in terms of the choreographic moves, Clavel had overall control. As Clavel notes on her website in relation to the dancer 'me complació dejándose moldear por mi idea, pero además añadió la música y el trazo coreográfico de toda la secuencia' [she pleased me by allowing me to mould her to my ideas, but she herself also added the music and came up with the choreography of the entire sequence]. The author's presence is felt throughout, in particular as Clavel appears as one of the actors of the performance in which she reads a number of excerpts of her book to the audience. As with the performance of *Cuerpo náufrago*, the concurrent multimedial interaction of various media — performance, voice, music, text, and image — serves to underpin the literary and non-literary sources of *Las Violetas*, as well as to the various themes of both the novella and the exhibition including (paedophilic) sexual violence, child sexualization, or spectator voyeurism/complicity.

The performance is highly self-referential, peppered with textual and visual references which thread together Clavel's novella, her photography, that of Cuéllar and Hans Bellmer, indirect allusions to Courbet's *L'Origine du monde* and to Nabokov's *Lolita*. Even as the performance underscores the view that all 'texts' are highly intertextual and therefore explodes the myth of the singular creative voice, so too does it transform multimedially not only the works of the aforementioned artists and writer, but also *Las Violetas* itself. The Lolitaesque theme of precocious nymphet which connects all of these works becomes apparent from the outset via the multimedial interaction of the various components. Thus, on the back wall of the stage one of Bellmer's photographs of a contortioned mannequin is projected. The dancer, dressed in school uniform, drapes herself against the image, as if she were the Bellmerian mannequin. Clavel and Cuéllar's image of the semi-nude of the cover of *Las Violetas* is also interspersed with various photographs of Bellmer, and so the dancer could similarly be seen as representing the female semi-nude depicted in the former work. The inert girl-doll becomes alive as the author reads about the 'Violetas prohibidas' [prohibited Violetas] and the section in which Julián discusses his vivified dolls (p. 94).

The girl-doll nymphet moves centre stage slowly removing each item of clothing, smiling provocatively. It is only when she strips down to her underwear that she begins the whole process of dressing again. Her performance of a striptease thus recalls the role of striptease in the *Cuerpo náufrago multimedia* canvas *La censura también es fuente*, discussed in Chapter 5. As mentioned here, the process of concealing and revealing is integral to erotic play and serves to highlight the *tease* in striptease. Clavel comments that making the decision for Fernández not to undress would be more suggestive (<http://www.violetasfloresdeldeseo.com/>), thus harping back to Barthes's view that the erotic is found in those spaces where the items of clothing part. The *tease* in striptease disturbs as it serves to position the spectator as (paedophilic) voyeur. It also produces discomfort as the underage stripper doll-girl is shown to be in control of her sexuality, particularly suggested in the manner in which she revels in her sexual power, and is therefore presented as an erotic subject rather than an objectified one. Even though striptease is typically directed at a heterosexual male audience, the *Las Violetas* performance invites both male heterosexual visual enjoyment as well as soliciting other gazes from a mixed gender audience with diverse sexual orientations. Yet it is undeniable that the girl-child stripper is set up for penile penetration by the male gaze. The online video performance particularly stresses this point given that the final shot we have is of Clavel and Cuéllar's female semi-nude. The metaphor of camera-as-penis becomes strongly apparent as the camera rapidly zooms in towards the vaginal area of the splayed-leg semi-nude. This particular technique highlights how multimedial intervention via camera, video, and computer technology serves to complement, and, it may be suggested, even improve, the reader-viewer's experience of the original text. It was mentioned earlier in relation to the front cover image of *Las Violetas* that clever photographic techniques of focus and framing devices force the viewer-reader's eyes to look towards the girl's pubic area. In this respect, the zooming technique is a clever visual enhancement.

Not only is the girl-doll encoded in terms of penetration by the implied male 'member' but she/it is also presented as the locus of (paedophilic) sexual brutality. This latter point becomes apparent as the doll-girl dancer becomes almost invisible to the eye as the projected images of Bellmer's horrifying scenes of brutalized dolls depicted in sombre forests and Clavel and Cuéllar's ambiguous semi-nude envelop her body. The disturbing images are also complemented by the dancer's choreography. At times her moves flow smoothly and graciously to the gentle beat of the ambient music from *The Album Leaf* (2001) in which the dream-like melody floats across the stage towards the spectator. On other occasions the dancer begins to jerk and jolt convulsively which has a rather unpleasant visual effect. Even the music's etherealness dissipates as it becomes melodically darker, pointing to the performance's own murky thematics. The possibility of rape is articulated as Clavel reads out the final lines of the excerpt 'He dicho ya que la violación empieza con la mirada. Maniatadas en el bosque de su placer, las ropas en jirones, la cabeza doblegada, las tres niñas [...] prodigándose con criminal e inviolable inocencia' [I have already said that rape starts with the gaze. Handcuffed in the forest of their pleasure, their clothes in shreds, their heads downcast, the three little girls [...] revelling in their criminal and inviolable innocence] (p. 95). The multimedial interaction serves to enhance the shock factor the spectator may experience as we are presented here with a highly problematic encoding of rape as enjoyable for the female victim, a perspective which the works of Cuéllar, Bellmer, and Clavel posit. Julián's view that the young doll-girl nymphet deserves such treatment because of her 'criminal e inviolable inocencia' utterly shocks, but such abomination may be understood as Clavel's tactic to critique the traditional patriarchal gambit of presenting sexual abuse victims as taking pleasure in being raped and therefore deserving it, as well as allowing the perpetrator to get off scot-free.

The recurrent theme of reader-spectator complicity in Clavel's novella and overall multimedia endeavour is also once again foregrounded in the performance. As Clavel reads her final words and the *Las Violetas* front cover with its title is projected onto the wall, the uncomfortable visual complicity forged between the various multimedial strands — narrative, performance, image — and spectator becomes apparent. As with the work of Bellmer, Cuéllar, and Nabokov and the *Las Violetas* multimedia project, the performance is nevertheless ambiguous as it is not always entirely clear what position the spectators are meant to occupy and therefore, taking my cue from Rose, the 'neat division of scopic labour' is often confused ('Making Space', p. 344). Thus, are these works exclusively addressed to men or to women, or both? Are we asked to take up the view that girls or women are complicit with the dominant gaze, or should we revile female sexual objectification by men? The performance is set up in such a way that it manipulates the position of the looked-at and spectator as voyeur: even as the girl-doll becomes the object of the spectator's gaze, this dynamic is flipped as the girl-doll, who is fully aware, and in charge, of her erotic power, suddenly steps off the stage and touches, looks at, and interacts with the audience, thus turning them into the objects of *her* gaze. Therefore the typical feminine and masculine 'positions are refused [...] the masculine gaze is deflected, the feminine object lost' (Rose, p. 344). Ultimately Clavel does not offer us the comfort of one stable perspective or subject position and so, to cite Mulvey, 'meanings shift and change their reference like shifting perceptions of perspective from an optical illusion' (Mulvey quoted in Rose, p. 344).

Clavel's performance and overall literary and multimedia endeavour thus appears to complement the works of Courbet, Bellmer, Nabokov, Duchamp, or Cuéllar in its ambiguous depiction of girl-woman as (sexually) passive or active, as object of (male) pleasure, or as complicit with the patriarchal gaze. I would argue nevertheless, that the notion of girl-woman as object of, at times brutal, male desire overrides in the main the more positive interpretation of femalehood which the works of all of these male writers or artists may suggest, and, in a sense, the performance seeks to rectify this imbalance, undoubtedly motivated by Clavel's strong feminist principles. Throughout the *Las Violetas* performance, the girl calls out the words 'quisiera ser mujer' [I would like to be a woman], 'quisiera ser persona' [I would like to be a person].[50] This of course links the performance to the text being read aloud by Clavel in which Julián asks himself: '¿qué piensa una muñeca cuando le haces el amor? ¿Acaso su carne dormida no soñará que es en verdad una muchacha?' (*Las Violetas*, p. 93). As mentioned in Chapter 6, this quotation underscores his terror at the dolls' silent thoughts of becoming human and thus at losing control over his products. He is also haunted by the prospect of their desire to become real, sexually mature women (p. 37). Clavel articulates this fear in the performance by vivifying the doll and giving a voice to her as well as to the generally voiceless women which Clavel/Cuéllar, Nabokov, Bellmer, and Julián create for themselves. As noted, Julián attempts in vane to deny his Violetas the power of speech in order to maintain his verbal and physical power over them. By bestowing on the girl-doll dancer the power to speak out, that is, to express her desire to be concomitantly a woman and her own person, Clavel reinforces the feminist thrust that advocates women's autonomy and their ability to create images of selfhood which shatter ideals of femininity as delineated by the patriarchy within which the works of Courbet, Duchamp, Nabokov, Bellmer, and Clavel/Cuéllar are strongly encoded. This particular point is powerfully bolstered via a number of intertextual references in the performance. As the dancer-girl dresses she approaches a mirror, steps through it, and disappears off the stage. Here of course Clavel is drawing from the mirror trope in Lewis Carroll's *Through the Looking Glass, and What Alice Found There* (1871) in which Alice discovers that she can step through a mirror into a 'Looking-Glass World'. The dancing doll-girl, whom Clavel refers to as Lulú-Violeta-Lucía-Soledad-Alicia, also becomes an allusion to Soledad and her alter-ego Lucía in Clavel's novel *Los deseos y su sombra*, examined in Chapter 2.[51]

Both the Chinese vase which Lucía and Soledad inhabit in *Los Deseos* and Alice/the girl-doll dancer's wonderland represent an ambiguous space of Dantesque horror and a place in which the female characters can take refuge from the external world where fantasy and the queer give vent to female imaginative freedom. In the context of the performance's own particular wonderland, Soledad's vase and, I would add, the 'third' space *Cuerpo náufrago* advocates for non-heteronormative sexualites become loci in which the self is able to be the self for itself and where cyborgs, ghosts, dolls, and queers can choose to be what they want emotionally, sexually, and bodily, as encapsulated in the girl-doll's plea to be a genderless 'persona'. These alternative spaces do away with phallo-centrism which seeks to establish its authority and specifically to regulate the body and identity via stereotypes. Rose notes that for feminists who dream of new kinds of subjectivity, then new kinds of spaces must also follow (p. 353). Clavel posits a new kind of spatiality which is 'constituted by, and itself constitutes, a different relationship to the body and the subject from that of everyday space and the master subject' (Rose, p. 354). In the fantasy world of Clavel's female and non-heteronormative subjects, as represented by the transgender Antón/ia and the various 'nons' s/he encounters, the author ultimately seeks to offer a different sort of space which challenges the 'objectification of everyday voyeurism', foments 'a relation between subjects rather than between the subject and his Others', and ultimately does away with 'the violence to which so many bodies are subjected (not just female bodies)' (Rose, p. 353).

It is true to say that despite the feminist potentialities postulated in *Las Violetas*, in either its literary or multimedia dimension, the outlook presented is far from comforting as there appears to be almost no space for girls or women which is beyond the reach of patriarchy. During our interview it became apparent that Clavel was very aware that her representation of women as the often complicitous victims of sexual violence in *Las Violetas* and its multimedia dimension was controversial and stated that 'muchas feministas me consideran como muy poco feminista' [a lot of feminists consider me as not very feminist].[52] Indeed, her work may be viewed as deeply problematic given the immediate context of the ferocious violence against Mexican women nationally and the history of gender construction in Mexico. It is interesting to note that *Las Violetas* was published after there were a number of high profile international rulings against Mexico for the nation's inadequate response to the violence against women particularly in the Juárez region. The book's publication date similarly coincides with a law which was passed in Mexico specifically trying to combat the unacceptable levels of gender violence in the country.[53] Clavel's dolls are particularly poignant in the context of the femicides in Juárez and the creation of the so-called 'maquiloca' dolls, Barbie-like constructs that are supposed to approximate the *maquila* workers. Clavel's exploration of feminine complicity and culpability is also deeply unsettling given the ways in which these views have predominated so much in media coverage of violence against women in Mexico, and therefore some may perceive Clavel as perpetuating 'real' sexualized brutality against women. Furthermore whilst this study has, and continues, to propose that Clavel's overall *oeuvre* is transgressive and refuses the comfort of one stable position, it is true that some of her perspectives on women are at risk of being critiqued by some who may view her posturing both as dangerous as it is dated. This latter critique may come about from the manner in which the 'playful' nature of Clavel's provocative questioning could be perceived as being located within an early twentieth-century European avant-garde transgressive aesthetic of pre-surrealist sadomasochism, of a kind that Lautréamont personifies perfectly. In a recent discussion I asked Clavel what her views were in relation to the antifeminist stance in her work suggested by certain critics, to which she responded:

> As with Albert Camus's character Caligula, I would like to be able to restore the freedom to all people, despite the mammoth effort this would entail. But such an endeavour is not in my capacity nor is it my task to do so. I am simply a writer who believes that literature is a kind of black mirror which allows one to imagine or reveal the possibilities and realities of humanity, and which goes beyond fashions, moralities, and what is politically correct. Given the level of violence and the awareness of the horrors which we are currently experiencing particularly in Mexico and other parts of the world, one could easily fall into the temptation of creating a literature of denunciation or social engagement — but which, in reality, is often falsely engaged. For this there are specific forms of writing such as proselytist literature, the journalistic chronicle, and sociological studies. There are also activist movements and initiatives fighting for human rights. 'Necessary' literature is another thing: just as with art, it is one of the few spaces in which there is true freedom of the imagination of the writer or artist, freedom to reveal or recognize via the medium of language/art the deepest contradictions of life in all its subtlety and complexity. In a world in which everything is sold to us, true literature is one of the few bastions where the writer does not want to sell anything to the reader. Authentic literature goes through us, it touches us, and stirs us in such a way that it removes us from a place in which we have felt protected with all our false sense of security.
>
> I am deeply incensed by the fact that, for example, the International Women's Day — which has at its roots the fight for women's human rights — has become confused in Mexico with a humdrum and antiquated celebration in which women are offered flowers and hearts merely for being female, as occurs on the 10th of May each year when we celebrate our 'saintly mothers', which is a very patriarchal tradition in Mexico. Such events contrast sharply and ironically with the recent reports of indigenous women having to give birth

> outside of hospitals because they are not admitted either because of negligence or racism; then there are the reported cases such as those of the woman Yakiri Rubio who has been imprisoned and is now facing charges for trying to defend herself against her rapist; or the ones relating to the trading of white female slaves who are being forced to prostitute themselves — this another form of slavery. Despite all the public denunciations and press coverage on these sorts of events these atrocities are continuing to happen in Mexico City because of the negligence and complicity of the authorities. But that indignation and that anger are not reflected in my work. What is present in my work is a rebellion against prejudices and false good intentions and consciences which has led me to delve into urges and specifically desire, which is something which I consider an utmost human trait. And that is the reason perhaps why my work is so disturbing, sometimes in a more obvious way, other times in a more subtle way. Furthermore my multimedia endeavours which have sprung from my books similarly continue with that rebellion, with that desire to transgress boundaries [...] But there is nothing special about what I am saying: I think that every true artist is, in his or her own way, transgressive and disturbing.[54]

Faced with the 'transgressive and perturbing' content of *Las Violetas* the viewer or reader may prefer to turn away, close the book or the web browser. The viewer's reluctance is likely to be further exacerbated by the extremely graphic content of *Las Violetas* in the depiction of the, especially underage, female body that is the subject of the paedophilic gaze or sexually brutalized. In similar fashion to the novel and multimedia dimension of *Cuerpo náufrago* with its abject viscerality, the visual element of *Las Violetas* causes 'a crisis in viewing in much the same way as watching a horror film' (Gear, p. 323). The viewer of Clavel's work may want to look away and re-establish the boundaries between that which is deemed proper versus the improper. But to do so would be to replicate the actions of a society which has so often looked away from the kinds of questions which Clavel's work brazenly takes on, including notions of taboo whereby certain types of desires, incest, and paedophilia specifically, are deemed unlawful. The viewer is thus caught between a desire not to see and the realization that a response is required in order not to be complicit with such denial, and it is this difficult position into which he or she is thrust that makes Clavel's literary and multimedia work so effective in making her reader-audience critically engage with the issues addressed.

Notes to Chapter 8

1. Lavery, unpublished interview with Clavel, 2008.
2. It was also exhibited in the Coordinación Nacional de Literatura del INBA, situated in República de Brasil 37, Col. Centro Histórico, from 3 July to 15 August 2008.
3. <http://www.violetasfloresdeldeseo.com/> [accessed 14 June 2014].
4. Michael R. Taylor, *Marcel Duchamp: Étant donnés* (New Haven: Philadelphia Museum of Art published in association with Yale University Press, 2009), pp. 108–11. Derek Sayer, 'Doll Parts, or, the Subject Reconfigured from the Point of View of the Mannequin', paper presented at 4S-EASST Conference, 26–28 August 2004, 1–29 (p. 19), <http://www.csi.ensmp.fr/WebCSI/4S/download_paper/download_paper.php?paper=sayer.pdf> [accessed 22 June 2014]. Bellmer and Duchamp shared Surrealism's long-standing interest in the theme of dolls and mannequins (Taylor, p. 39). Bellmer's dolls also had a deep impact on Duchamp's *Étant donnés* (Taylor, pp. 40–41).

5. McGrath, 'Re-reading Edward Weston: Feminism, Photography and Psychoanalysis', p. 331.
6. <http://www.violetasfloresdeldeseo.com/> [accessed 20 July 2014].
7. Creed, *Monstrous-feminine*, p. 106.
8. Mulvey, 'Visual Pleasure and Narrative Cinema', pp. 6–18.
9. Halberstam, *Female Masculinity*, p. 178.
10. Valerie Traub quoted in Halberstam, p. 178.
11. Such images hark back to the works of André Masson, Courbet, Bellmer, and Duchamp which evoke the idea of woman as nature.
12. <http://www.violetasfloresdeldeseo.com/> [accessed 20 July 2014].
13. Linda Clifton, 'The Gaze of Gustave Courbet's *L'Origine du monde* — A Response to Juan Davila', *Écritique*, Papers of the Freudian School of Melbourne, *Lacanian Psychoanalytic Writings*, 5 (2005), 39–46 (p. 40), <http://home.vicnet.net.au/~fsom/ecritique0405.htm> [accessed 22 June 2014]
14. James Rubin, *Courbet* (London: Phaidon Press Ltd, 1997), p. 208.
15. Day, 'Annie Ernaux and Courbet's *L'Origine du monde*', p. 209.
16. Ibid.
17. Clifton, 'Apropos Encore', p. 107.
18. Taylor, *Marcel Duchamp*, p. 41; Sue Taylor, *Hans Bellmer: The Anatomy of Anxiety* (Cambridge, MA: MIT Press, 2000), p. 2.
19. Suleiman, 'Dialogue and Double Allegiance', p. 136. Rosalind E. Krauss, *Bachelors* (Cambridge, MA: October Books, MIT Press, 1999), p. 156.
20. Alyce Mahon, *Eroticism and Art* (Oxford: Oxford University Press, 2005), p. 67.
21. Duchamp's *Étant donnés* also pre-programmed viewers to 'unthinkingly accept that (they were) spectators of a sadistic crime'. Michael R. Taylor, 'Body Matters: Marcel Duchamp's *Étant Donnés* Revisited', in Marc Décimo (ed.), *Marcel Duchamp and Eroticism* (Newcastle: Cambridge Scholars Publishing, 2007), pp. 33–42 (pp. 27 & 33). However, Taylor contends the perception of Duchamp's reclining nude as violated and views this woman — as has already been suggested of the female in Clavel's *El origen del juego* and Courbet's *L'Origine du monde* — in a state of post-coital bliss, suggesting the 'blossoming' of a woman who 'has reached the goal of her desire' ('Body Matters', p. 42).
22. Tanner, 'Reading Rape', p. 560.
23. Jukka Gronov, *The Sociology of Taste* (London: Routledge, 1997), p. 11.
24. Ibid., pp. 9 & 12. Colin Shaw, *Deciding What We Watch: Taste, Decency, and Media Ethics in the UK and the USA* (New York: Oxford University Press, 1999), p. 1.
25. Lavery, unpublished interview with Rogelio Cuéllar, 2008.
26. Jerrold Levinson, 'Erotic Art and Pornographic Pictures', *Philosophy and Literature*, 29:1 (2005), 228–40 (p. 232).
27. Clavel, 'Los caballeros las prefieren mudas', p. 65.
28. Abyss Creations RealDoll catalogue (2007).
29. 'RealDoll', <http://www.realdoll.com> [accessed 22 June 2014].
30. 'RealDoll', posted 11 December 2009, <https://secure.realdoll.com/testamonials> [accessed 22 June 2013].
31. 'RealDoll', no post date, <https://secure.realdoll.com/testamonials> [accessed 22 June 2013].
32. Quoted in Toshi Maeda, 'Japan's Lonely Hearts Turn to Dolls for Sex, Company', *Reuters*, 18 July 2007, <http://www.reuters.com/article/2007/07/18/us-japan-sex-dolls-idUSSP10422420070718> [accessed 22 June 2014].
33. David Levy, *Love and Sex with Robots* (New York: HarperCollins, 2007), p. 247.
34. Kate E. O'Neill, 'Female Effigies and Performances of Desire: A Consideration of Identity Performance Lars and the Real Girl', *Desire, Forum*, 6 (2008), <http://www.forumjournal.org/site/issue/06/kate-e-o-neill> [accessed 14 June 2014].
35. 'RealDoll', posted 6 April 2010, <https://secure.realdoll.com/testamonials> [accessed 14 June 2013].
36. Lavery, unpublished interview with Clavel, 2008.
37. Ibid.
38. Throughout the exhibition, as indeed in the exhibitions of *Los deseos y su sombra, Cuerpo náufrago*

and *Las ninfas a veces sonríen*, there was a clear foregrounding of authorial presence not merely to confirm Clavel as author of the book for which the book launch exhibition had been created, but also to establish her role as creator and choreographer of the exhibition with its various components. Arturo Buitrón's doll *Empiernada Violeta*, which was plastered with photocopies of the front cover image of *Las Violetas*, had had a CD and loudspeakers inserted into it from which the viewer could hear these same excerpts of the text also being read by Clavel. Clavel also came up with the names of the majority of the fourteen dolls which were artistically worked on by the various artists. Whilst Clavel wanted to 'control' the overall exhibition, the work of the various 'authors' who intervened artistically represented a collage of creative input.

39. <http://www.violetasfloresdeldeseo.com/>.
40. Lavery, unpublished interview with Saúl Kaminer, 2008.
41. Gear, 'All Those Nasty Womanly Things', p. 321.
42. Braidotti, *Nomadic Subjects*, p. 81.
43. Kristeva, *Powers of Horror.*
44. Finnegan, *Monstrous Projections of Femininity*, p. 102.
45. Brook, *Feminist Perspectives on the Body*, p. 5.
46. In relation to Caballero's doll and the others on display, Clavel notes that 'Los nombres de las muñecas se los puse yo, pero en el caso de la muñeca de Rocío, ella la llamaba Virginia, no Violeta, entonces decidí jugar con el significado de la palabra y añadí "Virginal" para parodiar la intención en una muñeca embarazada. Si te fijas, el asunto del embarazo en las muñecas, fue una propuesta de Rocío muy personal, que no tiene que ver con las muñecas que yo planteo pues son todas vírgenes violadas pero incapaces de embarazo por ser precisamente muñecas' [I gave the dolls their names, but in the case of Rocío's doll, she called her Virginia, not Violeta, so I thus decided to play with the significance of the work and added "Virginia" in order to parody the idea of a pregnant doll. If you notice, the question of the pregnancy of the dolls was a very personal one created by Rocío, which has nothing to do with the dolls that I have created given that they are all raped virgins but incapable of getting gregnant precisely because they are dolls], email to Lavery, 12 March 2014, 06:47.
47. Lavery, unpublished interview with Clavel, 2008.
48. Lavery, unpublished interview with Rubén Maya Moreno, 2008.
49. Fabiola Palapa Quijas, 'Inspira novela de Ana Clavel a 14 artistas para explorar las secuelas del deseo', *La Jornada*, 1 April 2008, <http://www.jornada.unam.mx/2008/04/01/index.php?section=cultura&article=a05n1cul> [accessed 22 June 2014].
50. During her reading of this chapter, Sarah Bowskill remarked in relation to this quotation that it could also be perceived as an intertextual reference to, and inversion of, the fairytale of *Pinocchio* in which the puppet yearns to become a real boy.
51. <http://www.violetasfloresdeldeseo.com/> [accessed 20 July 2014].
52. Lavery, unpublished interview with Clavel, 2008.
53. 'La Ley General de Acceso de las Mujeres a una Vida Libre de Violencia' [General Law on Women's Access to a Life Free of Violence], 1st February 2007.
54. Clavel, email to Lavery, 18 March 2014, 16:22.

CHAPTER 9

El dibujante de sombras
The Queering of Truth and a Poetics of Shadows

Although *El dibujante de sombras* (2009) has not received the same level of critical acclaim as *Las Violetas son flores del deseo* or *Las ninfas a veces sonríen,* the novel has nevertheless been praised by cultural critics in the few reviews of it which have been written.[1] Whilst thematically unique, *El dibujante* continues many of the existing concerns of her overall *oeuvre.* Indeed, the novel has deep resonances with Clavel's previous works in its exploration of notions of replica, origins, intertextuality, (non-) conformity, erotic desire, human subjectivity, the shadow, and in particular its need to queer certain 'givens', whether these be religious, moral, sexual, cultural, or historical. Anamari Gomis similarly notes how *El dibujante* 'recurre a dos constantes en la obra de Ana Clavel: las artes plásticas, en este caso, la camera obscura previa a los experimentos que desembocarían en la fotografía, y el deseo vinculado al erotismo' [draws from two recurring themes in the work of Ana Clavel: the visual arts, in this case, the camera obscura which was developed before other experiments which would give rise to photography, and erotic desire].[2] In *El dibujante* diverse forms of desires become apparent, such as the need for power or the desire for creative, intellectual, and sexual self-determination in the face of repressive cultural, ideological, religious, and moral forces which seek to curtail such freedoms. Whilst sexual desire is an important concern in the novel, it is not central to the work's overall thematic and therefore contrasts sharply with *Cuerpo náufrago, Las Violetas,* and *Las ninfas* which are driven primarily by the erotic. Although the use of images throughout *El dibujante,* with its interaction between the written and visual forms, has strong parallels with the technique used by Clavel in *Cuerpo náufrago,* of all the texts examined in this study *El dibujante* perhaps has most in common with *Los deseos y su sombra.* I propose here that as a multi-genre text in which the dividing line between fact and fiction is blurred, *El dibujante,* like *Los deseos* as discussed in Chapter 2, challenges traditional notions of the historical past, biography, and selfhood which can be placed alongside contemporary notions of subjectivity. Set in the Enlightenment period, Clavel examines in *El dibujante* the life and thinking of the historical figure, Johann Kaspar Lavater, an eighteenth-century Swiss Protestant pastor, theologian, physiognomist, and poet, as well as his fraught relationship with another historical-fictional figure, one of his apprentices whose real name remains unknown in the annals of history but is fictitiously named by Clavel as Giotto de Winterthur. Clavel is interested in exploring not the official version of Lavater's life but rather the underside of the history of this man, which is full of paradoxes. The novel thus suggests that the only way to reconstruct the life of Lavater and his assistant 'Giotto' is through postmodernist and new historical treatment.[3] As will become apparent, the inconsistency of Lavater's character, which derives from the contrast between and merging of the historical and the fictional, connects *El dibujante* not only to the new historical and the postmodern but also to the queer. This study will also show how, in similar fashion to *Los deseos*, the correlation between the individual and the historical becomes enmeshed as a means of queering traditional notions of 'truth'. As explored previously, in *Los deseos* the defiance of monological versions of political 'truth' and the drive to reconstruct alternative conceptions of national identity are linked to the creation of a multiple female 'sujet en proces' and a non-patriarchal conception of female subjectivity. In *El dibujante* Clavel appears to seek to challenge notions of singular biographical 'truth' and to propose instead that multiple biographical truths become interrelated with the creation of a male character whose identity is similarly presented as inchoate. In this respect, Clavel's apparent interest in a postmodern, unstable, and contradictory subjectivity in *El dibujante* is one which is a recurring feature in her *oeuvre*. Indeed, as we have seen in *Los deseos*, *Cuerpo náufrago*, *Las Violetas* and in some of Clavel's short stories, the notion of an originary or stable selfhood is challenged. Thus the internal inconsistencies as seen in Lavater share some broad commonalities with the split selves of Clavel's other characters. The notion of a split identity can be seen in the context of, for example, the heterosexual/homosexual Samuel in 'Una advertencia' or the transgender Antón/ia in *Cuerpo náufrago*. Split identity is often linked to the notion of the performance of self. In 'Una advertencia', 'Tu bella boca rojo carmesí', or *Cuerpo náufrago* it was discussed how the Butlerian notion of 'doing gender' signals the view that gender and sexuality are not innate but rather socially constructed. In *El dibujante* the performance of self is linked specifically to Lavater's saintly public persona, which, as we will discuss further on, contrasts sharply with his scheming, unsaintly private self. The split self often leads to a sense of anguish as seen for instance in the characters of Lavater, Samuel ('Una advertencia'), María ('Cuando María mire el mar'), or Soledad (*Los deseos*). Lavater's tormented character can be compared in some respects to Julián Mercader's own anguished being in *Las Violetas*, as will be briefly discussed further on.

Following analysis of Lavater's incongruous character, the study then turns its focus to Clavel's obsession with the 'poética de las sombras' in *El dibujante*, and which, as we have already seen, also permeates *Los deseos*, and to an extent her other works. This notion is inexorably linked to the opposition between shadow and light and such antithesis serves as a metaphor for a series of binary contrasts which are at play, including carnality versus spirituality, embodiment and disembodiment, truth versus masquerade, the (double-) self and non-self, proper and improper, reason and emotion, mind and body, life and death. The contrasting notion of the shadow as lack or a Duboisean luminous presence, as seen in both *Los deseos* and

El dibujante, will be similarly discussed. Yet the fusing of both light and dark in an ambivalent chiaroscuro suggests the impossibility of keeping any fixed categories apart. Although shadows represent negativity, so too do they have a positive valence in Clavel's novel, as she unqueers the negative otherness attached to the shadow in the history of art. The proliferating references to shadows, shadow art, the 'camera obscura' [dark room], as well as Clavel's use of illustrations throughout *El dibujante* similarly raise fascinating questions in relation to notions of 'essence', 'aura', 'authenticity', authority, mechanical reproduction, imitation, (digital) replication, and intertextuality. In this respect, *El dibujante* once again positions Ana Clavel as a multimedia writer whose work is defined by the fusion of the written and non-written forms.

Queered Truth

Los deseos and *El dibujante* have in common Clavel's ability to queer official versions of truth by blurring both fact and fiction. As in *Los deseos,* the historical credentials of *El dibujante* are enhanced by ample references to historical texts, figures, locations, and events. Yet even as Clavel provides a sense of 'historicalness' in both fictive worlds, so too is the real imbued with the unreal. But as is common with historiographic metafiction, the author merges reality and fiction, leaving the process of distinguishing the two to the judgement of the reader. By fusing the real and unreal in both works, Clavel can be seen to seek in postmodern fashion to chip away at mono-logical concepts such as 'essence', 'authenticity', and 'truth'. *El dibujante* (like *Los deseos*) is thus a prime example of postmodern historiographic metafiction, or new historicism, as it focuses on the 'historia no oficial' [unofficial history], and on that side of 'truth' which some of the existing official biographical texts on Lavater appear to have omitted.[4] In *El dibujante* Clavel notes that P. I. Heisch's *Memoirs of John Caspar Lavater* (1842) presents Lavater as a benevolent religious figurehead (p. 60). By noting that 'hay que tomar las *Memorias de Lavater* escritas por el reverendo Heisch con reservas' [We must read the Reverend Heisch's *Memoirs of Lavater* with reservation] (p. 62), Clavel appears to undermine staunchly the manner in which some biographies present their facts as the definitive truth without offering alternative interpretations. Clavel's imagination was particularly captured by Lavater's involvement in 'escándalos callados' [silenced scandals],[5] as well as by a quotation in Stoichita's critical work on Lavater in which the art historian draws from various biographies which allude to the shadier side of Lavater's persona.[6] Stoichita thus notes in relation to Lavater that 'there were strange events in his personal life and immediate environment: these were not without their neuroses, suicides and exorcisms' (p. 163). Clavel's presentation of Lavater as a man whose occasional kindness is overridden by intransigent moral, religious, and philosophical ideology counters those versions which emphasize his unreserved compassion. Clavel is seen to have little empathy for Lavater whom she depicts as a zealous promoter of his own benevolent efforts, and so for the author 'había necesidad de parodiarlo y tomar una distancia crítica' [there was a need to parody him and to assume a critical distance].[7] Another significant reference Clavel came across was to that of Lavater's apprentice, who inspired the character of Giotto, 'murió en circunstancias poco claras' [died in very unclear circumstances].[8] The exploration of Giotto represents for Clavel a kind of 'poetic justice' which allows her to 'reclamar desde las sombras ese personaje histórico' [reclaim that historical person from the shadows].

Traditional historical and biographical discourses have typically been assessed according to the persuasiveness of their presentation of claims of truth, a concept which is queered by Clavel who examines the unofficial version of Lavater's life. The author posits that history and biography may be seen as a kind of fiction. According to Linda Hutcheon, the separation between literary and historical (and, by extension, biographical) discourse is questioned by postmodern theory and art: both are 'linguistic constructs [...] not at all transparent in terms of language or structure, and they appear to be equally intertextual, deploying the texts of the past within their own complex textuality'.[9] Truth therefore is always mediated, a perspective which Clavel constantly draws our attention to via the queer specifically in the context of the blurring of fact and fiction and intertextuality. The mediation of truth is particularly underscored in the context of Nussbaum's discussions on the new historical argument which posits the view that rather than 'knowing history directly, as objective intractable fact, we can know it only in textual artefacts [...] While a category of the real exists, our access to it is constrained and held within certain textual and ideological bounds'.[10] For Clavel it appears that the historical or biographical past must therefore be reinvented or '"emplotted" in the manner of a literary text, because what really happened remains largely beyond the grasp of the historian' and biographer.[11] *El dibujante* gives voice to those critical theories of (auto)biography which challenge authoritative writing and aim to question the humanist conception of a stable self. By incorporating manifold interpretations of Lavater's self into the narrative, via the inclusion of multiple and often incongruous narrative techniques and discourses, Clavel's approach to the construction of subjectivity is in line with contemporary practices of biographical writing where 'practitioners and readers alike acknowledge the genre's employment of documentary and novelistic techniques, biographical and autobiographical material to present a kaleidoscopic version of an ever-elusive subject'.[12] Clavel shares much in common with new historical Spanish American writers such as Tomás Eloy Martínez or Elena Poniatowska who focus on the 'proliferation and diversity of texts, highlighting their chaotic and discontinuous forms. They often give priority to the unofficial, the marginal, the exotic and anecdotal aspects of the historical record'.[13] The primary and secondary sources upon which Clavel draws are used to portray the varying representations of the 'official' and 'unofficial' life of Lavater. The intermingling of discourses thus suggests that there may be on the part of Clavel a feminist questioning of patriarchal structures of knowledge in her desire to represent alternative versions of historical or biographical 'truth'. *El dibujante* is truly heteroglossic: Bakhtin's 'heteroglossia', which refers to the conflict between 'official' and 'unofficial' discourses, serves to undermine the official historical discourse surrounding the public Lavater and is present in the clash between imaginative reconstructions of this man's story and the official record.[14] Whilst

Clavel's text is not claiming to be historically accurate, it is via this dialogic collision of discourses that the author ultimately seeks to bring to our attention the notion of multiple, rather than singular, 'truths'. This perspective also aligns *El dibujante* to *Los deseos* in which, as discussed previously, emphasis is placed on the idea of historic 'truth' as an imaginative construct.

Given that Clavel draws from historical texts, such as biographies of Lavater or primary sources written by the clergyman, and then juxtaposes such existing sources with fictional reconstruction, it is important in the following sections to make the links between the 'real' and 'unreal' in order to provide the reader with a comprehensive understanding of Lavater's paradoxical personality. Two areas in particular seem relevant when exploring his split persona. Firstly, an examination of his physiognomical work will highlight contradictory views of both his public persona and his study, and ultimately underscore his status as imposter and vainglorious character. Secondly, an analysis of his physiognomical work as well as a number of historical sources such as biographical texts or the infamous 'caso Grebel' [Grebel affair] will consider the clergyman's moral-theological agenda which is driven not so much by piousness, as some may believe, but rather by a ruthless desire for public recognition, a religious fanaticism verging on fascism, and deceit.

Lavater as (Imposter) Physiognomist

The incongruity of Lavater's person and his thinking is best highlighted in the context of his four-volumed *Physiognomische Fragmente zur Beförderung der Menschenkenntnis und Menschenliebe* (1775–78) and its reception, which Clavel, not without irony, mentions 'le atraería admiradores y enemigos por igual' [would attract admirers and enemies alike] (*El dibujante*, p. 17). She notes that *Physiognomische Fragmente* was significant for being the first 'grandiosa "poética de la interioridad"' [grandiose 'poetics of interiority'] (p. 94) of the Enlightenment to explicate the human soul via the physiognomical silhouette. However, as will be discussed below, Clavel highlights the manner in which Lavater's physiognomics was similarly widely derided for its pseudo-scientific claims and its prejudices. Clavel thus presents the clergyman as a kind of imposter in the context of his physiognomical work. The author suggests that the physiognomic illustrations officially attributed to the clergyman were not created by him or by other intellectuals such as Lips or Zimmerman but rather by his assistant Giotto, who remains unrecognized in the annals of art history (p. 57). Given the scant information which exists on the real 'Giotto', it is impossible to verify whether Clavel's inference is rooted in fact or fiction, but raises in any case interesting questions relating to notions of authority. As discussed in Chapter 5 in the context of *Cuerpo náufrago*, the signature traditionally bestows attribution or 'aura'. Clavel can be seen to mock such notions and to problematize the concept of the work of art as being linked to a unified authorial source. Lavater was widely considered the father of physiognomy, an attribution he was keen to promote, and his success owed much to 'a culture characterized by a new obsession with the notion of "genius"'.[15] Yet his physiognomical *oeuvre* belies the idea of singular genius, since the volumes are composed of elements taken from works of other intellectuals and artists, including those of former physiognomists such as Aristotle and Giambattista della Porta. By reinforcing the heteroglossic nature of Lavater's *Physiognomische*, Clavel is also pointing to her novel's own heteroglossic qualities, and hence its constructedness. The self-conscious foregrounding of the intertextual process highlights, as in the case of Clavel's overall literary and multimedia output, that texts are not stand-alone artefacts but rather a mosaic of previous works.

Through the notion of imposter, Clavel also links Lavater to wider questions of replication and reproduction, both of which of course are central concerns in *Cuerpo náufrago* and *Las Violetas.* Whilst Lavater perceived his physiognomics as embedded in scientific truth, others saw him as a pseudo-scientist, a position Clavel appears to uphold. Lavater's use of copies in the form of physiognomical profiles thus places him at the heart of two divergent eighteenth-century trends, namely, scientific replication, on the one hand, and aesthetic reproduction, on the other.[16] Even as Lavater strives for scientific replication, the physiognomist privileges aesthetic reproduction and the aura it lends him, as it permits him to reproduce himself as mediator of truth (Lyon, p. 240). During the Enlightenment, physiognomy came to be perceived as a pseudo-science, but, as Clavel observes (*El dibujante*, pp. 67–68), Lavater was intent on proving that his particular mode of physiognomics was embedded in 'respectable' scientific paradigms by making sustained appeals to scientific replication which 'demands that original and copy be identical, and relies on engineering and technology to ensure this identity. It produces a sense of objectivity and credibility' (Lyon, p. 259). Clavel reproduces various illustrations found in *Physiognomische Fragmente* to highlight some of the methods Lavater used in order to emphasize this notion of replication. Thus, the image of *Machine for Drawing Silhouettes* by Thomas Holloway and others (1792), which appears in *El dibujante*, underpins Lavater's obsession with demonstrating that if a mechanical process is used, silhouettes can replicate nature exactly, ensuring that the original and copy be identical and so 'bolstering the scientific credibility' (Lyon, p. 263). Even as Clavel appears to reinforce such a perception, so too does she undermine it when she suggests that Lavater in fact derides any kind of machine such as the silhouette apparatus or other types of Enlightenment methods of reproduction for capturing images (*El dibujante*, p. 123). The other example which Lavater used to promote physiognomics as a respectable form of science was the use of geometric quantification of physiognomies through the silhouette (Lyon, p. 263). In *El dibujante*, there are two identical facial silhouettes, one in white and the other in black (p. 96). The white silhouette is subdivided into various geometrical sections. As immediate imprints of nature, Clavel indirectly highlights via the use of such images the manner in which Lavater sustains the view that no other art is able to attain the truth of a well-made silhouette and that therefore physiognomics has no more reliable proof of its objective truthfulness than the silhouette (Lyon, pp. 262–63).

Despite Lavater's desire to use such methods to underpin the scientific credibility of physiognomics, *El dibujante* highlights the manner in which this field is embedded in questions of aesthetic reproduction. Influenced by eighteenth-century aesthetic discourse whereby all human culture is defined in terms of imitation,

Lavater believed that imitation is not exact replication, but imperfect reproduction of the eternal original spirit (Lyon, p. 265), as his words in *El dibujante* suggest: 'El hombre es el dibujo más perfecto hecho por la mano de Dios' [Man is the most perfect image made by God's hand] (p. 97). For Lavater the physiognomist belongs to a privileged category who possess a unique ability as mediator in unravelling the truth of nature, of the character of mankind, and ultimately of God. Lavater thus aligns himself to the artist and his artwork:

> The artist as reproducer creates a copy that is itself a new creation, an ideal [...] the artist becomes the original; he acquires the aura of authenticity usually associated with the artwork. Lavater blurs the distinction between original (nature, imagination) and mediator (artist). The artist becomes both mediator and original for Lavater. (Lyon, p. 270)

Whilst scientific reproduction appeals to the absence of its creator (Lyon, p. 274), Clavel underlines the manner in which Lavater emphasizes the presence of the artist-physiognomist as 'original' mediator-creator which aesthetic reproduction demands. This is captured in *El dibujante* in the black and white silhouettes which are reproductions of Lavater himself. Here, the act of self-reproduction underpins Lavater's desire to assert himself, like the artist, as an original and so reinforce the authenticity and authoritativeness associated with aura, as well as to present himself to his readers as authoritative mediator between original and copy. It thus confers on him in his capacity as physiognomist 'an aura of authenticity similar to that of aesthetic productions' (Lyon, p. 273). Clavel nevertheless can be seen to parody the alignment of any text with a single auratic 'genius' given that, as noted earlier, Lavater's *Physiognomische Fragmente* is a multi-authored feat. Unlike Lavater, whose insertion of his own image suggests a kind of 'anxiety of influence', Clavel, as evinced in *El dibujante* as well as her other texts such as *Cuerpo náufrago* or *Las Violetas*, celebrates intertextuality as a means of leading to creative renovation.

Clavel similarly appears to ironize Lavater's justification for the reproduction of his own image in his work. Critics of Lavater's physiognomy posited the view that rather than being based on impartial and empirical observation, his work was underpinned by 'physiognomic sense' whereby the physiognomist can discern people's character based on innate intuition or 'eye and heart' (Lavater quoted in Lyon, p. 271). The reason why Lavater inserted reproductions of himself into his own work was precisely to refute the critique that his physiognomy was 'that of a judgemental person' and instead it provided accurate analysis (Lyon, p. 272). With ironic effect, Clavel juxtaposes the black and white silhouettes with the description of a physiognomical profile of Lavater himself, which he personally wrote about:

> revelaba 'un carácter poético, muy sentimental y sobre todo sensible, una bonhomía que podía llegar a la imprudencia...'. Por eso, para no pecar de imprudente y soberbio, añadía también que el largo intervalo que separaba la nariz de la boca demostraba, por otra parte, 'una falta de prudencia y una tendencia a la precipitación'. (*El dibujante*, p. 95)
>
> [revealed a 'poetic character, very sentimental and above all very sensible, a bonhomie which verged almost on imprudence ...' In order to not be seen as being imprudent and arrogant, he thus added that the long gap which separated

> the nose from the mouth demonstrated, on the other hand, 'a lack of prudence and a tendency to be precipitous']

In the above passage, Lavater's analysis undermines any form of modesty, revealing an inflated self-promoter of his own apparent kindness. Ironically too, whilst the insertion of the black and white silhouettes of Lavater suggests the idea of physiognomy's impartiality, bolstered by their appeal to geometric precision, the analysis of his own profile underpins the biased predisposition of the physiognomist. Indeed, as Clavel notes:

> A pesar de que el pastor suizo se defendía de sus detractores diciendo que no pretendía juzgar a los hombres, sino conocerlos, lo cierto es que siempre había un halo de valorización en sus cartillas fisiognómicas. (*E lDibujante*, p. 95)
>
> [Even though the Swiss pastor defended himself from his detractors by saying that he did not seek to judge men, but rather get to know them, the truth is that there was always an aura of valorization in his physiognomic cards]

What is also significant about Clavel's purposeful juxtaposition of the black and white images with his physiognomical self–analysis is that they reveal his opposing pious and unpious selves, which is particularly apparent in the context of his religious persona.

Lavater as 'Pious' Religious Seer, Zealot, and Master of Subterfuge

Just as *El dibujante* draws our attention to the inherent paradoxes in Lavater's physiognomical work and his status as physiognomist, so too does the novel highlight the ambiguities surrounding his religious persona, in both the public and private spheres. Such incongruities ultimately serve to queer official versions of the pastor as pious religious entity and to offer instead an alternative representation of Lavater, namely, the clergyman as a zealot and master of subterfuge.

Through the juxtaposition of the 'real' and 'unreal', Clavel can be seen to reveal to her reader the manner in which Lavater's ideological and intellectual thinking, as well as his public/private persona, are informed by a staunch moral-theological agenda. Whilst the subtitle of Lavater's *Physiognomische Fragmente* emphasizes its desire to impart scientific truth about mankind, it also informs us that physiognomy is a means of promoting Christian benevolence and instructing readers in how to love human nature. In order to do so, Clavel's Lavater seeks to assert himself as a mediator of divine truth. Therefore, 'to give his readers insight into the manifold grace of God' Lavater must reproduce himself as 'an oracle of God' (Lyon, p. 274). Lavater perceives himself as a kind of religious seer, as noted by Clavel: 'la gloria de saberse elegido él, pastor de Zurich, para desempeñar altas tareas encomendadas por el Redentor' [the glory of knowing that he, the pastor of Zurich, had been chosen to carry out tasks of utmost importance entrusted to him by the Redeemer] (p. 9), which he applies, not only to his role as physiognomist, but also, as we shall see further on, to his role as clergyman. Whilst Lavater may wish to be perceived as acting unselfishly on God's behalf in order to sponsor Christian benevolence, his intellectual thought and actions in fact reveal a man who is driven by an almost arrogant desire to compete with God's powers. For Lavater the physiognomist is endowed with the privileged divine gift of reading appearances via one's shadow, which thus enables him to communicate to others God's divine truth. Lavater's physiognomics is rooted in the religious concept of the body as transparent, whereby the pastor, taking his cue from the German philosopher Johann Gottfried Herder, perceives man, as Clavel notes, as an 'espejo mágico donde se manifestaba [...] la Divinidad presente pero asimismo escondida. Se trataba, a partir de los signos visibles, de descubrir lo no-visible: el alma verdadera de los seres' [magical mirror where present yet hidden Divinity manifested itself. By observing the visible signs, the aim was to discover that which is not visible: the true soul of beings] (p. 94).[17] There are strong parallels here between Lavater and Julián Mercader in *Las Violetas*. Both Lavater and Julián aspire to embody God's divine powers. Whereas Lavater's discernment of the human soul via his shadow can be seen as his aspiration to possess God's divine knowledge, Julián's production of dolls can be understood as a desire to replicate God's unique power of human creation.

In the context of Lavater's apparently 'do-gooder' physiognomics, Clavel reveals how his work in fact reveals an obsessive drive for power in the form of public recognition as well as revealing, albeit unwittingly, quasi-fascist beliefs. For Lavater the legible body was connected to the Renaissance concept of the 'Great Chain of Being' and believed that the world was ordered according to a divinely inspired and universal hierarchy ranking all forms of higher and lower life, as suggested in his view in *El dibujante* that 'cada cosa en su sitio, cada ser en el lugar exacto del corazón de Dios' [each thing in its place, each being in the right place in the heart of God] p. 81). In this sense, the pastor's physiognomy assumes and reinforces the physical, moral, and spiritual superiority of humans over animals and refutes the possibility of transmutation.[18] This is manifested in *El dibujante* when Lavater acquires the sixteenth-century physigonomical work *De humana physiognomia* (1586) by Giambattista della Porta, who presented caricatures of human faces which resembled various animal profiles, with the objective of comparing animals and humans on the basis of their psychic characters. Here Clavel includes a series of sketches taken from Della Porta's work illustrating the heads of men placed alongside those of a range of animal heads, namely, a bird of prey, a goat, and a ram. Lavater warns Giotto: 'No creas todo lo que esos dibujos revelan: el hombre nunca podrá ser comparado con una bestia. El hombre es el dibujo más perfecto hecho por la mano de Dios' [Don't believe everything that those pictures reveal: man will never be able to be compared to a beast. Man is the most perfect image created by God's hand] (pp. 86–87). Lavater's rebuttal of della Porta's work is linked to the former's desire to set his own physiognomics apart from the latter's work for two reasons. Firstly, Lavater's refutation not only signals his desire to assert his authority but also his obsession with affirming his credibility amongst scientific circles. Despite the widespread popularity of della Porta's physiognomical work in Europe, both *De humana physiognomia* and *Magiæ naturalis* (1558) and their author had been subjected to inquisitorial processes, as Clavel notes, because of their interest in the occult sciences and folk medicine (p.86). Ironically Lavater, like della Porta, was later criticized for quackery and his physiognomics came under attack for being a form of divination (Stoichita, p. 163).

Clavel also explores the second reason why Lavater rejects della Porta's work by highlighting their differences in opinion in relation to the theological notion of the 'Great Chain of Being', or 'scala naturae', and man's status within the 'order of things'. In *El dibujante* even though Lavater embraces the principles of the 'scala naturae', he paradoxically appears to be threatened by the classical idea that all living creatures could be placed on a scale from the lowliest creature to humans as the highest, since it could be perceived as denying humankind's uniqueness. Lavater refutes the della Porta suggestion that a clear separation of humankind from animals cannot be taken for granted, a perception that Giotto is nevertheless clearly in agreement with: 'Giotto escrudiñaba las imágenes del libro y no le parecían tan erradas: cómo no reconocer al cabarellango Rudi en aquel hombre carnero de barba velluda hasta la quijada' [Giotto examined the images of the book and he did not think that they were that misguided: how could one not recognize Rudi, the stableman, in that ram-man with a hairy beard up to the jawbone] (pp. 86–87). Clavel's Lavater is visibly disturbed by della Porta's celebration of the inexorable interconnectedness between man and beast, a reflection perhaps of the historical Lavater who was at odds with the increasing tendency of new evolutionary systems of classification to challenged man's unique place in the universe. Lavater's response to such developments was to create his own chain of 'evolution' in some 800 illustrations in *Physiognomische Fragmente* in order to prove that men were unique and the most beautiful and moral 'creatures' on earth. It is on this basis that for many, Lavater's physiognomics came to reveal not only Christian religious zealotry but also a deeply-ingrained bigotry (Smith, p. 204). According to Lavater, the conformation of the skull and the features of the face revealed an individual's intellectual and moral qualities. Gray discusses how such thinking influenced materialist forms of physiognomy which came to be used as the basis for racial ideologies in general and Nazi racial theories in particular.[19] Whilst Clavel notes that Lavater unwittingly contributed to Nazi ideologies she, like countless other critics of Lavater, nevertheless underpins the physiognomist's quasi-fascist aesthetics of a superior race which posits the belief that physical beauty and ugliness are indications of a person's moral condition. Clavel notes that in relation to Lavater:

> Sus estudios fisiognómicos derivaron hacia una cuestión doctrinaria y maniquea al afirmar que la belleza de un rostro corresponde a una alma bella, del mismo modo que la fealdad, si no ha sido causada por un accidente o enfermedad, revela las faltas de un ser. De ideas semejantes se nutriría esa aberración y esa vergüenza que el siglo XX conocería con el nombre de naczismo en su exaltación de la raza superior — aunque por supuesto, Lavater estaba lejos de imaginar tales consecuencias. (*El dibujante*, p. 95)
>
> [His physiognomic studies resulted in doctrinaire and Manichean questions since they confirmed the idea that just as facial beauty corresponded to a beautiful soul, so too did ugliness, if it had not been caused by an accident or illness, revealed the faults in one's essence. It was such ideas which nurtured that shameful aberration which the twentieth century would come to know as Nazism with its ideological exaltation of beauty. Of course, Lavater was far from imagining that such consequences could be possible]

Despite the inadvertently dangerous materialist implications of Lavater's work, it seems hard for Clavel's modern day reader to comprehend how Lavater was not capable of recognizing the fact that many of his physiognomical judgements, as elicited in the above passage, far from promote a love for one's fellow man.[20]

Lavater's oscillating identity, marked on the one hand by piousness, and on the other hand by zealotry, bigotry, self-adoration, and obsession with fame, continues elsewhere in *El dibujante*, as seen in the context of his public role as clergyman and his involvement in 'escándalos callados'. Clavel draws from widespread historical sources in which frequent mention is made of Lavater's fame as Protestant pastor and which depict the celebrated religious figure as a pious and charismatic personality who had a lasting influence on his religious adherents. The author refers to Lavater's magneticism — 'no era mal orador y sus prédicas iban ganando fama entre los feligreses por su pasión y su poder de convencimiento' [he was not a bad orator and his sermons were gainin amidst his followers notoriety for their passion and power of persuasion] (p. 25) — and to his outward benevolence, in particular via his intentions (in appearance at least) to 'promote love towards humanity' (p. 17), the Christian doctrine of love for one's neighbour, in his self-perceived capacity as religious seer. Clavel similarly can be seen to seek to underpin another characteristic, namely, the idea of masquerade. Lavater delivers his sermon from the pulpit to the churchgoers congregated at Saint Peter's with 'su ágil razonar, la suavidad o vehemencia de su tono, un aire de mesurada dignidad, su convincente habilidad gestual' [his agile reasoning, the mildness and strength of his tone of voice, his air of measured dignity, his convincing gestural skill] (p. 140). The word 'aire' underscores the clergyman's prodigious faculty of performance. Here Clavel unmasks Lavater's manicured performance by revealing his religious zealotry which is marked by a paternalistic drive to guide the souls of the masses towards the path of Christian goodness (p. 141). Elsewhere she draws from Heisch's *Memoirs of Lavater* in order to critique public discourses which blindly uphold the clergyman's virtuousness: 'También para aquellos, como el reverendo Heisch, que veían en la existencia de Lavater la vida de un santo, y a quien no se cansaban de ofrendar orlas y coronas en el mausoleo de su recuerdo' [Those people, such as the Reverend Heisch, who also saw in Lavater the life of a saint, and who never tired of offering garlands and wreaths for the mausoleum of his memory] (p. 60). Clavel presents Lavater as a vainglorious man by remarking mockingly that 'lo del mausoleo fue el propio pastor zurichense quien no se cansó de erigirlo, como lo atestiguan los numerosos retratos que mandó hacer a su persona' [it was the pastor from Zurich himself who never tired of erecting the mausoleum, as seen in the number of portraits of himself which he commissioned] (p. 60). This comment is followed by the inclusion of a physiognomical silhouette of Lavater surrounded by a wreath of flowers which he himself had drawn and which was often distributed amongst his friends and strangers alike, clear testament, not only of Lavater's self-adoration, but also of his longing for posthumous celebrity (p. 61). Pre-empting her modern-day reader's response to the image which underpins the clergyman's self-importance, Clavel comments that Lavater's 'devotos y defensores nos acusarán de perjuros. Para nosotros resulta revelador el retrato en sombra chinesca' [devotees and supporters will accuse us of being perjurious. For us this Chinese shadow portrait is quite revealing] (p. 61). The word 'revelador' serves to peel away the layers of public masquerade with which Lavater shrouds himself. Clavel's depiction of Lavater as a deceitful masquerader is seen in the context of his relationship with the German poet Johann Wolfgang Goethe. Of all the acquaintances Lavater had, it is Goethe who best understood that Lavater's public person promoting the benign love of humanity via the Christian doctrine of salvation was no more than a façade concealing an overwhelming affectation, as well as the mind of a religious fanatic. Clavel describes how the historical Goethe despised the physiognomist's vanity of which he thought the silhouettes of Lavater were a prime example (p. 61).

Goethe's observations highlight Lavater's obsession with public recognition. Lavater was particularly keen to make his mark in the ecclesiastical domain and nowhere is this better demonstrated than in two very public historical incidents, the so-called 'Grebel case' and the 'Lavater affair' (or 'Mendelssohn case'), which *El dibujante* explores. Whilst Clavel only briefly alludes to the Grebel case (pp. 35–37), it contributes to the overall picture of Lavater as a man whose actions in the public sphere, whilst apparently enacted for the greater good of society, reveal an intrinsic self-interest in his desire to place himself firmly in the public eye as a religious saviour and to enhance the reputation he was gradually gaining as a figure of controversy. This is also exemplified in the 'Lavater affair' which serves to reveal Lavater's calculating nature and in particular his religious intransience which is underpinned by his view that Christianity is the one 'true' religion. Clavel recreates the public written exchange between Lavater and the Jewish intellectual Moses Mendelssohn (pp. 75–79). Through irony Clavel derides the callous tactics informing Lavater's dispute with the Jewish scholar in order to mock the Lavaterian idea of 'love thy neighbour' (pp. 76–77). She similarly captures, with irony, the mixed reception of Lavater's attack on Mendelssohn: 'Aplaudido por almas tan vehementes y crédulas como la suya; criticado por las mentes más lúcidas y sensatas del medio intelectual, entre cuyos miembros hubiera deseado contarse' [applauded by vehement and credulous souls like himself; critiqued by the lucid and sensible minds of intellectual circles, amidst whose members he would have liked to have been part of] (p. 79).

The religious fanaticism and scheming nature of Lavater which are apparent in the public and intellectual sphere are also mirrored in the realm of the private in the context of his particular conception of friendship. Clavel demonstrates how for Lavater friendship does not embody so much the traditional features associated with it, such as mutual trust and respect, but is rather a kind of 'Werkstatt der Tugend' [workshop of virtue].[21] In *El dibujante*, key to Lavater's friendship is the search for the divine in man and his respective 'friendships' with Goethe, Felix Hess, and Giotto exemplify, each in their own way, the clergyman's endeavour to seek out the virtuous side of these men. Clavel describes indirectly Lavater's failed attempt to convert his friend Goethe, a polytheist, to Christianity, and it is thereon that their friendship ended. In *El dibujante*, Lavater recalls their separation, not without regret (p. 198). Following their separation, Goethe historically described Lavater as a kind of imposter who not only deceived himself but equally sought to deceive those whom surrounded him, including himself.[22] Clavel explores the manner in which Lavater treats his friends Felix Hess and Giotto as if they were part of his physiognomical experiments, at the heart of which masquerade is also key.[23] For Lavater, the body was intrinsically deceptive because everything externally associated with it, such as social standing, education, and behaviour, 'masks the "real" person, who is hidden behind these disguises'.[24] According to Lavater, the science of physiognomy uncovers the soul and thus the physiognomist possesses a unique power as 'arbiter of "true" feelings and "true" character. He alone is the judge, the spy, who can discern these signs and penetrate the mask of consciousness' (Moore, p. 178). Clavel similarly presents her fictional Lavater as a sort of spy who through subterfuge seeks to unmask the real self. This becomes particularly apparent with Giotto, with whom Lavater shares a kind of paternalistic friendship between mentor and mentored, religious steer and disciple. On one occasion, Lavater spies upon his young apprentice, who appears not to be aware that he is being observed by the clergyman. As he is taking a dip in the Limmat river one hot summer's day, Giotto's torso casts a shadow onto the water's shimmering surface (pp. 81–82). Lavater believes that he can discern in the young boy's shadow his essential being, which is marked by angelic qualities. His observation that Giotto's self merging with his shadow is the embodiment of a 'Dios en dos' (p. 81) bolsters Lavater's idea that God can be encountered in man's shadow. Whilst Lavater initially marvels at such a perception, he almost immediately realizes that the idea of God split in two is sacrilegious (p. 83). Such back-peddling is particularly telling in the context of the historical Lavater's theories on shadow-analysis. Stoichita remarks that what Lavater was looking for was not the positive, divine side of man, as Lavater himself claimed, but rather the demonic, sinful side of man (Stoichita, p. 161), for the 'shadow was the imaginary area where the soul revealed itself full of sin' (Stoichita, p. 164). Therefore to propose that God can be split into two is profane for it suggests that not only does God possess a shadow and is therefore an embodied mortal, but equally that he has a sinful side to him. The shadow or 'dark stain' was the epitome of the Devil. In this respect, Stoichita notes that Lavater 'identified the devil within, not without [...] The devil within was visualized in Lavater's science of physiognomy, projected in the shadow'.[25]

The role of Lavater's mastering gaze on deviant, monstrous bodies becomes significant in this respect. Whilst it may appear that he is seeking the saintly in Giotto's shadow/self, he paradoxically is searching for 'the fallen man' in him, and Giotto's sinful nature, as with Hess, has its roots — in the view of the clergyman — both in superciliousness and carnal lust. In this respect we can find another parallel between Lavater and Julián Mercader. Julián's own mastering gaze on Violeta is informed by conflict. As we saw in Chapter 6, even as he perceives his daughter and doll replicas as embodying innocent purity, he similarly views them as 'flores del mal' (p. 111). In his mind it is the sexual precociousness of his daughter (and of the Violetas) that defines her intrinsic evilness and makes the nymphet an 'irremediable violada' (p. 47). By finding deviant qualities in others, both Lavater and Julián can, for the most part of their lives, at least, ultimately pursue their own 'unacceptable' desires and ambitions guilt-free, thus relieving themselves from the responsibility for their immoral conduct.

In *El dibujante*, Lavater's conflicting attitude towards Giotto becomes apparent from the outset of the novel. Upon first discovering Giotto's flourishing artistic talent in shadow art, he sees the young boy as 'un diamante oscuro que habrá que pulir' [a dark diamond that will have to be polished] (p. 20). Taking Giotto under his wing thus forms part of Lavater's personal project both in his capacity as artistic mentor and religious saviour. Whilst Lavater's adoption of the orphaned Giotto can be seen as a selfless act, it becomes apparent that self-interest is at the heart of such 'benevolence'. Lavater's fondness for Giotto is undeniable, perhaps because of the young boy's resemblance both physically and in character to his beloved friend Hess. Lavater finds in both males angelic and sinful qualities simultaneously and he describes them as embodying such antithesis almost word for word in similar terms (pp. 20 & 30–31). It becomes apparent that as with Hess, Lavater sees the possibility of finding God in Giotto's mortal, embodied, and imperfect being and therefore is able to save him from perdition.[26]

Yet Lavater's hopes of salvation are dashed for his grip over Giotto loosens as his friend/apprentice becomes increasingly free-spirited, both sexually and creatively. Giotto's 'no-deseos' are awakened, ironically and inadvertently, by Lavater himself. Lavater becomes familiarized with the triptych entitled *The Garden of Earthly Delights* (c. 1504) by Hieronymous Bosch, whose fantastical sexual and violent imagery here served to fuel images of Hell in the popular conscience of the Enlightenment. The impressionable Lavater uses this painterly example in his sermons as a moral warning to his parishioners whom, he cautions, could be tortured in Hell 'por desear, pero sobre todo, por gozar el vicio de un cuerpo que no ha sido santificado' [for desiring, but above all, for taking pleasure in the vice of a body which has not been sanctified] (p. 51). Amidst the churchgoers Giotto 'escuchó como si fuera la única alma pecadora en el mundo' [listened as if he were the only sinful soul in the world] (p. 46) and is left in a state of feverishness propelled, on the one hand, by his nascent sexual instinct and, on the other, by the self-castigating repression of that same impulse which religious proselytizing incites. Despite the clergyman's God-fearing repressive measures directly aimed at taming Giotto, the latter's carnal thirst is unquenchable. Giotto becomes exposed to the temptations of the flesh when Lavater's maid Hilde places Giotto's hand on her pubic area and masturbates in front of him (pp. 48–50). Giotto similarly becomes infatuated with the Huber twin sisters. Upon discovering a shadow drawing of the twins in Giotto's sketchbook, Lavater realises that Giotto 'era ya un hombre [...] hubiera querido abrazarlo y pedirle: "Detente, Giotto. Vuelve a ser otra vez un niño" [...] presintió que ya lo había perdido' [had become a man [...] he would have liked to embrace him and to ask him, 'Stop Giotto. Go back to being a little boy'] (p. 109). Giotto not only develops sexually, but also creatively. Whilst Lavater considers Giotto's dabbling in this 'shadow' technique of the camera obscura as an example of religious aberration and specifically his apprentice's erring towards the path of evil, Giotto perceives the discovery of the gadget as offering exciting possibilities in the faithful reproduction of reality, especially of the human form and its shadow. It is ironic that Lavater sees Giotto as a 'fallen man', since the clergyman embodies this very characteristic not so much for reasons discussed earlier, such as his bigotry or arrogant nature, but more for his manslaughter of Giotto (pp. 193–99).

It becomes apparent from the above analysis of Lavater and his oscillating character that his personal ambitions, such as his drive to achieve divine power or public recognition, override any attempt to be pious or maintain and nurture friendships and his love for others. His life is therefore characterized by loss, and this is particularly captured, as discussed further on, when he is lying on his deathbed regretting the loss of his friendships and anguishing over his possible manslaughter of Giotto. In this regard, Lavater shares some synergies with Julián Mercader whose life is also characterized by loss. Like Lavater, Julián oscillates between good and evil. Lavater appears to be saintly yet his piousness masks sinful qualities, including the manslaughter of Giotto. Julián is torn between his carnal desire for his daughter Violeta and drive to rape her and his refusal to commit the act, but ultimately decides not to commit the deed. Whilst both characters may be condemned for their respective 'crimes', the reader may feel an element of empathy towards them. In the case of Lavater, when he is on his deathbed at the end of the novel, he is able to show remorse in relation to his behaviour which has led to the loss of friendships and to the manslaughter of Giotto. Here his waning faith in God and his death are ultimate forms of loss. Julián, whose obsession with his daughter and doll replicas similarly causes a breakdown in his human relations with his wife and daughter, is also remorseful, and like Lavater he experiences loss, but this time in the form of a metaphorical death, namely hyppereal madness, pushed towards insanity by the anguish of his unfulfilled desire for his daughter and the guilt generated by it.

The Shadow

The shadow as both a uniting and dividing force in Lavater and Giotto's professional and emotional relationship becomes a metonym for Clavel's exploration of the shadow in art history. The same can be said of course of the role of the shadow in Clavel's *Los deseos*. As examined in Chapter 2, the shadow is a defining element in the relationship between Soledad and Péter. Both characters are drawn towards each other given their interest in the role of the shadow in photography. At the same time, Péter's 'shadow poetics' alienates Soledad as she is cast into an unfeeling object-shadow of his own creativity. It is through their shadow relationship, that Clavel also explores her wider interest in photography. In the context of both *Los deseos* and *El dibujante*, Clavel is particularly interested in the shadow as it has been a neglected area of interest in art history criticism, perhaps because of its archetypal connotation of death, the demonic, and otherness which are encompassed in Lavater's concept of the shadow as a 'dark stain' (Stoichita, p. 162) and the representation of Soledad in *Los deseos* as lack.[27] Its absence from art history criticism may also be explained because in traditional Western thought it has been difficult to accept that representation originates 'in the absence of light, in a dark spot' (Stoichita quoted by Turner). Taking her cue from Stoichita, Clavel surveys the negative valence of the shadow as well as reclaiming its positive element in *El dibujante* in order to explore the myth of origins in relation to the birth of art, knowledge, representation, and projection by drawing from a rich array of visual and written sources, such as Pliny the Elder's story about the daughter of Butades and Chamisso's *Peter Schlemihl.*

In *El dibujante* the shadow as a positive force can be traced back to the myth of origins. It is thought that art was born when the outline of a human shadow was cast onto a wall and then traced out so as to capture it in the form of a silhouette. Pliny the Elder's fable, in which the daughter of Butades draws the outline of her lover's face which is projected onto a wall by the light of a lamp, is often considered as embodying the invention of art and the origin of representation. This Greek legend also has an important role in Clavel's *Las Violetas* given that the author uses it in order to explore the novel's central theme of substitution and notions of simulacra. In *El dibujante*, an image which Clavel draws from to explore Giotto's burgeoning shadow art is the engraving *The Origin of Drawing* by Anne-Louis Girodet-Trioson (1820), which is directly influenced by the Plinian myth. In Pliny's myth and Girodet-Trioson's visual representation of it, the shadow becomes a sublimation of desire. In the Plinian fable the shadow came to be perceived not as a primitive mode of pictorial expression but rather a primitive language of love through which love can express itself (Stoichita, p. 153). As Clavel points out in relation to Girodet-Trioson's engraving, 'era amorosa la mano de la muchacha en plasmar el perfil fugitivo, pero más amorosa la sombra que así se dejaba dar luz' [she captured his fugitive profile with her loving hand, but even more loving was the shadow that allowed itself to be cast into light] (*El dibujante*, p. 46). Thus even though the birth of Western artistic representation is 'in the negative', the shadow is imagined in a positive way. In the context of this quotation, the positive value attached to the shadow is similarly demonstrated in the manner in which Clavel proposes that the shadow represents a Duboisean desiring luminous trace. In *El dibujante*, the shadow as affirmative source of representation is further bolstered when Goethe explains to Giotto that representation, like human essence, knowledge, and freedom, originates in the shadow: 'todo lo que hacemos proviene de su venia [...] es ahí donde comienza la libertad y nuestra obligación: en conocer las semillas secretas que nos fueron confiadas y hacerlas crecer a todo lo que puedan dar' [everything that we do stems right from it [...] it is there where freedom begins and our responsibility: in discovering the secret seeds which were entrusted to us in order to make them grow the most they can] (p. 99).

Despite the positive approach to the shadow in Pliny's story, the myth was gradually forgotten, and the shadow in Western representation came to be imbued with negativity. This was perhaps in part because for the Ancient Greeks 'the shadow was one of the metaphors for the *psyche*, the soul. A dead person's soul was compared to a shadow, and Hades was the land of shadows, the land of death' (Turner). One myth which contributed to this negative validation was Plato's cave myth. Although the shadow is placed at the origin of duplication in both Plato's and Pliny's fables, the shadow, unlike in the Plinian myth, is imagined in a negative way in Plato's story since the projected shadow comes to be associated with a copy of reality and which consequently came to have a very negative charge in Western art. Furthermore, in the Platonic myth, in order to attain true knowledge one has to forsake the shadow and exit the cave into the sun (Turner). Stoichita counterposes a shadow phase with Lacan's mirror phase. For Lacan, whereas the mirror stage involves the identification of the 'I', for Stoichita the shadow stage involves primarily the identification of the 'other' via the projection of the shadow. In *El dibujante*, Plato's allegory is alluded to indirectly in the observation that man's quest is to 'abrirle paso a la luz del conocimiento' [to give way to the light of knowledge] (p. 67). For Lavater one's encounter with divine knowledge can be achieved via the unravelling of the sinful in the shadow and the renunciation of that demonic other, but the shadow cannot be ultimately banished. It therefore brings to mind Kristeva's gloss on Freud's notion of the uncanny, as discussed in Chapter 6. Once, upon discovering Giotto sketching his master's profile, Lavater is incensed at feeling spied upon (p. 93). Lavater's reaction may be understood perhaps because of his fear that Giotto has uncovered in the projected shadow the very essence of his being: 'Creyó entonces vislumbrar la esencia de su alma' [he thought that he could make out the essence of his soul] (p. 93). Here Clavel has inserted a copy of 'The Shadow Dance' (1675) by Dutch painter Samuel van Hoogstraten. This engraving is emblematic of the works of many artists such as Jacques de Gheyn II and Athanasius Kircher where they present a study of the distorted, monstrous, and demonic projections produced by shadows. The overwhelming negativity with which the shadow is invested is linked to the status of a person's negative otherness with which representations of the cast shadow are endowed in Western art (Stoichita, pp. 132 & 134). In *El dibujante*, the juxtaposition of text and Van Hoogstraten's image functions to suggest that Lavater appears to have identified his otherness in his shadow and thus recognized that his own being is flawed like that of other humans, comprising both light and dark, the virtuous and the shadow other or the 'devil within' (Turner), ambiguously fusing with one another. But such recognition is only short-lived (until the end of the novel at least) as Lavater denies the uncanny side to his being as shown in the manner in which he continues to perceive those who surround him as objects onto which he can project his internal demons and violence.

The negative valence attached to the shadow as duplicate and as embodiment of alterity continues in Clavel's exploration of the double, a theme which, as we have seen, is widely explored in *Los deseos* and *Las Violetas*. *El dibujante* suggests the manner in which the (shadow) double is an uncanny 'thing of terror' (Freud quoted in Stoichita, p. 133), recalling Soledad's ghostly otherness in *Los deseos* or Violeta's doll replicas in *Las Violetas*. In his drive to save Giotto from ruin, Lavater recounts to his disciple Chamisso's story of *Peter Schlemihl* (1814) in which the eponymous Schlemihl loses his shadow to the devil in exchange for a magic purse which makes Schlemihl incredibly wealthy. Chamisso's novel has been interpreted as the story of the symbolic loss of determination (Stoichita, pp. 171–72). Lavater no doubt uses this story as a warning to Giotto about the consequences of moral waywardness. Whilst one can be steered towards the path of goodness with the help of religious guidance, the selling of one's shadow to the devil denotes for Lavater the erring from that path, resulting in the loss of one's righteous soul which is the core essence of being. Here being robbed of one's shadow is also akin to 'a sort of ghostly living death' (Turner). Drawing on Chamisso's story, Lavater cautions Giotto that '¡Las personas decentes tienen la costumbre de llevar consigo su sombra!' [Decent people are in the habit of carrying their shadow around with them!] (p. 53). For the clergyman to be 'somebody' (with shadow in tow) can only be achieved via one's strict adherence to the Christian faith and its doctrine of moral behaviour. Lavater's views on determination are deeply imbued with religious proselytizing and have a profound impact on Giotto's conception of (non-) self. Even after he has become physically and (almost entirely) emotionally detached from the clergyman, such perceptions continue to haunt him. Following his amorous affair with the twins and the death of Elise, about which he feels deeply guilty, he recalls how Lavater would often show him one of Giotto's paintings, *The Expulsion of the Demons from Arezzo* (1297–99), in order that his apprentice 'regresara al camino de la fe y de la obediencia' [return to the path of faith and obedience] (p. 174). Upon recalling the fresco, Clavel's Giotto is particularly struck by one of the demons which, overwhelmed by the terror caused by the driving out of fellow devils under the command of Francis of Assisi, holds its head in its hands in desolation. Clavel has included the image of this devil alongside the passage. Giotto takes pity on the spirit for he sees himself projected in this uncanny other. Having erred from the path of faith and obedience as sermonized by Lavater, Giotto visualizes himself like the demon, 'una sombra doliente y desesperanzada' [a sorrowful and despairing shadow] (p. 174), whose apparent sinfulness leads to a sense of 'undetermination'.

Clavel reworks Chamisso's shadow story which informs one particular nightmare Giotto has. In it the man in grey who buys Schlemihl's shadow is none other than Lavater himself, and Peter Schlemihl is Giotto. Here Giotto is not offered a magic bag full of gold in exchange for his shadow, and instead 'aparte de no poder ya consolarse en los brazos de su propia sombra, era no saber a cambio de qué la había cedido' [apart from not being able to console himself in the arms of his own shadow, it was not knowing for what it was that he had actually given it up] (p. 54). This dream becomes a mirror reflection of Giotto's life given that under the auspices of Lavater he loses his sense of creative and emotional self-determination. The loss of his shadow double in the dream epitomizes a source of terror, specifically Giotto's anxieties at the possibility of not being able to overcome his condition as a 'nobody'. Just as Giotto's sexual self-determination is initially quashed by Lavater's fanatic proselytizing, so too is his artistic freedom and recognition nullified by his mentor. In the private sphere, Giotto's work is given its due recognition by various intellectuals and artists, including Goethe and Heisch Füssli. Whilst Lavater is fully cognisant, and deeply admiring, of his apprentice's inherent artistic genius, he will not allow Giotto to develop as an autonomous artist nor to receive public recognition for his contributions of the silhouettes to *Physiognomische Fragmente*. Indeed:

> ¿Y por qué no firmaría Giotto sus dibujos? ¿Acaso porque cuando conoció la vida del Giotto original [...] supo que su nombre era un eco, una suerte de doble que volvía un tanto irreal su propia existencia y lo hizo sentir que la vida que tenía no era suya sino que en realidad era una vida prestada? ¿Sería también por esas oscuras razones que [...] no se sintió con derecho para ejercitarse en el arte de la pintura? (*El dibujante*, p. 57)
>
> [And why was it that Giotto did not sign his images? Was it when he discovered the life of the original Giotto [...] that he knew that his own name was nothing

> but an echo, a kind of double which made his own existence unreal and made him feel that he was in fact living a borrowed life? Was it also for those dark reasons that he [...] felt that he did not have the right to practice the art of painting?]

The above passage gains relevance in the context of another. When Giotto decides to leave Zurich to follow Giuseppe Calabria and his cabinet of scientific curiosities, Lavater becomes enraged as his attempts to hinder the young apprentice from leaving fail, and shouts out: 'Tú, Giotto de Winterthur, tú, carbonero de nombre inexistente, tú no tienes derecho a nada' [You, Giotto of Winterthur, you, charcoal drawer with an inexistent name, you have no right to anything at all] (p. 169). Lavater perceives Giotto as a 'product' of his own making upon which he seeks to inscribe his fatherly signature, in similar fashion to Julián Mercader with his doll replicas or Péter Nagy with Soledad, whom he sees as an object of his creativity. To suggest that Giotto's name is irrelevant is a stinging reminder of the irony inherent in Giotto's name: Lavater originally named Giotto after the Italian painter of the same name, the father of the Italian Renaissance. If a name signifies the unitary self, then to deny its significance is to refute one's social recognition upon which the 'I' relies to achieve a sense of self.[28] Lavater thus disallows Giotto's sense of creative self-determination and public acknowledgment by relegating him to the status of a shadow, the negative double of the original Giotto. He is 'el otro Giotto. El desconocido Giotto' [the other Giotto. The unknown Giotto] (p. 16).

A Chiaroscuro 'Shadow Poetics': Light and Darkness as 'Primeval Dialectic of Life'

Clavel's 'shadow poetics', as explored in Chapter 2 in relation to *Los deseos*, becomes a prime concern in *El dibujante*. Stoichita comments that our conception of history as influenced by the thinking of Hegel, and our conception of representation as determined in Plato's cave allegory, have encouraged us to approach a 'history of light' from diverse angles but has nevertheless circumvented the possibility of a 'history of the shadow' (*A Short History of the Shadow*, p. 8). Drawing from Hegel's view that 'light is determined by darkness and so is darkened light, and darkness is determined by light, is illuminated darkness' (Hegel cited in Stoichita, p. 8), Stoichita states that Western representation must be approached as a 'history of chiaroscuro' (p. 9). As was discussed in relation to *Los deseos*, Soledad's clair-obscure existence becomes a primer of Clavel's poetics of shadows which also notably comprises a chiaroscuro dialectic of light and shadow. Thus, as in *Los deseos*, in *El dibujante* even as the shadow often connotes all that is negative such as death, ignorance, or the sinful, in contradistinction to light which connotes positive values such as life, knowledge, or the angelic, Clavel can be said to draw our attention to the fact that light depends on darkness as much as darkness on light, thus intermingling in an ambiguous chiaroscuro whereby time-honoured associations are challenged or reinforced. Clavel's chiaroscuro shadow poetics can be linked to Tymieniecka's discussion of light and darkness as a 'primeval dialectic of life':

> When we refer in any way to light and/or darkness, their essential conjunction is necessarily surmised — conjunction and opposition. This very opposition indicates a primal relationship. [...] The dialectic of light and darkness appears [...] in all [...] sectors: organic, vital, psychic, societal, spiritual and religious.[29]

Tymieniecka's reference to the primal relationship of the opposition of light and dark in relation to the 'organic' and the 'vital' can be linked to Clavel's appropriation of the Dubois notion of the shadow as 'luminous trace' which reveals a pulsating, 'organic', 'vital', and desiring presence.

Nowhere is Clavel's shadow poetics or Tymieniecka's 'primeval dialectic' better explored than in Giotto's experiences within the camera obscura. As a darkened room that admits light only through a small hole, the camera obscura depends as much on light as it does on darkness. This intermingling of darkness and light is linked to Giotto's creative and sexual self-determination which is realized via the camera obscura. Giotto's burgeoning interest in early photographic techniques is sparked primarily by his exposure to Maese Calabria and his mobile 'camera admirabilis' (*El dibujante*, p. 124), which the latter has developed after becoming acquainted with the works by the pioneers of this optical device, specifically, Athanasius Kircher's seminal *Ars magna lucis et umbræ* (1656). As was common in the seventeenth and eighteenth centuries, Calabria uses his optical gadget for creating spectacular entertainment. Here the narrator addresses the modern day reader familiarized with the notion of replica and virtual reality:

> Para nosotros, hombres y mujeres acostumbrados al imperio de la imagen duplicada y reproducida *ad infinitum*, no es comprensible en su real magnitud la impresión que podía provocar en aquella gente el espectáculo maravilloso de contemplar en miniatura, apresada en un cuarto de reducidas proporciones, la grandiosa obra del Señor. Parecía cosa de magia o brujería. (*El dibujante*, p. 118)
>
> [For us men and women used to the domain of the duplicated image and its reproduction *ad infinitum*, we cannot comprehend the sheer magnitude of the impression that that wonderful spectacle could have on people as they were able to contemplate the Lord's grandiose work in miniature, trapped in a small-sized room. It was almost like an act of magic or witchcraft]

The association of the gadget with the occult is similarly made by Lavater. When the clergyman discovers Giotto's cabin converted into a life-sized optical device and sees one of the images captured with silver salts, he warns his apprentice of the dangers of meddling in 'las artes demoniacas de los alquimistas y esos otros herejes que, réprobos y blasfemos, quieren compartir los secretos de Dios' [the demonic arts of alchemists and those other heretics, reprobates and blasphemers who want to share the secrets of God] (p. 165). It is ironic that even as Lavater reviles the optical gadget, it has striking similarities to his science of physiognomy. In the view of the clergyman at least, both serve to visualize the 'devil within' (Turner) via the projected shadow. His demonization of the 'camera lucida' is reinforced because of his familiarization with della Porta's *Magiæ naturalis* and Kircher's treatise on light and shadow, *Ars magna lucis et umbræ*, in which both associate the gadget with the devil. More than its apparent relationship to the demonic, the camera obscura threatens Lavater because of its capacity to create shadows and to mirror reality faithfully. For the clergyman, as Clavel notes, its ability to replicate God's divine power is an aberration and though 'la ciencia puede ayudar al humano, uno no puede superar el conocimiento divino' [science can help humans, one cannot supersede divine knowledge].[30]

Unlike Lavater, both Calabria and Giotto see, overall, affirmative qualities and infinite possibilities in the camera obscura. Influenced by Plato's theories of duplication which held that the physical world was a reflection of a more perfect, abstract world which contained unchanging truth, Calabria is mesmerized by the possibility of being able to compete with God's creative powers in faithfully capturing and replicating reality thanks to Johann Heinrich Shulze's method of capturing images with silver salts: 'por fin el hombre podía participar un poco de los dones de la divinidad' [at last man could finally partake somewhat in the gifts of Divinity] (p. 126). As with Calabria, Giotto experiments with capturing diverse images from the natural world in his life-size camera obscura, as well as the frescos by his namesake with the help of a miniature optical device. Whilst their method of recording images foregrounds the mutual dependence of light and darkness, so too does it highlight the destructive effects of light on darkness. To their great frustration both men discover the silver image's proneness to fade through exposure to light: 'estas visiones estaban destinadas a desvancerse a la luz del día' [these visions were destined to disappear in the light of day] (p. 145).

The dialectic of light and darkness which is comprised in the camera obscura and its photographic methods becomes a prime feature of the 'poiesis of life' (Tymieniecka, p. viii), given that Giotto's burgeoning artistic creativity with the optical device coincides with his flourishing emotional and sexual life. In this respect, there is a strong parallel with *Los deseos*. Soledad's character shares similarities with that of Giotto in the context of the expression of repressed sexual desire and artistic freedom via the medium of photography and its interrelationship with light and dark. With his discovery of the camera obscura, Giotto starts to feel that he has achieved a sense of self-determination free from Lavater's grip: 'se sentía colmado de fe. La certeza de caminar al lado de su propia sombra' [he was full of faith. The certainty of walking along next to his own shadow] (p. 143). His shadow is, overall, not one which is determined by Lavater's religious conception of (non-) being, but rather increasingly fashioned according to Giotto's own particular vision of selfhood which encompasses sexual, emotional, and artistic freedom. The same can be said of Soledad in *Los deseos*, as we saw in Chapter 2. Her photographic exploration leads to a sense of artistic fulfilment and her shadow/light self similarly begins to flourish independently of Péter's patriarchal conceptions of the self. In *El dibujante* the shadow/darkness is similarly endowed with affirmative qualities as the camera obscura comes to represent primal drives. Here Giotto feels safe from the external world and the dark enclosure becomes associated with the maternal. Giotto yearns 'vivir en su vientre gestante para sentirse pleno' [to live in the gestating womb so as to feel complete] (p. 132), implying his repressed need for the archaic mother. As in the Plinian fable, the shadow also comes to embody a kind of primordial language of love, thus revealing a Duboisean desiring presence.

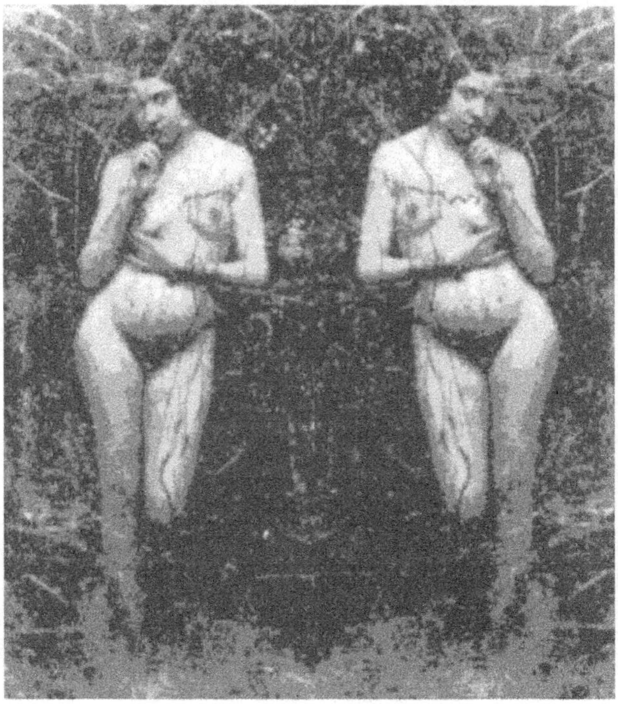

FIG. 9.1. *Desnudo de gemelas* — created after an anonymous daguerreotype. Ana Clavel. Digital image. Courtesy of Ana Clavel

But in the camera obscura this love is expressed through the conjunction and the opposition of darkness and light. Giotto's experiences of carnal lust with the twins in his camera obscura are described as a form of chiaroscuro desire (p. 116). Clavel's apparent celebration of the replica via the camera obscura is metonymically expressed in Giotto's ability to hanker after two women at once who are doubles of each other. The basic principle of using a negative and positive to create the final image in analogue photography is embodied in the twins, who are complementary and opposite: 'como dos caras de la misma moneda [...] cuerpo y sombra, positivo y negativo de una dualidad intercambiable' [like two sides of the same coin [...] body and shadow, the positive and negative of an interchangeable duality] (p. 154). Obsessed with capturing photographically the (naked) beauty of the twins and their desiring luminous shadows, Giotto's creative energy becomes a sublimation of sexual desire, powerfully embodied in two images. In the first image (figure 9.1), we see two identical women posing fully naked in the fashion of Ingres's nymph in *La Source*, a clear intertextual allusion to Clavel's *Cuerpo náufrago*.

This illustration has been digitally manipulated by Clavel to give it the appearance of a daguerreotype, and the female 'twins', who represent the Huber doubles, are not twins per se but rather one of the females is the negative or inverted image of the same woman. This process of inversion reinforces the view of Elise and Clara as the interchangeable negative and positive sides of each other. In many ways these twin doubles complement our reading in *Los deseos* of the female character Soledad and her (non-)being and her doppelgänger Lucía. Both Soledad and Lucía represent a duality of light and shadows as well as the internal conflict of Soledad's split selves.

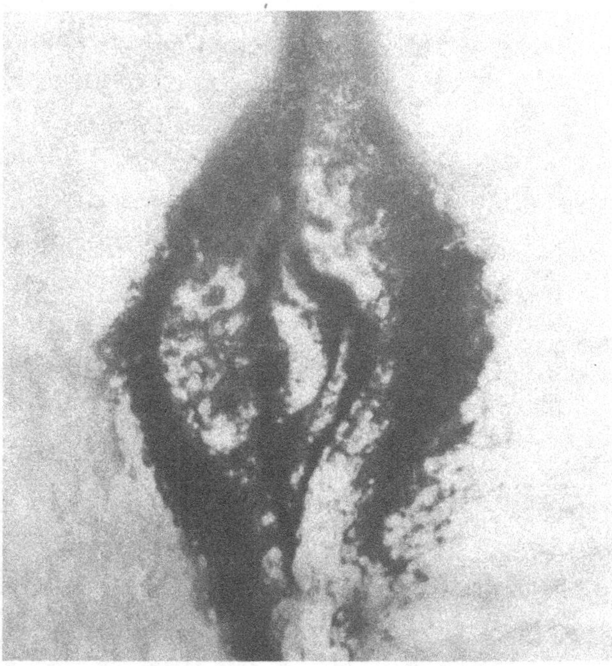

FIG. 9.2. *El origen del mal según Lavater* after 'Une des "deus mille photos du sexe d'une femme"' by Henri Maccheroni. Ana Clavel. Digital image. Courtesy of Ana Clavel.

However, Soledad and Lucía equally mirror each other in many other respects and, unlike the Huber sisters, finally fuse with one another in order give way to Soledad's sense of completed self, free of symbolic repression. In *El dibujante*, Giotto visually recreates in his mind the image of the naked women as if using the camera obscura and the notion of art as the sublimation of desire is emphasized: 'su interior [...] era una *cámera obscura* donde se dibujaba el recuerdo sublime de las gemelas [...] sombras sometidas a la voluntad de la mano que las delineaba según la luz espesa de su deseo' [The interior was [...] a dark room where the sublime memory of the twins was apparent [...] shadows obeying the command of the hand which sketched them according to the intense light of desire that emanated] (p. 156).

Another image which serves to make clear links between creative expression and carnality is the image which Giotto captures of Clara's naked vaginal area with the aid of the camera obscura (figure 9.2). The image, which graphically depicts the labia and vaginal slit, serves as an intertextual reference to Clavel's references in her previous works to Courbet's *L'Origine du monde*. Whilst Clara's shadow-light image has a positive valence for it serves as a kind of trace of her love for Giotto (p. 161), so too does it take on demonic qualities. When Lavater discovers the various illustrations of the naked twins in the cabin, he is particularly horrified by the image of the exposed pubis: 'un haz de luz, o más bien, un haz de sombras. ¿Qué podía ser aquello sino el ojo del maligno, la boca del infierno?' [a shaft of light, or rather, a shaft of shadows. What could that be other than an evil eye, the mouth of hell?] (p. 191). This oscillating perspective of the female genitals as a source of pleasure on the one hand, and as a source of terror on the other, is reminiscent of Kristeva's notion of the abject as discussed throughout this study in relation to Clavel's *Cuerpo náufrago* and *Las Violetas*.[31] In particular, Lavater's view of the female genitals as terrifying recalls Julián Mercader's fear of the vaginal 'wound' of Violeta and her doll replicas. Lavater's description of Clara's vagina as a castrating 'mouth of hell' evokes Creed's notion of the monstrous-feminine that describes the female vagina in equally demonic and castrating terms from a patriarchal perspective.[32]

In *El dibujante*, the camera obscura's positive association with a chiaroscuro of creativity and sexuality becomes overridden with negativity whereby the intermingling of light and dark is soon subsumed in total darkness, associated with destruction and death. This of course provides a counter-reading to *Los deseos*, in which the clair-obscure fusion of light and shadow and Soledad's opposing selves have a positive valence as they give rise to a female self-assertion, independent of patriarchal notions of feminine identity, as well as coinciding with Clavel's affirmation of her creative voice. It is ironic perhaps that the last section of *El dibujante* is entitled 'Sólo luz' [Only light], given that although this section celebrates Giotto's creativity and love life, it is overwhelmingly desolate. Elise, deeply in love with Giotto, is unable to cope with the idea of sharing her lover emotionally and sexually with her sister. When Elise discovers Clara and Giotto making love in the cabin 'esa luz niebla se hizo oscuridad' [the nebulous light became darkness] (p.162), and shortly after she hangs herself. The chiaroscuro which informs the twins' relationship, based on the positive and negative of each other, is inexorably broken by permanent darkness. Elise's death also signals the end of Giotto and Clara's relationship. When Clara joins Giotto in Italy, their meeting suggests the possibility of rejuvenation and redemption. Yet this possibility is only fleeting for Clara dies soon after from ingestion of silver salts. Shortly before dying, Clara explains to Giotto that the reason for her consumption of the lethal chemical was an act of love (p. 181). Clara, whose name is a metonym for light, becomes subsumed in deathly darkness. Her evanescence also becomes a symbolic reference to the manner in which Giotto is unable to halt the chemical reaction which darkens the image. Giotto's own life, which embodies a symbol of light via its associated affirmative values of irrepressible sexual drives and creativity, is also overcome by darkness as his life, following a scuffle in his cabin with Lavater, is extinguished when he is killed in a fire in which his images are also destroyed (p. 193). Ultimately Giotto's observation that both beauty and happiness are ephemeral like the images which dissolve when exposed to light (p. 173) underpins the overall creative, emotional, and ontological darkness which surrounds his life. Even though he survives the blaze, Lavater's life also descends into a permanent gloom. Clavel captures his dying moments when the clergyman is depicted as an anguished man reflecting upon a life which is characterized by loss. He mourns over the loss of the friendships of those he most cherished including Goethe, Hess, and Giotto, as well as anguishing over his possible manslaughter of Giotto (pp. 193–99). On his deathbed there is also the realization that his faith in God, which had given him steadfast conviction in terms of his actions and beliefs, is quickly eroding, leaving him in a state of anguished obscurity: 'buscó [...] a Dios como un refugio, pero solo encontró oscuridad' [he sought [...] in God a refuge, but only found darkness] (p. 199).

Photography: (Digital) Replication, Mimesis, and Authority

The last words of Clavel's *El dibujante*, 'una fértil y exultante oscuridad' [a fertile and jubliant darkness], are followed by the insertion of an image depicting utter blackness (p. 199). The final lines in a piece of fiction can often serve to add to the sense of closure and resolution of the novel as a whole. In *El dibujante*, however, the final words and the black rectangle provide instead a sense of contrasting ambiguity. Given the prototypical association of darkness with death and its finality, the image functions to contribute to an overwhelming negativity. It acts too as a reminder of Lavater's sinful soul and of Giotto's fate, his woeful love life, and in particular his status as the 'other' Giotto, the shadow artist who remains in the shadows of oblivion in the annals of art history. But in postmodern fashion, just as Clavel can be seen to find the negative in the positive, so too does she find the positive in the negative, as 'una fértil y exultante oscuridad' suggests. Giotto's frustration at the inability of silver salts to halt the process of the darkening of an image upon exposure to light, metonymically embodied in the black rectangle, is turned into something affirmative by Clavel. The image of the black rectangle serves to remind us that Lavater's, or Giotto's as Clavel would have us believe, physiognomic process of capturing as faithfully as possible the profile's negative image represents 'ese arte previo a la fotografía' [that art which preceded photography] (p. 57). Giotto's creative exploration in the methods of the camera obscura, a natural extension of his shadow art, is also a forerunner of photography. The black rectangle represents however what the camera obscura could not obtain, that is, the permanence of the image, a seminal breakthrough in the nineteenth century which coincided with the invention of photography as we know it today. As a digital reproduction, Clavel's image similarly attests to the view that just as photography 'telescopes backward into earlier modalities based in painting, drawing, cartography and geometry', so too does it project 'forward into cinema, television and digital media'.[33] Clavel celebrates the mechanized form of representation for it allows for endless creative possibilities, particularly in its digital dimension, as we see throughout many of her works. Clavel explained to me that the black rectangle is a homage to Tristram Shandy's 'black page' from Laurence Sterne's *The Life and Opinions of Tristram Shandy, Gentleman* (1759–67) and a digital reworking of Kazimir Malevich's painting *Black Square* (1915).[34] *El dibujante*'s chiaroscuro's thematics are mirrored specifically in Malevich's piece, literally a square of darkness with splatterings of white, embodying the conflict between light and darkness ending in the 'implacable triumph of night' (Stoichita, p. 188). Malevich's painting was initially conceived of as a kind of stage curtain which embodied not representation but rather what it conceals or, by raising it, what makes representation achievable. In this respect Stoichita notes that Malevich is undoubtedly advocating the anti-representational nature of *Black Square*. Clavel reworks Malevich's work in order to focus not on the notion of the anti-representational but rather on the idea that representation is not mimetic and thus provides an 'embryo of infinite possibilities' (Stoichita, p. 188). As we have seen, Clavel can be seen to challenge the idea of mimetic representation by reworking the life of Lavater and Giotto via postmodernist and new historical treatments. Examples of mimesis abound in *El dibujante* such as the art of physiognomy which involves faithfully replicating the profile, or the instance when Clavel alludes to the idea that during the Renaissance many young artists would flock to Italy to produce 'copias de aprendizaje' [copies for learning] (p. 43) of paintings by great artists such as Da Vinci. But the anti-mimetic also becomes apparent in the author's use of digital technology, specifically, Corel Photo Paint which Clavel used to solarize the images. The proliferation of images suggests blind replication given that many of these are reproductions of 'originals' as seen in the inclusion of the demon from Giotto's *The Expulsion of the Demons from Arezzo* or the section from Michelangelo's *Pietá* in which we see the Mother of Sorrows holding her son Jesus. Unlike the *Fuente* images in *Cuerpo náufrago* which have been subjected to a number of clever intermedial, digital alterations and thus depart quite radically from the 'originals', the majority of the images in *El dibujante* have been modified only minimally. For instance, the *Pietá* piece has been manipulated to appear like a negative image. Here Clavel uses digital photographic techniques in which a negative image becomes a total inversion of a positive one, whereby the bright areas of the image become dark and the dark areas become light. With the physiognomic profiles of Lavater's own image Clavel also inverted them. Whereas in the original text the profiles were dark, in *El dibujante* some became white.

The greatest intervention is seen in the image of the Huber twins (figure 9.1). Clavel found the image of the woman by an anonymous artist in a book on daguerreotype photography. The author appropriated the image in order to transform it by duplicating the image of the woman and inverting her as well as using digital photo-editing software. Clavel uses the original as a means to transform it by adding new meanings and to expand visually our understanding of the textual thematics of *El dibujante*. In this context, Clavel notes that she produced a daguerrotype which was very different from the original one and used various photo paint techniques to transform the original into something new: 'para darle tratamiento alquímico, de daguerrotipo para sentir la alquimia del dibujo de sombras o del propio Giotto cuando estaba en la camera obscura' [in order to give it an alchemical treatment in the form of a daguerreotype so as to enhance the alchemy of the image of shadows or of Giotto himself when he was in the dark room].[35]

The image of the twins on the front cover of *El dibujante* differs from the one which appears in the text. The cover illustration, digitally created by Leonel Sagahón and reworked from Clavel's image in the novel, has been subjected to further manipulation. An additional feature appears, namely, the shadow of a hand which has been placed on the twins, partially occluding their nudity. The shadow of the hand alludes to shadow art, to Giotto's shadow drawing of the twins, as the words 'sombras sometidas a la voluntad de la mano que las delineaba según la luz espesa de su deseo' [shadows obeying the command of the hand which sketched them according to the intense light of desire that emanated] (p. 156) emphasize. The shadow hand could equally be a metonym for the lack of recognition of Giotto's contribution to the science of physiognomy with his silhouette drawing. As noted earlier, the image of the naked twins posing in the fashion of Ingres's nymph becomes an intertextual allusion to *Cuerpo náufrago*. The shadow hand similarly functions as an intertextual reference to this text. As we discussed in Chapter 7, Alfaguara, the publisher of *Cuerpo náufrago*, asked for Clavel and Paul Alarcón to add the ribbon to the Ingresian nude on the book cover as the image could be deemed inappropriate by Sanborns and thus potentially affect the sales of the book. In the cover image of *El dibujante* the contours of the breasts of the two women have been faded and the shadow hand covers strategically, albeit partially, the pubic area of both females. Whilst *El dibujante*, also published by Alfaguara, was not subjected in any way to the censorship imposed on Clavel's previous novel, the image of the Huber twins has a parodic intertextual function, teasingly harping back to *Cuerpo náufrago* and the bowdlerizing context in which its front cover illustration was produced and manipulated.

Unlike the images in *Cuerpo náufrago*, those in *El dibujante* have not been accredited. When I made this particular observation to Clavel, the author said that she did not feel the need to acknowledge the images as in all cases she had digitally manipulated them and so in a sense they had become her own. For Clavel then both the replica and digital technology frees art from traditional ascriptions such as those of 'origins' or 'authority', a view which aligns *El dibujante* to *Cuerpo náufrago*. Clavel mentions that it is through the particular transformation that the images in *El dibujante* had undergone (however minimal) that they had become original in their own right, even as replicas of other replicas.[36] This viewpoint harps back to an almost Duchampian aesthetic discussed in Chapter 5. For Duchamp, even as his ready-mades confounded concepts of origins and uniqueness, each of his replicas was subjected to minimal alterations which, according to the artist, conceded it an element of originality. The un-naming of images in *El dibujante* can be perceived as an exemplar of the transformative possibilities of intertextuality. Even as a text absorbs prior texts, these are imbued with new meaning(s) as the author builds them creatively into his or her own particular mode of imagining the world. The reason Clavel did not acknowledge the images in *El dibujante* was also in part a protective measure against potential censure from literary critics who view her straddling of diverse fields such as multimedia as not being true to, or in some way contravening, her literary roots:

> El no acreditar es un poco para protegerme de la crítica literaria en el sentido de que a menudo los críticos que analizan mis obras no entienden cuál es mi propuesta al meterme en nuevos territorios y la ven como una suerte de prótesis a la obra literaria.[37]
>
> [Not accrediting the images is something I have done in order to protect myself somewhat from literary criticism, in the sense that critics often examine my work and do not understand what my intention is when I move into new areas and see it as a kind of prosthesis to my literary work]

Clavel may also believe that the concession of authority in *El dibujante* may be perceived as an exemplar of the uninventive absorption of prior visual texts, which ultimately serve to hinder rather than enrich her narrative. It would appear then that lack of attribution in conjunction with the process of creative (digital) reworking liberates Clavel from the notion of 'blind' mimesis and unoriginality. Clavel also inserts unaccredited visuals into her text as a way of engaging the active participation of both reader and literary critic:

> Lo que me interesaba era poner a prueba la movilidad que pudiera tener el lector o crítico especializado en la lectura literaria, es decir, qué capacidad tiene de moverse entre diferentes territorios y de poder conceptualizarlos. El incluir las imágenes en general y el hecho de no acreditarlas era como un reto al lector para ver qué es lo que iba a pensar de las imágenes y sobre qué relación tienen con el texto, de qué parte del discurso son, de quién son. ¿Sólo ilustran o se vuelven parte de la propuesta escritural? ¿No transforman al libro mismo en una suerte de *cámara oscura*? El multimedia de *El dibujante*, que no se realizó por falta de recursos económicos, se proponía armar una gran cámara oscura en el espacio de exhibición: una suerte de matriz en penumbras donde se proyectaran las imágenes de la novela 'intervenidas' por las siluetas de los propios visitantes al recorrerla.[38]
>
> [Here I was interested in testing the flexibility of a reader or literary critic, that is, their ability to move between different disciplines and understand them. The images as a whole and the lack of accreditation of these was a challenge for readers, meant for them to see what they made of the images and to think about what relationship they could have to the text, what part of the discourse they were and who had created them. Are they there just to illustrate or are they part of the writing rationale? Do they not simultaneously transform the book into a kind of camera obscura? The multimedia exhibition of *El dibujante*, which was not able to happen because of a lack of funding, was going to involve the creation of a life-sized camera obscura in an exhibition space: it was going to be a kind of partially shaded womb onto which images of the novel would be projected and which in turn would be 'intervened upon' by the silhouettes of the visitors as they walked around in the space]

This particular comment strongly underpins Clavel's postmodern playful aesthetic. Clavel does not perceive herself as a trained photographer or a visual or digital artist, but her passion for these fields has made it almost a prerequisite for her to work and toy with the visual and digital technology in and beyond her literary work. Indeed, as will be discussed in Chapter 10, this particular enthusiasm of Clavel is signalled in the development of her literary works *El dibujante* and *Las ninfas* as online multimedia endeavours in the form of YouTube videos; and these, along with her other multimedia activities, raise interesting questions in relation to reader/user participation, consumer persuasion, and her use of cyber technology to promote both her *oeuvre* and public persona.

Notes to Chapter 9

1. See for example, Ana García Bergua, 'De sombras y espejos', *La Jornada Semanal*, 986, 14 February 2010, <http://anaclavel.com/entrevistas/dibujante/El_dibujante_de_sombras_por_Ana_Garcia_Bergua_en_Jornada_Semanal.pdf> [accessed 14 June 2014], or Élmer Mendoza, 'Ana Clavel', *El Universal*, 30 September 2010, <> [accessed 14 June 2014].
2. Anamari Gomís, 'Dibujanta de Sombras', *Nexos*, 10 March 2010, <> [accessed 14 June 2014].
3. For an overview of new historicism within a postmodern theoretical framework and the new historical novel in Latin America, see Magdalena Perkowska, *Historias híbridas: la nueva novela histórica latinoamericana (1985–2000) ante las teorías posmodernas de la historia* (Madrid: Iberoamericana, 2008).
4. Lavery, unpublished interview with Clavel, 2011.

5. Ibid.
6. Victor I. Stoichita, *A Short History of the Shadow*, trans. by Anne-Marie Glasheen (London: Reaktion Books, 1997), in which he refers on p. 11 to Georg Gessner, *Johann Kaspar Lavaters Lebenschreibung von seinem Tochtermann G.G.*, 3 vols (Winterthur: Steiner, 1802–10), and on pp. 213–34 to Rolf Christian Zimmermann, *Das Weltbild des jungen Goethe: Studien zur hermetischen Tradition des deutschen 18. Jahrhunderts*, 2 vols (Munich: W. Fink, 1969–79).
7. Lavery, unpublished interview with Clavel, 2011. This lack of empathy provides an interesting contrast with Clavel's *Las Violetas* in which the author appears to avoid taking a moral stance with her morally dubious character Julián Mercader.
8. When I asked the author where she had found this reference to the death of 'Giotto' she could not remember specifically and mentioned to me in an email exchange that 'busco el dato de ese ayudante de Lavater que murió de una manera misteriosa, y no lo encuentro... es como si el dibujante que alentó a mi Giotto [...] no quisiera salir a la luz' [I have searched for that piece of information about Lavater's assistant who died in a mysterious way, but cannot find it ... it is as if the artist who inspired my Giotto [...] did not want to appear], Clavel, email to Lavery, 26 October 2011, 15:00.
9. Linda Hutcheon, *The Politics of Postmodernism* (London: Routledge, 1989), p. 7.
10. Felicity A. Nussbaum, *The Autobiographical Subject: Gender and Ideology in Eighteenth-Century England* (Baltimore: The John Hopkins University Press, 1989), p. 11.
11. Lloyd Hughes Davies, 'Portraits of a Lady: Postmodern Readings of Tomás Eloy Martínez', *Modern Language Review*, 95:2 (2000), 416–23 (p. 416).
12. Beth E. Jörgensen, 'Light-Writing: Biography and Photography in Tinísima', in Ibsen (ed.), *The Other Mirror*, p. 58.
13. Lloyd Hughes Davies, *Projections of Peronism in Argentine Autobiography, Biography and Fiction* (Chicago: Chicago University Press, 2007), p. 82.
14. Mikhail Bakhtin, 'Discourse in the Novel', in Michael Holquist (ed.), *The Dialogic Imagination: Four Essays*, trans. by Caryl Emerson and Michael Holquist, University of Texas Press Slavic Series, I (Austin: University of Texas, 1981), pp. 259–422.
15. Martin Porter, *Windows of the Soul: Physiognomy in European Culture 1470–1780*, Oxford Historical Monographs (Oxford: Clarendon Press, 2005), p. 129.
16. John B. Lyon, '"The Science of Sciences": Replication and Reproduction in Lavater's Physiognomics', *Eighteenth-Century Studies*, 40: 2 (2007), 257–77 (p. 240).
17. Lavater's religious pseudo-science is also underpinned by the semiotic which entails 'decoding internal life from the external signs on the body, particularly the face', Fae Brauer, 'The Transparent Body: Biocultures of Evolution, Eugenics and Scientific Racism', in Jane Kromm and Susan Benforado Bakewell (eds.), *History of Visual Culture: Western Civilization from the 18th to the 21st Century* (Oxford: Berg, 2010), pp. 89–103 (p. 91).
18. Jonathan Smith, *Charles Darwin and Victorian Visual Culture*, Cambridge Studies in Nineteenth-Century Literature and Culture (Cambridge: Cambridge University Press, 2009), p. 204.
19. Richard T. Gray, *About Face: German Physiognomic Thought from Lavater to Auschwitz* (Detroit: Wayne State University Press, 2004).
20. In this context, Rivers remarks sardonically that, due perhaps to the jaundiced perspective of contemporary society's cynicism, 'it is unlikely that many present day readers could follow the logic that tells us that recognizing our neighbour's sloth and stupidity from his large ears and bulbous nose will lead us to greater ability to love him', Christopher Rivers, *Face Value. Physiognomical Thought and the Legible Body in Marivaux, Lavater, Balzac, Gautier, and Zola* (Madison: The University of Wisconsin Press, 1994), p. 69.
21. Ursula Caflisch-Schnetzler, 'Biography and Works', University of Zurich, Institut für Schweizerische Reformationsgeschichte, Lavater-Edition, trans. by H. Bociek, 2001, <http://www.irg.uzh.ch/lavater/jclavater/bio_en.html> [accessed 14 June 2014].
22. Johann Peter Eckermann, '1829', in *Conversations of Goethe*, trans. by John Oxenford, digital production by Harrion Ainsworth, <http://www.hxa.name/books/ecog/Eckermann-ConversationsOfGoethe-1829.html> [accessed 14 June 2014].
23. In the context of Lavater's friendship with Hess, the idea of deceit becomes apparent in *El dibujante* when Lavater sketches a portrait of Hess in order to reveal his 'true' soul (pp. 30–32).

24. Evelyn K. Moore, 'Goethe and Lavater: A Specular Friendship', in Evelyn K. Moore and Patricia Anne Simpson (eds.), *The Enlightened Eye: Goethe and Visual Culture*, Amsterdamer Beiträge zur neueren Germanistik, 62 (Amsterdam: Rodopi, 2007), pp. 165–92 (p. 174).
25. Christopher Turner, 'A Short History of the Shadow: An Interview with Victor I. Stoichita', Shadows, 24 (2006/07), <http://cabinetmagazine.org/issues/24/stoichita.php> [accessed 14 June 2014].
26. Lavater's philosophical palingenesis, which posits the idea that the human soul does not die with the body but is born again in new incarnations, instils in him the hope that he will re-encounter Hess, reborn and spiritually cleansed of all sin (*El dibujante*, pp. 75 & 197).
27. For psychologist Carl G. Jung whilst the shadow archetype embodies 'negative' qualities a person may not want to recognize in himself, it is also important in terms of individuation and the development of self, Carl G. Jung, 'The Psychology of the Unconscious', in *Collected Works, Volume 7: Two Essays on Analytical Psychology*, ed. by Herbert Read, Michael Fordham and Gerhard Adler, trans. by R. F. C. Hull (London: Routledge & Kegan Paul, 1953), pp. 3–117 (p. 103).
28. (Un-)naming from a patriarchal perspective also has an important function in relation to providing a sense of the female (un-)unitary self in the context of Soledad's character in *Los deseos* and the dolls in *Las Violetas.*
29. Anna-Teresa Tymieniecka (ed.), *The Elemental Dialectic of Light and Darkness: The Passions of the Soul in the Onto-Poiesis of Life*, Analecta Husserliana, 38 (Dordrecht: Kluwer Academic Publishers, 1992), pp. vii-viii.
30. Lavery, unpublished interview with Clavel, 2011.
31. Kristeva, *Powers of Horror.*
32. Creed, *Monstrous-feminine*, p. 106.
33. Ali Hossaini, 'Vision of the Gods: An Inquiry into the Meaning of Photography', *Logos*, 2:3 (2003), <http://www.logosjournal.com/hossaini.pdf> [accessed 23 June 2014].
34. Lavery, unpublished interview with Clavel, 2011.
35. Ibid.
36. Ibid.
37. Ibid.
38. Ibid.

CHAPTER 10

Further Queer Literary and Multimedia Interventions

Having provided the reader with an in-depth overview of Ana Clavel's literary and wider multimedia endeavours, this study clearly demonstrates that her *oeuvre* is queer, as Kaminsky, Halperin, and Rubin Suleiman would understand the word. Via her ambiguous, and often controversial, oscillating feminist and queer positionalities, her works are united by an interest in exploring both heteronormative and 'outlaw' sexual desires such as homosexuality, bisexuality, transgender, and paedophilia. In doing so, even as Clavel appears to uphold 'compulsory heterosexuality' so too is the writer drawing our attention to that which has been silenced as a means of questioning the notion of the acceptable or originary sexual and gender identities and as a way of exposing (Mexican) society's disavowed fears or desires. Her focus on shadow, the urinal, ghosts, human-like dolls, and the fantastical similarly demonstrate Clavel's apparent interest in the non-normative as a way of challenging set religious, artistic, literary, moral, sexual, or ideological conventions. Via her exploration of the queer Clavel seeks to defy as well as confuse the borders between, for instance, the proper and improper, sanity and insanity, male and female, saintly and unsaintly, fact and fiction, real and hyper real, self and other, high and low, authenticity and inauthenticity. But what makes Clavel stand out particularly as queer is her status as multimedia writer. Her interventions are unprecedented in relation to other Mexican female writers who on the whole stick to the conventional print medium. It is precisely because of Clavel's unique queer status as writer-artist and her multimedia endeavours, that this particular area warrants further analysis in this chapter through reference to Clavel's other (literary) multimedia interventions.

As discussed throughout this study, Clavel's trajectory as a writer has been queered as she has moved from using the exclusively written form to combining both the literary form with the non-literary. Clavel's *Los deseos y su sombra*, *Cuerpo náufrago*, *Las Violetas son flores del deseo* and *El dibujante de sombras* have been used as springboards to various multimedia projects involving an array of forms including photography, art installation, performance, and cyber technology. Clavel's further engagement with multimedia in the broad sense of the word is seen in her regular blog, Twitter, and Facebook interventions; her creation of YouTube videos for her books *Amor y otros suicidios*, *El dibujante*, and *Las ninfas a veces sonríen*, and lastly a multimedia exhibition based on *Las ninfas*. In addition to these multimedia endeavours, Clavel has exploited intense marketing strategies and technologies, including book launches, interviews, media advertising via radio and television to increase her authorial presence and book sales.[1] Clavel's dynamic involvement in such media signal the author's extensive media exposure and the diverse tools she uses to promote, at both local and global levels, both her *oeuvre* and her public persona as a multimedia writer.[2]

Blog, Social Networks, and YouTube Book Trailers

As mentioned in the Introduction, Clavel's blogging endeavour forms part of a wider cultural context of blogging by other Mexican writers. These blog sites attest to a newly emerging literary genre, as Edmundo Paz Soldán explains:

> The blog is a travel log in cyberspace, a textual practice which combines elements of the diary, the notebook, literary criticism, the opinion column, the short story, the epigram, and whatever other literary genres we might care to add [...] Thanks to the appearance of a new technological format we are witnessing, in 'real time', the birth of a new literary genre.[3]

Clavel's blog combines a number of the literary features mentioned by Paz Soldán, including short stories or newspaper column 'crónica' [chronicle] style essays written by the author, with non-written forms such as image or video. Clavel also uses her blog to promote her public persona and works, as do most writers of fiction who exploit such a medium. But her blog differs markedly with that of, for instance, Ángeles Mastretta.[4] Mastretta has used her blog site primarily as a vehicle to maintain her (literary) media celebrity status and to encourage her hundreds of adoring fans to uphold her self-constructed iconicity. Clavel's posts are characterized by their intellectual thrust. Her blogs include biographical details of other writers and provides critical comments on their works. Clavel has included links of articles published on her work in various newspapers, her acceptance speech for a literary prize for her *Las ninfas* book prize and reflections on her literary work. She has written scholarly essays on the role in the humanities of, for instance, the female nude, carnality, or the Lolita figure, and such academic ponderings in a sense act as intertextual extensions of Clavel's overall literary and multimedia *oeuvre* which explores similar topics.[5] Clavel uses various social networking mediums, namely Twitter and Facebook, in similar fashion to her blog. Indeed, she notes that:

> Uso internet y las redes regularmente. Me sirvo de ellas para darle difusión a mi trabajo [...] busco que mis posteos en fb y tw tengan el atractivo de brindar algo novedoso, de actualidad, apoyar a otros creadores, aportar una dosis de belleza a través de poemas de otros, música, fotografías, pequeños descubrimientos cotidianos.[6]
>
> [I use internet and social networks regularly. I use them to promote my work [...] I seek for my Facebook and Twitter posts to be interesting by talking about things which are new, current, by supporting other artists, by offering a dose of beauty through the poems written by others, music, photography, and tiny discoveries in everyday life]

In this regard, Clavel's Facebook account shares some similarities with that of

Mastretta's blog entries in its oscillation between a 'bítacora frívola' [frivolous blog] and discussion characterized by its intellectual engagement. Thus Clavel's posts range from an occasional discussion of quotidian-type experiences with comments, for instance, about her night out with friends, to mainly posts with links to her blog containing essays written by her of an academic kind, or entries promoting her works or the works of other writers or artists.[7] An element which thus becomes apparent in this virtual space is the way in which Clavel straddles the boundary between self-publicity and literary creation and also between the high and low, in Bakhtinian heteroglossic fashion, by discussing mainly serious topics alongside frivolous matters.

Clavel has similarly created and conceived YouTube videos for book launch events and for general marketing purposes, as well as making them available in various languages, including Chinese.[8] For Clavel the online videos are a natural extension of her texts given her general interest in the visual. It made particular sense for Clavel to create the *El dibujante* video since the photographic — a key component of this novel — projects forward into other visual forms such as television, cinema, and digital media.[9] In relation to *El dibujante* Clavel notes that:

> No me queda más que esa opción de lo visual. El libro simplemente ofrecía otra posibilidad de insertar imágenes y jugar con ellas y luego hacer lo del videíto en forma de fotomontaje que permitiera una suerte de avance de la novela.[10]
>
> [I have no other choice but to embrace the option of the visual. The book simply offered the possibility of inserting images and playing with them and then later the possibility of making the little video in the form of a photomontage which acted as a kind of preview of the book]

The videos for a number of her texts have been created by Clavel in the form of book trailers and are representative of a surge in popularity in the exploitation of this technique in the publishing industry. Both publisher and writers are increasingly using book trailers as the prime launching pads for the marketing campaign of a book. Books are often promoted via video in which the author features being interviewed and/or reading excerpts from his or her work. This latter format has been adopted for the promotion of *Amor y otros suicidios* in which Clavel is reading the short story/recipe entitled 'Caldo largo de cola de sirena' in a bathtub.[11] As an extension of her *Amor y otros suicidios*, the video establishes Clavel's drive to transgress literary generic boundaries.[12] The short story, written in recipe format, can be situated in the context of a long-established literary history in which the traditional recipe format is parodied, such as Laura Esquivel's *Como agua para chocolate* (1989). The preparation of the aphrodisiac mermaid soup, which becomes a metonym of desire itself, suggests the idea that heterosexual desire can only be fulfilled by following strict instructions, as if following those of a recipe. This also implies that desire is a singular form of expression. But by parodying the strict recipe format, Clavel also suggests that desire is multifarious as illustrated in all of her works, in which she provides the reader with a range of expressions of sexuality from the heterosexual and the incestuous to the bisexual and gay, for instance. The video also demonstrates Clavel's drive to establish her public persona as multimedia writer. By becoming an actress in the video Clavel foregrounds her authorial presence not only as a means to assert herself as author of the collection of short stories but also to establish her role as creator and choreographer in this multimedia endeavour. Authorial self-reference also becomes apparent in the manner in which Clavel uses the multimedia format as a platform from which she can make witty intertextual references to other works she has written and provide comments on the process of writing.[13]

With the advent of new digital technologies videos have become increasingly sophisticated to the point that book trailers have become rivals to movie trailers. There are numerous examples of fiction which have been professionally made by production companies, such as Simone Elkeles's *Rules of Attraction* (2011) which was produced by Spotlight Films. But this route is very costly and whilst some publishers will cover the costs, it is often the case that authors have to pay for the trailers out of their own pocket. To avoid such an expense the authors themselves will often create their own book trailer videos, as is the case with Clavel. Whilst Clavel's trailer was not commissioned by Alfaguara, Clavel included the name of the publisher of *El dibujante* in the video credits in order to give it the appearance of an official promotional trailer and thus 'lending it the appropriate weight'.[14] The book trailers of *El dibujante*, *Amores* and *Las ninfas* are not as showy as many professionally-assembled versions. None of these features, for instance, the seductive voiceover of a professional actor, live action featuring equally attractive performers, or complex visual effects. Both *Las ninfas* and *El dibujante* videos are a 'fotomontaje', that is, a simple photographic slide show created with appropriate movie maker software and interspersed with music, text, and stills. Despite their simplicity, both contain distinct movie/book trailer techniques which have been used successfully and which demonstrate Clavel's commendable facility to span different fields.[15] These techniques include the use of understated but alluring motion graphics in the form of moving text.

The success of a book trailer is similarly often measured in terms of its capacity for consumer persuasion. The trailer blurb of *El dibujante* has been cleverly pieced together with image and music in order to provide us with an idea of what the book is about but without giving too much away, thus compelling us to want to find out more. But what ultimately piques (but may also dissuade) the potential reader's interest is the emphasis on the emotional which is achieved via the multimedial interaction of text, image, and sound.[16] In this respect, Clavel's book trailer has broad commonalities with certain movie or book trailers which adhere to the genre of romance or melodrama and require strong emotional, even physical, involvement in viewers and therefore demand a 'low' cultural mode of response, to borrow from Pierre Bourdieu (*Distinction*). In the trailer of *El dibujante*, text and image are accompanied by the sorrowful music of the 'Stabat Mater' (1736) by Giovanni Pergolesi. The music, the visual and textual storyline all stir in us an emotional response, the different media all working in conjunction. Pergolesi's 'Stabat Mater' is described by Richard Will as exemplifying an 'expressivity so powerful that listeners react as though to a text from eighteenth-century sentimental literature or drama, whose signature was to make people cry'.[17] The theme of Pergolesi's work is the sorrowing Virgin at the crucifixion of her son and at first may seem unrelated to the storyline of *El dibujante*, which alludes to Giotto's fall from grace as he is exposed to carnal desire and Lavater's inability to save his apprentice from perdition. However the parallels between music and text become inexorable as both elicit the idea of a tension, at the heart of which is human emotion and depth of feeling. Pergolesi's sacred composition deeply moves us not so much because it emphasizes the Virgin Mary's virtue and commitment to the greater good of Christianity, but rather because we are left with a sense of deep empathy for the very human experience of the suffering of a distraught woman over the loss of her son. In this regard, Pergolesi's music's 'beauty, melancholy, and unabashed sentimentality exert undeniable power, drawing listeners into a world where compassion and endurance matter more than judgement or redemption' (Will, p. 609). Through the interplay of words and image, the slide show of *El dibujante* emphasizes how religion, shadow art, pictorial techniques, and human desire are inexorably intertwined. But above all the trailer is geared towards the emphasis on feeling, as attested in the first lines: 'No hay laberinto más intricado que el corazón de un hombre' [there is no more complex a labyrinth than the heart of a man], and in particular in the multimedial interaction of music, text, and image. When listeners hear the first stanza of Pergolesi's hymn, sung by a narrator who provides us with a picture of the Virgin's harrowing suffering as she witnesses Jesus's death, the focus is on human emotion. Specifically, music enriches the meaning of the written text which describes the conflict between Lavater and Giotto, the clergyman's obsession with his apprentice's talent, and his efforts to prevent his assistant from deviating from (religious) purity, and Giotto's suggested emotional and sexual turmoil. The written form is explicated visually as images which fit the storyline appear, such as that of the Huber twins, signalling Giotto's experiences of carnal lust. It is at this point, when we also hear the sorrowful voice of the narrator, that the Virgin's conflicting experiences of grief over her son's death and the view that his death is the proper path towards Christian salvation become metonymically embodied in Giotto's chiaroscuro emotions of 'la culpa y el dolor' [guilt and sorrow] and 'el éxtasis y el delirio' [ecstasy and delirium]. In similar vein to *El dibujante*, music, text, and image in the *Las ninfas* trailer work multi-medially to entice the spectator to want to read Clavel's novella.[18] At the same time, the edgy thematics of the combination of images of a child-nymphet posing seductively against various statues of goddesses, Led Zeppelin's 'Stairway to Heaven' (1971), and the textual allusions to the autoerotic experiences of the child protagonist Ada of the novella, may equally dissuade certain readers.

It is nevertheless easy to understand why Clavel has chosen to create YouTube book trailers for her various texts and, by extension, her other social networking mediums and blog. Besides being used as a platform from which to promote Clavel's books, both the blog and the various social networks which the author uses serve to entice new readers and to engage a broad audience with the content of her books. In relation to YouTube, Susarla and others note that 'the usability and functionality of YouTube makes it easy for users to create their own channel and to post content that can be shared almost instantaneously to a wide audience across the world'.[19] Because of the ease of creating a personalized page or channel, a user on YouTube 'can engage in self-expression [...] as well as obtain peer recognition' (Susarla &

others, p. 2). YouTube, Facebook, and Twitter alike promote user inclusivity and spontaneity as well as providing the possibility to generate a space for a virtual community. The boundaries between creator and consumer are truly blurred since these social media encourage a collective process in which both creator(s) and users intervene. With YouTube, subscribers or friends can rate and comment on videos, add videos to a list of favourites, and even enter contests of interest. Such choices also 'serve as signals to other users, driving the popularity of content' (Susarla & others, p. 2). With YouTube, Facebook, and Twitter, both author(s) and readers similarly can intervene by adding their comments and views to create a complex and multi-layered narrative. Here everyone is (or can be) both author and reader. The opportunities afforded by new internet technologies like Twitter and Facebook have been fully exploited by Clavel in the creation of a space that permits 'real interaction' with her readers.[20] Clavel's Facebook account in particular has garnered extensive interaction between author and her followers as seen in the regular posts sent between author and fellow writers and academics (for example Martin Camp, Ana García Bergua, Ethel Krauze) or the general public.

As yet though, the full potential of Clavel's book trailers has not yet been harnessed as they have garnered to date few hits, ratings, and comments. In the specific case of the trailers, it is very difficult to ascertain whether using the latest trend in book marketing is more effective in helping to generate sales over more traditional methods of promoting a book such as author tours, printed advertisements, or book fairs. However, where book trailers may well help to sell is when they are geared towards an existing fan base. In other words, many authors promote their books via trailers pre-publication. This helps to build anticipation, particularly if there is an existing group of devotees. Clavel is gaining increasing recognition and it could be argued that the book trailers for *El dibujante* and *Las ninfas*, which were created pre-publication, were developed with the aim of whipping up support from current Clavel enthusiasts as well as building upon her existing fan base.

Las ninfas a veces sonríen and Multimedia

In 2013 Ana Clavel received the prestigious *Premio Iberamericano de Novela Elena Poniatowska* for her novella *Las ninfas a veces sonríen*, attesting to her outstanding skill as a writer and to her increasingly important status in contemporary Hispanic letters. This study was coming to an end at the point at which *Las ninfas* was published and so for reasons of space and time it was not possible to carry out an extensive study of this work.[21] However it is important to mention briefly this novella as it evinces, once again, the author's continued interest in the queer and drive to break boundaries, in terms of the work's thematic and multimedia dimension. With her powerful stylistics, Clavel manages to disturb, yet again, the pleasurable reading experience of the reader of *Las ninfas* by delving into prohibited 'no-deseos'. The narrative is told from the perspective of the female adult narrator Ada, who recounts in graphic detail her sexual experiences from childhood through to adulthood. From the outset, the author disturbs traditional conceptions of children's literature in which childhood is portrayed as a time graced by (sexual) innocence and play. Its focus on the flourishing carnal desire of a young child may be perceived as taboo by some readers, in particular as Ada's experiences range from the autoerotic to the paedophilic. As we mentioned in relation to *Las Violetas* in Chapter 7, the notion that under-aged girls can be sexually experienced challenges society's drive to maintain an ideology of 'natural' female modesty and its unthreatening and infantilized image of female children. In contrast to *Las Violetas*, where women or their replicas are seen almost exclusively as the often brutalized objects of male desire, Ada is primarily seen as agent of her own desires. She is a 'ninfa en plenitud de poderes' [nymph in full command of her powers] (book blurb). In some instances though, the reader may find this agency disturbing since Ada appears to revel in being the sexual object for the use of the paedophile. Clavel similarly incites discomfort with her exploration of rape or so-called 'abnormal' or unexpected sexualities, including carnal desire between cousins or siblings, incest, sapphism, or sexual intercourse between a doctor and the pregnant adult Ada. Like in many of her previous works, the queer dimension is evinced in Clavel's recourse to the fantastical in the form of fairy tales, legends, and myths, and the unearthly characters which inhabit these bizarre worlds contribute to Ada's multifarious sexual desires and experiences and to her discovery of 'eso que algunos llaman perversiones' [that which some may call perversions] (book blurb).

As with the majority of Clavel's works, the author could not resist the temptation of creating a multimedia event for the book launch of *Las ninfas*. The exhibition, entitled *Las ninfas a veces sonríen: cinco rutas para explorar el misterio de una sonrisa*, was held in the Centro Cultural Bella Época in Mexico City between 11 and 28 April 2013.[22] Clavel enlisted the help of four female artists, Rocío Caballero, María Eugenia Chellet, María José Lavín, and Maribel Portela, to participate artistically in the event. In similar fashion to the *Las Violetas* multimedia exhibit, Clavel asked these artists to read her novella first and then create their particular vision of the text in artistic form by drawing from their own artistic traditions, illustrating once again how Clavel's multimedia endeavours are a fusion of voices that champion the idea of multi-authorship. Thus painter Rocío Caballero created ten 'cajas-objeto' and visual artist María Eugenia Chellet eleven collages. Both their works depict an array of angelic nymphets in ethereal worlds underscored by sexual pleasure in the form of, for instance, lesbian carnality or autoeroticism (figures 10.1 and 10.2), harping back to Ada's own particular world of sensuous discovery of a multitude of sexual experiences.

Maribel Portela produced an enormous tulip out of red paper and it hung from the ceiling of the gallery. Here the flower is a vital trope for Ada/girl/woman's burgeoning sexuality. Plastic artist María José Lavín created a number of pieces, including two abstract, plaster female deities which were developed as a way of underscoring the central role of the goddess as object and agent of desire in *Las ninfas*. Many of the art pieces on display were also emblazoned with textual excerpts from, or had references in their titles to, Clavel's work, highlighting the important role of intertextuality. Even as the exhibition reflected the idea of art as collaboration, so too did it mark Clavel as choreographer and active creative participant, a tension which is similarly present in the author's other multimedia

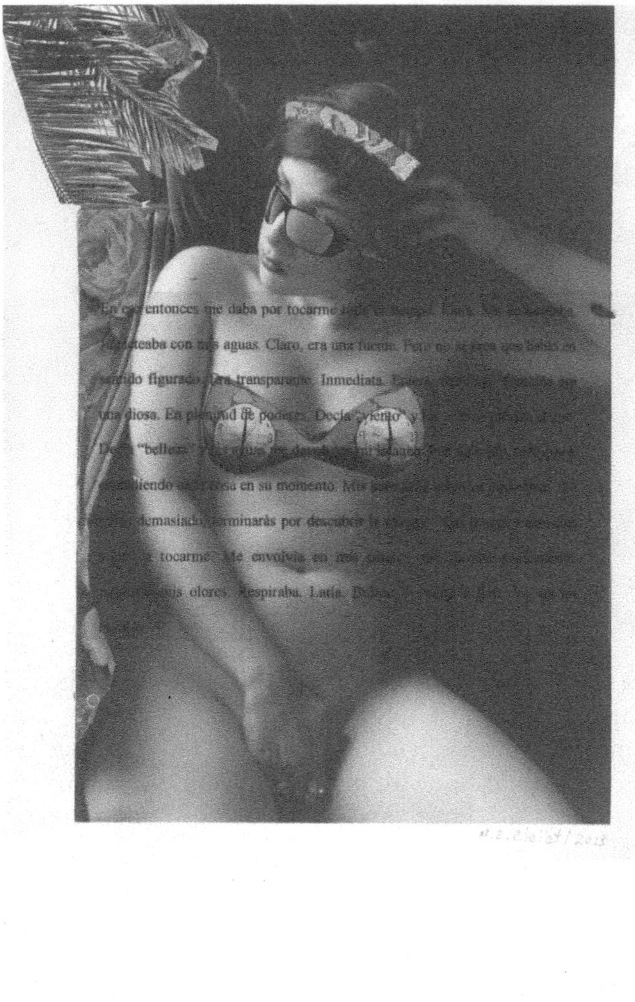

Fig. 10.1. *Dios castiga a las ninfas malas.* Rocío Caballero. Acrylic, paper, ink and collage. 28 × 21.5 cm. Photo: Rocío Caballero. Courtesy of Ana Clavel

Fig. 10.2. *Apenas tenue.* María Eugenia Chellet. Collage. 21.5 x 28 cm. Photo: Ana Clavel. Courtesy of Ana Clavel

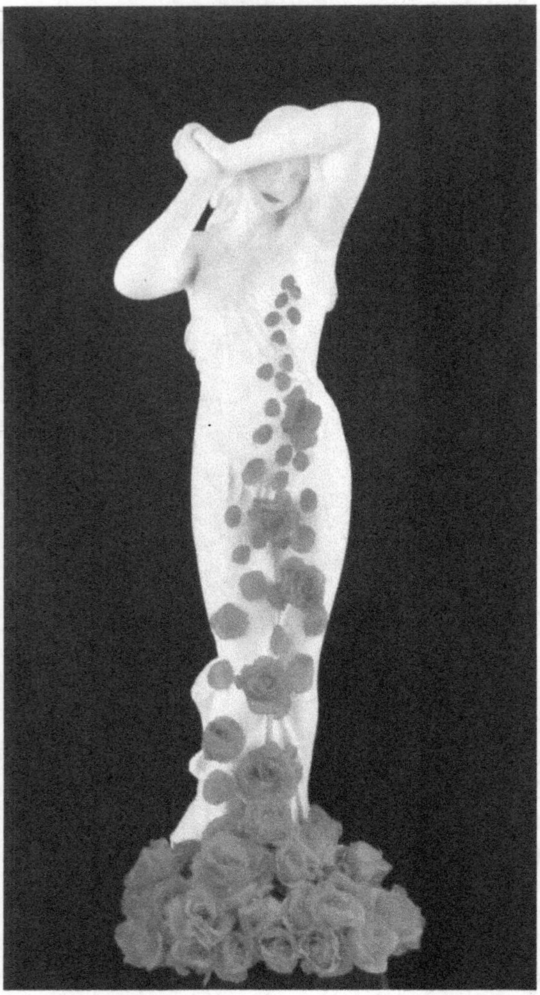

FIG. 10.3. *Yo era mi paraíso* 1. Ana Clavel. Alabaster sculpture intervened with lipstick and artificial flowers. 115 × 35 × 35 cm. Photo: Ana Clavel. Courtesy of Ana Clavel.

endeavours. Thus Clavel participated in all of Lavín's works by selecting which excerpts from the text would be inserted onto the artworks, and therefore both artist and writer decided that Clavel's name would also appear next to the exhibited items. The author-artist similarly created her own artworks by intervening on the torso and head of a mannequin as well as an alabaster statue of a goddess of antiquity. This latter artwork features on the cover of *Las ninfas* (figure 10.3). All three pieces were displayed in a darkened area of the gallery on plinths and had special lighting effects to enhance the artworks.

Clavel came up with the idea of having a performance for the inaugural presentation of the novella. In the performance, the actress nymphet-child is seen standing in seductive poses on a plinth with roses but then stands down, starts walking around the room, and subsequently invites spectators to stand on the plinth. She is then seen displaying a poster with the words 'espacio disponible para cualquier dios o diosa' [space available for any god or goddess]. Clavel came up with this idea as a means of harping back to the novella's vision of sexual self-

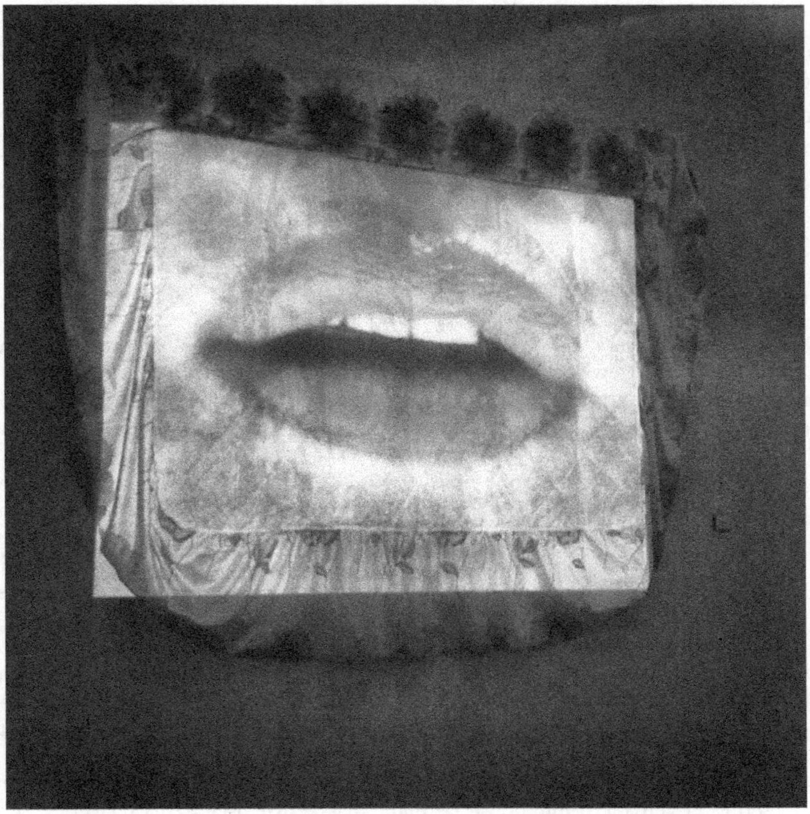

FIG. 10.4. *Las ninfas a veces sonríen.* Ana Clavel. Video-Installation. Queen size mattress: 2 × 1.75 m. Photo: Alina López-Cámara. Courtesy of Ana Clavel

empowerment. By encouraging both men and women to stand on the plinth and pose in any position they wanted, this playfully invited them to counter traditional images of the Ingresian-like nymph as passive object of the gaze and to reflect on the notion of being gazed upon but equally of returning the gaze. This particular element of the performance had many spectators in fits of laughter and Clavel may well have intended for it to have such an effect. Indeed, it served perhaps as a means of parodying the 'high' notion of art's uniqueness and inaccessibility in order to celebrate the 'low' intention of installation art which encourages the physical interaction of the spectator with the artwork.[23] The final piece which Clavel developed herself was the video installation in which the author-artist placed a mattress on the wall surrounded by a flower-embellished frame made from a sheet. Projected onto the installation are images of poppies which then morph into bloodstains and then into speaking lips (figure 10.4).

The lips are those of Clavel and we hear the author reading a number of excerpts from *Las ninfas* relating to Ada's sexual desires. The references to the flowers in this piece multi-medially link back to the other art pieces of the exhibition in which red or white coloured flowers of diverse kinds predominate, and which in turn, are intertextually connected to the floral tropes in both *Las ninfas* and *Las Violetas*, and in this latter's multimedia dimension. Both in text and multimedia the flower symbol embodies a range of themes such as those of desire, love, beauty, flourishing sexuality, virginal purity, deflowerment, or maternal reproduction.

Having provided here an overview of Clavel's engagement with diverse literary and multimedia forms, this study now turns to the Conclusion which will discuss the manner in which Clavel's queer multimedia interventions and blurred role as writer-artist confirm her status as a 'contrabandista'.[24]

Notes to Chapter 10

1. In the context of Clavel's websites, apart from their value in helping to promote author credibility, the positive reviews of her books (and indeed the eye-catching visuals of the websites) act as important selling points and a consumer trend capitalized upon by Clavel. Online book reviews are becoming the standard as the internet is able to reach wider audiences than print-based mediums such as specialist journals or newspapers. A good and reliable review will often prompt readers to purchase the book online or at bookshops. Furthermore the sample chapters on both the *Cuerpo náufrago* and *Las Violetas* websites could be seen as an imitation of Amazon and the features it has for sampling books. Clavel may thus be catering for the expectations of the contemporary reader as consumer. Thus, even as her overall websites are motivated to underscore the cultural value of literature, its creative processes, and its inexorable interrelationship with multiple media or mediums, so too do they accentuate Clavel's work as commodity.
2. The term multimedia writer is one which I have personally coined to describe Clavel and her works. In an article on Clavel published in *El Universal*, Clavel embraces this notion: 'A Ana Clavel le gustó que la investigadora inglesa Jane Elizabeth Lavery la llamara "multimedia writer" porque en esos terrenos se ha movido en los últimos años' [Clavel endorsed the fact that the British researcher Jane Elizabeth Lavery described her as a 'multimedia writer' because it is precisely in this area that the writer has been working on in the last years]. Yanet Aguilar Sosa, '"El Deseo es el verdadero mundo de las maravillas', Entrevista a Ana Clavel', *El Universal*, 9 April 2013, <http://www.eluniversal.com.mx/cultura/71506.html> [accessed 20 June 2014].
3. Edmundo Paz Sóldan, 'A Cyberliterary Afterward: Of Blogs and Other Matters', in Taylor and Pitman (eds.), *Latin American Cyberculture and Cyberliterature*, pp. 257–62.
4. <http://lacomunidad.elpais.com/puerto-libre/posts> [accessed June 20 2014].
5. Ana Clavel, 'Mujeres al desnudo' (31 October 2013), 'Otros labios, otros paraísos' (14 November 2013), 'Territorio Lolita' (9 July 2013), <http://anaclavel.com/blog/> [accessed 14 July 2014].
6. Clavel, email to Lavery, 24 November 2013, 15:37.
7. See for instance, 17 November 2013, 21 November 2013, and 19 November 2013, <https://www.facebook.com/ana.clavel.18> [accessed 14 July 2014].
8. Clavel commissioned me to translate the book trailer for *El dibujante* into English which has still to be made available to the general public.
9. Hossaini, 'Vision of the Gods', <http://www.logosjournal.com/hossaini.pdf> [accessed 23 June 2014].
10. Lavery, unpublished interview with Clavel, 2011.
11. <http://anaclavel.com/multimedia.html> [accessed 2 December 2014].
12. Clavel also created another promotional video for the *Amor y otros suicidios* collection. This time an actress is reading the short story 'Después del paraíso', similarly in a bathtub, <http://anaclavel.com/multimedia.html> [accessed 23 June 2014].
13. Clavel, email to Lavery, 7 July 2012, 14:00.
14. Lavery, unpublished interview with Clavel, 2011.
15. Clavel's ability to 'smuggle' herself into other mediums becomes apparent in the credits section of the book trailers in which, in the style of movies or their trailers, a list of the different contributors appears, including, for instance, Carlos Cantú as producer and Clavel as director and scriptwriter.
16. Whilst audio-visual and textual techniques are more important perhaps than timing, length is

nevertheless a key factor in the ability to sway an audience. If a book trailer is too long, it risks losing the audience's attention and turning off potential buyers. At 3 minutes 37 seconds, *El dibujante*'s relative brevity contributes towards maintaining one's interest in the book's plot.

17. Richard Will, 'Pergolesi's Stabat Mater and the Politics of Feminine Virtue', *Musical Quarterly*, 87:3 (2005), 570–614, doi:10.1093/musqtl/gdh021, <http://mq.oxfordjournals.org/content/87/3/570.citation> [accessed 20 June 2014], p. 570.
18. <http://anaclavel.com/multimedia.html> [accessed 23 June 2014].
19. Anjana Susarla and others, 'Social Networks and the Diffusion of User-Generated Content: Evidence from YouTube', *ISRE* (2011), DOI 10.1287/isre.1100.0339, 1–9 (p. 1), <http://isr.journal.informs.org/content/early/2011/04/08/isre.1100.0339.full.pdf+html> [accessed 20 June 2014].
20. Holdom, 'Literary E-magazines in Latin America', p. 146.
21. Clavel also published two further books as this study was being finalized: *Material de lectura: Ana Clavel. Cuento contemporáneo*, 126 (Mexico City: Dirección de Literatura Coordinación de Difusión Cultural/ UNAM, 2013), and *CorazoNadas* (Mexico City: Posdata (La Hormiga Iracunda), 2014) (Trifling Matters of the Heart).
22. It was also exhibited between 5 and 12 June 2013 in the lobby of Radio Educación, situated in Angel Urraza 622, Col. Del Valle, Mexico City.
23. See also the discussion of Bourdieu in relation to notions of high and low art in Chapter 5.
24. O'Connell, *Prospero's Daughter*, p. 35.

CONCLUSION

Some Final Thoughts

Following on from the previous chapter, what becomes apparent in the *Las ninfas a veces sonríen* video installation is Clavel's desire to assert her authority both as the mastermind of the overall multimedia exhibit and creator of *Las ninfas.* The notion of authority has relevance in the broader context of Clavel as consecrated writer of the queer and the explicit in her literary *oeuvre* and as a 'contrabandista' multimedia artist.[1] Whilst Clavel's literary work has been praised for its innovation and contribution to Mexican and more widely Hispanic letters, her multimedia enterprise, however, has had at times a lukewarm reception, perhaps because she has straddled, or rather smuggled herself, into other fields which are not perceived as her expertise. Clavel mentioned to me informally that a number of critics were somewhat disparaging of the *Cuerpo náufrago* and *Las Violetas* multimedia projects for their unoriginality and for their amateurish quality, even though they unreservedly praised her literary works. She explained that she invited a number of visual art critics to the multimedia exhibition of *Cuerpo náufrago,* including José Manuel Springer, and remarked that 'aunque de pronto se sabe de autores que se van hacia otros campos' [although it is known of authors to veer into other fields], these particular critics found the event interesting but 'muy inusitado' [very unusual].[2] In Springer's review of *Cuerpo náufrago proyecto multimedia* the critic enthusiastically extols the novel for its originality in its exploration of the urinal-fetish, its gender bending thematics, and their interrelation with the visual dimension of the novel, but he was less enthusiastic about the multimedia event, in particular, the photographic display and installation:

> El trabajo fotográfico y la instalación de Ana son menos radicales, quizá porque existe toda una genealogía del baño y el mingitorio en el arte del siglo XX, y porque en ocasiones su discurso visual sufre de ataques de hipo que lo hacen saltar del descubrimiento notable hacia el *déjà vu.*[3]
>
> [Ana's photographic work and installation are less radical, perhaps because a whole genealogy of twentieth-century toilet and urinal art already exists, and because her visual discourse suffers from occasional glitches which turn it from noteworthy invention to *déjà vu*]

Although Springer himself champions 'alternative' art forms which overlap various fields in the form of art installations, for instance, his reservations here may be linked to a broader anxiety about the crossing-over of diverse disciplines conventionally kept apart, evidenced in particular in the encroachment of so-called new media or contemporary art forms, such as art installation, art (video) performance, digital technology, and cyber technologies, on traditional art forms including print-medium literature or painting. Clavel's venturing 'hacia otros campos' and dabbling in areas which are not perceived as being within her area of expertise were critiqued by internationally renowned painter Arturo Rivera who contributed to the *Las Violetas* exhibition. Whilst he eulogized her literary work and described it as of the calibre of Juan Rulfo, he thought the multimedia dimension was rather shabby, particularly the performance element.[4] He noted that he collaborated with Clavel because he endorsed her literary skills and she is a close friend, but compared her meddling with the non-literary to his conducting an orchestra as a painter. But Rivera's viewpoint is, as Clavel notes:

> permeada de una visión clásica que niega toda aportación al arte contemporáneo post-conceptual. Él, junto con la crítica Avelina Lésper, se han convertido en los enemigos acérrimos de todo arte situacionista, performance, instalación, es decir, todo aquello que no sea pintura retiniana, pintada en la acepción tradicional.[5]
>
> [permeated by a classical vision which negates any type of contribution by contemporary post-conceptual art. He, alongside Avelina Lésper, has become the staunch enemy of all Situationist, performance, and installation art. In other words, of all that which is not retinal painting that draws from traditional forms]

There were undoubtedly elements of the *Cuerpo náufrago* and *Las Violetas* multimedia exhibitions which had certain slapdash aspects to them: for example, the CD placed in Arturo Buitrón's Violeta doll stopped working after a few hours and the somewhat gimmicky air freshener scent emitted from Clavel's doll was barely perceptible and soon vanished completely. The signs which read 'Firme Aquí. R. MUTT' on the images of the *Cuerpo náufrago* photographic installation had been sloppily written by hand in black marker pen and occasionally peeled off. But despite these somewhat rudimentary failings, Clavel has a strong artistic sensibility and vision, as demonstrated by the participation of the numerous internationally acclaimed artists in her multimedia projects who have endorsed her not only as a writer, but as an artist too. Clavel sees herself primarily as a writer, but she is nonetheless an artist in her own right who not only has conceived the various multimedia projects, but also creates queer art herself. A good example is the image which dons the cover of this book, explicitly created by Clavel for this study. The urinal-mannequin, entitled *Un Duchamp reinstalado* (2012), may well be an intertextual collage of the artists Duchamp, Bellmer, and Courbet, but it exemplifies the idea of 'creative plagiarism' (like some of Clavel's other pieces as discussed elsewhere), in which the writer-artist has dynamically borrowed previous voices or traditions in order to create something new. Upon being shown this image, many colleagues and friends reacted immediately with an expression of surprise, horror even, accompanied by perplexion and a desire to understand its meaning. This reaction marks Clavel out as an accomplished multimedia writer-artist for it is precisely this response that she seeks and successfully elicits in her reader-spectators, both in her written work and multimedia art. In other words, she foments in us via her literary and artistic work a sense of abjection, that is, initial shock and curiosity or fascination, which then leads us to reflect upon notions of what constitutes the normal vis-a-vis that which is standardly considered abnormal.

Clavel's multimedia interventions have served to both multiply and magnify her literary works by providing a 'sort of heteroglossia or multiple voices' realised through linking text, image, sound, and physical interaction, which have thus enabled diverse readings and levels of interpretation of both text and multimedia.[6] Just as Antonia's transgender in *Cuerpo náufrago* defies rigid gender and sexual categorization, so too do Clavel's overall works in their textual and multimedia formats give way to a type of transgendered (non-) writing which challenges rigid boundaries maintained between, for instance, technology and culture, the humanities and the social sciences. In her analysis of Laura Esquivel's multimedia novel, *La ley del deseo* (1995) in which the text is interspersed with images and accompanied by a CD, Rodríguez-Vivaldi enquires whether Esquivel's novel should be perceived as the harbinger of the end of traditional print-medium literature (p. 31).[7] The critic notes that:

> The transformation of culture in our last century and the present has been fuelled by new technologies, and we will have to learn to integrate them aesthetically because art and culture, very much like Esquivel's work and like life itself, are dynamic concepts. (Rodríguez-Vivaldi, p. 31)

Like Esquivel (Rodríguez-Vivaldi, p. 31), Clavel is greatly in tune with these transformations and is thus calling for writers, and artists alike, to integrate new media and different disciplines, a process which can only serve to enrich rather than impoverish the individual areas. Clavel's intentional blurring of strict disciplinary divides is an attempt to propose her particular vision of the future of literature which she envisions as an interdisciplinary and often 'inter-medial' fusion of the cultural and the technological, the fictive and the non-fictive, in the form of different artistic disciplines (photography, sculpture, art, performance) and new cyber technologies, hyper texts, and realities. As discussed in the Introduction, Clavel is not unique in her interest in the interrelationship between literature and new mass media and can thus be added to a long list of Latin American writers such as Manuel Puig, Rosina Conde, Cristina Civale, and Albert Fuguet, to cite only but a few. Even as they seek to reaffirm the authority of the literary intellectual, these media-conscious writers engage creatively with contemporary mass cultural forms.[8] In line with such writers, Clavel's use of an array of disciplines and new mass media (the internet, digital/video technology, photography, and commercial culture), can thus be understood as a means of decentring writing's 'representational privilege', that is, its 'monopoly in the processing, storage and transmission of data' (Paz Soldán & Castillo (eds.), pp. 13 & 16).

Finally, Clavel's overall literary and multimedia projects make a lasting impression because they are driven, in a kind of 'McOndista' spirit, by a desire to create a more inclusive form of art by taking into account the experience of life in the age of cyber and (audio)visual culture.[9] Ultimately, by engaging with our intellect, emotions, and fears, as well as our physical senses Clavel has captured the visceral, pulsating human condition in a way that is deeply effective precisely because it is 'replete with the substance of life'.[10]

Notes to the Conclusion

1. O'Connell, *Prospero's Daughter*, p. 35.
2. Lavery, unpublished interview with Clavel, 2008.
3. Springer, 'Imaginar el deseo masculino desde lo femenino y viceversa'.
4. Lavery, unpublished interview with Arturo Rivera, 2008.
5. Clavel, email to Lavery, 12 March 2014, 06:47.
6. Rodríguez-Vivaldi, 'Shaking the Soul', p. 31.
7. Esquivel's use of multimedia is not as broad-ranging as that of Clavel given that *La ley del deseo* is Esquivel's only multimedia text, and Clavel of course exploits multimedia forms which extend beyond solely the illustrative.
8. Paz Soldán and Castillo (eds.), *Latin American Literature and Mass Media*, p. 16.
9. For an examination of Latin American McOndo writers see Alfonsina Lorenzi, 'In Search of the Lost Time: Intellectuals, Media and Narrative', in *Latin American Literature and Mass Media*, Hispanic Issues, 22 (New York: Garland, 2001), pp. 222–31.
10. Rosenthal, *Understanding Installation Art*, pp. 26–27.

BIBLIOGRAPHY

❖

Ana Clavel: Published Works

A la sombra de los deseos en flor. Ensayos sobre la fuerza metafórica del deseo (Mexico City: Universidad Autónoma de la Ciudad de México, 2008)
Amor y otros suicidios (Mexico City: B. de Bolsillo, 2012)
Amorosos de atar ([Culiacán]: Dirección de Investigación y Fomento de Cultura Regional del Estado de Sinaloa, 1992)
'Los caballeros las prefieren mudas', *Nexos* (March 2008), 61–65
CorazoNadas (Mexico City: Posdata (La Hormiga Iracunda), 2014)
Cuerpo náufrago (Mexico City: Alfaguara, 2005)
——*Shipwrecked Body*, trans. by Jay Miskowiec (Minneapolis: Aliform Publishing, 2008)
'Un deseo realizado', *Revista de la Universidad de México*, 65 (2009), 68–69, <http://www.revistadelauniversidad.unam.mx/6509/conten.html> [accessed 8 June 2014]
Los deseos y su sombra (Madrid: Alfaguara, 2000)
——*Desire and Its Shadow*, trans. by Jay Miskowiec (Minneapolis: Aliform, 2006)
El dibujante de sombras (Mexico City: Alfaguara, 2009)
——*Le Dessinateur d'ombres*, trans. by Brigitte Jensen (Paris: Éditions Anne Carrière, 2013)
Fuera de escena (Mexico City: Letras Nuevas, 1984)
'La imagen del espejo', in Yolanda Medina Haro (ed.), *Antología* (Mexico City: taller de creación Colegio de Bachilleres # 1, plantel El Rosario, 1979), pp. 11–15
Material de lectura: Ana Clavel, Cuento contemporáneo, 126 (Mexico City: Dirección de Literatura Coordinación de Difusión Cultural/ UNAM, 2013)
Las ninfas a veces sonríen (Mexico City: Alfaguara, 2012)
Paraísos trémulos (Mexico City: Alfaguara, 2001)
Las Violetas son flores del deseo (Mexico City: Alfaguara, 2007)
——*Les Violettes sont les fleurs du désir*, trans. by François Gaudry (Paris: Métailié, 2009)
——Arabic translation (Lebanon: Dar-Al-Farabi, 2011)

Ana Clavel: Other Material

<http://www.anaclavel.com/> [accessed 14 June 2014]
——'Mujeres al desnudo' (31 October 2013), <http://anaclavel.com/blog/> [accessed 14 July 2014]
——'Otros labios, otros paraísos' (14 November 2013), <http://anaclavel.com/blog/> [accessed 14 July 2014]
——'Territorio Lolita' (9 July 2013), <http://anaclavel.com/blog/> [accessed 14 July 2014]
<http://anaclavel.com/blog/>
<http://www.anaclavel.com/multimedia.html>
<http://cuerponaufrago.com/fachada.htm> [accessed 14 June 2014]
<https://www.facebook.com/ana.clavel.18> [accessed 14 June 2014]
<http://www.violetasfloresdeldeseo.com/> [accessed 14 June 2014]

Emails to Jane Lavery

——20 April 2011, 16:29
——21 April 2011, 14:24
——22 April 2011, 14:52
——26 October 2011, 15:00
——7 July 2012, 14:00
——24 November 2013, 15:37
——8 March 2014, 16:29
——11 March 2014, 01:33
——11 March 2014, 04:19
——12 March 2014, 06:47
——18 March 2014, 16:22

'Intervención artística de Ana Clavel en Zona Rosa: *La censura también es fuente* o como el arte público transgrede', CONACULTA, FONCA, unpublished material courtesy of Ana Clavel

Works by Other Authors

Abyss Creations, RealDoll catalogue (2007)

Adams, Jeffrey, 'Narcissism and Creativity in the Postmodern Era: The Case of Patrick Süskind's *Das Parfum*', *The Germanic Review*, 75:4 (2000), 259–79

Aguilar Sosa, Yanet, 'Le da voz propia al incesto y sus abismos', *El Universal*, 7 November 2007, <http://www.eluniversal.com.mx/cultura/54563.html> [accessed 22 June 2014]

——'"El deseo es el verdadero mundo de las maravillas', Entrevista a Ana Clavel', *El Universal*, 9 April 2013, <http://www.eluniversal.com.mx/cultura/71506.html> [accessed 20 June 2014]

Allmer, Patricia, 'La Reproduction interdite: René Magritte and Forgery', *Papers of Surrealism*, 5 (2007), 1–19, <http://www.surrealismcentre.ac.uk/papersofsurrealism/journal5/index.htm> [accessed: 10 June 2014]

Anderson, Danny, 'Creating Cultural Prestige: Editorial Joaquín Mortiz', *Latin American Research Review*, 31:2 (1996), 3–41

Andersson, Johan, and Ben Campkin, '"White Tiles. Trickling Water. A Man!" Literary Representations of Cottaging in London', in Olga Gershenson and Barbara Penner (eds.), *Ladies and Gents: Public Toilets and Gender* (Philadelphia: Temple University Press, 2009), pp. 208–17

Anonymous:

——'Ana Clavel asegura que está al margen del "best seller"', *Informador*, 8 March 2009, <http://www.informador.com.mx/cultura/2009/161631//ana-clavel-asegura-que-esta-al-margen-del-best-seller.htm> [accessed 8 June 2014]

——'Los 10 libros más vendidos de la semana', no pagination, <http://espanol.news.yahoo.com/s/ap/071116/entretenimiento/esp_lib_los_diez_libros> [accessed 22 June 2014]

——'Los éxitos y las críticas', *Clarín*, 2 September (2003), <http://edant.clarin.com/diario/2003/02/09/ s04003.htm> [accessed 10 May 2014]

——'Ganan mexicanos Premio Internacional Juan Rulfo', <http://www.terra.com.mx/articulo.aspx?articuloId=177386> [accessed 22 June 2014]

——'Prevalecen contenidos sexistas en medios: Segob', September 2010, <http://www.eluniversal.com.mx/notas/709542.html> [accessed 10 June 2014]

——'Sobre la Ley de fomento para la lectura y el libro', <http://www.leydellibro.org.mx/Ley_de_Fomento_para_la_Lectura_y_el_Libro.pdf> [accessed 14 June 2014]

Aranda, Alberto, 'El Centinela de las buenas conciencias', 2 May 2008, <http://www.noticias.canal22.org.mx/noticia.html?n=12283> > [accessed 14 June 2014]

BAKHTIN, MIKHAIL M., 'Discourse in the Novel', in Michael Holquist (ed.), *The Dialogic Imagination: Four Essays*, trans. by Caryl Emerson and Michael Holquist, University of Texas Press Slavic Series, I, (Austin: University of Texas, 1981), pp. 259–422

——*Problems of Dostoevsky's Poetics*, ed. and trans. by Caryl Emerson, Theory and History of Literature, 8 (Minneapolis: University of Minnesota Press, 1984)

——*Rabelais and his World*, trans. by Hélène Iswolsky (Bloomington: Indiana University Press, 1984)

BARTHES, ROLAND, *Camera Lucida: Reflections on Photography* (New York: Hill and Wang, 1981)

——'From Work to Text', in Josue V. Harari (ed.), *Textual Strategies* (New York: Cornell University Press, 1979), pp. 73–81 (Barthes first published in 1971)

——*Mythologies,* selected and trans. by Annette Lavers (New York: Hill and Wang, 1972) (first published in 1957)

——*The Pleasure of the Text*, trans. by Richard Miller, note by Richard Howard (New York: Hill and Wang, 1975) (first published in 1973)

——*S/Z,* trans. by Richard Miller (New York: Hill and Wang, 1974) (first published in 1970)

BATE, DAVID, *Photography & Surrealism: Sexuality, Colonialism and Social Dissent* (London: I. B. Tauris, 2004)

BAUDRILLARD, JEAN, *Simulacra and Simulation*, trans. by Sheila Faria Glaser (Ann Arbor: University of Michigan Press, 1994)

—— *Simulations* (New York: Semiotext(e), 1983)

BEARDSELL, PETER, *Europe and Latin America: Returning the Gaze* (Manchester: University of Manchester Press, 2000)

BEAUVOIR, SIMONE DE, *The Second Sex*, ed. and trans. by Howard M. Parshley (London: Vintage, 1997) (first published in 1949)

BECERRA, LUZMA, 'Otra forma de estar en el mundo, o la ciudad subterránea en *Los deseos y su sombra*, de Ana Clavel', Instituto Tecnológico y de Estudios Superiores de Monterrey, *Revista Iztapalapa*, 52 (2002), 245–59

BENJAMIN, WALTER, 'The Work of Art in the Age of Mechanical Reproduction', in *Illuminations* (London: Pimlico, 1999), pp. 211–44 (first published in 1968)

BERNAERTS, LARS, LUC HERMAN, and BART VERVACEK, 'Narrative Threads of Madness', *Style*, 43:3 (2009), 283–90

BEST, VICTORIA, 'The Uses and Abuses of Children: Fairy Tales and The Pornographic', in Anna Fahraeus and Annkatrin Jonsson (eds.), *Textual Ethos Studies, or Locating Ethics*, 26, Critical Studies: Critical Theory, Literature & Culture (Amsterdam: Rodopi, 2005), pp. 229–44

BILBIJA, KSENIJA, '"Las Hortensias" by Felisberto Hernández: The Fabrication of Desire', in Giovanna Covi (ed.), *Critical Studies on the Feminist Subject* (Trento: University of Trento Press, 1997), pp. 245–63

——'"The Youngest Doll" by Rosario Ferré: On Women, Dolls, Golems and Cyborgs', *Callaloo: A Journal of African American and African Arts and Letters*, 17:3 (1994), 878–88

BLOOM, HAROLD, *The Anxiety of Influence: A Theory of Poetry*, 2nd edn (New York: Oxford University Press, 1997) (first published in 1973)

BOURDIEU, PIERRE, *Distinction: A Social Critique of the Judgement of Taste*, trans. by Richard Nice (London: Routledge & Kegan Paul, 1984) (first published in 1979)

BRAIDOTTI, ROSI, *Nomadic Subjects: Embodiment and Sexual Difference in Contemporary Feminist Theory* (New York: Columbia University Press, 1994)

BRAUER, FAE, 'The Transparent Body: Biocultures of Evolution, Eugenics and Scientific Racism', in Jane Kromm and Susan Benforado Bakewell (eds.), *History of Visual Culture: Western Civilization from the 18th to the 21st Century* (Oxford: Berg, 2010), pp. 89–103

BROOK, BARBARA, *Feminist Perspectives on the Body*, Feminist Perspectives (London: Longman, 1990)

BROWN, SARAH ANNES, *The Metamorphosis of Ovid: From Chaucer to Ted Hughes* (London: Duckworth, 1999)

BÜCI-GLUCKSMANN, CHRISTINE, *Baroque Reason: The Aesthetics of Modernity*, trans. by Patrick Camiller (London: Sage, 1994)

BUTLER, JUDITH, *Bodies that Matter: On the Discursive Limits of 'Sex'* (New York: Routledge, 1993)

—— *Gender Trouble: Feminism and the Subversion of Identity* (New York: Routledge, 1990)

—— *Undoing Gender* (New York: Routledge, 2004)

CAFLISCH-SCHNETZLER, URSULA, 'Biography and Works', University of Zurich, Institut für Schweizerische Reformationsgeschichte, Lavater-Edition, trans. by H. Bociek, 2001, <http://www.irg.uzh.ch/lavater/jclavater/bio_en.html> [accessed 14 June 2014]

CANAVILHAS, JOÃO, 'Hypertext Newswriting Effects on Satisfaction, Comprehension and Attitudes', (2008), 1–17, <http://online.journalism.utexas.edu/2008/papers/Canavilhas.pdf> [accessed 10 March 2014]

CARRIER, JOSEPH M., 'Mexican Male Bisexuality', in Fritz Klein and Timothy J. Wolf (eds.), *Bisexualities: Theory and Research* (New York: Haworth Press, 1985), pp. 75–85

CASTILLO, DEBRA, *Talking Back: Toward a Latin American Feminist Literary Criticism* (Ithaca, NY: Cornell University Press, 1992)

CERTEAU, MICHEL DE, *The Practice of Everyday Life*, trans. by S. F. Randall (Berkeley: California University Press, 1984)

CHANADY, AMARYLL BEATRICE, *Magical Realism and the Fantastic: Resolved Versus Unresolved Antinomies* (New York: Garland, 1985)

—— 'The Territorialization of the Imaginary in Latin America: Self-Affirmation and Resistance to Metropolitan Paradigms', in Lois Parkinson Zamora and Wendy B. Faris (eds.), *Magical Realism: Theory, History, Community* (Durham: Duke University Press, 1995), pp. 125–44

CHANT, SYLVIA, 'Single-Parent Families: Choice or Constraint? The Formation of Female-Headed Households in Mexican Shanty Towns', in Denise A. Segura and Patricia Zavella (eds.), *Women and Migration in the U.S.-Mexico Borderlands: A Reader*, Latin America Otherwise (Durham, NC: Duke University Press, 2007), pp. 360–68

CHAPMAN, CHRISTOPHER, 'Piss Art: Images of Urination in 20th Century Art' (1998) <http://ensemble.va.com.au/array/chap_00.html> [accessed 10 March 2011]

CHARNEY, MAURICE, *Sexual Fiction* (Routledge: London, 2003)

CHIAPPE, DOMÉNICO, 'Creative Processes in Hypermedia Literature: Single Purpose, Multiple Authors', in Claire Taylor and Thea Pitman (eds.), *Latin American Cyberculture and Cyberliterature* (Liverpool: Liverpool University Press, 2007), pp. 216–26

CIXOUS, HÉLÈNE, 'The Laugh of the Medusa', trans. by Keith Cohen and Paula Cohen, *Signs*, 1:4 (1976), 875–93 (first published in 1975)

CLIFTON, LINDA, 'Apropos Encore', in David Pereira (ed.), *Anguish & Erotics*, Papers of The Freudian School of Melbourne, *Lacanian Psychoanalytic Writings*, 22 (2004), 91–108

—— 'The Gaze of Gustave Courbet's *L'Origine du monde* — A Response to Juan Davila', *Écritique*, Papers of the Freudian School of Melbourne, *Lacanian Psychoanalytic Writings*, 5 (2005), 39–46, <http://home.vicnet.net.au/~fsom/ecritique0405.htm> [accessed 22 June 2014]

CONNELL, RAEWYN W., *Masculinities* (Cambridge, MA: Polity, 1995)

COON, DENNIS, and JOHN O. MITTERER, *Introduction to Psychology: Gateways to Mind and Behavior*, 12th edn (Belmont, CA: Wadsworth, Cengage, 2010)

CORONA, IGNACIO, and BETH E. JÖRGENSEN (eds.), *The Contemporary Mexican Chronicle: Theoretical Perspectives on the Liminal Genre*, Suny Series in Latin American and Iberian Thought and Culture (Albany: State University of New York Press, 2002)

Creed, Barbara, *Monstrous-feminine: Film, Feminism, Psychoanalysis* (New York: Routledge, 1993)
Cubitt, Tessa, *Latin American Society* (London: Longman, 1995)
Cuddon, John Anthony, *A Dictionary of Literary Terms and Literary Theory*, rev. by Claire Preston (London: Blackwell, 1998) (first published in 1976)
Davies, Lloyd Hughes, *Allende: La Casa de los espíritus*, ed. by Alan Deyremond and Stephen Hart, Critical Guides to Spanish Texts, 66 (London: Grant and Cutler, 2000)
——'Portraits of a Lady: Postmodern Readings of Tomás Eloy Martínez', *Modern Language Review*, 95:2 (2000), 416–23
——*Projections of Peronism in Argentine Autobiography, Biography and Fiction* (Chicago: Chicago University Press, 2007)
Day, Loraine, 'Annie Ernaux and Courbet's *L'Origine du monde*: The Maternal Body, Desire and Filial Identity in *Je ne suis pas sortie de ma nuit* and *Passion simple*', *French Forum*, 25:2 (2000), 205–26Domenella, Ana Rosa, ed., *Territorio de leonas: cartografía de narradoras mexicanas en los nóventa* (Mexico: Casa Juan Pablo Centro Cultural, 2001)
Douglas, Mary, *Purity and Danger: An Analysis of Concepts of Pollution and Taboo*, in *Collected Works*, 2 vols (London: Routledge, 2003), II (first published in 1966)
Dubois, Philippe, *L'Acte photographique et autres essais* (Brussels: Média Editions Labor, 1990) (first published in 1983)
——'Photography Mise-en-Film: Autobiographical (Hi)stories and Psychic Apparatuses', in Patrice Petro (ed.), *Fugitive Images: From Photography to Video*, trans. by Lynne Kirby (Bloomington: Indiana University Press, 1995), pp. 152–72
Ebergenyi, Emilio, 'Entrevista con Ana Clavel, quien habla de la instalación *Cuerpo náufrago* ready-made multimedia', 'Su casa y otros viajes', Radio Educación, 1060 AM, 19 September 2005, 9.35am, radio interview script
Eckermann, Johann Peter, '1829', in *Conversations of Goethe*, trans. by John Oxenford, digital production by Harrion Ainsworth, <http://www.hxa.name/books/ecog/Eckermann-ConversationsOfGoethe-1829.htm> [accessed 14 June 2014]
Edelman, Lee, 'Men's Room', in Joel Sanders (ed.), *Stud: Architectures of Masculinity* (New York: Princeton Architectural Press, 1996), pp. 152–61
Ekins, Richard, and Dave King, 'Telling Body Transgendering Stories', in Kathryn Backett-Milburn and Linda McKie (eds.), *Constructing Gendered Bodies* (Basingstoke: Palgrave, 2001), pp. 179–203
Elias, Norbert, *The Civilizing Process: Sociogenetic and Psychogenetic Investigations*, transl. by Edmond Jephcott (Oxford: Blackwell, 2000) (first published as *Über der Prozeß der Zivilisation*, I, in 1939)
Eveleigh, David J., *Boggs, Baths & Basins: The Story of Domestic Sanitation* (Stroud: Sutton Publishing, 2002)
Farrier, Stephen, 'Ga(y)zing at Soap: Representation and Reading-Queering Soap Opera', in Bruce Carson and Margaret Llewellyn-Jones (eds.), *Frames and Fictions on Television: the Politics of Identity Within Drama* (Exeter: Intellect Books, 2000), pp. 86–99
Finnegan, Nuala, *Ambivalence, Modernity, Power: Women and Writing in Mexico since 1980* (Oxford: Peter Lang, 2007)
——'"Light" women/"light" literature: women and popular fiction in Mexico since 1980', *Donaire*, 15 (2000a), 18–22
——*Monstrous Projections of Femininity in the Fiction of Mexican Writer Rosario Castellanos* (Lewiston: Edwin Mellen, 2000)
Finnegan, Nuala, and Jane Elizabeth Lavery (eds.), *The Boom Femenino in Mexico: Reading Contemporary Women's Writing* (Newcastle upon Tyne: Cambridge Scholars Publishing, 2010)
Flores, Angel, 'Magical Realism in Spanish America', in Lois Parkinson Zamora and

Wendy B. Faris (eds.), *Magical Realism: Theory, History, Community* (Durham, NC: Duke University Press, 1995), pp. 109–24 (Flores first published in 1955)

FOSTER, DAVID WILLIAM, *Sexual Textualities: Essays on Queer/ing Latin American Writing* (Austin: University of Texas Press, 1997)

FRANCO, JEAN, *The Decline and Fall of the Lettered City: Latin America After the Cold War* (Cambridge, MA: Harvard University Press, 2002)

FRIEDMAN, KEN, 'Intermedia: Four Histories, Three Directions, Two Futures', in Hans Breder and Klaus-Peter Busse (eds.), *Intermedia: Enacting the Liminal* (Norderstedt: Dortmunder Schriften zur Kunst, 2005), pp. 51–62

GALVÁN, AGUSTÍN, <http://duendecallejeroelemental.blogspot.com/2008_11_01_archive.html> [accessed 22 June 2011]

GARBER, MARJORIE, *Vested Interests: Cross-dressing and Cultural Anxiety* (London: Penguin Books, 1992)

GARCÍA BERGUA, ANA, 'De sombras y espejos', *La Jornada Semanal*, 986, 14 February 2010, <http://anaclavel.com/entrevistas/dibujante/El_dibujante_de_sombras_por_Ana_Garcia_Bergua_en_Jornada_Semanal.pdf> [accessed 14 June 2014].

——'Y ahora paso a retirarme, "Comida, Mingitorios y Zapatos"', *La Jornada Semanal*, 546, 21 August 2005, <http://anaclavel.com/jornada/anagarcia.htm> [accessed 10 March 2014]

GEAR, RACHEL, 'All Those Nasty Womanly Things: Women Artists, Technology and The Monstrous-Feminine', *Women's Studies International Forum*, 24:3–4, (2001), 321–33

GEISDORFER FEAL, ROSEMARY, 'Queer Cortázar and the Lectora Macho', in Susana Chávez-Silverman and Librada Hernández (eds.), *Reading and Writing the Ambiente: Queer Sexualities in Latino, Latin American, and Spanish Culture*, ed. by (Madison: University of Wisconsin Press, 2000), pp. 239–56

GELPÍ, JUAN G., 'Walking in the Modern City: Subjectivity and Cultural Contacts in the Urban Crónicas of Salvador Novo and Carlos Monsisváis', in Ignacio Corona and Beth E. Jörgensen (eds.), *The Contemporary Mexican Chronicle: Theoretical Perspectives on the Liminal Genre*, Suny Series in Latin American and Iberian Thought and Culture (Albany: State University of New York Press, 2002), pp. 201–20

GENETTE, GÉRARD, *Paratexts: The Thresholds of Textuality*, trans. by Jane E. Lewin, Literature, Culture, Theory, 20 (New York: Cambridge University Press, 1997) (first published in 1987)

GERSHENSON, OLGA, and BARBARA PENNER (eds.), *Ladies and Gents: Public Toilets and Gender* (Philadelphia: Temple University Press, 2009)

GESSNER, GEORG, *Johann Kaspar Lavaters Lebenschreibung von seinem Tochtermann G.G.*, 3 vols (Winterthur: Steiner, 1802–10)

GOFFMAN, ERVING, *The Presentation of Self in Everyday Life* (New York: Anchor Books, 1959)

GOMÍS, ANAMARI, 'Dibujanta de Sombras', *Nexos*, 10 March 2010, <http://anaclavel.com/entrevistas/dibujante/El_dibujante_de_sombras_en_nexos.pdf> [accessed 14 June 2014]

GÓNGORA, LUIS DE, *Obras completas*, ed. by Antonio Carreira, 2 vols (Madrid: Biblioteca Castro, 2000)

GONZALEZ RODRÍGUEZ, SERGIO, 'Mejores libros del 2005', Suplemento Cultural de Reforma, *Reforma*, 8 January 2006

GONZÁLEZ RUIZ, EDGAR, *La Sexualidad prohibida: intolerancia, sexismo y represión* (Mexico City: Plaza y Janés, 2002)

GRAY, RICHARD T., *About Face: German Physiognomic Thought from Lavater to Auschwitz* (Detroit: Wayne State University Press, 2004)

GREEN, MARY, *Diamela Eltit: Reading the Mother* (Woodbridge: Tamesis, 2007)

GRONOV, JUKKA, *The Sociology of Taste* (London: Routledge, 1997)

GROSZ, ELIZABETH, *Jacques Lacan: A Feminist Introduction* (London: Routledge, 1990)

——*Sexual Subversions: Three French Feminists* (St Leonards, NSW: Allen and Unwin, 1989)

—— *Volatile Bodies. Towards a Corporeal Feminism* (Bloomington and Indianapolis: Indiana University Press, 1994)

HALBERSTAM, JUDITH, *Female Masculinity* (Durham, NC: Duke University Press, 1998)

HALPERIN, DAVID M., *Saint Foucault: Towards a Gay Hagiography* (Oxford: Oxford University Press, 1995)

HARAWAY, DONNA, 'A Cyborg Manifesto: Science, Technology, and Socialist-Feminism in the Late Twentieth Century', in *Simians, Cyborgs and Women: The Reinvention of Nature* (New York: Routledge, 1991), pp. 149–81 (first published in 1985)

HARRIS, PAULINE, 'At the Interface Between Reader and Text: Devices in Children's Picture Books that Mediate Reader Expectations and Interpretations', AARE Conference Paper, Parramatta (2005), 1–17, <http://www.aare.edu.au/05pap/har05606.pdf> [accessed 22 June 2014]

HARRIS, PAULINE, and BARBARA MCKENZIE, 'Inviting Dissent: Classroom Practices for Nurturing Communities of Readers in the Early School Years', AARE Conference Paper, Parramatta, (2005), no pagination, <http://www.aare.edu.au/05pap/har05289.pdf> [accessed 22 June 2014]

HARRISON, CHARLES, *Painting the Difference: Sex and Spectator in Modern Art* (Chicago: University of Chicago Press, 2005)

HAYMES, EDWARD R., 'The Sexual Stranger: The Sexual Quest in Wolfram's *Parzival*', in Frank R. P. Akehurst and Stephanie Cain Van D'Elden (eds.), *The Stranger in Medieval Society*, Medieval Cultures, 12 (Minneapolis: University of Minnesota Press, 1997), pp. 80–91

HERNÁNDEZ, FELISBERTO, 'Las Hortensias', in *Obras Completas*, 6 vols (Montevideo: Editorial Arca, 1967), v (first published in 1949)

HERRERA, JORGE LUIS, 'Escritora de deseos y sombras: entrevista con Ana Clavel', [n.d.], <http://www.uaemex.mx/plin/colmena/Colmena%2051/Conversaciones/Ana.html> [accessed 3 June 2014]

HIGGINS, DICK, 'Intermedia', *Something Else Newsletter*, 1:1 (1966), 1–66

HIND, EMILY, 'After Hours: Six Mexican Women Writers on Borrowed Time', unpublished PhD dissertation, University of Virginia (2001)

—— *Femmenism and the Mexican Woman Intellectual from Sor Juana to Poniatowska: Boob Lit*, Breaking Feminist Waves (New York: Palgrave Macmillan, 2010)

—— 'Pita Amor, Sabina Berman, and Antonio Serrano: Camp in DF', in *Latin American Urban Cultural Production*, ed. and intro. by David William Foster, *Hispanic Issues On Line*, 3: 7 (2008), 136–62, <http://spanport.cla.umn.edu/publications/HispanicIssues/pdfs/Hind.pdf> [accessed 10 June 2014]

—— 'Six Authors on the Conservative Side of the Boom Femenino, 1985–2003: Boullosa, Esquivel, Loaeza, Mastretta, Nissán and Sefchovich', in Nuala Finnegan, and Jane E. Lavery (eds.), *The Boom Femenino in Mexico* (Newcastle upon Tyne: Cambridge Scholars Publishing, 2010), pp. 48–72

HOESTEREY, INGEBORG, *Pastiche: Cultural Memory in Art, Film, Literature* (Bloomington: Indiana University Press, 2001)

HOLDOM, SHOSHANNAH, 'Literary E-magazines in Latin America: From Textual Criticsm to Virtual Communities', in Claire Taylor and Thea Pitman (eds.), *Latin American Cyberculture and Cyberliterature* (Liverpool: Liverpool University Press, 2007), pp. 140–60

HOLM, LORENS, 'eS aitcH eYe Tee', *The Journal of Architecture*, 12:4 (2007), 423–36

HOSSAINI, ALI, 'Vision of the Gods: An Inquiry into the Meaning of Photography', *Logos*, 2:3 (2003), <http://www.logosjournal.com/hossaini.pdf> [accessed 23 June 2014]

HOULBROOK, MATT, 'The Private World of Public Urinals: London 1918–1957', *London Journal*, 25: 1 (2000), 52–70

HOWSON, ALEXANDRA, *The Body in Society: An Introduction* (Cambridge, MA: Polity, 2005)

HUTCHEON, LINDA, *The Politics of Postmodernism* (London: Routledge, 1989)

IDEL, MOSHE, *Golem: Jewish Magical and Mystical Traditions on the Artificial Anthropoid* (Albany: State University of New York Press, 1990)

IRIGARAY, LUCE, *This Sex Which Is Not One*, trans. by Catherine Porter and Carolyn Burke (Ithaca: Cornell University Press, 1985)

IRWIN, ROBERT MCKEE, 'The Famous 41: The Scandalous Birth of Modern Mexican Homosexuality', *GLQ: A Journal of Lesbian and Gay Studies*, 6:3 (2000), 353–76

JAMESON, FREDERIC, 'Postmodernism and Consumer Society', in Hal Foster (ed.), *The Anti-Aesthetic: Essays on Postmodern Culture* (Port Townsend, WA: Bay Press, 1983), pp. 111–25

JONES, ANN ROSALIND, 'Writing the Body: Towards an Understanding of *L'Écriture féminine*', in Elaine Showalter (ed.), *The New Feminist Criticism: Essays on Women, Literature and Theory* (London: Virago Press, 1986), pp. 361–77

JÖRGENSEN, BETH E., 'Light-Writing: Biography and Photography in Tinísima', in Kristine Ibsen (ed.), *The Other Mirror: Women's Narrative in Mexico 1980–1995*, Contributions to the Study of World Literature, 80 (Westport, CT: Greenwood Press, 1997), pp. 57–72

JUDOVITZ, DALIA, *Unpacking Duchamp: Art in Transit* (Berkeley: University of California Press, 1995)

JUNG, CARL G., 'The Psychology of the Unconscious', in *Collected Works, Volume 7: Two Essays on Analytical Psychology*, ed. by Herbert Read, Michael Fordham and Gerhard Adler, trans. by R. F. C. Hull (London: Routledge & Kegan Paul, 1953) [first pub. 1917], pp. 3–117

KALLBERG, JEFFREY, 'The Harmony of the Tea Table: Gender and Ideology in the Piano Nocturne', *Representations*, 39 (1992), 102–33

KAMINSKY, AMY, 'The Queering of Latin American Literary Studies', *Latin American Research Review*, 36:2 (2001), 209–19

KAVIOLA, KAREN, 'Revisiting Woolf's Representations of Androgyny: Gender, Race, Sexuality, and Nation', *Tulsa Studies in Women's Literature*, 18:2 (1999), 235–61

KELLY, LORRAINE, "'La pieza desquiciante de la jerarquía': Reading the Work of Brianda Domecq as a Philosophy of Feminism', in Nuala Finnegan, and Jane E. Lavery (eds.), *The Boom Femenino in Mexico* (Newcastle upon Tyne: Cambridge Scholars Publishing, 2010), pp. 149–65

KRAUSS, ROSALIND E., *Bachelors* (Cambridge, MA: October Books, MIT Press, 1999)

KRISTEVA, JULIA, *Black Sun*, trans. by Leon S. Roudiez (New York: Columbia University Press, 1989)

——*Desire in Language: A Semiotic Approach to Literature and Art*, ed. by Leon S. Roudiez, trans. by Thomas Gora and others (New York: Columbia University Press, 1980)

——*The Kristeva Reader*, ed. by Toril Moi (New York: Columbia University Press, 1986)

——*Powers of Horror: An Essay on Abjection*, trans. by Leon S. Roudiez (New York: Columbia University Press, 1982) (first published in 1957)

——*Revolution in Poetic Language*, trans. by Margaret Waller (New York: Colombia University Press, 1984) (first published in 1974)

——*Strangers to Ourselves*, trans. by Leon S. Roudiez (Hemel Hempstead: Harvester Wheatsheaf, 1991)

—— 'Le Sujet en procès', in *Polylogue* (Paris: Seuil, 1977), pp. 55–106

KUHN, ANNETTE, *The Power of the Image: Essays on Representation and Sexuality* (London: Routledge and Kegan Paul, 1985)

LACAN, JACQUES, 'The Agency of the Letter in the Unconscious or Reason since Freud', in *Écrits: A Selection*, trans. by Alan Sheridan (New York: W.W. Norton & Co., 1977) [first pub. 1957], pp. 146–78

——*Écrits: A Selection*, trans. by Alan Sheridan (New York: W.W. Norton, 1977) (first published in 1957)

——*The Four Fundamental Concepts of Psycho-Analysis*, ed. by Jacques-Alain Miller and trans. by Alan Sheridan (Harmondsworth: Penguin, 1987) (first published in 1977)

LANDOW, GEORGE P., 'Hypertext' (1996), <http://www.cyberartsweb.org/cpace/ht/jhup/writerly.html> [accessed 10 March 2014] (first published in print in 1992)

LAPORTE, DOMINIQUE, *History of Shit*, trans. by Nadia Benabid and Rodolphe El-Khoury, intro. by Rodolphe El-Khoury (Cambridge, MA: MIT Press, 2000) (first published in 1978)

LAURETIS, TERESA DE, *Alice Doesn't: Feminism, Semiotics, Cinema* (Bloomington: Indiana University Press, 1992)

LAVERY, JANE ELIZABETH, 'Ana Clavel's *Las Violetas son flores del deseo* and Peritextuality', *Hispanic Research Journal*, 14:2 (2013), 159–74

——*Ángeles Mastretta: Textual Multiplicity* (Woodbridge: Tamesis, 2005)

——'The *Superescritora* Ángeles Mastretta: The Strategies of a Best-Seller Writer in Projecting and Maintaining (Literary) Superstardom', *Journal of Iberian and Latin American Research*, 16:2 (2010), 117–31

——unpublished interviews with Ana Clavel, 2008–11

——unpublished interview with Arturo Rivera, 2008

——unpublished interview with Rogelio Cuéllar, 2008

——unpublished interview with Rubén Maya Moreno, 2008

——unpublished interview with Saúl Kaminer, 2008

LEAL, LUIS, 'Magical Realism in Spanish American literature', in Lois Parkinson Zamora and Wendy B. Faris (eds.), *Magical Realism: Theory, History, Community* (Durham, NC: Duke University Press, 1995), pp. 119–24 (Leal first published in 1955)

LECHTE, JOHN, and MARY ZOURNAZI, *The Kristeva Critical Reader* (Edinburgh: Edinburgh University Press, 2003)

LEITCH, VINCENT B., and OTHERS (eds.), *The Norton Anthology of Theory and Criticism* (New York: W. W. Norton, 2001)

LEVINSON, JERROLD, 'Erotic Art and Pornographic Pictures', *Philosophy and Literature*, 29:1 (2005), 228–40

LÉVI-STRAUSS, CLAUDE, *The Savage Mind* (Chicago: University of Chicago Press, 1966) (first published in 1962)

LEVY, DAVID, *Love and Sex with Robots* (New York: HarperCollins, 2007)

LÓPEZ, IRMA M., '"The Will to Be": Mexican Women Novelists from the late 1960s to the 1990s', in Nuala Finnegan, and Jane E. Lavery (eds.), *The Boom Femenino in Mexico* (Newcastle upon Tyne: Cambridge Scholars Publishing, 2010), pp. 26–47

——*Confluencias y demarcaciones: generaciones literarias y expresiones estéticas en la novela mexicana, 1998–2008*, 18, Ensayo (Mexico: Ediciones y Gráficos Eón, 2011)

LÓPEZ GONZÁLEZ, ARALIA, ed., *Sin imágenes falsas, sin falsos espejos. Narradoras mexicanas del siglo XX* (Mexico: El Colegio de México, 1995)

LORENZI, ALFONSINA, 'In Search of the Lost Time: Intellectuals, Media and Narrative', in *Latin American Literature and Mass Media*, Hispanic Issues, 22 (New York: Garland, 2001), pp. 222–31

LYDENBERG, ROBIN, 'Marcel Duchamp's Legacy: Aesthetics, Gender, and National Identity in the Toilet', in Olga Gershenson and Barbara Penner (eds.), *Ladies and Gents: Public Toilets and Gender* (Philadelphia: Temple University Press, 2009), pp. 151–66

LYON, JOHN B., '"The Science of Sciences": Replication and Reproduction in Lavater's Physiognomics', *Eighteenth-Century Studies*, 40: 2 (2007), 257–77

MACÍAS-GONZÁLEZ, VICTOR M., 'Scrubbing the Queer Away, or Homosexuality and Mexico City Bathhouses, 1880–1920', unpublished paper presented at I Congreso Mexicano de la Comunidad Lésbica, Gay, Bisexual, Transgénero y Travestí, LGBTT, *Memorias*, Monterrey, N.L. México, 20 and 21 October 2001, 1–13 <http://lasa.international.pitt.edu/Lasa2001/MaciasGonzalezVictor.pdf> [accessed 10 March 2014]

MAEDA, TOSHI, 'Japan's Lonely Hearts Turn to Dolls for Sex, Company', *Reuters*, 18 July 2007, <http://www.reuters.com/article/2007/07/18/us-japan-sex-dolls-

idUSSP10422420070718> [accessed 22 June 2014]
MAHON, ALYCE, *Eroticism and Art* (Oxford: Oxford University Press, 2005)
MARCIAL, ROGELIO, 'Identidad y representationes del cuerpo en jóvenes gays de Guadalajara', *Revista de Estudios de Género, LaVentana*, 3:29 (2009), 7–31
MÁRQUEZ , CARLOS F., 'El Cambio de género se ha dado para evadir las reglas del destino: Ana Clavel', *La Jornada Michoacán*, 10 November 2009, <http://www.lajornadamichoacan.com.mx/2009/11/10/index.php?section=cultura&article=012n1cul> [accessed 19 July 2014]
MARTIN, BIDDY, 'Sexualities without Genders and Other Queer Utopias', *Diacritics*, Critical Crossings, 24 (2–3), 104–21
MARTÍNEZ-ALCE, GRACIELA, 'La Apropiación y sus formas: las violetas de Ana Clavel', in Miguel Rodríguez Lozano (ed.), *Nada es lo que parece: Estudios sobre la novela Mexicana 2000–2009* (Mexico City: Universidad Nacional Autónoma de México, Instituto de Investigaciones Filológicas, Centro de Estudios Literarios), pp. 107–21
MARTING, DIANE E., 'Dangerous (To) Women: Sexual Fiction in Spanish America', in Sara Castro Klarén (ed.), *Narrativa femenina en América Latina: Prácticas y Perspectivas Teóricas/Latin American Women's Narrative: Practices and Theoretical Perspectives*, Theory and Criticism of Culture and Literature (Princeton: Markus Wiener, 2003), pp. 197–219
MASTRETTA, ÁNGELES, <http://lacomunidad.elpais.com/puerto-libre/posts> [accessed June 20 2014]
MCGRATH, ROBERTA, 'Re-reading Edward Weston: Feminism, Photography and Psychoanalysis', in Liz Wells (ed.), *The Photography Reader* (New York: Routledge, 2003), pp. 325–37
MENDOZA, ÉLMER, 'Ana Clavel', *El Universal*, 30 September 2010, <http://anaclavel.com/entrevistas/dibujante/Elmer_Mendoza_El_universal.pdf> [accessed 14 June 2014]
MENDOZA, VICENTE T., 'El Machismo en México: a través de las canciones, corridos y cantares', *Cuadernos del Instituto Nacional de Antropología*, 3 (1962), 75–86
MENTON, SEYMOUR, *Magic Realism Rediscovered, 1918–1981* (Philadelphia: Art Alliance Press, 1983)
MESSINGER CYPESS, SANDRA, *La Malinche in Mexican Literature: From History to Myth* (Austin: University of Texas Press, 2000)
MILLER, BETH K., *A la sombra del volcán: conversaciones sobre la narrativa mexicana actual* (Guadalajara: Universidad de Guadalajara/Xalli, 1990)
MOLINA RAMÍREZ, TANIA, 'Explora artista el diálogo entre el cuerpo y el alma de la cámara', *La Jornada*, 8 September 2007, <http://www.jornada.unam.mx/2007/09/08/index.php?section=cultura&article=a04n1cul> [accessed 21 May 2014]
MOLLOY, SYLVIA, and ROBERT MCKEE IRWIN (eds.), *Hispanisms and Homosexualities*, Series Q (Durham, NC: Duke University Press, 1998)
MONTIEL, DAVID SÁNCHEZ, 2008, <http://www.cfc.gob.mx/index.php?option=com_content&task=view&id=2447&Itemid=206> [accessed 20 June 2014]
MOORE, EVELYN K., 'Goethe and Lavater: A Specular Friendship', in Evelyn K. Moore and Patricia Anne Simpson (eds.), *The Enlightened Eye: Goethe and Visual Culture*, Amsterdamer Beiträge zur neueren Germanistik, 62 (Amsterdam: Rodopi, 2007), pp. 165–92
MOORE, HENRIETTA, 'The Problem of Explaining Violence in the Social Sciences', in Penelope Harvey and Peter Gow (eds.), *Sex and Violence: Issues of Representation and Experience* (London: Routledge, 1994), pp. 138–55
MORRIS, MEAGHAN, 'Banality in Cultural Studies', in John Storey (ed.), *What Is Cultural Studies? A Reader* (London: Arnold, 1996), pp. 147–67
MULVEY, LAURA, 'Afterthoughts on "Visual Pleasure and Narrative Cinema" inspired by King Vidor's *Duel in the Sun* (1946)', in *Visual and Other Pleasures*, 2nd edn (Basingstoke: Palgrave Macmillan, 2009), pp. 31–40 (first published in 1989)

——'Visual Pleasure and Narrative Cinema', *Screen* 16:3 (1975), 6–18
Nabokov, Vladimir, *Lolita* (London: Penguin, 1980) (first pubished in 1955)
Nelson, Theodor H., *Literary Machines 93.1* (Sausalito, CA: Mindful Press, 1992) (first published in 1980)
——'Replacing the Printed Word', in Simon H. Lavington (ed.), *Information Processing 80, Proceedings of the IFIP Congress* (Amsterdam: North-Holland, 1980), pp. 1013–23
Nobus, Dany, and Lisa Downing (eds.), *Perversion: Psychoanalytic Perspectives/Perspectives on Psychoanalysis* (London: Karnac Books, 2006)
Núñez Noriega, Guillermo, *Masculinidad e intimidad: identidad, sexualidad y sida* (Mexico City: UNAM y Miguel Ángel Porrúa, 2007)
Nussbaum, Felicity A., *The Autobiographical Subject: Gender and Ideology in Eighteenth-Century England* (Baltimore: The John Hopkins University Press, 1989)
O'Connell, Joanna, *Prospero's Daughter: The Prose of Rosario Castellanos*, Texas Pan American Series (Austin: University of Texas Press, 1995)
O'Neill, Kate E., 'Female Effigies and Performances of Desire: A Consideration of Identity Performance Lars and the Real Girl', *Desire, Forum*, 6 (2008), <http://www.forumjournal.org/site/issue/06/kate-e-o-neill> [accessed 14 June 2014]
Orr, Mary, *Intertextuality: Debates and Contexts* (Cambridge: Polity, 2005) (first published 2003)
——'Intertextuality', in Michael Ryan (ed.), *Encyclopaedia of Literary and Cultural Theory: Vol. II, Literary Theory from 1966 to the Present*, ed. by Robert Eaglestone (Chichester: Blackwell, 2011), 1–4 (first published in 2010), <http://www.literatureencyclopedia.com> [accessed 10 March 2014]
Oxford English Dictionary, 'Multimedia' (2011), <http://www.oed.com/viewdictionaryentry/Entry/123564> [accessed 10 June 2014]
Paredes, Américo, 'The United States, Mexico, and Machismo', in Américo Paredes and Richard Bauman (eds.), *Folklore and Culture on the Texas-Mexican Border* (Austin: University of Texas Press, 1993), pp. 215–34
Paz, Octavio, *El Laberinto de la soledad* (Mexico City: Colección Popular, 1950)
——*El Laberinto de la soledad, Postdata y Vuelta a El laberinto de la soledad*, 2nd edn (Mexico City: Colección Popular, 1992)
Paz Soldán, Edmundo, and Debra A. Castillo (eds.), *Latin American Literature and Mass Media*, Hispanic Issues, 22 (New York: Garland, 2001)
——'A Cyberliterary Afterward: Of Blogs and Other Matters', in Claire Taylor and Thea Pitman (eds.), *Latin American Cyberculture and Cyberliterature* (Liverpool: Liverpool University Press, 2007), pp. 257–62
Penner, Barabara, '(Re)Designing the "Unmentionable": Female Toilets in the Twentieth Century', in Olga Gershenson and Barbara Penner (eds.), *Ladies and Gents: Public Toilets and Gender* (Philadelphia: Temple University Press, 2009), pp. 141–50
Peralta, Violeta, and Liliana Befumo Boschi, *Rulfo: la soledad creadora* (Buenos Aires: F. García Cambeiro, 1975)
Perkowska, Magdalena, *Historias híbridas: la nueva novela histórica latinoamericana (1985–2000) ante las teorías posmodernas de la historia* (Madrid: Iberoamericana, 2008)
Petersen, Alan, 'Sexing the Body: Representations of Sex Differences in Gray's Anatomy, 1858 to the Present', *Body & Society*, 4:1 (1998), 1–15
Pifer, Ellen, 'The Lolita Phenomenon from Paris to Tehran', in Julian W. Connolly (ed.), *The Cambridge Companion to Nabokov* (Cambridge: Cambridge University Press, 2005), pp. 185–99
Porter, Martin, *Windows of the Soul: Physiognomy in European Culture 1470–1780*, Oxford Historical Monographs (Oxford: Clarendon Press, 2005)
Prieur, Annick, 'Domination and Desire: Male Homosexuality and the Construction of

Masculinity in Mexico', in Marit Melhuus and Kristi A. Stølen (eds.), *Machos, Mistresses, Madonnas* (London: Verso, 1996), pp. 83–107

QUIJAS, FABIOLA PALAPA, 'Inspira novela de Ana Clavel a 14 artistas para explorar las secuelas del deseo', *La Jornada*, 1 April 2008, <http://www.jornada.unam.mx/2008/04/01/index.php?section=cultura&article=a05n1cul> [accessed 22 June 2014]

RAFFAELLI, MARCELA, and LENNA L. ONTAI, 'Gender Socialization in Latino/a Families: Results from Two Retrospective Studies', *Sex Roles: A Journal of Research*, 50: 5/6 (2004), 287–99

RAJEWSKY, IRINA O., 'Intermediality, Intertextuality, and Remediation: A Literary Perspective on Intermediality', *Intermedialites*, 6 (2005), 43–64

RAMOS, SAMUEL, *El Perfil del hombre y la cultura en México* (Mexico City: Imprenta Mundial, 1934)

REEDS, KENNETH, 'Magical Realism: A Problem of Definition', *Neophilologus*, 90:2 (2006), 175–96

RESTUCIA, FRANCES L., '"Untying the Mother Tongue": Female Difference in Virginia Woolf's *A Room of One's Own*', *Tulsa Studies in Women's Literature*, 4:2 (1985), 253–64

REYES, JUAN JOSÉ, 'Seducciones múltiples de Ana Clavel', *Siempre!*, LIV: 2858 (2007), 70–71

RICH, ADRIENNE, 'Compulsory Heterosexuality and Lesbian Existence', *Signs, Women: Sex and Sexuality*, 5:4 (1980), 631–60

RICHMOND ELLIS, ROBERT, 'Introduction', in Susana Chávez-Silverman and Librada Hernández (eds.), *Reading and Writing the Ambiente: Queer Sexualities in Latino, Latin American, and Spanish Culture* (Madison: University of Wisconsin Press, 2000), pp. 3–20

RIVERS, CHRISTOPHER, *Face Value. Physiognomical Thought and the Legible Body in Marivaux, Lavater, Balzac, Gautier, and Zola* (Madison: The University of Wisconsin Press, 1994)

RIX, ROB, 'Julio Cortázar's Rayuela and the Challenges of Cyberliterature', in Claire Taylor and Thea Pitman (eds.), *Latin American Cyberculture and Cyberliterature* (Liverpool: Liverpool University Press, 2007), pp. 194–206

RODRÍGUEZ MONEGAL, EMIR, 'Surrealism, Magical Realism, Magical Fiction: A Study in Confusion', in Peter G. Earle and Germán Gullón (eds.), *Surrealismo/ Surrealismos: Latinoamérica y España* (Philadelphia: University of Pennsylvania, 1977), pp. 25–32

RODRÍGUEZ-VIVALDI, ANA MARÍA, 'Shaking the Soul, the Mind, and the Reader: Laura Esquivel and the Multimedia Novel', *Pacific Coast Philology*, 38 (2003), 25–32

ROJAS, MARTHA AVELINA, 'Periodismo', 27 April 2008, <http://avelina-tropos.blogspot.com/2008/04/ana-clavel-me-dej-atnita-con-su-novela.html> [accessed 26 June 2014]

ROSE, GILLIAN, 'Making Space for the Female Subject of Feminism: The Spatial Subversions of Holzer, Kruger and Sherman', in Steve Pile and Nigel J. Thrift (eds.), *Mapping the Subject: Geographies of Cultural Transformation* (New York: Routledge, 1995), pp. 332–54

ROSENTHAL, MARK, *Understanding Installation Art: From Duchamp to Holzer* (Munich: Prestel, 2003)

ROSIQUE, JESÚS ANAYA, 'Estadísticas del sector editorial: problemas y perspectivas — I', *Libros de México*, 19 (1996), 63–70

RUBIN, GAYLE, 'Thinking Sex: Notes for a Radical Theory of the Politics of Sexuality', in Carole S. Vance (ed.), *Pleasure and Danger: Exploring Female Sexuality* (Boston: Routledge, 1984), pp. 267–319

RUBIN, JAMES, *Courbet* (London: Phaidon Press Ltd, 1997)

RYCENGA, JENNIFER J., 'Endless Caresses: Queer Exuberance in Large-Scale Form in Rock', in *Queering the Popular Pitch*, ed. by Sheila Whiteley and Jennifer J. Rycenga (New York: Routledge, 2006), pp. 235–47

SAID, EDWARD W., 'Foreword', in Ranajit Guha and Gavatri Chakravorty Spivak (eds.), *Selected Subaltern Studies* (New York and Oxford: Oxford University Press, 1988)

SALZINGER, LESLIE, 'Manufacturing Sexual Subjects: "Harassment", Desire and Discipline on a Maquiladora Shopfloor', *Ethnography*, 1:1 (2000), 67–92

SANOUILLET, MICHEL, and ELMER PETERSON (eds.), *Salt Seller: The Writings of Marcel Duchamp* (New York: Oxford University Press, 1973)

SAYER, DEREK, 'Doll Parts, or, the Subject Reconfigured from the Point of View of the Mannequin', paper presented at 4S-EASST Conference, 26–28 August 2004, 1–29, <http://www.csi.ensmp.fr/WebCSI/4S/download_paper/download_paper.php?paper=sayer.pdf> [accessed 22 June 2014]

SCHAEFER, CLAUDIA, *Textured Lives: Women, Art and Representation in Modern Mexico* (Tucson: University of Arizona Press, 1992)

SCHMIDT, BETTINA E., *Caribbean Diaspora in the USA: Diversity of Caribbean Religions in New York City*, Vitality of Indigenous Religions Series (Hampshire: Ashgate, 2008)

SCHNEIDER, REBECCA, *The Explicit Body in Performance* (London: Routledge, 1997)

SCHWEDER, ALEX, 'Stalls Between Walls: Segregated Sexed Spaces', in Olga Gershenson and Barbara Penner (eds.), *Ladies and Gents: Public Toilets and Gender* (Philadelphia: Temple University Press, 2009), pp. 182–88

SCHWEITZER, DAHLIA, 'Striptease: The Art of Spectacle and Transgression', *The Journal of Popular Culture*, 34:1 (2000), 65–75

SHAW, COLIN, *Deciding What We Watch: Taste, Decency, and Media Ethics in the UK and the USA* (New York: Oxford University Press, 1999)

SHAW, DEBRA A., 'Bestsellers', in Verity Smith (ed.), *Encyclopedia of Latin American Literature* (London: Fitzroy Dearbourn, 1997), pp. 115–18

—— 'Men in High Heels: The Feminine Man and Performances of Femininity in *Tacones lejanos* by Pedro Almodóvar', *Journal of Iberian and Latin American Studies*, 6:1 (2000), 55–62

SHAW, DONALD L., *The Post-Boom in Spanish American Fiction*, Suny Series in Latin American and Iberian Thought and Culture (Albany: State University of New York Press, 1998)

SHOWALTER, ELAINE, *A Literature of Their Own: British Women Novelists from Brönte to Lessing* (Princeton: Princeton University Press, 1997)

SLACK, DAWN, 'Cristina Pacheco's Narratives: Multimedia Chronicles', in Ignacio Corona and Beth E. Jögensen (eds.), *The Contemporary Mexican Chronicle: Theoretical Perspectives on the Liminal Genre*, Suny Series in Latin American and Iberian Thought and Culture (Albany: State University of New York Press, 2002), pp. 221–39

—— 'If a Mexican Woman Wrote, and No One Read Her, Did She Really Write? An Examination of Cristina Pacheco's Contributions to the *B(l)oom Femenino* in Mexico', in Nuala Finnegan, and Jane E. Lavery (eds.), *The Boom Femenino in Mexico* (Newcastle upon Tyne: Cambridge Scholars Publishing, 2010), pp. 92–107

SMITH, JONATHAN, *Charles Darwin and Victorian Visual Culture*, Cambridge Studies in Nineteenth-Century Literature and Culture (Cambridge: Cambridge University Press, 2009)

SPIELMANN, YVONNE, 'Synesthesia and Intersenses: Intermedia in Electronic Images', *Leonardo*, 34:1 (2001), 55–61

SPRINGER, JOSÉ MANUEL, 'Imaginar el deseo masculino desde lo femenino y viceversa: Cuerpo naúfrago de Ana Clavel', *Réplica*, 17 October 2005, <http://www.replica21.com/archivo/articulos/s_t/384_springer_clavel.html> [accessed June 2014]

STALLEYBRASS, PETER, and ALLON WHITE, *The Politics and Poetics of Transgression* (London: Methuen, 1986)

STEELE, CYNTHIA, *Politics, Gender and the Mexican Novel, 1968–1988: Beyond the Pyramid* (Austin: University of Texas Press, 1992)

STEVENS, EVELYN P., 'Marianismo: The Other Face of Machismo', in Ann Pescatello (ed.), *Female and Male in Latin America: Essays* (Pittsburgh, PA: University of Pittsburgh Press, 1973), pp. 89–103

STOICHITA, VICTOR I., *A Short History of the Shadow*, trans. by Anne-Marie Glasheen (London: Reaktion Books, 1997)

STRAAYER, CHRIS, *Deviant Eyes, Deviant Bodies: Sexual Re-Orientations in Film and Video* (New York: Columbia University Press, 1992)

SUCRE, NATALIA, 'Distracting Art: Reading Shock in Felisberto Hernández's "Las Hortensias"', *Hispania*, 86:3 (2003), 482–92

SULEIMAN, SUSAN RUBIN, 'Dialogue and Double Allegiance: Some Contemporary Women Artists and the Historical Avant-Garde', in Whitney Chadwick (ed.), *Mirror Images: Women, Surrealism, and Self Representation* (Cambridge, MA: MIT Press, 1998), pp. 128–55

SUSARLA, ANJANA, and others, 'Social Networks and the Diffusion of User-Generated Content: Evidence from YouTube', *ISRE* (2011), DOI 10.1287/isre.1100.0339, 1–9, <http://isr.journal.informs.org/content/early/2011/04/08/isre.1100.0339.full.pdf+html> [accessed 20 June 2014]

TAMIR-GHEZ, NOMI, 'The Art of Persuasion in Nabokov's *Lolita*', *Poetics Today*, 11:2 (1979), 65–83

TANNER, LAURA E, 'Reading Rape: *Sanctuary* and *The Women of Brewster Place*', *American Literature*, 62:4 (1990), 559–82

TAYLOR, CLAIRE, *Bodies and Texts: Configurations of Identity in the Works of Griselda Gambaro, Albalucía Ángel and Laura Esquivel*, MHRA (Leeds: Maney, 2003)

——'Laura Esquivel and the *Boom Femenino*: Popular Genres and Double Encoding', in Nuala Finnegan, and Jane E. Lavery (eds.), *The Boom Femenino in Mexico* (Newcastle upon Tyne: Cambridge Scholars Publishing, 2010), pp. 199–216

——'Virtual Bodies in Cyberspace: Guzik Glantz's Weblog', in Claire Taylor and Thea Pitman (eds.), *Latin American Cyberculture and Cyberliterature* (Liverpool: Liverpool University Press, 2007), pp. 244–56

TAYLOR, CLAIRE, and THEA PITMAN (eds.), *Latin American Cyberculture and Cyberliterature* (Liverpool: Liverpool University Press, 2007)

TAYLOR, R. MICHAEL, 'Body Matters: Marcel Duchamp's *Étant Donnés* Revisited', in Marc Décimo (ed.), *Marcel Duchamp and Eroticism* (Newcastle: Cambridge Scholars Publishing, 2007), pp. 33–42 5

——, *Marcel Duchamp: Étant donnés* (New Haven: Philadelphia Museum of Art published in association with Yale University Press, 2009)

TAYLOR, SUE, *Hans Bellmer: The Anatomy of Anxiety* (Cambridge, MA: MIT Press, 2000)

TÉLLEZ-PON, SERGIO, 'La Primera novela queer', *Tierra Adentro* 139 (2006)

TENORIO-TRILLO, MAURICIO, *Mexico at the World's Fairs: Crafting a Modern Nation*, The New Historicism: Studies in Cultural Poetics (Berkeley: University of California Press, 1996)

THORNTON, NIAMH, 'Being Fruity in the Big City: Re-membering the Past in Enrique Serna's *Fruta verde*', in Victoria Carpenter (ed.), *(Re)Collecting the Past: History and Collective Memory in Latin American Narrative*, Hispanic Studies: Culture and Ideas, 31 (Oxford: Peter Lang, 2010), pp. 145–65

TREJO FUENTES, IGNACIO, 'Ana Clavel: mujer con cuerpo de hombre', *Siempre!*, 22 January 2006

TURNER, CHRISTOPHER, 'A Short History of the Shadow: An Interview with Victor I. Stoichita', Shadows, Winter 24 (2006/07), <http://cabinetmagazine.org/issues/24/stoichita.php> [accessed 14 June 2014]

TYMIENIECKA, ANNA-TERESA (ed.), *The Elemental Dialectic of Light and Darkness: The Passions of the Soul in the Onto-Poiesis of Life*, Analecta Husserliana, 38 (Dordrecht: Kluwer Academic, 1992)

USSHER, JANE M., *Managing the Monstrous Feminine: Regulating the Reproductive Body* (London: Routledge, 2006)

Vaughn, Jeanne, '¿En dónde van a florear? *La "Flor de Lis"*, and the Problematics of Identity', in Kristine Ibsen (ed.), *The Other Mirror: Women's Narrative in Mexico 1980–1995*, Contributions to the Study of World Literature, 80 (Westport, CT: Greenwood Press, 1997), pp. 41–56

Velasco, Karina, 'Exhiben 32 desnudos de Rogelio Cuéllar y Ricardo Vinós en galería del Fonca', *La Crónica*, 29 July 2006, <http://www.cronica.com.mx/nota.php?id_nota=253545> [accessed 21 May 2014]

Velasco, Raquel, 'De amores marginales: el juego de la diferencia', *La Palabra y el Hombre*, Universidad Veracruzana, 135 (2005), 7–19, <http://cdigital.uv.mx/handle/123456789/451> [accessed 6 May 2013]

Velasco Gutiérrez, Luz Elena de, 'El Problema de la voz en la narrativa femenina mexicana', *Revista Iztapalapa*, 37 (1995), 175–82

Verstraete, Ginette, 'Intermedialities: A Brief Survey of Conceptual Key Issues', Acta Univ. Sapientiae, *Film and Media Studies*, 2 (2010), 7–14

Vézina, Richard, and Olivia Paul, 'Provocation in Advertising: A Conceptualization and an Empirical Assessment', *International Journal of Research in Marketing*, 14:2 (1997), 177–92

Viegas, Cláudia A., 'Contemporary Brazilian Fiction: Between Screens and Printed Pages', in Claire Taylor and Thea Pitman (eds.), *Latin American Cyberculture and Cyberliterature* (Liverpool: Liverpool University Press, 2007), pp. 207–15

Walters, Suzanne D., 'From Here to Queer: Radical Feminism, Postmodernism and the Lesbian Menace', in Iain Morland and Anabelle Wilcox (eds.), *Queer Theory* (Basingstoke: Palgrave, 2005), pp. 6–21

Weed, Elizabeth, 'Introduction', in Elizabeth Weed and Naomi Schor (eds.), *Feminism Meets Queer Theory* (Bloomington: Indiana University Press, 1997), pp. vii–xiii

Wichterich, Christa, *The Globalized Woman: Reports from a Future of Inequality* (London: Zed, 2000)

Will, Richard, 'Pergolesi's Stabat Mater and the Politics of Feminine Virtue', *Musical Quarterly*, 87:3 (2005), 570–614, doi:10.1093/musqtl/gdh021, <http://mq.oxfordjournals.org/content/87/3/570.citation> [accessed 20 June 2014]

Wilson, Elizabeth, 'Into the Labyrinth', in Linda McDowell and Joanne P. Sharp (eds.), *Space, Gender and Knowledge: Feminist Readings* (London: Arnold, 1997), pp. 277–84

Woolf, Virginia, *Orlando: A Biography* (London: Penguin, 1963) (first published in 1928)

Wyman, Leah M., and George N. Dionisopoulos, 'Transcending the Virgin/Whore Dichotomy: Telling Mina's Story in Bram Stoker's *Dracula*', *Women's Studies in Communication*, 23:2 (2000), 209–38

Zamora, Lois Parkinson, and Wendy B. Faris (eds.), *Magical Realism: Theory, History, Community*, (Durham, NC: Duke University Press, 1995)

Zimmermann, Rolf Christian, *Das Weltbild des jungen Goethe: Studien zur hermetischen Tradition des deutschen 18. Jahrhunderts*, 2 vols (Munich: W. Fink, 1969–79)

Websites

—— <http://mx.answers.yahoo.com/question/index?qid=20080610112612AAwHMdo> [accessed 22 June 2014]

—— <http://www.pmate.co.uk/> [accessed 14 June 2014]

—— <http://www.realdoll.com> [accessed 22 June 2014]

—— <http://www.tiempolibre.com.mx/blog/> [accessed 14 June 2014]

INDEX